This Is Amerikkka:

The Troublesome Life, Loves & Soul of a Conscientious Thug

Kamaj Tawhid

Still Waters Prose
Albuquerque NM

Copyright © 2020 by Still Waters Prose, LLC
All rights reserved.
StillWatersProse.com

Library of Congress Cataloging-in-Publication Data is available upon request.

ISBN

978-1-7355890-1-5 (First paperback printing)

978-1-7355890-2-2 (Ebook epub version)

978-1-7355890-3-9 (Ebook mobi version)

PRINTED IN THE UNITED STATES OF AMERICA

Cover design by agnesam

Book design by accuracy4sure

First hardcover/paperback edition 2020

www.ThisIsAmerikkkaBook.com

DEDICATION

For the Ancestors: Brother Nat, Sister Harriet, Brother Marcus, El-Hajj Malik, Brother Huey, Brother Kwame, Comrade Geronimo, Madiba Mandela, Sister Afeni, "The Greatest" Ali, "Phenomenal Woman" Maya, my uncle Wolf, my loving father JT, and (the still indomitable) Sister Assata, Imam Jamil, Brother Mumia, Brother Mutulu, and Sister Nikki G. – your love is my love, your struggle is my struggle, your life is my life. I stand on your shoulders, walk with the strength of your spirits, and carry you in my heart. Forever and always…

For my family. So that you may understand…

Editor's Note

Throughout this book the reader may notice the unusual spelling of certain words and/or the uncapitalization of formal nouns; despite being well aware of the "rules," this is at the author's express insistence as a sign of his utter disdain for the subject in question. Similarly, the capitalization of usually informal nouns expresses the author's utmost love, reverence, and upliftment...

ACKNOWLEDGMENTS

Writing this book, for me, was painful at times. Variously I laughed, I cried, I smiled and I frowned revisiting those dramas, traumas and relationships that I wouldn't wish on any man's heart or soul, and reliving those precious times and precious people that make all of the other bullshit of life seem so worthwhile. So for all of the handholding, words of encouragement, and lending of an ear or shoulder throughout all of my misguided years in the streets, jails, and prisons of this kkkountry, I would like to thank the following people: Mr. Mick B., Ms. Nikki B., Ms. Felicia B., Mrs. Jennifer B., Ms. Shameka B., Ms. Stacey B., Ms. "Granni" B., Ms. Donna B., Ms. Joy C., Ms. Melissa C., Mrs. Stephanie A.C.-M., Mr. Adrian D., Ms. Deborah D.,Ms. Latoya B.F., Ms. Beverly F., Ms. Karen G., Mrs. Rhyanna G.-F., Ms. Terri G., Mrs. Tricia G.-A., Mrs. Melissa G.-H., Ms. Xenia G., Ms. Sukari H., Mr. Royce H., Mr. & Mrs. Todd & Peggy H., Ms. Markessa H., Ms. Alicia H., Mr. Mark H. & family, Ms. Tonzia H., Mrs. LaTrecia J., Ms. Marie J., Dr. Jeff Kersey, Ms. Seniqua K., Ms. Margeaux L., Mr. Brian L., Ms. Traci "Tiki" L., Ms. LeEricka L., Dr. Shana M.-H., Mrs. Talia M.-S., Ms. Ramell M., Mrs. Nikechia M.-A., Ms. Kwame & Mama M., Master Chef Mark Morton (I could whip a meal out of *sand* stranded on a deserted island with all you taught me! Love and respect forever!), Ms. Kim M., "Mama Tee Tee" O., Ms. Eileen Parrish (one of the two best attorneys in the world!), Ms. Carmen P., Mrs. Brandie P., Ms. Stephanie P., Mr. Jeffrey O. Powell (the other great attorney!), Mr. John P., Ms. LaKesha R., Author Mimi Renee, Ms. Denise R., Ms. Lisa S., Ms. Tameka S., Ms. Tanika S., Mr. Greg S., Mr. Jeff Swink, Dr. Ervin Tinnon (you tried your best – I was just hard-headed as hell!), Mr. Mike Valentino (the most patient and understanding editor in the

Acknowledgments

world!), Ms. Amira W., Mr. DeAndre W., Ms. Senita J.W., and Ms. Toya W. Although the seasons may change, my love and gratitude for you never will. I thank you all for being such a positive and encouraging part of my life...

And of course, my family whom has been so patient with me and my travails throughout the years: my mother Paula, my brothers Carvin and John, my sisters Devonne and Shawanda, my sons Kyree and Kalii, my oldest nephews Darieon, DeAngelo, and Kantreze, my oldest nieces Perryona and Jiya, my aunts Tricia, Fattie, Deborah Ann, Net, Paulette, ("play aunts") Jackie & Bridget, and great aunt Bibbie, my uncles Sweet Pea, John Lawrence, Vary, Poochie Kennedy, and Moochie Davis, my stepsons Avant'e and LaMichael, my godson Khahlil, my oldest goddaughters Maviya and Nikyra, my "play sister" Alex, the entire Jemison family, and last but not least, my "brothers from other fathers and mothers," Mkuu, Lil M4nst3, Cheanie, Lo Zo, Glocc, J Deuce, Hasan Ali, Wimp, Lil Lee, and Dreamer. Words alone could never properly express my gratitude and love...

A special shout-out to some of my favorite cousins that have *always* been in my corner no matter what or *who* I was up against: Raymond C., Dajuan W., Stacey T., John W., Jolonda W., Katrina C., Shotgun, Mandingo, Shotti, Keeta C. & Steven B., Justin W., Tiffany S., Nukie, Lil Rodney, Christa W., Brian K., Lil Don L., Shaunte K.-B. & Gerard, Sandy, Shack, Big B., Tim C., Lil T.C., Sheila L.-O., Angelia (Bee Bee), Angela E.-W. (Mook), Maury, Dough, Hunkas, Vonqua & Lil Dee, Chris (Bodi), Latisha D., Lee Lee W., Gerald M., Tracy C., Ariko, Dominique & Bryce H., and J. Eric W. Know that I love everyone in my family, so if I didn't single *you* out by name, don't trip; *these* are just some of the ones I have had strong and special relationships with over the years. Y'all know how it is – we all

Acknowledgments

have our favorites for one reason or another and *these* cousins have *always* been "down"…

Love, appreciation, and all due respect to the mothers of my children for allowing me to experience the blessing that is fatherhood. Although I recognize that our relationships may not be "ideal" (though, whose *is*, I ask you?!), understand that I will always love, care for, and thank you for the gift you shared with me…

As well, I would be remiss if I didn't send at least "three times the love" to all the righteous cats that have stood "ten toes down" beside me at various times throughout my life: Tre Ball, Money Bags Tre, Treacherous Tre, J Holla, Whispers, Gangsta Wayne, D-Boy, Lil Delo Thrice, Dee Smilz (The Queen!), C Fox, Bullit Tre, Tre Nightmare, Geno Tre, C-Fo, Tre Cali (Baby Madroc), Wacco, Bear Loc, Tear Drop, Big Tre G, Lil Tre G, Tre Money, Lou Loc, Pistol Loc, Choppa Loc, G Wood, Smiley Tre, Tre Face, Tre Smalls, Baby Ray Ray, Yikes, Lil Icey, Lil Gizz, Tre Beast, Cash Flow, June June & the rest of my TN M4v3n Gang Family; the homies G4ngst8 Loco, Havoc 93, Vitto, 47 T.Y., Ghost Tre, Big Joe from Kitchen, O.C., Al Bundy, Scab, Calico from Twenties Long Beach, the Twins from Palmer Blocc, Tac Loc from Trouble Squad (get at me fam!), G4ngst7 Doo Loc (find me Move!), and Macc 90; Youngsta & BK from ETG; "Richie Rich" Lil Reggie, Van Damn, Murder, Groundsta, Seven Wicced, Big Tank & Fat Rat from Underground; M-Loco, Killa Charles, J-9, Joe Cool, Carleon, and Smooth from Main St.; Sin Ball, Cross, Baldhead, Big T. Crutcher, Don P., Concrete & Chuccie from Forties Darcside; Goldie, Lil Ronnie, and Evil from Grape St.; Tre D, Awol, Big Hurk & Blacc Mafia from 307 Underworld; Gr10v7rs Trouble Bug, Gee Patton, Columbia Vic & Shooter; Harlem Mike, R30, Slim 30 & Baby Harlem from Thirties; Gr52vers Lil

Acknowledgments

V., Hoover J. (get at me fam), Hoover Joe, Gator, Casey Loc, ToJo, Big Ju (keep putting that poetry down Gangsta!), Groovy Blue (you're the next generation Lil brother! We're counting on you!), Crook, and V. Tyson; Gr83vers Crim, BK, Killa, True Blue & Tae Bae; C. Bang, Blue Cheese, KD, Big V-Murder, Tez Macc, C Villian, (old ass!!!) Doocie Loc, T-60 & J. Hall from Sixties; Damus Rolie Mac from Kansas City, Kendu from MadSwan, Courtney "Money" Ru & Killa from Skyline; Playas M. "Rod" Ford, Montana (you *still* can't handle me on that chessboard Playa!), Knockout, and Black Ty (Keep pushing Playa! Freedom will come soon!); Macs "Big Joe" W., G-Wiz, Chi-Town, and (my twin!) Dot; Dirty & Gambino from New Breed; all-around "thorough" cats Jasper "J-Red" McCoy, Jerome Sawyers, Mario Hambrick, Brett "Pat" Patterson, J. Michael Stanfield (even imprisoned, the most honest and thoughtful journalist in the world!), Fred "Justice" Sledge, Frank Adams, Joshua Bush, Mark Applegate, Scott "Outkast" Bickford, Marlo "P-Lo" Parham, Carl Byars, "John-John" Oglesby, Leon Robbins (what up fam!), "Big George" Bell, Pooh Dunn, Lavely X, Steve Stokely, LaDon Ervin, Kenneth Parham, K-Fed, D-Shot, Ro (but make that shit *right* cuz!), Dame Mac (you too Dame!), Marty Holland, Tim H. & Rudy C. from the Southside, Lil Murdoc & Deon L., Gabriel "Black" Ayuel from South Sudan, Roel G. from Laredo, Amir Taariq (my brother in the struggle), Carlos Hardy (I see you on that Deen cuz!), Terrence "Mansur" Davis (my fat cousin!), Kevin "KD" Davis (his even fatter brother! Just what in the hell have y'all been eating lately?! Or a better question may be, what *haven't* you been eating?!), Big Wu (no matter what we go through, it's still all love family!), A.C. (fam bam!), Shabazz (*37 years*! You're a much stronger man than I, but I'm glad to see you're finally home!), Corey Daniels, Big Ruck (find me fam!), and Young

Acknowledgments

Solid (*not* Oldhead Solid!) from Southside; and last but not least, the *Big* Big homies who always inspired me to *m4v3 smooth*: Big Scrap (C.I.P.), Big Loonie, T. Dopey, GhostTown, G. Mike, Coolaid & Bobby Louie. For anyone I may have missed, y'all know what it is, and you know the love is there and how I m4v3, so forgive me if I missed a name or three...

For all those souls lost too soon, a part of me left with you: Frederick "Putt-Putt" Blackwell; Thaddeus Eugene "Duck" Clay; Mrs. Carlene Walden-Lawrence (forever my favorite Auntie!); Ms. Deborah Nicole "Stinka" Thomas (love you always Stinka!); Mr. Freddie Marchbanks; Ms. Karen Comage (miss you "Mama Karen!"); Terry Chubb; Ronald Clay; Tahitian "Tee" Cristman; Kerry Pettus, Sr.; Shedrick "Sin" Britton; Keith Head; "Lil James" Odom; David Crenshaw & Donald Perry; Eric "Butt-Naked" Marthell; Tremaine "True" Caldwell; my uncle "Wolf" (Dennis Thomas, Jr.); Anissa "Nasa B." Blackwell, Marall "Rell" Edwards; Clarence "LaBo" Claybrooks; Lentonio "Whop" Swanson; Antoni "Tony Rony" Morton; Algernon "Big Joe" Cross; Antjuan "Lighter" Hughes; Tony "T" Rawls, "Cakemix" Swanson, "Hunchie" Lewis, "Lil Bryant" Crenshaw; Brad "Tre Loc" Gill; Richie "Lunchmeat" Anderson; my lil cousins Vernon "Jingle Bell" Robinson, Joseph "Lil Joe" Bass, Timond Chubb, & Isaac Lamont "Tre Cu Cu" Thomas; Dawn Dean; Benjanique Amos; Christopher Holland; Sheryl Watts; Greg "G Tre" McDaniel; Lonnie Layhew; Lamont Pitts; and attorney Ralph Newman (one of those rare gifts whom really took his duty to "defend the public" to heart!). I'll mourn and miss you all always...

Most heart wrenching for me was the loss of my father John Milton Thomas at 11:24 p.m. on Wednesday, November 20, 2019 as I was making the final edits to "tighten up" this book. For a host of reasons, you will see why it has taken me

Acknowledgments

longer than I would have liked to finish the manuscript – as it was my greatest wish for him and my mother both to read it before either one of their passing, and this failure of mine I will forever mourn. This man – my "Pops" – was my greatest living hero and no amount of words or tears could ever come close to expressing the love, admiration, and pride that I will forever feel for him. Sadly, for the rest of my living years, I don't think I'll ever be able to completely recover from not being able to hear his voice and wisdom, or feel his hugs, kisses, and "daps" again, and I honestly didn't realize how much of this was about him, our relationship, and of the things he taught me until after I lost him. Prior to his passing, I had been counseled more than once that I would not understand "loss" until I experience the loss of a child or parent, and no statement could have ever been more prescient. Even at 42-years-old, I can't help but to feel "lost" and adrift without him, and my heart goes out to all whom have felt (or is feeling) something similar...[1]

Finally – on an entirely different note – I would like to send thank-yous to all those whom without your conniving acts of betrayal, backstabbing, disloyalty and desertion, I would be a much weaker man mentally, physically, spiritually, and emotionally. Thank you for being such despicable persons and helping me grow into the man I am today. You all know who you are...

---

[1] Speaking of those gone too soon, I really feel like the world could use more kind, caring, and enlightened spirits like those of the late Anthony Bourdain, Ermias "Nipsey Hussle" Asghedom, and Kobe Bryant. I, of course, knew neither of these men personally, but you wouldn't believe the effect that their untimely passings had on not only myself, but a whole lot of other cats in cells alongside me in solitary confinement. Although we all, of course, did our best to not openly show it, it seemed as if we all lost a little bit of hope in the world when they departed...

CONTENTS

DEDICATION	I
ACKNOWLEDGMENTS	VII
PREFACE	XV
PROLOGUE	XIX
CORNERED	1
SOUTHSIDE	3
CAPTURED	15
EDGEHILL	25
CAGED	45
POPS	65
TRIAL & TRIBULATIONS	87
YOUNG & THUGGIN	101
RUNNING	117
JUVENILE	139
LOVING & LIVING	151
HUSTLING	181
BODY BLOW	209
DUCK	219
FIGHTING	231
FISK	243
CONVICTED	271
SURVIVING	279
DETAINER	305
EILEEN	309
PRISON	335
AWAKENING	355
APPEAL	373
HOPE	383
TO LIBERATION OR *DEATH*	403
AFTERWORD & PROPER RESPECTS	437
FAVORITE BOOKS	445
AUTHOR BIO	452

"I'm for *truth*, no matter who tells it. I'm for *justice*, no matter who it's for or against…"

El-Hajj Malik El-Shabazz
(b.k.a. Malcolm X)

PREFACE

Initially, none of what follows in this book was intended for release to the public in any shape, form or fashion; I wrote this memoir, originally, as a collection of letters to my sons, nephews, nieces, brothers, and sisters to explain certain incidents and quell rumors that kept coming up whenever my name was brought up in the streets and/or by some in my extended "family." I have always been (and will *always* be) an extremely private person who doesn't like others to know "my business" unless you were in some way *involved* in "my business" – and even then, you only knew what was necessary to *your* part, ya dig? At times, however, that has been used against me because I would not only *not* acknowledge the truth to some of the things heard, but I would, as well, *not* expend energy quashing whatever the particular rumor floating around was. I've learned over the years, however, that my ignoring of the nonsense can sometimes cause unforeseen problems and misconceptions best avoided if possible,[2] and I therefore realized that if I didn't address the truth/untruth of a whole lot of bullshit that has repeatedly reared its head, then I would forever have questions of my character, integrity and actions, and rumor would follow me wherever I go. So here I finally answer all, once and for all. And never again will I discuss what

---

[2] Mostly for others – me, I don't particularly give a fuck *what* others have to say, nor do I have *any* qualms dealing with *whatever* "problems" arise in whatever manner *I* see fit!

you find in these pages...

Nonetheless – as I will *not* allow *anyone* to mischaracterize what you are to read in the pages that follow – I want to stress to you that in no way do I seek to glorify and/or advocate needless, indiscriminate, nor unwarranted violence against *anyone* nor *any* group in *any* way. Yet, let me be clear: As you are to read, I stand firm in my belief that not only is there a *right*, but also, in fact, an *obligation* of individuals and/or groups to adhere to the tenets of self-defense *whenever anyone* seeks to wrongly do them harm. So if you're looking herein for *any* of that "turn the other cheek" bullshit, this *ain't* that...

Lastly, understand that *not one word* in this book is meant to make it appear that I am/was "harder," more "gangster," or more "street," "thorough," or any of that other unrighteous bullshit that means *absolutely nothing* to me, *nor* is there *even one word* written to disparage *anyone* – this simply is meant to express the truths of my life. As such, to avoid damaging others, certain names, nicknames, and quite a few well-known incidents have been excluded from *Amerikkka*, and for that same reason I've used pseudonyms for some of the people I have chosen to include in this book. Otherwise, the story I tell – *every single word* – is true. And with the preceding things in mind, for anyone who may not like something I had to say (or even *how* I said it), well hell, I'm not hard to find – come get at me. Just make sure you come correct...

Kamaj

This Is Amerikkka:

The Troublesome Life, Loves & Soul of a Conscientious Thug

Prologue

"Change will not come if we wait for some other person or some other time. We are the ones we've been waiting for. We are the change we seek... "

President Barack Hussein Obama

"Soul is about authenticity. Soul is about finding things in your life that are real and pure. The things that you know are at your core. The things you were put on this Earth to do..."
Grammy, Oscar, Emmy, and Tony-Award winning artist John Legend *(Commencement Address to the University of Pennsylvania, College of Arts & Sciences, 2009)*

"The seal and the kkkonstitution reflect the thinkkking of the Founding Fathers: that this was to be a nation by white people and for white people; Native Americans, Blacks, and all the other non-white people were to be the burden bearers for the real citizens of this nation..."
             The Honorable Minister Louis Farrakhan

> It's a long narrow, lonely path
> Looking over your shoulder
> Saw my shadow, saw my past
> Looked over my shoulder
> And it said you better move fast
>
> *Once I was a Panther*
> *by* Melvin E. Lewis

CORNERED

Skirrrrrrrtttt!!!!!!! A car had just run us off the road. Yet another occurrence in a long line of strange shit that had been happening all day. However, this time I wouldn't take it; this time I would open fire.

Click, click, click, click, click, click, click, click. Suddenly, I noticed the sound of multiple car doors flinging open and guns being cocked – followed by a lot of shouting:

"*I'VE GOT HIS HEAD!!! I'VE GOT HIS HEAD!!!*"

"*DON'T MOVE!!!! DON'T MOVE!!!!!*"

"*GET YOUR FUCKING HANDS UP!!! GET YOUR FUCKING HANDS UP!!!*"

Now are you thinking now what I was thinking then? How in the hell could I get my "fucking hands up," and not "move" all at the same motherfucking time???

So yeah, I figured it out rather quickly – this was the stupid ass metro police – and they were coming to *kill!* Now everything that day all made sense – the truck and two cars creeping past when I stopped at my cousin's house; the feeling that Freckles had that someone was following us; the strange-looking white man at the bowling alley minutes ago – all punkkk ass *metro police!*

And there I was surrounded on a dark side street on a gloomy rainy night with no witnesses in sight – what choice did I have but to shoot it out???

"I grew up in the ghetto and for a long time I had a ghetto state of mind and spirit..."

The Ghetto Solution
by Roland Gilbert & Cheo Tyehimba-Taylor

SOUTHSIDE

The "streets" will whisper that I shot my first three people at the age of 14, but that's not exactly true – as far as *I* understand, I only *grazed* those cats. However, had I been a better, more experienced and accurate shooter, then we'd be discussing three or more *deaths*. Because I sure as hell was trying to exterminate those motherfuckers.

"Oh shit! Damn, Delo! You almost shot me in the fucking head!"

I turned to the right to see my homeboy L.C. kneeling down, holding his head; I guess he'd got hit with the expelled shell from my .25 semi-automatic.

"SHIT. You cool cuz? You alright?"

"Yeah, nigga, damn! You shot too close to my muthafuckin' head!!!"

Seeing that the homie was cool, I looked up to discover, surprisingly, the fools I was gunning at, still standing there. These idiots either were stunned, stuck, or just plain fucking stupid – possibly all three.

Pat, Pat, Pat, Pat!!! I let off the rest of my shots, breaking them instantly from their suicidal paralysis. And as they ran their asses around the side of a house, L.C. and I ran our asses all the way back to the "Bricks"[3] nonstop, careful to avoid all of the main streets. Although, this was the first time that L.C. had went on a serious mission with me, it was actually the third time in two weeks that I had tried smoking those White Avenue cats.

---

[3] What we called "our" housing projects because of their red clay brick exterior.

Amerikkka

The first time I had wasted an entire night walking around with only one bullet in my pistol, with E.R.'s[4] unsuspecting brother attempting to help me find him. The second time – exactly three days before today – after growing frustrated at my inability to locate him, my homie White Lonnie and I let the clips go[5] at one of E.R.'s White Avenue homeboys standing out late night with a girl I went to school with – accomplishing nothing more than knocking the bark off of a tree. (As I said earlier, I was a terrible shot at that time.) Nevertheless, I was determined to get my man; he – along with everyone else – would early get the message that I *didn't play* concerning my family members. Because I'd be damned, before I lost another one...

Nine daughters and one son. Ten children. So many that for the first 17 years of my mother Paula's life, my grandmother Ann[6] mistakenly celebrated her eighth child's birthday on the wrong day. Not until I came along on the 26th of September in 1977 – exactly 3 weeks from the date of my mother's *actual* birthday – and my mother had to sign my birth certificate, did everyone realize that her birthday was on the *fifth* instead of the seventh. Amazing how an untruth can become gospel if enough people accept it as such, huh?

Anyway, I was given the name Kenneth Deangelo Walden. Kenneth from my mother's only brother (well, from my grandmother, that is; my mother's father also had another son and four more daughters in Ohio), Deangelo from God knows

---

[4] The cat whom that one bullet was for. What I would do after I let him have it, I honestly still don't know to this day.
[5] White Lonnie and I both had *full* ones this time!
[6] I've never known for anyone to call my grandmother anything but "Ann" – including her own children. Why, with ten children, not even one called her "Mama," I don't know. *Her* mother, however – my great-grandmother Nancy Blackwell – was whom we all called "Mama."

where, and Walden from Ann's husband.

Did you catch that, though? Ann's husband but *not* my mother's father. In fact, only the first three of Ann's children – my aunts Nancy, Virga, and Charlene – were Ann's and "Granddaddy" Bay Walden's biological children. My aunt Carlene followed with a father of her own, then came my grandfather "Johnny Boy" Johnson – the father of Tricia, Kenneth, Cheryl (whom we called "Fattie" despite her not being overweight), my mother, and Charlotte (whom the family called "Net") – lastly followed by the father of Scharnita (who was called "Mookie"). And although I've never been able to find out how true it was or not, it's been said that every time Bay Walden came home from the military – no matter how long or short he had been gone – somehow Ann was pregnant again. And since Ann and Bay stayed married until the day she passed, all of her children – and most of the grandchildren for a time – would carry his last name. This would later cause much "family" discord.

Since there were already two "Kenneths" in the family before me,[7] my aunt Tricia gave me the nickname "Delo" a few days after I was born. And for better or for worse, that's what I've been known by ever since.

My father, John Thomas ("Milton" – his middle name – to his family), also came from a sizable family. A year older than my mother, he was the fourth of seven children, four sons and three daughters, from my "Grannie" Mrs. Birdie B. Thomas; his father (who had passed away a couple of years before I was born), Dennis, Sr., also had two other daughters from a previous marriage. And with the exception of maybe 3 or 4 out of my combined 20-something aunts and uncles not having had numerous children of their own, I was blessed with at least 40-

---

[7] My aunt Virga had also named her oldest son after my uncle Kenneth; the family nicknamed him "Baby Brother" – pronounced in our southern vernacular as "BayBruh."

50 different first cousins of the same age, older, or younger. As a child, you couldn't ask for anything better. Always someone to play with, always somewhere to spend the night, always someone to look up to, always someone to fight beside, for, and with – yeah, I *loved* having a big family. And we were close-knit, too. Some of us cousins actually grew up like they were my brothers or sisters instead.

For a time after I was born, my mother and I lived with Ann in some projects in south nashville called "The Village," along with an ever-revolving cast of aunts and cousins. To this day, no one could probably tell you who "lived" there and who didn't, as those who didn't officially live there were always there anyway. Ann wouldn't have had it any other way, either. Children and grandchildren in and out, always welcome, always *loved*.[8] And even though we were all well-loved, I was especially my Aunt Tricia's favorite:

"*Always remember Auntie loves her baby, okay? Auntie loves her baby.*"

I heard that constantly. And I was always being showered with gifts of toy trucks and grape jelly sandwiches from both Tricia and Ann. Furthermore, at that time, no family politics had come into play over the different fathers – or at least any that a child would notice. To me, the "Walden Girls" and all of us cousins were one big happy family. However, I've come to realize since then, that I was the first nephew or niece from one of Tricia's "full sisters."

Surprisingly, I actually have no memories of my mother from those early years, although she likes to brag that I'm "so smart" because she was pregnant with me while finishing high school – even going so far as to take me to school with her after

---

[8] My nostalgia for this time in my life brings a smile to my face even as I write this. The atmosphere was one of love, happiness, and togetherness.

I was born. Nowadays, that isn't such a big deal – a teenage girl pregnant in her junior year of high school – but back then, that meant controversy. And I can only imagine the ridicule and bullshit she had to endure, inside *and* outside of home. Endure it she did, however, and she graduated with me right there on her hip, a son of 7 or 8 months old.

No early memories of my Pops, either, but I'm sure he was around. Hell, he had to be, because my brother Carvin came along in 1980, a couple of days after my third birthday. So maybe that's why I can't remember either of them from back then – because they were always off somewhere together, leaving me with Tricia, Ann, and my cousins. Can't blame them, though – two teenagers in love. I do hear that by the time I was born, that my Pops had dropped out of school to work and hustle the streets...

"Don't cry, Mama, don't cry. She just sleeping. She'll wake up in a minute."

Ann's funeral in 1981 is actually the first memory I have of my mother – and it's also my earliest memory of despair. I can clearly remember tugging on my mother's leg, trying to get her to stop crying somehow. In fact, *everyone* I knew and loved all seemed to be sobbing deeply in some kind of pain, with "my" Ann refusing to wake up from whatever dream she was having. At the time, I didn't quite realize *what* was wrong, but I knew that *something* was – the atmosphere didn't feel quite like what I was used to then. I also can't remember if I, myself, was in tears or not, but I do remember doing everything a 3-year-old could to calm my Mama's cries...

After Ann died, everything seemed to change. For some reason, I no longer liked the taste of grape jelly sandwiches, there were no more toy trucks, and my mother, Carvin, and I moved from The Village to some other housing projects on the "other part of South" named "J.C. Napier." Whereas (most of) The Village were stacked on top of one another 3 stories high and built more like apartments, "J.C." was the straight up brick projects that you see sprinkled all throughout the southeast united snakes. They were made like rows of townhomes, each home two levels, sidewalks in both the front and back yards, and even had manicured grass. There was also a small playground right outside in the front yard. Named after James Carroll Napier – a mulatto Howard University law school graduate and nashville sambo who helped to found in 1875 the Nashville Colored People's Cooperative Emigration Club to "improve the moral, intellectual, social, and material interests of the colored people" of nashville primarily by financing (with white money, of course!) the migration west to Kansas of Blacks they considered "ragged, loud, ignorant" (or just plain unemployed or embarrassing to the Black "elite"!), if you ask me, some urban planner really put some time and effort into making it seem like a community. Probably just to keep the residents from ever considering moving out of the projects or to another neighborhood. That at least was the effect for more than many.

Anyway, since this was the "other part" of south nashville where my father's side of the family was primarily from, I began to see my paternal cousins more often and grew closer to ones like Trina, T.C., and Shane. Trina and Shane were roughly my same age, but Trina's older brother T.C. was about 8 years older than I and rumored to be "crazy." I would often hear stories about him from some of the neighborhood kids or grownups gossiping:

"Man, yo cuz'n crazy."
"Un-uh, my cuz'n ain't crazy!"
"Un-huh. My big brother said he robbed the whole *dice game!"*

At the time I didn't know what a dice game was – or a

robbery, for that matter – but I sensed that "robbing a dice game" was considered something scandalous, remarkable, and, of course, "crazy." What was funny, though, was the admiration one heard in a person's voice when speaking of T.C. and his exploits. It seems the more "crazier" his actions, the more he was admired:

"*Girlll, you* know *that was T.C. who shot such-and-such last night.*"

"*Yeah, I heard. That boy crazy. What is he, 14 now? Maybe if I give him some of this grown woman pussy it'll calm his young ass down.*"

Amazing what grown folks will say when they don't think children are listening or can understand, huh? As if I didn't know what "pussy" was. Although I had never actually seen or had any at the time and didn't know the difference between regular pussy and "grown woman," I knew it was something that girls kept on them to give to boys when they were "good" or the girls wanted something from them. I think.

Anyway, the first time that I actually saw T.C. in action for myself blew my mind. Emptying the trash one night, I watched from the dumpster as he poured gas in the middle of the "drive"[9] and set it on fire; he also then burned the dumpster I had just thrown the trash in. Instantly, car traffic came to a screeching halt – as no one could pass through the flames without their car catching afire and possibly blowing up – and I watched for a couple of minutes mesmerized by the scene like everyone else. Then he noticed me.

"*Delo, what you doing out here? Get in the house before the police come.*"

His words broke my trance. I guess he wasn't worried about the police for himself, and despite the fact that I wanted

---

[9] The alleyway where everyone usually hung out that split through the projects leading to the parking lots.

to stay and watch like the growing crowd, I had, naturally, heard stories before about the police enough to fear them, and I, of course, always listened to my big cousin anyway, so I broke for the house.

"*Mama, Mama! T.C. set* EVERYTHING *on fire!*"

"*What, boy?*"

"*T.C. set* EVERYTHING *on fire!!! He* crazy!!!" I said proudly.

My mother looked out the door and saw all the smoke, fire, and the ever-growing crowd, then quickly shut and locked us in.

"*Boy, don't say that to nobody else! Don't tell nobody else he did that!*"

Up until that point I hadn't realized that I had said or did anything wrong; I was just doing like everyone else – saying how "crazy" T.C. was and talking about his exploits. But she taught me a valuable lesson that day and of course I listened to my Mama and never brought it up again. However, it would never leave my mind that "crazy" was good and "crazier" was even better...

Notwithstanding the newly heard (or just newly *noticed?*) gunshots at night sometimes, living in "J.C." was cool; I really felt a sense of community and friendship as I was growing up there. A lot of the people I met back then as an adolescent, I would still consider my friends today even as we haven't seen each other in years. In my front yard alone I had more than enough friends to play with like Wimp, Connie, and "Lil" Michael – not to mention all the other ones I made sneaking off to other yards and other sides of the projects when I *thought* I could get away with it.[10] And again, I had my cousins.

---

[10] When I thought *wrong* and for some reason or another got caught, my backside felt it. Which really didn't bother me much all the same, as I quickly learned that the pain of a "whooping" didn't last that long.

J.C. was also where I shared my first kiss – with Connie. Well, *kisses,* actually, because once I figured out that little girls were for more than playing toys with and getting beat up by, I couldn't get enough of either – the girls or the kisses. Neither of us couldn't have been no more than five or six years old or so when we learned with the guidance of one of her male teenage cousins the fine art of what he termed "French kissing." From that point on, whenever we got the chance to play together, invariably we would sneak off somewhere to "practice." I also taught and "practiced" with other girls whenever I could, as again, I say, I couldn't get enough of kisses or girls. Needless to say, I was probably not the little boy you would have wanted to leave your daughters around. Maybe even still to this day.

Anyhow, my first memories of my Pops are also from when we all moved to J.C.; I remember being especially happy those times when he'd ask me to ride with him to the store or to "make a run." Plus as I stated earlier, Pops was a hustler, so our "runs" took us all over the place it seemed. I had no complaints, though; I enjoyed all the personal time spent with my "Daddy" away from my mother and brother. Barely able to see over the dash of his sweet money green Chevy Monte Carlo with the big chrome Cragar rims, fuzzy dice hanging from the rear-view mirror, and pine-forest green air freshener reading "Gas, Grass, or Ass – No One Rides for Free," I was completely in awe of the man. I wanted to be just like him. And I was his spitting image, too:

"Boyyy, you look just like *yo' Daddy!"*

I was so proud. Everywhere we went, no matter who it was, that's all I seemed to hear whenever he and I were together. I wanted nothing more than to grow up and be just like my Pops, who was so cool in how he talked, how he walked – just being *him,* period.

I was also somewhat afraid of him, though. Or maybe I should say I was intimidated by him – which I guess is only normal between fathers and sons. Because it was never anything that I can remember seeing or hearing him having done that made me feel that way, but more so from my being so anxious of disappointing him in some way. In fact, the most afraid I can ever remember being in my life was a time where I felt I had let my Pops down: From time to time, either he or my mother would send me out to his car to retrieve something, and usually I'd sit for a while listening to the radio, imagining I was big and grown enough to drive a big car like my "Daddy." After one such trip that resulted in my leaving the radio on all night and running the battery down, my Pops returned to the house "cussing" shortly after leaving for work the following morning. I knew instantly that somehow or someway, *I* was responsible and had done something that I shouldn't have. Bursting out in tears, I wasn't even tripping about the "whooping" I knew I had coming, but was more so upset about how I knew I had upset *him*. I was worried for nothing, however, as Pops took it all in stride – after seeing the look on my face, he counseled me just to be more careful next time. And of course, I was...

Not long after we moved to J.C., I started attending school for the first time – Kindergarten at Cameron Middle. Cameron was a Kindergarten, 5th and 6th grade school named after a popular Black teacher from south nashville that had been killed in France misguidingly fighting for amerikkka in the First White World War. All of the neighborhood kids attended and I was so excited when it was my time to do so. From the first day, I was in love and pure heaven. Games and other children to play with, picture books to read – even a needed escape from my brother for a while – I *loved* school.

Every morning my Mom would walk me across "the Pike"

– the big street that separated the school from the projects – and I couldn't run fast enough to Mr. Hester's class. Some of us kids would make fun and occasionally laugh at how he reminded us of George Jefferson with glasses, nevertheless he never failed to make learning our numbers and letters fun for everyone in the classroom. We didn't realize at the time how lucky we were to have such an involved and caring teacher. Furthermore, a real rarity. Not only were Black male teachers a rare breed in nashville's public school system in and of itself, but a Black male *Kindergarten* teacher had to be at least doubly so. And although I was blessed to later be impacted by a couple of other Black male educators in my school career, Mr. Hester was the first and the one I remember the fondest. He truly seemed to make all us children believe that we could be whatever we chose to be when we got older as long as we worked at it.

Nevertheless, it wasn't all fun and games; Kindergarten would also be where I learned my family was "po." Up until that point, I had no concept of money, rich or poor, broke or wealthy. But I would soon enough learn on a day in which I was one of only a few students in class that didn't have a field trip paid for: After Mr. Hester implored us to inform our parents that we only had a couple more days to do so or we wouldn't be able to attend, I can remember having the most uneasy and strangest feeling. Especially since I had already been unnerving my mother about the trip as it was. At recess, a classmate would ask me:

"You not going on the trip? Is yo' family po' *or something?"*

She lived in the projects just as I did, but since *her* field trip was paid for and mine *wasn't*, I was whatever this "po" shit was.

That same night I would again ask my mother for the trip money, but pointedly never ask her the meaning of "po." Even with my 5-years-young mind, I could feel the negative connotations to this new word. Plus, I didn't want my mom to confirm to me if, in fact, we were "po."

Walked to the crossing guard the next morning as usual but again without the money for the trip, the little girl's remarks concerning my family being "po" would replay over and over again in my mind. Thinking it wise to skip school and re-cross the Pike alone, I have to admit to being absolutely petrified as all of the speeding cars zipped past. For some reason, though, I was much more terrified of being considered "po" than of getting hit by a car my first time crossing the street alone.

Turning up at home unexpectedly an hour or so after she had first taken me to school, it seemed as though my mother understood somewhat as she was beating my ass before she took me back...

"When times are good, your friends know you; when times are bad, you know your friends..."

Author Unknown

CAPTURED

From the time of its theft from the Shawnee "Indians" by white invaders[11] in the mid-1700s, the area along the banks of the Cumberland River now known as nashville, tennessee has long had a sordid and racist history. With a population of only 300 individuals in seven forts by 1780, nashville was granted a city charter in 1806 – just ten years after tennessee became a state. Eventually becoming tennessee's permanent capital in 1843, the city would be at the forefront of "keeping niggers in their place" before, during, and especially, after the South's defeat in the amerikkkan "Civil War." Cowardly fleeing the city and quickly laying down its arms to the approaching Union Army without even *one* bullet being fired, nashville would in fact be the first "major" Confederate city to fall. And just as any other humiliated bully does, in order to feel more like "men," the "good" nashvillians deemed to take their humiliation out on the usual scapegoats of this kkkountry: the Blacks.

With lynching being an integral aspect of perpetuating the hypocrisy of white "supremacy" in the wake of the South's defeat, the "good, white Christians" of the defeated confederacy would lynch more than one hundred Blacks a year between 1889 and 1918; white racial violence and animosity was especially rampant in and around nashville during this time, with innocent Black men and women sometimes even hung off the city's main bridge for hours at a time without trial, jury, or a lot of times

---

[11] Although normally referred to as "settlers" in amerikkkan propaganda to gloss over their genocide of the natives of the land, these skkkum would more properly be referred to as "invaders."

even the usual bogus-assed crime charged. Eye-openingly, the "good" white nashvillians were well-known for standing atop houses and buildings to watch the brutalized and murdered Black men and women as they were being tortured to death. Markedly, at least 200 of tennessee's Blacks would go on to be lynched between the years of 1890-1950.

The ku klux klan was also especially active in the area of nashville, with its members, associates, and accomplices commonly attacking Blacks, in sometimes the bright daylight, but especially after dark. Organized in nearby pulaski, tennessee, the KKK would go on to hold its first national convention in 1869 at nashville's Maxwell House Hotel. Nashville and nashvillians were so proud of the klan that even its newspapers would sing its praises, heroically highlighting and glamorizing the klan's activities "defending southern honor" and "keeping niggers in their place." Nighttime attacks on innocent Blacks became so rampant that the (not-so-necessarily-friendly towards Blacks!) Union Army patrols had to be re-instituted when torrents of Black complainants continuously arrived at nashville's Freedmen's Bureau office to file reports.

The local police and "judges" – the KKK outside of its white robes and regalia – also was used to target Blacks at this time, continuing throughout nashville's history. After the civil war, the newly "freed" Blacks were commonly "arrested" by the pigs for such minor offenses as "talking too loud," "using bad language," "speeding in a wagon," "driving a wagon on a sidewalk," "having a party without *permission*,"[12] "running and drumming," and other such "crimes" that were in no way illegal for a *white* person to commit. Local police also would arrest unemployed Blacks – men *and* women – and put them to

---

[12] Doesn't that say it all? "Permission" from *who* and for what??? I guarantee that no whites needed "permission"!

"work" again for the former slaveholders who faced "labor shortages." First established with the Tennessee Patrol Act of 1753 – which required *all* white persons, under penalty of fine, to arrest and chastise any slave away from his *"home"* plantation without a proper "pass" – these pigs would go on, and continue to be to this day, the last line of defense in the formal social control of Blacks.[13] By 1806, these searchers evolved into an elaborative preventive patrol force – the precursor to today's amerikkkan paramilitary police forces. And just as modern-day police officers, correctional overseers, and private security guards primarily come from "working-or lower-middle class" white families,[14] so too did these slave "paterollers" (patrollers) emerge from the ranks of less well-to-do and uneducated bakkkwoods whites. Nashville's pig police would throughout the decades earn a well-deserved reputation for beating, shooting, and/or killing unarmed and even nonresistant Blacks. Now these same bastards had me surrounded.

"PUT YOUR FUCKING HANDS UP GODDAMNIT!!!"

The way they were screaming and carrying on, it sounded as if we were surrounded by a thousand of those punkkk ass pigs. Running Freckles and I off the road, they now had us totally surrounded – one vehicle blocking our front, one vehicle to the driver's side, another vehicle to the rear, and nothing but an open field and clear shots to the passenger side where I was – nowhere for us to go. I honestly saw no way for me to come out of this situation alive.

Strangely, though, I wasn't afraid. Although I was consigned to my fate, I relished the chance to take as many of

---

[13] The Act also required appointed "searchers" to survey slave quarters four times a year in a check for "contraband," and most importantly, weapons to fight the whites back with. This continues to this day in amerikkka's prisons and jails, and during "routine traffic stops."

[14] In other words, poor white trash!

the punkkk motherfukkkers with me as I could.

However, I couldn't in good conscience allow Freckles to die with me – at least, not if I could in any way help it. Whatever brought on what was happening at that moment, I knew that *she* had nothing to do with. Hell, she and I had really just recently started kicking it tough. She seemed to be terrified, too. But honestly, who could blame her? The way those neanderthals were screaming bloody murder, no telling *what* was going through her mind. What young mother – what woman, period – *wouldn't* have been terrified in that same situation? Hell, most *men* would have been, too, for that matter. So I slowly put my hands up, trying to buy time and figure my next move.

Not taking long to figure out that if they wanted us *both* dead then we would have been so by now, I looked her way and told her to get out of the car and out of harm's way, as the pigs were now demanding:

"DRIVER! SLOWLY, WITH YOUR LEFT HAND, OPEN THE CAR DOOR AND EXIT THE VEHICLE!"

"I can't, I'm stuck by the seatbelt," she replied.

My head turned, watching as she opened the door and released the latch on her seatbelt. Distracted, I felt the passenger side door open behind me. Shit!

"I'VE GOT HIS GUN!!! I'VE GOT HIS GUN!!!"

My strap had slipped out of my waistband and onto the seat behind me; feeling it as it did, I also felt that that really was no problem – I had planned to duck down to give myself cover right before I let off my shots anyway. However, this sneaky bastard had snuck up behind me and taken my fucking gun! FUCK!

"IF YOU SO MUCH AS BREATHE WRONG I WILL SHOOT YOU IN THE MOTHERFUCKING HEAD!!!" the pig screamed.

Damn. I was fucked at this point: no gun to shoot back with, no witnesses to my impending assassination, and the crazy thing was, was that I didn't even have *any* idea of *why* I was being taken out! Let the streets tell it, though, and it could have been for a whole host of things. Fuck!

Surprisingly, however, instead of metal piercing my body and brain, I felt myself being pulled out of the car onto my knees into the pouring rain – the barrel of rifles, pistols, and shotguns still pointed at my head, of course. Maybe they just wanted to shoot me out in the open, is what I was thinking. Especially after a pig produced a knife and cut my body armor off of me.

"YOU ARE UNDER ARREST FOR CRIMINAL HOMICIDE!!! IF YOU SO MUCH AS MOVE, I WILL SHOOT YOU IN YOUR MOTHERFUCKING HEAD!!!"

Preparing myself mentally, still, for the bullets to strike my head and body, and clueless as to what he was referring to, my mind began to race tracing all the possibilities of whom I could have been suspected of killing; pathetic as it is for me to admit even today, I found more questions than answers. Then after a moment of realizing that I was still alive, I just had to ask, "How did you find me?"

"WE STALK PEOPLE! THAT'S WHAT WE DO!"

This was true, they had been stalking me all that day and night. I could feel it. The eerie feeling of being watched and followed. The peculiar feeling of Death being near. Had Freckles not been with me, they would have killed me long before this moment – of this, I'm sure. Why else would they have been following me all that day yet choose to take me down on a dark back road in the rain, away from all witnesses? Yeah, I'm positive that they would have killed me if given the slightest opportunity. Luckily, for me, though, they seemed to have gotten tired of waiting for a chance. Moreover, I guess they couldn't figure out how to explain Freckles' death along with mine. Other than that, I'm positive that I wouldn't be alive today. Head-Pig-in-Charge to Freckles somewhere in the background:

"*Do you* know *who you are with???*"

"*Yes. He's my friend.*"

"*But do you* know *him? Do you* know *what he does???*"

"*He's just my friend.*"

"*You are with a* very dangerous individual! *You don't realize how much your life was in danger!!!*"

Life in danger? Yeah, right. Sure as hell not from *me*. The danger came from being run off the road in the rain and darkness with guns drawn on us from *those* motherfukkkers!!! There *was* no danger from *me* – we were just kicking it for the night. So despite how they tried then and even more so later to turn her against me, to this day we remain good friends.

Within a few moments, a marked police car pulled up to transport me downtown to the "Murder Squad" office. The entire ride my mind was racing, trying to figure out just exactly whom they had charged me with killing and why tonight was the night they had come for me. It sounds terribly embarrassing to say, but I had been suspected in so many murders the preceding couple of years that I honestly had no idea as to which "body" I had been brought in for. Paraded through a gauntlet of pigs – the detectives laughing, joking, and high-fiving each other – and then set roughly in a chair at a long conference table, it would still be awhile before I would even find out. Detective Sambo to Detective Hillbilly:

"*Which ones you got him for?*"

Which *ones???* Fuck!!! Believe me, I was well aware of nashville's history of excessively pinning crimes on Black men once they had you in their clutches. Hell, this is a city that's even sent Black men to the penitentiary for *talking loud in public*!!!

"*I got him for such-and-such, and such-and-such.*"

I wasn't familiar with either of the two victim's names, but later I would learn that one of the names was that of "Old School" – the case in which I was now arrested on.

"*Well, I've got him on such-and-such, such-and-such, and such and such,*" Detective Sambo said with a bootlicking smirk on his face.

On-and-on the different pigs went, until they had called out what seemed to be at least ten bodies they said I would soon be charged with the murders of.[15] At one point, one of the pigs even gloated how I "would never see the outside of the penitentiary again." A couple of times I even heard reference to the "death penalty." Nevertheless, the more I thought about it, the bigger the smile that crept to my face; I could tell a bluff a mile away. Finally, once they realized that they couldn't rattle me, a pig frustratingly inquired:

"*Well, you got anything to say?*"

I smirked out my response:

"*Yeah, I got something to say* – talk to my muthafuckin' lawyer *that's what the fuck I got to say!!!*"

To say that that enraged the bastard is an understatement of the worst kind:

"*YOU WANNA TALK TO YOUR LAWYER, HUH?!? YOU WANNA TALK TO YOUR LAWYER???*"

BOOM! BOOM! BOOM!!! With my chair suddenly snatched out from under my legs, my shirt grabbed at its collar choking the hell out of me, and myself fiercely struggling against the handcuffs behind my back, I was dragged across the floor and my head soon made the acquaintance of a wall. Needless to say, I made the decision rather quickly not to say *anything* else.

---

[15] You would think that they wouldn't have as many unsolved murders if they actually got off their asses and *honestly* done some *investigating* of the *truth*, huh?

Furthermore, if by some chance I forgot to hold my tongue, the imminent headache would soon remind me of what could and *would* happen to a Black man "getting smart" in the eyes of the rednekkks, sambos and uncle ruckuses that made up a large part of the metro-nashville davidson county police department.

"You need to be careful with what you say and your attitude Delo, because you're the only nigger in here and these white boys'll kill you."

This from another detective sambo, named Al Gray – a known crackhead in the streets of nashville – whom came in a little later, saw me on the floor and I assume surmised what had happened. That was his way of letting me know that I was on my own in there – as if I hadn't already figured *that* out. Hell, the first sambo had witnessed the entire assault and said nor did nothing to stop it; he acted oblivious to the look of disgust I shot him. Bootlicking bitch.

For whatever reason after that, they kept me there awhile in their office – I guess in some misguided optimism that I would crack in fear or something. However, if they hadn't known beforehand, I'm sure it didn't take long for them to realize that they weren't dealing with the typical "nigger" they were used to. Even as the different pigs coming through were making their slick comments and boasting of all the time they would give me, I kept quiet. Fuck talking, fuck trying to explain myself, fuck trying to pump them for information concerning my charge; eyes and ears open, I would soon enough learn all that I needed to know. Particularly from the crackhead sambo.

*"You know your Aunt Nancy really believes you did that, don't you? She calls me almost every day, asking when are we finally gonna get you off the street*s!*"*

I guess he could tell from my eyes that he had caught my attention, but that I somewhat still didn't believe him, so he continued.

"Oh yeah, me and your Auntie are real good friends and she does all she can to help us get you. How do you think we knew about your lil dope house out north on 10th? We know every move you make."

Wow. Unbelievable. I had a feeling that something wasn't right with the newfound frequency of her popping up over my Mom's house and calling her all the time – probably on order of the police! Pitiful!

"She just can't understand why you would do her son like that," he said with a smirk.

Although I was shocked and hurt from my aunt's betrayal, still I kept quiet – no way would I dare give this crackhead sambo the satisfaction of knowing he had gotten to me...

After maybe an hour or so of my absolute silence following my "talk to my lawyer" statement and corresponding assault, I guess they finally got the message and I was then moved to an interrogation room. Surprisingly, though, it was already occupied – yet another ploy:

"Man what the fuck you doing in here?" I couldn't help but to ask.

That was the first time I had opened my mouth since getting my head cracked; I was so stunned at seeing *him*, though, that my curiosity forced the question.

"Th-th-th-they picked me up talking about some murders, and th-th-th-they kept as-asking me to tell them about you," he responded. *"Man they really want you."*

It was then that I noticed that although he was cuffed, too, *his* were in *front* of him – that meant that this bitch motherfucker had been signing something! Probably a statement on *me!* I knew right away that we were placed in the room together for no other reason than to trap me into saying something incriminating somehow. No way in hell was I falling for *that* bait, however! I knew from the way it was setup that there were cameras and microphones recording my every breath and move. So, hell, even if I *had* have known something about any murders, come on now – why would I be discussing it with *him* and in a *monitored police interrogation room*, at that??? How stupid does one have to be??? But I guess it couldn't hurt for them to try, huh? It's worked with enough idiots in the past.

"*Asking about me??? Motherfucka,* you *don't know* me," I menaced out.

Here I am already pissed off about being kidnapped, head banging from being assaulted, wondering what in the hell exactly was going on, and they've got this bitch-made motherfucker in here asking him questions about *me*! Just what in the fuck was *really* going on???

"*I-I-I-I know. I just kept saying I didn't* know *no Delo, I don't* know *no Delo! But they was talking like they knew your whole life story!*"

I grunted and turned my head away from him, laying it on the table – and said no more to that weak snitching bitch, nor anyone else for the rest of the night.

Finally taken in front of the Night Court Commissioner a few hours after my arrest, my charges were read off:

"*Kenneth Deangelo Thomas you are hereby charged with criminal homicide, to wit, that on or about January 9, 1999, said Defendant did cause the victim – a one James R. Ransom – to be murdered in the county of davidson, tennessee.*"

No bond. They charged the bitch-made motherfucker – Paul Eugene Talley – the same as I; that made him my codefendant – no bond for him either.

As I lay with my head against the wall of the crowded and moldy holding cell – shell-shocked somewhat – a few hours after I had first been arrested, I readied my mind for the struggle I knew lay ahead…

> twice in our lives
> we need direction
> when we are young and innocent
> when we are old and cynical
> but since the old refused
> to discipline us
> we now refuse
> to discipline them
> which is a contemptuous way
> for us to respond
> to each other…..
> *A Very Simple Wish* by Nikki Giovanni

EDGEHILL

I guess you could say I was born to be a "Street Star" – "Ghetto Celebrity" ran through my veins on both sides of my family. My older cousins Raymond, Duck, Ca-Carl, T.C., Waldo, Putt-Putt, and Shotgun among others – along with my oldest uncle "Wolf" and even my Pops – all had the streets ringing in one way or another all throughout the Southside while I was coming up.[16] Even "Mama" (my maternal great grandmother) was a prodigious and daring bootlegger during Prohibition, while my maternal grandfather, Johnny Boy, was an all-around hustler until the day he died.

So it was so that I was already respected somewhat through my familial relations when we moved in the summer

---

[16] Raymond got arrested in 1987 on drug trafficking and weapons charges and spent many years in federal prison. He finally got out in February of 2016.

before my 4th grade year, back to the "other part of South"[17] to "Edgehill."

Established as a "contraband camp" for runaway slaves during the height of the amerikkkan civil war in November of 1864, the Edgehill neighborhood in south nashville even to this day is primarily Black in spite of encroaching "gentrification." Located near Fort Negley – the largest Union fort west of Washington, D.C. at that time[18] – its strategic import would especially attract thousands of Blacks from the western and southern sections of tennessee and the ever-growing city of nashville following the breakup of the slave plantations in the war's aftermath. Under the shadow of the former Belmont plantation – sight of present-day Belmont University – from whence many of the former slaves came, Edgehill consists of three adjacent housing complexes known as the "The Village," "The Manors," and "The Projects" in addition to the single-family homes and duplexes that surround them. Acquiring notoriety for becoming home to nashville's first "housing projects" complex in the mid-1900s, this ill repute would grow after the "riots" in those projects following the death of Martin Luther King in April of 1968. And instead of back to The Village, these infamous projects – what would become known to me as "The Bricks" – is where my family would move this time. It was the summer of 1986, and unbeknownst to me, the height of the crack epidemic in amerikkka, and I would soon be right there in the midst of all the happenings.

However, it would be quite some time before I was able to perceive the socio-and-macroeconomic fuckery of Reaganomics

---

[17] To Edgehill and (another set of projects on the South Side) Vine Hill Manors, the J.C. / U.C. area is known as the "other part of South" and vice versa. To all other sides of the city, we are all just "South."

[18] Which was, ironically, built with the "forced labor" of Blacks kidnapped by the *Union* cavalry.

that was going on in my world at that time – all I could notice was that Edgehill was "live." In fact, it was *so live* that I was "tried" and tested within 48 hours of our moving in. Matter of fact, I had to fight the very first time my mom allowed me outside.[19] It was cool, though, because I wasn't "no punk" – I had had numerous fights walking back and forth to J.C. Elementary School while attending the 1st-3rd grades – so fighting wasn't anything new or something I was afraid of. In fact, I liked and almost *loved* fighting when I was growing up – fighting was the surest way to establish a respect factor where there was none before. Later, I would also learn that fighting could be mental and even emotional instead of physical all the time, however in those days all I knew was the *knuckles*. So knuckles, it was.

Anyway, to this day, I can't remember *why* I was fighting, but I can sure as hell remember *who*: Scoozie, a big fat fucker of a kid who I *knew* had to be at least 2-3 years older than me. Surrounded by a crowd of neighborhood kids that I hadn't met yet, most of them were "egging him on" to "beat his (my) ass." And as much as I hate to admit it, that fat motherfucker won the fight, too! Nevertheless, he and all the other kids out watching *did* respect me afterwards. And that's all I could ask for. It didn't even matter to the kids in the neighborhood that he was in fact a couple of years *younger* than me instead of older, as long as I *did* fight and take up for myself, I was cool. That way they knew I wasn't no "chump," and they could possibly accept me as one of their own.

But, of course, that first fight sure as hell didn't mean that I wouldn't have to fight any more after that. In fact, it seemed as though fighting was the neighborhood pastime. Mothers and

---

[19] I would soon notice that my mother seemed to be more comfortable with allowing me to roam more since we were back on "her side" of south.

fathers would fight each other, siblings would fight one another, friends would fight – all out in the yard in the open, sometimes, for everyone to witness. (We can only imagine what went on behind closed doors!) Afterwards, invariably, everyone would be right back cool with each other later on that day, if not later on that hour. Not at all unusual for the neighborhood, I'm almost sure I fought all of whom would become my friends in the Projects at least once. Fighting was just the way Edgehill handled its differences and/or just seemed like the thing to do.

But check it, I don't want you to think that I'm saying any of this in a *bad* way, because I'm not; I loved living in Edgehill, fights and all. I instantly noticed that there was a never-ending excitement in the Projects – many times involving one of my extended family members. In the Edgehill neighborhood alone, living in The Village was my great-grandmother "Mama"; her daughter (my great-aunt) "Bibbie" and her youngest daughter "Shack"; Bibbie's oldest daughter Paulette and her son "Putt" and youngest daughter "Sandy"; and Paulette's oldest daughter "Nasa B." with her twin girls. That was just on my mother's side of the family, with my father's brother "Wolf" living along with his wife "Patsie," daughter Deborah ("Stinka" to the family), and son "Man" (Dennis, Jr.) in The Village, also.

In the Edgehill Manors, our family had my (maternal) Aunt Carlene, along with her sons Lamont ("Shotgun" or "Shot"), Carl ("Ca-Carl"), John ("Punkin" – who was only a couple of years older than I), and daughter Jolonda.

Then, within walking distance, my Aunt Net lived in a home a street over from the Projects, and my aunts Fattie (with her son Juan who was Carvin's age and her daughter Shateka) and Tricia lived a few streets away on Hawkins St. So we all lived pretty close and, thus, all of us cousins would grow up together that way. By this time, also, my own immediate family had grown by two: In addition to myself and my brother Carvin, my mother and father had also had my sister Devonne in early February of 1983, followed shortly thereafter by my youngest brother John.

So we had an extremely large extended family throughout the Edgehill community, and although our family was huge, I'm not even sure it was quite the biggest in the neighborhood. There were a lot of 2nd and 3rd generation families in and around the Projects, Manors, and Village. What's more, usually when one did decide to move out of the public housing complexes, frequently it was to one of the houses or apartments within walking distance dotting the neighborhood. People in Edgehill didn't seem to want to leave. Edgehill was where it's "at." Furthermore, most of all of the large families would be inter-related through marriage or the birth of children.

With all of the large families in and around the neighborhood, Edgehill would be where I really learned the sense of "community" in spite of all the violence and chaos I witnessed. How? Well, in Edgehill, since everyone seemed to be kin or connected to one another's family in some kind of way, no matter *what* you were into, or *who* was into it, *it* usually involved some type of "family." So for the most part, through the majority of disagreements, those familial links kept all of the "deadly" shit down. Furthermore, the grownups of the neighborhood looked out for all of the children it seemed, meaning that no matter if somebody's mama was kin to you or not, she could and would still "beat your ass" if she saw you doing something wrong. Usually, though, the "kin" issue *wasn't* one because more times than not you were inter-related with everyone else whom you would come across.

What's more, for those children that by some off chance didn't happen to be kin to me (or kin to one of my cousins), usually we ended up being friends anyway. Hell, it's almost as if we had no choice with how close-knit the neighborhood was and the amount of us children that lived there. We all went to school and played together, our mothers and (a lot of times) fathers hung out with one another, and in later years, we ourselves would further the inter-relations of the families by having children by one another as well.

So as you can imagine, our house was always full of people, especially on weekends. It was mostly my extended family and my mom's friends. I was about ten and this arrangement put all of my favorite cousins around me to play too, which was pretty cool. All my teenage and young adult female cousins loved hanging out at our house too because my Mama was a cool aunt and they could see their boyfriends. I think probably half of them got pregnant as a result.

While we children "ran wild" upstairs and/or sometimes in the yard out front, the grownups would play cards and drink. When not doing so at our house, one of their (the adults) favorite haunts was the nearby Beer Barn. They would appoint one of the older cousins to babysit us and you can imagine how that went.

Similar to most of my peers, this would be a time when we were introduced in a peripheral way to alcohol, cigarettes, and drugs. However, I saw what they do to people and how it makes them act and rather than taking a liking to it like many other kids, I developed an aversion to it which lasts till this day. I tried it (alcohol) once and had such a negative experience, it was more than enough for me; I became a teetotaler.

With all that being said, Edgehill was always fun for a child. Having three different parks/playgrounds in the Projects alone, there was always, it seemed, a basketball, baseball, kickball, and football game to be had, or maybe even a game of "hide and go seek."²⁰ Our mothers would sit on the porch socializing with one another and watch our friendly competitions as we would race up and down the sidewalks or play "Red Light Green Light" until it was time to go in to eat or take a bath to get ready for the next day. Even the fights were fun – with, as I've said earlier, seemingly the entire neighborhood coming out to watch as if it was a prizefight.

One of my childhood memories is of a cat named "C." He had the sweetest whip (car) with a custom paint job of flashy colors. He was a local hustler and everyone loved "C." He used to cruise the neighborhood tossing out money, with us kids following him like the Pied Piper. We could now get a chance to get something that was a rarity to you as a Project kid at a candy store in the area: candy and snacks. A welcomed treat!

At night, for those of us who could stay out a little bit later than others, we had a game we called "Nig Knock" – short for "nigger knock," I later found out – wherein we would knock on other people's doors hard as hell like the police and run away before they could answer. Looking back on it now, I don't even understand what was so fun about it to us a kid because all it involved was, at best, irritating the hell out of someone by beating down their door, or, at worst, scaring the hell out of them if they actually thought that it was the police. We would run throughout the Projects, ruining people's peace and quiet and just generally acting a fool.

Which brings me to us neighborhood kids' favorite game: cops and Robbers. Cops and Robbers involved setting up a "base camp" – say, for instance, one of the benches in the park – choosing teams as to who would be the cops and who would be the Robbers, and then counting to, say, ten or twenty or some

---

²⁰ Or when we became pre-teens and young teenagers, "hide and go *get*," which involved finding the girl you "liked" and "winning" some kisses and/or "hunching" for your efforts.

other agreed upon number, and giving the Robbers time to run through the Projects and hide. The cops would then send out the majority of its team to track down the Robbers, while the Robbers would try its damnedest to stay "free" for as long as they could.[21] The most significant rule was, if you were caught by the cops, you would be escorted back to "Base" where you would have to sit for the remainder of the game guarded by one of the cops. However, you could be liberated from the jail base by one of the other Robbers coming up to free you by making it past the cop(s) and touching Base. It was basically like Hide-and-Go-Seek on steroids, with the game never ending until the entire team of Robbers were caught, with them sometimes being liberated two or three times – or maybe even never – before that ever happened. Girls and boys both played, with sometimes the agreed upon area allowed for you to hide involving the entire Edgehill neighborhood. We would hide beside, behind, or on houses, on or under cars, behind or in bushes, or just sometimes out in the open. (Matter of fact, those were usually the most fun times – because having the cops chase you yet you somehow getting away was a straight-up sugar rush! Crazy how that would foretell things to come, huh?) Sometimes the game would go on for hours in the summertime when we were all allowed to stay out later, with maybe ten or twenty or maybe even thirty of us boys and girls from all three housing projects involved in playing.

Another favorite pastime of ours was swimming. E.S. Rose Community Center on Edgehill Ave. across from the Manors had an adjacent open-air community pool that was free to all in the summer, and utilized almost every day by most of us neighborhood kids attempting to counteract the heat. The "Center" also gave out "free lunch," so lots of times us kids

---

[21] It's ironic how this would be a major theme of a lot of our *real* lives as we got older!

would get the free food (usually a bologna and cheese sandwich and a drink), wait a few minutes before jumping in the pool (because we were warned we would catch "cramps" and drown if we swam so soon after eating), and then swim all morning well into the afternoon. Normally we would all be tired as hell by the time the pool closed for the day, so after that, we would usually head to our respective homes to regroup with another meal, followed by coming back outside to the usual game of cops and Robbers. Furthermore, a lot of times, also, a few of us would later jump the fence and "hit the pool" (skinny dip) again after a robust game. That's how I and many others passed many a summer's day. Later, as a pre-teen, I would join the Center's swim team and go on to win many a match in my age division against other city neighborhoods.

I also picked up another love during that first summer back in Edgehill: the public library. Edgehill Public Library was directly across a small street from the Projects on 12th Avenue, and – reading proficiently since the age of four or five or so – I would find myself there at least once or twice a week on average after we moved back to the neighborhood. Loving the fact that I had a plethora of books and magazines to choose from, I would wile away hours lost in different worlds and times. (It didn't hurt that the library was air-conditioned, either!) My library card in my own name was, in fact, one of my most prized possessions. I checked out many books all summer long and probably to this day still have overdue/lost book fees owed.

My love affair with school continued, too, although more so after I started the 5th grade and was able to start attending Carter-Lawrence Middle School right across the street from the Projects. Not to say that 4th grade wasn't cool for the most part, but with us neighborhood kids being forced to attend Cole Elementary School's Annex – which was located a few miles south on Nolensville Rd. in a traditionally white part of town – most of us didn't necessarily feel "welcomed" there.[22] It's not that I can remember anything overtly racist or non-welcoming, but it was easy to sense that we were "out-of-place."

Compare that to Carter-Lawrence, which we knew was "our" school. Neighborhood parents were seemingly much more involved at Carter-Lawrence as opposed to Cole Annex as it wasn't unusual for mothers and/or fathers to eat lunch with their children, walk their children to their first class, attend open houses or parent-teacher conferences, or just drop in for a chat with the teachers and/or our principal, Dr. Jeff Kersey.[23] I can submit that the parents of Edgehill had a seemingly appreciated presence at Carter-Lawrence, with Dr. Kersey and teachers such at Mr. Jeff Swink and others greeting many of them by name and with a welcomed smile.[24] And although I can in some ways understand the case for the integration of schools during the time of my parents' adolescence, there has got to be a better way than taking children – black, white, Hispanic, Asian, Native American, whatever – and driving past a school within walking distance of home to be bussed to another neighborhood. That can't be the most intelligent and/or only way of doing things.

Furthermore – although we had just as much fun as at other schools that I had attended – Carter-Lawrence's teachers also nurtured our intellectual sides. Carter-Lawrence was, in fact, the first time I can remember the public school system identifying me as having "above-average" intelligence or being

---

[22] We were bussed all the way out there due to the city's "desegregation plan" then in federal court.

[23] Whether that had more to do with Carter-Lawrence's closer proximity, I don't know. But no matter how close it was would not have made any difference if it wasn't for the welcoming that Dr. Kersey and a lot of the teachers gave both us students and our parents.

[24] My favorite teacher Ms. O'Connor was a blonde lady who was very athletic and so nice to us kids. She always encouraged us to stay in shape and study.

"gifted." Not only were academics supported and encouraged at Carter-Lawrence, but also they were *expected* of *all*.[25] I would find myself being a part of "spelling bees" and other contests that were strictly academic and loving it.

Plus my cousin "Punkin" (my Aunt Carlene's son) and I were in the same classes and had already started to run together after we moved back to that part of South, so that just added to my comfort level. Usually he and I would spend just as much time together *after* school as we would in school. Many a weekend he would spend the night over my house in the Projects or I would spend the night over his in the Manors – even though we only lived a short five-minute walk away from each other. Being in the same classes just made us closer – to add to his mother being my mother's favorite sister. We would ride bikes, skateboards, or scooters, play football, basketball, or baseball, climb trees, or just generally act a fool like most young children do. It was fun.

But not everything was all fun and games at Carter-Lawrence; I also, in fact, remember it as the first place I was called a "nigger." Not that I had never heard the word, of course – I mean, how could you not growing up in the Projects? – but this time it came with *venom* from some fat wanna-be bully white boy.[26] And although I didn't understand at the time all the implications of what he had said, with the poisonous inflection in which he spit it, I couldn't help but to feel a certain kind of way. Besides, the little fat bastard had called me that after being unable to take a ball or something from me that I assume he felt

---

[25] Which is a hell of a distinction once you really think about it. Because children, especially, can only rise or fall below what is *expected* of them. If expectations are low, then so, usually, are the goals for life. But if *more* is expected, usually more is also achieved.

[26] As opposed to Cole Annex, the situations were in fact reversed in that the *white* children were bussed to *our* neighborhood now, and I guess more than a few hated the idea just as much as we did when faced with it.

he had a right to, but you know, of course, *that* wasn't what was happening. And when that shit didn't work out like he wanted, he and I had a little tussle, and that's when his true feelings and the epithet came. Me being me, and pulling him to the side in P.E. (Physical Education) class the very next day, he and I had a nice conversation about his actions and his words while I held a small army knife to his stomach.

So you know, no more problems out of the little bastard after that, of course – except him snitching on me like a little bitch when he ran home – I assume – and told his parents (who were probably the same people who taught him the word "nigger"), who, in turn, I guess complained to Dr. Kersey. Because that's sure as hell who was waiting on me the very next morning to question me about it. Nevertheless, although I admitted that we had in fact gotten into a "disagreement," I was smart enough to lie about the fact that I had a knife. Think my lying about the knife speaks to my character at an early age, huh? Or do you agree that it speaks to my developing grasp of the reality of the world I was born into? I myself, think so a little of both, but more so the latter than the former, because I could sense even at that age that had I admitted to having possessed the knife, it would've led to a-whole-nother ball game. Looking back, I'm positive that the police would have been called, resulting in my leaving school in handcuffs, with the possibility of me being expelled for the rest of that year at best – and for good at worst. All because I chose to answer a bully's force with (the necessary, in my opinion!) counterforce of my own.

Thankfully, though, it didn't happen that way and Dr. Kersey took me at my word. I think. Plus, I could sense that none of the teachers liked the little fat ass bully anyway, as he was always a problem for them and other students. Either way, that was the end of it and I never even told either of my parents any of what had transpired.

After that, though, Dr. Kersey and Mr. Swink (my math and science teacher and Dr. Kersey's best friend, I think) seemingly took an interest in me and started giving me more attention. They took me to college football games at Vanderbilt University (where they were both alumni) or sometimes just out to get a bite to eat on the weekends. Looking back, I think it was just to get me out of the "Project environment" every little now and again and expose me to something else. Anyway, those two and the memories of how they looked out for me will always be with me...

Sadly, shortly after moving back to Edgehill, my family life would change drastically after my father left our household. I can't remember exactly why or when he and my mother broke up, but I *can* remember how distinctly different things were afterwards. Notwithstanding the fact that we children were used to our father being an everyday presence in our lives, I soon noticed that we also didn't have some of the basic material things we were used to. What's more, I'm not sure if we had always received "public assistance" and "food stamps" or not, but I *do* remember us using/having them at that time. In fact, my first pangs of hunger and hearings of "child support" all come from then. We seemed to only have enough food towards the beginning of the time of the month in which my mother "got her food stamps," which left us borrowing a "$5 book" of them from a neighbor or my Aunt Carlene until my mother again got her own. Which was so embarrassing. I don't know if it was more so from not getting enough for a mother and her four kids, or just from that mother not having enough money management skills to make it, but every single month we struggled.[27]

However, not as much as some other families did. Some of the children we played with would be back to starving within a week of their mother receiving their monthly allotment of food stamps and/or "check." How? Well, usually from what I witnessed it was because the mother was strung out on drugs – which meant in my neighborhood "base" or as it's more widely known, "crack cocaine." So either she would sell her food stamps for pennies on the dollar as soon as she received them, or she would already owe them out to the "dopeman" beforehand. Either way, the children starved and were the ones to suffer the most. Shit was (and still is!) crazy.

I know it may sound strange coming from a person who grew up on public assistance himself, but I for one am all in favor of the drug testing of *any* and *all* those whom receive welfare of the kind where it's a direct cash payment (or its equivalent). Why? Because no way in hell should someone else pay for people choosing to get "high" for any reason whatsoever.[28] Yet, time and time again I witnessed money that should have directly went for the benefit of children, instead go to fill up a neglectful mother's lungs or veins with an intoxicating

---

[27] It was about this time that I and a kid named Rodney began our career of "crime." Mostly it was stealing candy bars and things from the local stores. We were candy starved, having to rely on food stamps, which ran out all too fast, for any such treats. We also went down to Sears to snatch GI Joe and other toys. We even did our biggest job at Vanderbilt University, stealing bikes. But my career ended when Rodney got grabbed. That was enough for me.
Just like booze and drugs, the experience eventually turned into a lifelong aversion to stealing. I felt bad sneakily taking what was the property of someone else. I knew I wouldn't like it myself.
However, taking something by *force?* – somehow or another that became something altogether different. Something that my parents could never understand nor condone when they became aware of my inclinations. Something that I myself can't even understand nor justify as I look back on it.
[28] However, whatever you choose to do to *your* body and in *your* life with money *you* earned is *your* business in my opinion. Get high as a cloud, for all I care. It's your life – I just don't want to have to help pay for it.

substance. And by no means am I saying that this was the case in *most* instances, but in the same vein, *any one* case is a case too many. So in order to safeguard the few who need it, the many will have to be slightly inconvenienced.

Furthermore, the hassle of monthly or bi-weekly drug testing would encourage those on public assistance to get off of it and become self-sufficient much more quickly in my opinion. To me, what amounts to basically free money should *always* come with a stipulation in my eyes. No way in hell am *I* working hard or even taking "penitentiary chances" just for someone else to misuse *my* hard-earned funds. And I think most of the practical thinkers of this country think this way, also.

Moreover, although "welfare reform" is something that's customarily touted by the republikkkans of this kkkountry, I don't think that that should automatically discount a great idea. The "Welfare System" of this kkkountry is undoubtedly broken in that instead of teaching people *to* fish, it's constantly providing fish *for* them. Nonetheless I seriously feel as if that's *without a doubt* by *design* in order to keep us dependent upon (white) amerikkka *begging* it for table scraps. And *that* is a major reason behind a lot of multi-generational "poor" families, consistently staying poor. In my opinion the aims of the Welfare System should be to *empower* people to *do for self* so that they can live their lives the way they *aspire* to. And I recognize that some libertarian republikkkans have a time or two forwarded these ideas. Yet as "they" say, even a broken clock tells the right time twice a day. Moreover, you can learn profound truths from even your worst enemies.

But I digress – back to my Pops and his involvement in our lives after he moved out. Because I don't want you to get it twisted about him, as if he was neglectful or unsupportive, as he was still *actively* involved in our upbringing. No doubt that we hated not seeing him as much as we were used to (which is, in fact, normal when there's been a divorce or some type of breakup within families), but we *did* spend a lot of time with him, nonetheless. Him not really moving far away when he did so, my mother would a lot of times walk my brothers, sister, and I to his apartment right down the street across from Belmont University and drop us off – whether he knew we were coming or not. Sometimes this would end in an argument between the two, but not once can I remember him turning us away or not letting us spend the night when we wanted to. Moreover, he himself would come to get us most times.

And our times with him were *fun*. While we were there we would run around the apartment complex much like we did in the Projects, and watch movies and play video games all day. Plus, he had a whole host of characters for friends constantly stopping by when we were there (more on that later) who used to give us candy, money, and sometimes even tell a crazy ass story to entertain us. Never did we want for anything whether it was food, peace, or something to do when we were with him. So all in all, we enjoyed the time spent at our father's house.

All in all, my Pops seemed to adjust to living apart from us fairly quickly. However, my Mom's adjustment was a totally different story. Although she tried to hide it from us children, she was seriously emotionally damaged by the breakup of her and our father. And, inevitably I guess, that started to effect the relationship we had with him.

Hating to admit it but wanting to be fair, looking back on things now I can see how my Mom's bitterness at their separation started to poison the relationship we children had with our father. My mother would key in on any discrepancy in what he said or what he did – even if it only meant he was a few minutes late in picking us up when he said he would – and we would never fail to hear the fact of his failings if he didn't provide something at the time in which he said he would. And no child wants to see his mother upset or angry or crying all the time (even though she thought she was hiding it from us), yet nor can a child continue to hear statements such as "your Daddy ain't shit," or "why ask that man for anything – all he gonna do is lie to you" without it poisoning his or her mind. However, that's what we had to deal with regularly. But to be fair, I'm not even sure she realized (or even realizes to this day) the effect she was having, nor was it fair to her or us children for my father to say or do something and not keep his word.

Yet, in reality, that's the real world. My experiences as I've grown older are that what happened with my mother, father, and us is unfortunately not an uncommon occurrence. Far too many women (and men in some cases when the positions are reversed!) poison the relationships children have with their fathers just because the parents are no longer together. Most times, I would say, this is done so subconsciously, but a lot of times women do this willfully realizing the damage she's causing in some sick plot of revenge or punishment. And with the women usually supported fully by the kkkourts, a lot of men allow this to push them away from their children. But I'm glad that my father never gave up on us like that. Shamefully, however, I can't honestly say that I didn't do the same in not giving up on him:

Like most children at that age, one of the things I didn't understand was the value of money and the concept of my father having to work hard for all the things he provided us. All I knew – like other kids – was what *I* wanted, which was to have all of the same things the other kids did. Especially my cousin Punkin who – as I said earlier – was my peer at home and at school and who I hung out with the most. So when his father bought him some "BKs" – British Knights shoes – for our upcoming school year, I wanted some also – even though I had never even *heard* of BKs before he said something to me about them.[29] My father was, of course, going to buy me, my brothers, and my sister clothes, shoes, and all the other things we needed in order to properly start school. But what he *wasn't* going to do was blow his hard-earned (or hard-*hustled*, which is the same thing, in my eyes!) money on some BKs that I would more likely than not tear a hole in within a month like I did all my other shoes. And although I don't blame him one iota for his decision now, I sure as hell blamed him then.

With the help of my mother, of course. After he refused to buy me what I wanted (the BKs) as opposed to what I needed (some sensibly-priced and decently made shoes), my mother scolded me that I "knew not to ask that man for anything." That was it for me. My eleven or twelve years young mind made itself up that not only would I not ask him for anything ever again, but that I also would never even speak to him again. Sad to say, that seemed to be exactly what my mother wanted, too. It was like I chose her side or something in whatever else was going on between them.

So the next time my father called to talk to us, I was the only child that didn't. The next time my father came to pick us up for the weekend, I was the only child that didn't go. Soon, the bullshit would start to take on a life of its on, too. When asked by some of the neighborhood kids why I didn't go with

---

[29] Same thing with the Troops, and the Filas, and the Diadoras, and the Ellese, and the Pumas, and Adidas, and all the other bullshit "name brand" shoes I and others coveted back then. What we didn't realize at that time was that *we* made the brand, the brand didn't make *us*. So many companies have been built up upon the backs of young, Black kids like myself making them into something that it's hard to even fathom. I'm sure glad that as I became older you had Black entrepreneurs like Marc Buchanan, Sean Combs, Russell and Kimora Lee Simmons, Daymond John, and others capitalize off of our setting of the trends that run not only this country but the world. But I, again, digress.

the rest of my siblings, I took to replying that "he wasn't my Daddy" or that "my Daddy is dead." Sickening, right? And I have to be fair to my Mom and say that I don't think she was the one whom actually put those statements in my head explicitly — because it was clear to anyone who took even a cursory glance at my father and I that I *was* in fact *his* child — but she also didn't discourage me from making them when she heard them. In fact, she thought it was funny. But it wasn't.

I *hurt* my father in treating him the way that I did. Forget about anything you've ever read or heard about men in general, and Black men specifically not giving a damn about their kids and/or not having any feelings. Because that's simply not true. For my father to know that his oldest *child*, his oldest *son*, basically abandoned him for *nothing* would keep him up at night, crying, sobbing, and drinking himself to sleep. How do I know? Because not only would my brothers, sister, and cousin Trina constantly tell me about it, but I could also *feel* it as I was doing the same thing (crying) every time my siblings left for his house without me. I mean, me being saddened about it would happen without fail. I would go on to miss some valuable times with my father behind all of that bullshit. Valuable time with my brothers and sister while they were gone on without me, valuable time with most of my father's side of the family, just valuable time growing up period.

I wouldn't let my Mama see me down or discouraged about it, though, because I didn't want to disappoint her. And to be honest, I didn't understand why my father just couldn't come back home with us all anyway. That's what would have made everything alright in my young eyes. And I know that's what she wanted, also.

But that wasn't to be. And I can't even blame him, either. Someone turning *my* child against *me* would make me in turn,

turn against *them*.[30] My father and I would go on to lose close to two years, I think, of valuable time with each other as a result, and this would affect our relationship in both good and bad ways for the rest of our lives.

---

[30] The parent / person, not the child. Although in some cases, sadly, that happens a lot of times, also.

"Although the Black community is persistently fractured by the sudden removal of its members through either the calculated strategy or the mere whim of their white controllers, the community always patches itself back together drawing from its common suffering and anger a common strength..."
Robert Crossley, Reader's Guide Critical Essay on Octavia E Butler's *Kindred*

CAGED

Classified to the 5th floor of the "Justice Center" along with the rest of the accused murderers and other so-called "worst of the worst," I would for the next few months spend most of my time reading the newspapers, magazines and books I had my family purchase me, "hooping" (playing basketball), and playing chess. Matter of fact, I spent more time than any engaged in chess battles – accepting all challengers and challenges – as it seemed to allow me to keep my mind fresh and somewhat of use in that misery pit known as the "cellblock." Picking it up during my first trip to the Justice Center at the age of 17, I had before then always considered chess to be a "whiteboy game" as I had never seen anyone but whiteboys on television playing it. But in fact, chess was a *thinking* man's game, and above all else I've always been a "thinker."

And, by then, I considered myself somewhat of a "chess master," too. I would purposely psyche my opponents out by going so far as to continue reading while I was whooping their asses. Most cats initially would think that there was no way I could be paying attention to the game, or in the alternative, I couldn't actually be reading the paper, but after so many times seeing me both win the game and simultaneously hold a conversation with onlookers concerning what I was reading, cats knew that they would have to bring their "A-game" just to even compete.[31] Furthermore, my antics and arrogance made cats want to beat me that much more, and made me pick my game up as a consequence by doing my damnedest not to let anyone defeat me.

As a result, I didn't lose many games. And when I did, I was that much more determined to demolish the person who had the audacity to defeat me.[32] Most cats, for the most part, I had no trouble with. Yet, no matter what strategy I used, I just couldn't seem to consistently be able to best this older gentleman named "Butch." The old cat's eyes were so squinty that half of the time they looked completely closed, but he was so smooth as hell and so observant that for the longest time I couldn't figure out how he got out of almost every jam I happened to corner him in. My inability to dominate him as I did the rest frustrated me to all ends, so there was never a time when the cell doors were open that I wasn't challenging him to a game or two. I knew to defeat him I had to be up on all my "Cs" and "Ts" at all times. Nevertheless, I wouldn't (and couldn't!) stop until I had this cat's game figured out.

Resolving myself to remembering every move he made on the board every time we played a game, I one day peeped his strategy: Thinking he was distracting me by regaling me with old street and penitentiary tales, he would move one or more pieces into the positions he needed them in to win. I busted him. You should've seen the look on his face when I was able to replay not only every move we had made that game, but also every move we had made the two games before it.

From that point forward, he was never able to win more than one game out of five – I had broken the only advantage he

---

[31] Not to sell any of the cats' in jails and/or prisons short, either, because a lot of these individuals are more intelligent than the average.
[32] As you've probably noticed by now, sometimes my arrogance back then could get the best of me. But you'd better believe, I've been humbled by life more than needed.

ever had on me: the ability to break the rules of the game due to my being distracted. And I'll always appreciate 'Ol Butch for that lesson; he taught me to pay closer attention to details and everything around me at all times (especially when being wooed with words!), to keep my focus no matter the chaos of my surroundings, and to not allow anything or anyone to knock me off the path to accomplishing my goals. Butch also made me accept the fact that people can and will cheat you if they think they can get away with it – no matter how much they profess to "follow the rules." Important lessons that would help me later in my many unforeseen battles in the kkkourtrooms and streets of this kkkountry.

So, yeah, I learned a lot from Butch. Yet, although he and I would become cool as hell, I would always maintain somewhat of a wariness towards him. And sometimes that wariness could manifest itself quickly and aggressively.

Like the time he mentioned that I was a "sensitive brother." Immediately taking offense because of his reputation of being a "booty bandit" from his previous bids in the penitentiary, fury instantly hit my eyes. And although I was arrogant enough to think that he wouldn't dare try me, I was always on high alert for him or anyone else who was foolish enough in making the mistake of doing so. So I "checked" him.

"What the fuck you mean 'sensitive,' *muthafucka???"*

Peeping the balled up fists that went along with the murderous face in front of him, he quickly reassured me that he simply meant that I wore my heart on my sleeve. Luckily, for him, he was right. I could be your best friend or your worst enemy – there was no in between with me. And it was all up to you in my eyes. Furthermore, I've never been the type of person able to "fake" how I feel about someone; even if never verbalized, there's never a question as to where someone stands with me.

Making sure then that we had an understanding that he wouldn't attempt suicide by trying to "play" me, we continued our match while I soaked up all the game and knowledge he chose to bless me with. And, of course, from then on, he was much more careful with his words...

Butch wasn't the only "Old Head" I was able to soak up game from during this otherwise awful time in my life – in fact, a lot of them took a liking to me, seeing in me the potential to be all that they used to be, wished they were, or saw others become. In listening to their tales, I received hustling tutorials of all kinds – drug dealing, robbery, kidnapping for ransom, scamming, and even white-collar crime. You wouldn't believe what most cats had gotten away with, let them tell it. The common attributes to success they expressed were fearlessness, the ability to improvise, and above all else, outthinking your adversaries. All qualities I had in droves.

Brazenly, I was very interested in the reasons for them being caught those times they were. Most of the time it had something to do with them being "high" off something, not following their instincts, or overconfidence – all mistakes that one could avoid. Even in regards to those times when someone else had snitched on them could be attributed to not following their instincts – a weak person always gives off a certain kind of vibe I was to learn later. Whether we choose to take heed to it or not, is on us.

However much I kicked it with the Old Heads, I fucked with the cats of my generation, too. Coming through the door of the county jail, most of them either knew me or knew of me through all of the gossip of my dealing, robbing, or killing in the streets of nashville – and usually the rumors involved at least some combination of the three. I had always known, of course, that my street exploits had my name "ringing," but truthfully, I didn't know to what extent I was being gossiped about in nashville's street lore until this particular incarceration. All kinds of shit was attributed to me or my hand, so much so that if I didn't know myself, then *I* would have been afraid of me! Pathetic, right? However, as a consequence of my reputation, all of the young cats gave me my respect, as they either dug the way I got down, or at least didn't knock it. Well, not to my face, anyway.

Nevertheless, those that only knew of *me* usually didn't believe at first glance that I was the one that everyone had been talking about – I was too clean-cut and studious looking, always with something to read in hand until those that *knew* me confirmed that, yeah, I was "that muthafucka." To the uninformed, I looked more as if I belonged in a classroom instead of a cell, and hell, I was in total agreement with them feeling as if I didn't belong. Nonetheless, let the punkkk bitch d.a. tell it, I not only belonged in a cage just as they had me, but for the rest of my life, as well. And truth be told, it was hell to pay for any fool who made the mistake of taking my humble appearance for some type of weakness…

Astoundingly, there was a time or two when fools would even go so far as to discuss my exploits without even realizing that I was the cat that they were talking about. I remember one occasion while playing chess in the back of the cellblock overhearing my name; a new cat in the pod was mentioning to another how he had been "going to meet" some "dude named Delo who drives a black Expedition." My opponent heard him, too. And seeing how he (my chess opponent) was a homeboy from San Diego that had heard of my reputation but never actually seen me in action, I could tell that he was peeping as to how I would handle the situation. Letting the new cat talk a little bit more until I noticed a subject change, I then "fronted him out":

"*Hey, you know Delo?*"

He could tell from my manner that somehow he had talked himself into some shit; too late for him to be nervous now, though.

"*Uhh, yeah, I – I met him one time.*"

"*Dig that,*" I said, "*where you know him from homie?*"

"*I – I – I was supposed to be selling him some guns one time, but I got busted with 'em first,*" he stammered.

Talking too fucking much. Didn't even know who in the hell I was and running his mouth like that. That made me get even more aggressive.

"*Oh, for real? I know him, too. Who you used to kick it with? Who you know him through?*"

He mentioned the names of some friends of mine that I then went to the phone to question. Turns out, the cat and I really *had* met before and he really *was* supposed to sell me some Mac-90s once upon a time. I simply didn't remember his name or face. Nor, of course, did he remember mine. And that's not as unusual as it sounds when dealing with jails and prisons – you see so many different faces that you sometimes don't remember how even those that were close to you look like after so long.

Anyway, calling him up to the front of the cellblock and handing him the phone, I then let him know that I was in fact the "Delo" that he had been talking about and to quit running his mouth so fucking much. He was surprised and embarrassed, but quickly apologized, and he and I would end up being good friends. We became so cool that he would even stand up alongside me and the homie from San Diego a few months later when a "set-tripping-related" melee jumped off in the cellblock one day…

Speaking of some of the bullshit that you're faced with in jail, if I haven't been clear enough, let me say this: Jail is a literal hell, so you do all you can to make the best of it. Some cats "ride" the phones harassing their wives and girlfriends to keep other men out of them, others live visit to visit, and some cats dedicate themselves to either working out, "the Lord," or either to their cases. However, even throughout the midst of the bullshit, you can meet some real cool cats.

Gravitating to what I considered the "real thorough" cats, I made many lifelong friends during this time including Whop, Big E, Keith Head, Lil Danny, and a whole host of others. Most are in prison indefinitely or either dead now: Whop died in his sleep somehow while on "23 & 1" lockdown[33] in the state penitentiary; Big E was extradited back to California to serve out the remainder of his parole from his sentence out of San Diego; Keith Head was killed after his acquittal and release on the murder case he was then currently locked up on (his second, in fact); and Lil Danny was released with his charges dropped after the main witness against him was murdered the night before his trial, only to be re-arrested and convicted years later after his "friend" found himself in some trouble and sold him out to the pigs like a bitch. All of them are/were good dudes, all not the monsters the nashville media, pigs, and "justice" system would have you to believe, and all in some way or another lost to the system. Just like I was.

Being around those cool ass cats who understood what I was going through made the time we sat languishing in jail more bearable and helped it to pass quicker. As did the visits from my loved ones. Every week without fail it seems, I received at least one out of the two we were allowed per week. Freckles had come that first week to let me know that she was still in my

---

[33] 23 hours in cell, 1 hour allowed "out" per day for "recreation."

corner despite the way the pigs tried to convince her I was Jeffrey Dahmer or something, going around and just massacring people for no reason. My mother had come also in those first few weeks, bringing my son Kyree along with her. That visit didn't last long, though; after five, maybe ten minutes or so, I asked her to leave – I couldn't stop myself from breaking down crying as my son – only 1 ½ years old at the time – kept trying to press through the glass to get to me. He was so used to being able to jump up on me, play, or just be held by me. But I couldn't touch him, he couldn't touch me – and of course he was too young to even understand why we couldn't. That shit was too much to bear; it hurt too much.

My female friends came, too – especially my girlfriend Jannah. In fact she came regularly, at least 2-3 times a month when she wasn't back home for the summer in Pittsburgh. Even then, she still made the trip and flew down at least once a month to show me she was still there for me.

She also brought along some of our mutual friends from school with her sometimes. As a matter of fact, more than a few of my Fisk friends made the trip downtown to see me. And I still to this day appreciate all the love shown me then; not everyone would take time out of his or her lives to go visit someone in jail – especially a person not really used to that type of lifestyle. So every one of those people that did, forever will have a place in my heart.

Speaking of Fisk, one of the most embarrassing things I've ever had to do in life was call my faculty advisor informing her of my incarceration and the fact that I'd have to drop out of school indefinitely. Not able to answer some of the questions she had because of my impending legal battles, she seemed to understand and offered to do for me all that she could. And though she tried to hide it, I could tell her disappointment in me

– losing what she felt was another bright, young Black man to "the system."

Yet sad to say, it's not like I was an anomaly, either; I soon noticed what seemed like a never-ending parade of cats – bright, intelligent Black men much like myself – in and out of the cellblock, herded off to the penitentiary, to do "numbers"[34] greater than the entire amount of time I had been on this earth. And it was more depressing than I can even begin to describe now. Seemingly every time someone came from kkkourt from "resolving" their cases, you could feel the life deflated out of him almost to the point of nausea. I couldn't help but to think at the time that this was the way our captured and kidnapped ancestors must have felt: deflated, devoid of all hope, consigned to whatever fate their tormenters deemed them to have. Totally powerless. Shit was sickening. All of these cats – sons, fathers, brothers, uncles, cousins, and friends to someone – treated and abused in a kkkourtroom of "law" they no more had an understanding of than physics...

I was able to help alleviate some of the bullshit and fuckery, however. Spending a lot of time studying up on my own case, I quickly acquired the reputation of being "good with the law," so a lot of cats would come to me asking for help in fighting their way out of their own predicaments. So what I would do is help those cats to help themselves by pointing them in the right directions via showing them how to research their cases and issues. And similar to myself when I first picked up a law book, most were surprised at how uncomplicated the law was when you actually took the time to learn something about it – reading, researching, and writing could actually mean the difference between losing your life and *living* your life. (Although making the amerikkkans to actually *follow* their own law is a

---

[34] The amount of years to serve in prison.

totally different story!)

I can't even begin to explain to you the pleasure I got out of helping cats to fight back at some of the numerous injustices I noticed around me. Furthermore, what made me even more determined to help all whom I could, was the fact that some of these cats were actually innocent. Do you find that hard to believe? Surely not so much nowadays with the epidemic of innocent Black and Brown men being released from wrongful imprisonment after having had *decades* of their lives stolen! Plus, in more than one instance I read in other people's cases and charges "crimes" that I, in fact, either had committed myself or in which I knew the identities of the actual perpetrators! Sad, but true.

However, as I've said about nashville before, the police department usually clears its backlog of cases when they have someone convenient to pin something on. Any "nigger" is just as good as the actual guilty one when filling up the prisons for a little slave labor. Besides, the pigs seem to figure that they'll get the actual "guilty nigger" one way or another someday, anyway, so he hasn't really gotten away. Because sad to say, most Black men in nashville will not escape the clutches of the system in some shape, form, or fashion.

Additionally, "solving" the backlog of old "cold" crimes saves the pig police from actually having to do any investigative work while simultaneously giving "the state" (i.e. prosekkkutors) even more leverage to force a plea "bargain":

Court-appointed Attorney: *"You're charged with seven aggravated robberies; the d.a.[35] is willing to let you plead out to three of them for 10 years apiece with parole eligibility after serving 30%, all running concurrently."*

Defendant (Black or Brown man, usually!): "Three

---

[35] Short for district attorney, i.e., the prosekkkutor.

robberies! Ten years apiece! *I admit that I did the last one they got me for, but I didn't do none of them other six! I'm not pleading out to that!"*

Attorney: *"Well, it's not what you've* done; *it's what* they *can* prove. *This last robbery that they caught you red-handed for is in the same neighborhood as the other ones, with a similar m.o.,*[36] *and you* will *get convicted of them if you go to trial."*

Implied in that is that your attorney – and I use that term loosely – *won't* be breaking his/her neck to fight your case. Already she or he is not getting paid anything more than a pittance that won't increase regardless of how much or how little she or he does working on your case – not to mention whether you're found guilty or not – plus you just confessed to committing the last crime you were charged with, so they probably think that you're lying about being innocent of the other ones anyway! (Not that that makes any sense once you think about it – I mean, why confess to only one if you're guilty of them all? You would either keep your mouth shut or spill the beans completely, I would think.) So what choice do you think most of these cats feel that they have?

Defendant: *"Okay, tell them I'll take the deal, then. And you* sure *that I'll be able to make parole after serving 30%?"*

An unscrupulous attorney will then confirm this misconception to the uninformed defendant, while the (too) rare honest one will make the defendant aware that he's only *eligible* to go up for parole at that time – whether he makes it or not is entirely up to a totally different group of slave masters. Unknowingly, the defendant has just consigned himself to 10 years of forced slavery – and a lifetime of the detested label (and new euphemism for "nigger") of "convicted felon." Thinking about this bullshit that I witnessed an untold amount of times

---

[36] Modus operandi – which usually only means that the assumed perpetrators were also Black or Hispanic!

makes me sick to my stomach even today! But what can we do about it, right?

For one, we as Black and Brown people in this kkkountry have a *responsibility* to start teaching the "law" and a minority's supposed "legal rights" from the time our children are able to read; only then will the injustices like the one discussed above (and the untold thousands that happen similar to it every day!) be stopped. Furthermore, not only will it inform our misguided youth as to the ins and outs of the law, but it may in fact even also stop a lot of them from falling into the "justice" system's traps in the first place. Nothing like knowledge to prevent a catastrophe, ya dig?

What's more, if I had my way, there would in fact be legal education classes held every single week near every "projects" and/or "hood" in this kkkountry. These would be held in or near neighborhood community centers that would be at least partially devoted to giving people access to law books and law cases to *help us help ourselves*. They would not be formed, fronted, nor financed by any local, state, or federal government agency of this kkkountry (you know, the same government that has proven itself time and time again not to be trusted in regards to our "rights" or livelihoods), but by *ourselves* and *our own* colleges and schools. Furthermore, I would do completely away with the plea bargain system and force *every* charged crime to trial – including misdemeanors – with all possible resulting sentences after conviction imposed by the *jury* with "truth in sentencing" where three years means three years, ten means ten, so on and so forth. The judge will/would only be there as the *arbiter* to ensure *fairness* – and not yet another prosekkkutor against the defendant whose life is at stake like in the system in which we have now. Additionally, everyone over the age of fifteen would be compelled to participate on juries at least every couple of years; this will insure community involvement, community awareness about "crime" and its perpetrators and causes, and will help to open people's eyes about (and eventually stop!) the warehousing of certain groups of this kkkountry's population currently in place. Only then will we make some type of dent in the enslavement of our people. Only then will we really have some semblance of "equal justice" for our men, women, and children in this kkkountry.

Moreover, I know that this would work because many times in my helping cats help themselves, we had some impact – sometimes great! – upon their cases. Such as times when I would help a cat to prove that not only was his stop by the pigs unwarranted, but that this mere fact made the subsequent search of his vehicle illegal and thus the evidence seized was "ill-gotten fruits of the poisoned tree." However, since prosekkkutors hate to dismiss charges even in cases that clearly warrant it (less they give hope and inspiration to others to fight back), more often than not this only made for a better bargaining position when taking a plea deal. Yet at other times we would find information that would go towards proving a cat's *innocence*.

Say for instance, the only eyewitness to a crime says that the perpetrator was 6'4" tall and 250 lbs. while you're only 5'10" and weigh 180; that's a major discrepancy if I've ever met one, ya dig? However, just because both the arrested suspect and the alleged perpetrator just happen to share the characteristic of dark colored skin, the prosekkkution in the case will scream to all hell (usually after kkkoercing the witness to agree) that the witness has made a positive identification of whomever the defendant just has the bad luck to be. Yet this is not the end all and be all, ya dig? That same "evidence" the prosecution is attempting to use against you can also be used to help you, if only you know to look for it, where to look, and know what to do with it once you have it. The evidence is/was always there, however usually the defendant's attorney – more times than not, appointed by the "honorable kkkourt" – won't take the time to investigate even this most glaring of discrepancies. Nor would even acknowledge the defendant's pleas of innocence. Their view is usually, "Who has the time or patience when I know he/she's guilty of *something*, anyway?"

However, if a defendant actually researched the applicable law, the issues surrounding the law, and the facts of their life-altering cases themselves, surprisingly, a lot of court-appointed lawyers would jump at the chance to fight for you. (It's not often that court-appointed attorneys are presented with winnable cases considering the circumstances, ya dig?) A smart man or woman would help someone help you. If more cats took this approach, then it would make it so much harder for the system to stroke us all with "no Vaseline." The more cats that fight, the more of a fight they would have to bring to us. And besides, whose life is it anyway that's on the line? Yours or your attorneys? If more cats thought about it like that then maybe things would change. Unfortunately, most cats don't have that attitude. But those whom do/did usually ended up in better situations than they were initially facing...

"Death," unfortunately, never stopped stalking and surrounding me, even after I was incarcerated. One night, I dreamt that as I was opening some door to leave some unfamiliar house, as soon as I attempted to step through it, Death suddenly grabbed me from behind. Spinning me around with His skeletal hands atop my head to face Him, I began attempting to swing my fists in an attempt to fight Him off. Nevertheless, the more I exerted myself in trying to escape His clutches, the more sinister His expression became and the more I could feel myself fading... fading... fading... Awakened by the sound of my cellmate's voice noticing that I was having some type of nightmare, I thanked him for "saving my life" as I knew that without him I would have died in my sleep. He thought I was nuts, of course. Especially after I wouldn't dare to fall asleep for at least two days as I knew Death was still chasing me...

In spite of my always fighting Him off when going up against Him, personally, I've never really been afraid of Death. In some ways I can't wait until He wins and I move on to the next chapter of life, and in fact, I've had premonitions and dreams of dying for as long as I can remember. And while having these dreams and premonitions, I could *feel* Death. I could *feel* the bullets or knife enter my chest or head; I could *feel* the breath leaving my body. One of the most vivid of these memories comes from the time I was no older than 13 or 14 years of age and dreaming about myself shot on a basketball court. In that dream, every single bullet that entered my chest, I felt; and as I took my last breath, I died, waking up to find myself at home in bed with pangs at every single spot the bullets pierced my body...

Sadly, Death was also still stalking my family and friends. David and Donald were two of the coolest young cats you could ever want around you; the months before I got incarcerated, I used to have them with me at least a couple of times a week. Not only were they fearless when it came to "putting in work," but they were also attentive and able to take direction. One evening watching the news in the cellblock, I saw that a major car accident had taken place resulting in the loss of three young lives; come to find out that the driver of the SUV was drunk and had lost control of the vehicle, killing David, Donald, and another cat.[37] I was crushed. Losing your loved ones while

---

[37] Yet another reason why I have *no tolerance* for those who choose to drive (or fly!) while intoxicated. Do what you do – get as high or drunk as you like, who cares, it's

incarcerated is one of the greatest fears that any prisoner has. I hadn't even been gone a couple of months, and I know it hadn't even been a couple of days after I spoke with them last.

To top it off, the driver was someone I didn't even care for much before the accident; matter of fact, I had beat his ass on one occasion for being a chump who liked to beat on women and children. Once I heard that, I was looking for a reason to kick his ass. And of course, he never gave me one so I had to find one. Since he was dating David's sister, the opportunity presented itself to finally be at their house at the same time he was. Somehow or the other, the subject came up of what he had been doing to her and her daughter so I requested of him to leave:

"Get the fuck out," I calmly said.

Can you believe that this chump actually tried to *man up and defend himself?*

"This is my *house,"* he said incredulously.

"I don't give a fuck; I said get the fuck out."

I guess he noticed the look in my eyes then. Because he got up like the sucker he was and got the fuck out. Of his own home. What a bitch. The simple fact of him being such a coward pissed me off even more because he would kick a woman's ass in a second but wouldn't defend himself against some random man in his *own home?!* I followed his chump ass outside to his SUV – the same one he would later wreck and kill my lil homies in – and commenced to beating his ass. Sometimes I wish I would have killed him. Then maybe my lil homies would be alive today...

Nonetheless, though, my most distressing encounter with Death came on a day that I will never in my life forget again:

---

your life – but don't put anyone else in danger with your bullshit junkiness and/or drunkenness, is my way of thinking.

January 31, 2000. As soon as Carvin didn't make it to see me before the end of visitation that day, an unexplained uneasiness completely enveloped me. I thought it entirely possible that I may have been overreacting, but still it didn't sit well with me knowing that he had never missed a visit when I was expecting to see him. To put my mind at ease, I just told myself that maybe something had come up at the last minute and tried to ignore the disturbed feeling I was having, spending the rest of my day as usual – chess, dominoes, a few games of spades, watching a few videos – and even decided not to call home that evening.

When night fell, however, the most foreboding feeling kept me from closing my eyes and resting for the longest of time. Finally forcing myself to sleep, what little I did receive wouldn't at all be peaceful. In the middle of the night, an awful, eerie feeling awakened me again – a combination of anger, fear, sadness, I felt as if Death was near somehow, but not coming after me this time – someone close to me was in danger. Never making it back to sleep, I didn't know what was wrong, but I knew that *something* was.

When morning came at last, the cell doors couldn't open fast enough so I could rush to the phones to check on everyone. However, my mad dash was quickly interrupted by the television news reporting a quintuple shooting resulting in at least one death.[38] Averting my eyes from the phones and to the television, I could see a man being placed into an ambulance on a stretcher – and it was my brother. The news didn't release any information concerning his identity, nor could I see his face, but somehow, I recognized him. I felt it.

Not recalling right now whom exactly I forced off the phone or how I forced him out of the way, I can, however, recall

---

[38] I even heard a few cats gossiping about what went down like always – even though those fools had no way of knowing what went down and with whom no more than I did. But lack of information has never stopped that type of fool before, now has it?

my sister Devonne answering on the other end:
"*What's going on?*" I frantically asked her.
Silence.
"*Where the fuck is my brother???*" I asked my little sister, with less patience.
Again, silence.
"*Please,* PLEASE, *lil sis, just tell me my brother is going to live!*"
"*We don't know yet.*"

My heart dropped. I could hear the tears in my sister's voice and feel her despair through the phone. As I know she could feel and hear my own. Had there been a way for me to have broken free and escaped that very moment, I would have with no regard or concern for the consequences. I just needed to get to Carvin, to get to my family; to see my brother, to hold him, hug him, help him somehow. But there I was stuck, hopeless and helpless to be there for my loved ones, as my lil brother fought for his life in some cold and uncaring hospital room.

The more that I thought about what he was going through – what my mother, my father, my sisters, and my brother John must have been feeling – the more a complete rage engulfed every fiber and stitch of my being. I vowed right then and there – in that moment of powerlessness and fear of losing my brother to the streets – that *every single person* even remotely involved in the shooting of my brother would die the most horrible death I could think of if he didn't pull through. Fuck praying, fuck crying out to "God" – if my brother died then *every other motherfucker would, too!*

"*Lil Sis, my brother* BETTER *live!*" was all I could cry as I choked back the tears.

Nothing can describe the feeling of not knowing whether my brother would live or die; of imagining the pain he must have been in, the fear he must have felt. Even to this day I hate to revisit those feelings. I was a volatile mixture of anger at God, anger at the world, anger at who shot him and how he got shot, anger at myself for not being there, anger even at him – just anger at life period. My *brother* man. *My little brother.* Can you imagine losing someone so close to you???

You know, it's amazing that so many of our people in this kkkountry experience something all too similar and familiar every day; it's a damned shame (isn't it?) what we've accepted as "normal." Because think about it: How many of our people have had to endure this same pain, feel this anger, experience those fears? Think of all the hearts broken every time one Black or Brown man kills another, every time we foolishly allow this society to pit us against one another to the point of each of ours' demise. The mothers, the fathers, the brothers, the sisters, the daughters, the sons, the uncles, the aunts, cousins, friends – all affected tragically by the death of their loved one before their time. We all need to think about that. And more importantly, we *all* need to *do* something to change and prevent this in any way possible. If not, we will continue to lose entire generations to early graves and enslavement in prison.

However, at that time, I wasn't thinking about all of that; my mind was on making others feel the pain I and my family was. We were hurting. And I wanted to hurt (someone else) in return. Yet even the house where it all went down mysteriously burning to the ground shortly thereafter didn't make me feel any better…

Carvin was in such a critical condition that he even flatlined at least once that night; I now realize that that was what my spirit felt in waking me up – my brother and I are so closely connected that I could sense his spirit slipping away from us.

Thankfully, though, something pulled him back and he

survived intact, less a spleen. He likes to say that it was "God's Grace," but no matter Who or What it was, all I know is that motherfuckers better be thankful that "God" was merciful in this situation because *I* sure as hell wouldn't have been had he died. Able to visit with him a week or so later after his release from the hospital followed by arrest related to his shooting, it was impossible for me to stop the flood of emotions, the tears of joy at seeing him alive and breathing in spite of our both being decked out in jail attire. I hugged him so hard, he had to remind me of his soreness and stitches. But he survived. And to be honest, his survival saved a lot of other peoples' lives...

But Death was still taunting – especially within the span of the twelve days from January 31 with Carvin's shooting through February 11 with the passing of both of my grandmothers. First there was the word I got that we had lost our great-grandmother "Mama," and while viewing her body handcuffed and shackled inside the church, unbeknownst to me my paternal "Grannie" passed away, too. Also – in the same incident involving my brother – Arkie (Vell's brother, and ostensibly my "cousin" in the streets' eyes) wasn't as lucky as Carvin in keeping his life; he died on the floor of the house where most of the shooting took place. Vell, however, survived as my brother did – along with the two other people my brother shot in order to save his own life, "Turtle" and "D. Salt."

Twelve days. Three deaths, one near-death of the lil brother I shared bunk beds with, and the shooting of Vell by whom I would later find out was my brother. Death and disaster seemed to have my world crashing down around me.

Heart learning how to love…
Head learning who to hate…

Assata Shakur

POPS

All I could assume is that Lil Kenny's bitch ass wanted to die. How else would you explain him trying to "fuck with" me? He was one of those chumps that acted cool when alone, but a fool with a crowd. Well, he made that mistake in trying to pull that move on me – and I pulled his card.

It couldn't have been no more than a couple of months or so since we moved from the Projects to Vine Hill – but the Bricks was where I continued to spend most of my time when not over my Aunt Carlene's house. And don't get me wrong, I was under no illusion that Lil Kenny and I were "friends," but at least I thought we were "cool." Although we had fought more than a few times – with him actually winning more than losing – I thought at least there was a mutual respect factor involved in our relationship. Evidently, I was wrong. But that would be *his* mistake, not mine.

Coming out of the store, for some reason I was the chosen person to fuck with that day; I saw Kenny, Fat Walter,[39] and a couple of other cats near my bike. I guess they were about to steal it. As I went near it, Kenny jumped on the bike and started to peddle off. Well I yanked his ass off the bike and we commenced to fighting. As we were scrapping, each time it seemed as though I was getting the best of him I would feel a push or grab from behind throwing me off balance and letting Kenny's bitch ass then "get out" on me. Every time I recovered, the same shit would happen all over again. After a few times, I

---

[39] Who is actually the first cousin of some of *my* first cousins.

peeped what was happening.

"*Alright, y'all got that.*"

"*What you mean y'all, nigga? It's just me!*" Kenny said.

"*Yeah, aw-ite. Y'all got that. You don't wanna see me one-on-one, though.*"

"*Yeah, whatever, nigga! We can go again right now!*"

"*Naw, y'all got that. But I'll be back, though.*"

"*Nigga, you don't even live over here no mo!*"

Riding off on my bike (motherfucking right they didn't get it!), with a few rocks thrown in my direction, all I could think in my mind was *wait until they saw what I had to throw at them.*

Later that evening, I (along with my cousin Reggie) made my way back to the Bricks and headed straight to my partner Lee's house. Lee and I used to hang pretty tough, doing more than our fair share of dirt together, but since I had moved out of the projects, he had started to hang with Kenny every day. And, of course, he had already heard about what happened. News travels fast in the projects. Especially fight news.

"*Man, go tell that bitch Kenny that if he wanna fight one-on-one then here I go!*"

Even though Kenny lived all the way over on the other side of the projects, it seemed as though he was coming through the big field huffing and puffing in only a couple of minutes; I guess Lee *ran* to get him, or something – you know how project people love to see a fight. Fools were in for a lot more than that *tonight*, though!

My cousin Reggie and I calmly sat on the slide as Kenny and Lee walked side-by-side crossing the drive and entered the playground; when they were less than 10 feet away – BOOM!!! – everything and everyone stopped. Kenny stood frozen mid-stride with my .38 pointed at his face. Lee quickly moved to the side.

"So, bitch, *you thought y'all hoe asses was gone get away with ganging me???*"

There was nothing but fury and murder in my eyes – and there was nothing but terror and tears in his. He seemed too petrified to even *breathe*, let alone capable of moving his mouth to speak.

"*Pu-pu-pu-pu-put the gun down.*"

"*Shut up, bitch!*" I said, cracking him upside his head with my pistol. "*Bitch, I'll kill all y'all hoe ass niggas for that shit y'all tried to pull earlier!*" I hit his bitch ass again. "*PUNK ASS BITCH!!!*" I hit him again and again and again.

I was filled with such unexplainable rage and anger; even to this day, I don't quite understand it. I mean, I had been ganged before – what kid in the projects hadn't? – and Kenny and I had fought numerous times prior to this one, but for some reason I just felt so *furious*. I truly wanted to *kill* this dude! Maybe it was the way I felt disrespected by his "you don't even live over here no mo'" statement. Like *I* was no longer welcome? Fuck that! *No one* could tell *me* where to go, *when* to go there, nor where I *belonged!* Fuck that! This bitch was about to *die!*

"*Delo, please don't kill him. Please don't kill him baby.*"

Lee's older sister Theresa broke me from my murderous thoughts. I was so zoned in on the bitch Kenny that I hadn't even noticed the growing crowd. The police could've been there the entire time and I wouldn't have been aware. Allowing my eyes to glance quickly around me, I noticed everyone in the drive staring at me with a mixture of shock and awe, wondering what I would do next. And I know Kenny felt The Reaper near the more his head bled from my pistol's blows – because I sure as hell felt Death using me to get at him. It seemed as if his soul, somewhat, was already readying its escape from his body. None of us knew – Kenny and I included – whether he would live or die.

"Delo, baby, please just let him go. Please, *baby. You're too* smart *for this,"* Theresa pleaded.

Truth being told, Lil Kenny and I both should thank Theresa for being out there that night. Because if not, he probably wouldn't have lasted a couple more heartbeats – and I would've been on my way to prison at the age of 14.

"You lucky, bitch," I said, hitting him in his head again, *"next time, I'mma kill yo hoe ass!"*

I cracked him upside his head a couple more times for good measure, and then let him back away with tears running down his face. You could tell by the look in his eyes that he knew how close he had actually come to dying that night. Walking away amped up, I was so inexperienced with guns that I had to shoot the pistol into the ground since I didn't know how to uncock the hammer...

From there, my late summer/early fall just got wilder and wilder. Every day, all day, I was into something, somehow, someway. Not really out looking for trouble per se, nevertheless I was *always* game for anything that seemed "fun," exciting, or gave me the opportunity to make some money. And it didn't matter how dangerous it was. I felt like nothing or no one could fuck with me, anyway. And I *stayed* strapped at all times.

I didn't have any more "issues" out of Lil Kenny or his crew ever again – and, for sure, I was constantly in the Projects where they continued to live. But they knew what was up. Matter of fact, the whole projects did – it doesn't take long for word to spread when somebody is "on one." And "on one" I was. Plus, a couple of weeks after the Lil Kenny incident was when I went gunning for the White Avenue cats. So from there, everyone gave me a wide berth – even the old school cats that I had come up looking up to. But not in a bad way, though – everyone just knew not to in any way try to play me close. And soon cats started paying me for putting in strong arm work with my pistol.

Wanted your competition robbed? – I was your man. Wanted a house shot up? – call on me. Wanted someone that owed you money to know how seriously you took their debt? – just point me in their direction. And I *guaranteed* results.

Culminating in this mentality of madness I realize I had back then, L.C. and I had stopped by his house one day so that he could change clothes or something. Right before we were about to leave, something on television caught my attention: a multi-million dollar bank robbery being shown on *America's Most Wanted* or some similar show. And what was the first thought that popped into *my* head? – Hey, *I* could do that! Crazy thought, huh? Not exactly normal that a 14-year-young kid, who had never even touched a thousand dollars before, would think that he could pull off a million dollar bank heist, right? But I was young, wild, and rambunctious – and in every way "with it."

Sharing my thoughts with L.C., a few days later he introduced me to this older cat named B.J. whom informed me that he had a bank in north nashville that he had already been casing. I naively wanted to do it *then* if at all possible, but (un)fortunately for us all, it was a Friday night when we were first introduced, so the bank was already closed. However, I was so gassed up at the possibility of pulling that type of move as soon as possible, that I gassed *them* up for us to pull a move – *any move* – that night to make some money.[40] I was hyped up off of adrenaline just at the thought of robbing the bank, and B.J. had just the place for us to test our robbing skills out – along with a single-shot sawed-off shotgun for good measure. It was

---

[40] Initially B.J. may have thought he had two young impressionable teenagers he could manipulate and send on random missions such as the one we were then discussing, but I think he quickly realized that it would be hard if not impossible to rein us in in any way once started – especially me.

on!

Pulling up in the alley behind a Lee's Chicken fast-food restaurant with no plan besides "go in there and get the money," B.J. let us out and parked in a predetermined area to wait on us. Time to make the move.

"Set that shit out!" I screamed the moment I came in through the side door with L.C. trailing me. *"Come on with all the muthafuckin' money!"*

I guess these motherfuckers thought it was a joke or something, because no one moved or even seemed to acknowledge us. Hell, there were even a couple of customers sitting in the dining area that looked up for *maybe* a millisecond, and then just turned back to eating their chicken. Couldn't really blame them, though – I was maybe 5'3" tall, 125 lbs. with clothes on, with a voice still cracking at times that in hindsight may not have been all that intimidating. Okay, cool.

"Bitch. I. Said. Set. That. God. Damned. Money. Out. NOW!!!" I said to the clerk nearest me. *"NOW GODDAMNIT!!!!!"*

My not-to-be-fucked with demeanor – along with the shotgun now pointed at her head – made everyone sit up and take notice. Except the couple eating their greasy-assed chicken. They *still* didn't pay me any mind.

Anyway, (whom I'm assuming to be) the manager took over and asked me and everyone else to remain calm and instructed all of the clerks to give me the money; I was so unprepared and the robbery was so spur-of-the-moment that I was, at first, literally grabbing the money out of their hands and putting it in my pockets. Then someone came up with the bright idea to use one of the bags used to carry the food, and L.C. held that.

So that was it – my first "store robbery." I had and held no fear, no compunction about what I had just done, no fear or care of getting caught, no consideration of what I had just put those innocent people through. All I thought of was the wad of money I now had in my pocket and what I was to do with it. I can't even remember how much money it was, but after the split it couldn't have been any more than $4-500. If that. But it sure felt good.

How and why I became this person who could do something like this with no remorse? I don't know. I have asked myself that repeatedly over the years.[41] Is there something

---

[41] In elementary school (5th and 6th grade), I had a relatively prosperous business selling candy, (Lemonheads, Laffy Taffy, Mike and Ikes, Red Hots, etc.) to white classmates with money at the time. I never knew of any blacks (whom the vast majority of were "project kids" like myself) who ever had any money to spend. I would buy the candy the day before at a store called "Mr. Whitt's" across the street from Carter-Lawrence School for 5-10 cents apiece and in turn sell them for 25 cents or sometimes even double that! Where I got the initial idea, I don't really know, maybe it came to me after some kid offered to buy the candy they noticed me eating, but I would take my profits to buy ice cream and chocolate milk at lunch, and also extra candy for myself and my siblings to eat.

In junior high school at Wright Middle (7th-8th grades), I had progressed to selling the answers to homework, pop quizzes, and tests again to what I thought were "well to do" white kids, who seemingly had an immense amount of pressure from their parents to get "good grades." The white kids in my "honors classes" always seemed to be stressed out and wanted desperately to get as good as if not better grades than me (there usually weren't many other blacks in my class, especially the girls for some reason, but after realizing that they really couldn't beat or match me intellectually, they invariably would pay me to help keep their grades up (with different pricings for an "A" or a "B," of course!). In fact, the only person I remember that could match me intellectually was my good friend Hung La, a son of Laotian refugees, and that seemed to bother a lot of the other kids (again, especially the white girls) to all hell.

I was 13 years young at the start of 9th grade in high school at Hillsboro and somehow slowly but surely on my way to full-fledged "thuggism" and the "gangsterism" of the projects in which I grew up. Although my mother and siblings had moved from Edgehill projects to Vine Hill projects at the beginning of the summer and I was essentially living with my Aunt Carlene and my cousin Punkin (Carlene's son, two years older than I) by then, a few weeks before the start of high school, my cousin Putt (a favorite of mine) was killed and I remember being just so angry. I was in a quiet, seething rage all the time, yet I didn't think anyone ever even noticed. My cousin Punkin may have noticed the change to some extent, but I doubt even he could understand my thoughts and feelings and reactions to Putt's death because I didn't even understand it all myself. I felt so powerless to prevent something like that from happening to someone else I loved, and in response, I in turn turned dangerous, in hindsight.

inherently "criminal" about myself and those like me or is that the only way we know (or choose to know!) how to rage at the many injustices we see and experience every day. I wonder. And that will forever be on my mind until I figure it out...

Anyway, we got away. But L.C. was soon bragging to other people all around the projects about what we had done. It was always "Man, Delo *crazy* cuz! He made them *come up off of it!*" or something to that effect. Soon I was the talk of the Southside with my "headcutting" of Lil Kenny, my shooting of the White Avenue cats, and now my robbery of businesses. Rightly so, I wouldn't last too much longer without being arrested for, at least, this horrible transgression...

My mother will always love my father; any man choosing to be in a relationship with her will have to deal with this fact. Even now as my parents are both married to other people, if my father was to express that he wanted to be with my mom, she would be willing. She may deny so, but all of us children know the truth.

But me? – for a time, I couldn't *stand* the man. My mom always says it's because he and I are so much alike, and although that's partly true, her poisoning of his and my relationship had a great deal to do with that (me not "liking" him) and was not easily forgiven nor forgotten on my part. Nonetheless, yes, my Pops and I are a lot alike. And so much of what my father always tried to teach me, I understand now and agree with. Amazingly,

---

So, by the end of my first year in high school (I was 14 by then!) I had a reputation for being a "nerd" in honors classes (something I prided myself on, the "nerd" label never bothered me) who was also known for being involved in numerous shootouts and robbing for and/or stealing Starter coats/jackets around the city and this didn't bother me at all. I suspect my thinking was, the "harder" I was then, the less likely someone would "fuck with" one of my loved ones and/or friends.

But something is very wrong and tragic with the trajectory I took in so short a matter of years, and needs to be examined by all in our society. Because I was an intelligent, sensitive, spiritually hungry child and look at what I became for a time.

almost everything I hated about him when I was a child I now greatly appreciate now that I'm a man.

But then? – hell no! I felt like the man didn't know *shit* about what I was going through "coming up in the streets," nor could he understand the way I thought and "got down." Not really realizing that all I was going through – all that I would go through in the future, my Pops had already been there and done that.[42]

That being said, *this* was the motherfucker that the state sent me to live with. I mean, we had just then began to get cool again after our separation, and I still (unjustifiably, I now readily admit) felt animosity towards him somewhat. But it was the only way I could get out of Juvenile – no way was the judge about to allow me to again live with my mother in the projects; those with the power to say so, saw something in that situation that was deemed "unfavorable," I guess. So I accepted it, and we tried to make it work. But there's a big difference between staying the night over the weekends and living together, I would soon learn.

At first, I was on house arrest – with an electronic monitor attached around my ankle – unable to go farther than the porch of the house. And to be honest, it wasn't really that bad. It was the summertime so my cousins and friends would come by – Ro, Brian L., Mac, Punkin, Vell – and I would also get visits from my girlfriend Shameka.

Late that summer I had court on my charges, with the end result being I was taken off house arrest and formally placed on something called "intensive probation" — the last possible opportunity someone my age could get before a forced incarceration and the taking of custody away from my parents. I have to give a lot of thanks for that second chance to Dr. Kersey, who somehow was informed of my predicament and

---

[42] Parents are indeed "great examples" and/or "horrible warnings" to a child.

came to testify to my character as he knew it. Needless to say he was more than mortified as to what he found out I had done, but he surmised that it had more to do with my environment than anything else. Dr. Kersey testified that I was one of the brightest and most gifted students he had known in his entire teaching career and that he had noticed early on that I was being pulled in a tug of war between athletics and academics. Partly he was right about that, but he had missed something that he had inadvertently alluded to: the "allure" of the streets and the grip it was beginning to have on me.

Anyway, I got my second chance and Dr. Kersey even arranged for my acceptance again to the most prestigious academic magnet school that the city offered to public school students – in spite of my turning down attendance the previous year so that I could attend school with my cousins and friends. Also, somehow, my Pops arranged it to where his ex-girlfriend Linda was my probation officer. So, how could I possibly fuck all this up, right? Leave it to my headstrong ass to find a way:

Second semester of my sophomore year, now enrolled at Hume-Fogg Magnet School, my grades and life seemed to deteriorate; for the first time in my life, I didn't really seem to have much interest in school outside of getting the hell out of the house and away from my father. Not really understanding or digging all that my Pops was trying to teach me and show me,[43] I mistakenly felt as if my environment was becoming more oppressive than bearable and that in some odd way I was being punished without being punished. If that makes sense. Going home was dreadful for me; school was a misery, too, outside of the girls.

I just couldn't concentrate, I was never at peace, and

---

[43] Not to keep harping neither on a tired subject nor to makes excuses for my actions, however I seriously think that all of the derogatory bullshit I heard about my father from my mother directly contributed to this.

always had an unexplainable, sullen attitude. Who knows? In hindsight, maybe it was all just my teenage hormones at work, or something. Possibly that explains some of it, but surely that's not the explanation for the rage I sometimes felt, is it? I don't know. Or maybe my ire came from all the newfound rules I had to follow and the disciplined environment my Pops had in place. Sounds more likely, doesn't it?

Yet even amidst my Pop's demanded discipline, I recognize now that he afforded me luxuries and leniency that most in my position (on an intensive form of probation for a violent crime) and/or at my age would not have been allowed. For one, I was allowed to get a weekend job with my cousin, Punkin, at a local newspaper plant in spite of my being underage and thus legally not allowed to work.[44] And, even better, I was allowed to have girls over and in my room alone with the doors closed where there was no possible way for him *not* to know that we were having sex.[45] We were young men (my Pops was only 33 at the time) and I was an even younger man (I was 14, then turned 15) living in a nice big house with more room than we needed, so in that my Pops was "cool." Hell, my Pops himself always had numerous women around, who (more than a couple of times) unwittingly brought their teenage daughters with them whom I would have sex with while our parents were off doing the same. Crazy, right?

Furthermore, (although I probably really didn't deserve it because of my attitude), my Pops bestowed upon me more

---

[44] I think I had paid someone to list my I.D. as me being a year older than I actually was so the company was technically "unaware" as to my "real age." But in all actuality, every single one of my supervisors knew how old I was.
[45] In my experience, a lot, if not most, of us children that grew up in the projects had already lost our virginities before our early teens came around. And I was more advanced than most, with a couple of older girls (first a white one that lived near the projects, and later, a black one that lived on the other side of them) teaching me more than I probably needed to know shortly before I became a teen.

freedoms the deeper we got off into the school year. On some *weekdays* (can you believe that?!) I would be allowed sometimes to walk to Vine Hill to see my mother and siblings.[46] After school, and on the weekends he began to allow me to go out. Where again a lot of times, embarrassingly, I was involved in a lot of shit that I *shouldn't* have been with Punkin, Ro, Mac, Brian L., and others he trusted me with. Great, right?

Well, unbeknownst to my Pops I had purchased two "accessories" that would soon cause us both some grief: a pager (or "beeper" as we called them) that he specifically forbid me to buy when I asked him, and I also sported a .25 caliber pistol.[47] And although my Pops was kept in the dark about the existence of my pager, my Mom *wasn't* and one Friday night during Christmas break "out and about" with Punkin and Ro, I received a "911" beep from her – something was wrong!

"*What's wrong, Mama?!*" I asked frantically, returning her call.

"*Delo, yo Daddy cut me and…*"

"*What?!*" I said cutting her off, "*don't worry about it! I'm on my way!*"

What else did I have to hear? My *Daddy* had *cut* my *Mama*! Like *what the fuck?!*

So we headed over to my Mom's house to pick her up, then furiously drove home so that I could confront my father!

"*Daddy, why the fuck you cut my Mama?!*" I menacingly shouted, opening the door and stomping up the stairs.

---

[46] Me being me, I would also involve myself in a lot of shit that I had no business doing, but that's another (more than a few!) stories for another time.

[47] A new one, *not* the same one as the year before. I had somehow lost the other one in some way that I don't remember now. But it's a damned shame that I and anyone else (including teens my age or younger!) could purchase a gun anytime I wanted to "off the streets." However, you'd be a damned fool if you thought this was by anything other than "amerikkkan design." Check the situation in *any* and *every* "hood" in the united snakes. Cool with me though. My only objection is that we've had our guns trained on the *wrong* targets for far too long.

Pops

    Suddenly, my Pops appeared at the top of the stairs waiting on me. But let me share with you something about my father. He. Is. Not. A. Man. To. Talk. To. Like. *That* in any shape, form or fashion! No matter *who* you are, Black, White, man, woman, child, civilian or pig that is *not* something I would recommend! Remember what I said earlier about my Pop's name ringing on the Southside? Well, let's just say that I got my "gangster mentality" honest! And I had *fucked up*! As sure as I know that water is wet, I *knew* I had fucked up. In hindsight, I should have more thoroughly asked my Mom what happened instead of flying off the handle the second she said he had "cut" her. Or at least asked to see the cut on her hand, which turned out to be more of a *scratch* (than anything) that she had gotten when he had *tried taking away the knife she* had *pulled on him*! Only later did I ask myself what she was doing over our house to get cut anyway, and I would soon find out that they had been "creeping" for quite some time, and started arguing after my Mom came by unexpectedly and found another one of his women there. This is what started it all, but I didn't know that then. I wish I had, however! Nevertheless, she and my cousins were (smartly!) still downstairs at the door watching our confrontation with my *pride* now involved (I am my Father's and Mother's child, after all!) so somebody (me!) was stupidly causing my feet to keep going up the steps! But I *knew* I had *fucked up*.

    "*Who the* fuck *you think you talking to like that in my goddamned house?!*" he said to me snatching me off my feet, jacked up by the front of my shirt as soon as I reached the top of the stairs! Within a second I was thrown into a chair like a rag doll and scolded even more, *"Don't you* ever *in your* goddamned life *again talk to me like that in my muthafuckin house,*" he continued. "*Now tell them to get the fuck out my house and lock my goddamned door*!" I could tell he was tipsy, but he meant *business*.

Now I was pissed. I mean, like, *highly upset* if you know what I mean. But more importantly at the moment, I was deathly afraid of this motherfucker! I mean, like *for real*! I don't think you even understand! Like I said, I *knew* I had fucked up!

So, I walked my scary ass down the stairs with my Pops a few steps behind me, doing my *damnedest* wracking my brain trying to figure out how to survive the night. Picking up my pace as I neared the bottom, I reached in Ro's waist for the gun I had given him to hold on the ride over.

Then I turned around with the .25 against the side of my leg. He saw it. My mother saw it even though she tried to act as if she never saw it. Everybody saw it – then time stopped.

"*Alright, you got that, Delo*," my Pops said, backing up the stairs.

All I could do was look on silently for a couple of seconds until we four left out the door hurriedly before my Pops could get to *his* gun.

Not that he would have. Because my father would have *never* seriously harmed me. Nor would I have ever seriously harmed my father, despite the situation turning out the way it did. I did then and have *always* loved my father, so grabbing my gun was my way to make it out of there. And although I had gone home with the express intent of "confronting" my Pops (which meant, get beat by him "protecting my Mom's honor," most likely!) I gave my gun to Ro before we got there and never pointed it at my father for a reason: I would have never fired it. It wasn't even "cocked," and I just (irrationally) wanted to scare him away in order to *get* away like I did. Nevertheless that still doesn't excuse it. Nor could I possibly ever ask my father enough times to forgive me. In my defense, however, at the time I wasn't so sure about my father hurting me or my mother. And

Pops

it pains me to admit (even now, over a quarter century later!), that I ever even once considered that my father would purposely hurt either one of us. And for this I am terribly embarrassed, as I should be. But that's what enough poison will do to you...[48]

I was terrified to go home to my father after that incident; it seemed inescapable that he would kill me. But Linda saw to it that I would not be going back to live with my mother in the projects.

"That's not a good environment and I can't allow you to go back there. You either go back home to your dad or I'll be forced to put you in State custody."

What could I do? – she had my entire life in her hand. So taking me back to my father's house a few days afterwards, that day, she had a talk with us both. Pops to his credit, never uttered a word about the incident, what I had said and done, nothing; he only stared at me with an indescribable expression. The initial fear I was feeling didn't totally subside either – I was still scared shitless at this point – yet I sensed somehow that I just might survive after all. Once my Pops did finally speak, he let me know in no uncertain terms that I would follow his rules and listen to what he had to say or I would suffer the consequences. I was miserable. I sensed, somehow, that he and I wouldn't last too much longer in the same household. We should all be more careful what we wish for, however...

---

[48] Even today I don't think my parents (especially my mother) realize the gravity of all of this awfulness of pitting parent against parent, parent against child, and child against parent and how it all stems from the "Willie Lynchism" of slavery. Nonetheless, *I* could never adequately express all of its terrible ramifications in this forum, so please, I implore all of you whom have any Black or Brown person in your life that you love and/or care for (parent, child, sibling, spouse, friend, companion) to read the book *Black Love Is A Revolutionary Act* by Umoja. And no, I have *no* affiliation whatsoever with the authors of the book (although I would love to meet them one day!), it's just well received and well overdue in our community to help heal our ills...

With all of the emotional and familial turmoil I was experiencing at home, I just couldn't "cut it" at Hume-Fogg.[49] My principal, my favorite teachers and fellow students all did their best to support and encourage me, but my heart and motivation simply wasn't there.

So at the beginning of the second semester I transferred schools, first to a high school (where I was "zoned") named after one of tennessee's largest slave "owners" for half a day, then to Glencliff (on a "special transfer") for the second year in a row. Nevertheless, either school would have turned out the same mistake for me as would all of the other Southside schools as well. Where as athletics were indeed encouraged at Hume-Fogg,[50] academics were and would always be the first priority there; in comparison were the Southside high schools (McGavock, Glencliff, Hillsboro, and the aforementioned "overton" where football and/or basketball reigned supreme, and academics were seemingly *not* a priority at all. Hell, academics wasn't even a distant second as far as I could see, as the "secure" babysitting of the future prisoners of amerikkka fought for supremacy with sports at all times. But I digress. Me? – I prioritized nothing other than all of the readily available trouble (locker room dice games, girls, and just general hooliganess), and (although not at school) I would soon again find myself "in trouble with the law."

The day started as ordinary as any could in my life (school, then home and supposedly homework and chores), yet this day was special in two key areas: It was Tuesday so I would receive my check from my job, and it was also my sister Devonne's

---

[49] Yet, somehow (because of my test scores, I think), I still made the cut for listing on the prestigious *Who's Who of America's High School Students.*
[50] In fact, I was even personally asked by our head basketball coach to try out for the team after he witnessed me playing against the starting varsity in an intramural game. I made it to a couple of practices, however, my effort wasn't there, weakened behind all the depression I experienced every day going home.

birthday. So after taking care of what I was supposed to at home, I would be allowed to head to Vine Hill to visit with her and my brothers for a while. Rushing my responsibilities, I then left to cash my check and hurry my happy-go-lucky ass to the projects.

Stupid me, I wasn't even in the projects good before I was distracted by a dice game. Nonetheless I still headed first to see my siblings for a while and share with them a few dollars. However it didn't take me long to get outside to the "drive." And wouldn't you know it! I quickly hit a "hot streak," busting up the pockets of all the others in the game, except one motherfucker, who was down to his *last* $5 and wouldn't you believe my greedy ass had to have it!?[51] Big mistake because greed will bite you in the ass every time. Which it did.

Can you believe that this motherfucker used that *last $5* to win not only *his* money back from me but *everybody else's and mine too*!? I mean, *every single dollar*! Leaving me not only feeling stupid, but also trying to figure out how I would pay for the "big birthday present" that I had promised my baby sister for that weekend! God damn it!

Yet who could I blame other than myself? Not only did no one force me to enter the dice game in the first place, but neither did anyone force me to be greedy (and petty!) after I had already won the majority of everyone's shit! Hell, at the very least, I could have stopped after my "luck" had turned around, and still walked away with half of the winnings, but no no! My *pride* wouldn't allow it! There's a lesson there.

And I would soon learn it. Even as I was emptying my clip into a tree out of frustration, rattling some cats.

---

[51] All the other participants (about five in all) were between the ages of 13-16 like I was. I had joined the game with maybe $100 myself, and we generally shot between $5 - $20 a "fade," with maybe another $5 - $20 on the various side bets. But with them all having already started selling marijuana and/or cocaine, (and most growing up to make some fairly decent money as we became adults) there was easily a little less than a thousand dollars floating around in the game.

"*Fuck!*" I exploded, reloading my clip, "*y'all come with me so I can make this money back.*"

Was it a request? Well, yes and no. But did anyone *object*? Well, not openly they didn't. However, can you blame them? It's not like I seemed as if I was thinking all that rationally at the time. Plus, it's not as if I was making my demand (oops! I mean "request") of some perfect angels, but instead to my peers who matched me in recklessness, rambunctiousness, and budding "criminality," if not necessarily (at that time!) in my propensity for violence. Hell, I didn't even have to explain to any of the cats what "make this money back" meant. Can you dig it?

We headed towards the back of the projects all brainstorming as to whom or what I could "hit."[52] Once we neared the hole in the fence separating the projects from the railroad tracks, I had it! The fast food pizza joint in the nearby strip mall![53] It was only a short walk away and I knew its entire layout from patronizing the place. In fact, at least a couple of times I remember taking my gun and spinning it on the counter in the blind spot of the surveillance cameras and commenting to a couple of the workers (whom I knew from school and the neighborhood) how I was "going to come in and rob (them) one day." We all just laughed it off as a "joke" of how I felt the store "was slipping."[54]

We all (or at least they) should have taken my comments

---

[52] In hindsight, I suspect the cat whom had won all of our money was just trying to keep me off of *his* ass. But he had no need to worry – I considered him a "homeboy" at the time. And the one thing no one has ever been able to say about me in this lifetime is that I've *ever* stabbed anyone in the back. That's not my style. And although my brother would have to shoot this particular individual a couple of times in the leg and hip a few years later, that was an entirely unrelated situation and in my eyes, totally necessary and justified.

[53] Even though it was in Berry Hill, one of the most heavily policed areas of my city. In fact, Berry Hill was actually its own city (with its own mayor, council and police force) completely encapsulated by the City of Nashville and known to all Blacks as a "police trap."

[54] Who *thinks* like this, right? How embarrassing!

more seriously, because now I was crossing tracks, heading under the underpass, and taking notice of the police patrol as we trooped along the way. Stationing a few cats across the street as a "warning system" and directing a couple of others outside the store as the same, I commenced to "get with the bullshit":

"*Set that shit out!*" I demanded, coming through the door.

Some girl was working the back, and a cat named D.S. was working the register; no one else seemed to be there, just us three teenagers. I could sense immediately that D.S. recognized me, but I didn't expect anything less than the strictest of cooperation from him, as he was a White Ave. cat (or at least "ran with" them), so he knew what was up. Plus, I didn't come in there to "hurt" anyone, anyway – entirely ignorant of the fact that I was causing emotional and traumatic harm to these two innocent people that would last longer than most physical wounds.

D.S. caught on quickly, and attempted to open the register. Unsuccessful, he tried again, getting the same results. However, he wasn't stalling for time; the cat was just nervous. But who wouldn't be (nervous) with a damned fool waving a gun in *your* face! He tried again, still the register refused to open and I could tell from the shaking of his hands that he was starting to panic.

"*Get the fucking register open!*" I demanded, more agitated than menacing.

He tried again, but his hands just wouldn't cooperate with his brain and push the correct sequence of buttons, until, finally, his entire motor skills seemed to shut down, and mouth only thing working, he called for help from his coworker:

"*Afya!*" he pushed out fearfully, "*come get this register open!*" he pleaded.

But she couldn't either; she was too afraid herself. So, after giving Afya a couple of times herself to open it, I told them both to step back and opened fire!

Boom! Boom! But two shots *still* didn't open up the register. And, luckily, neither of us three were hit by a ricochet and/or a flying cash register key! So, panicking now myself, I picked the entire register off the counter and ran out the door with it!

You heard that, right?! My. Dumbass. Took. The. Entire. Fucking. Cash. Register. And. Ran. Out. The. Fucking. Store. With. It!! How? I don't know! Because the damned thing was about half my size!

And wouldn't you know it? As soon as I make it outside I hear the "warning alarm" because a cop car was coming down the street on a routine patrol! Unbelievably, however, I pressed against a parked tractor trailer and watched it pass right by me with the cash register still in hand!

Imagine the sight of a short and slight 15 years young kid lugging a cash register across a wide (normally busy) city thoroughfare! Well, somehow, someway, there I was! And I made it across to the side of a building where the rest of my compadres awaited me, then smashed the cash register a couple of times until it revealed its treasures! Eager to leave the scene, I dished out a few small dollars to a couple of cats for looking out for me, yet, unsurprisingly, most didn't want a dime! And can you blame them? They had no idea *what* had went on in there, but they heard shots and saw that I had taken the register (like, what the hell, right?!) so they couldn't *wait* to get the hell away from my ass!

So we separated, them heading back towards the projects and me heading towards home. As if I was just going to go about the rest of my nightly routine and go to bed as if I hadn't just caused all of the chaos that I did! How unrealistic was that, right? Not far from home, a discomforting feeling knocked me from

Pops

this insane way of thinking as I witnessed a police car turn from the street on which my Pops and I lived, so I turned around and somehow covertly made my way back to Vine Hill without being stopped by the dozens of pigs in cars (and even a helicopter) seeking me whom already knew my full identity![55] Seeking comfort and safety in my mother's home and bosom (you know, just like any other "badass!"), instead, I found out (from my brothers and sister) that she, my father, and Trina had just left "looking" for me! Kissing my siblings before rushing back out, I (somehow) ducked the searchlights of the cop cars and helicopter(s) and made it safely to my homie Brian L's house near Edgehill before catching a breath!

If I had not have been the ripe old age of 15 years young (and thus, not have known everything there was to know about the world!), then I would have been in a pretty fucked up situation, wouldn't I? Because I could no longer go anywhere near either my mother's *or* my father's home, or *anywhere* in nashville, so good thing that I "knew it all." Or I would have been "fucked!" Yeah, I would have been "fucked" had I been a lesser "man" but since I wasn't, I knew what to do: Run forever! With a pistol and a few hundred dollars in my pocket, there was no telling how long I could live off of that!

So thinking along that vein, I called my cousin Punkin to pick me up and take me to a hotel for a couple of days.[56] I

---

[55] This shit is going to sound hard to believe but I swear *every single word* is true! After I had committed my awful misdeed, my cousin Trina pulled up shortly thereafter to pick up pizza she had ordered from the place! (How much of a coincidence was that?!) Catching wind of what happened and my involvement when Afya (who attended Glencliff with both Trina and I!) mentioned my name to the responding police officers, Trina hurried up the street to inform my father a few minutes before the cops got there! Someone or another informed my Pops that I was considered "armed and dangerous" (meaning the pigs would "shoot to kill on sight"), so he and Trina sought to find me before the police did.

[56] Because, of course, my 15 year old "bad" ass didn't *even* really know how to drive a car (let alone, did I *own* one!), nor could I even *get* a hotel room since I was under 18!

needed to lay low, then I would make my way to one of the other cities/states where I and my family had deep roots and from there I would be safe! Yeah, that was it!

Nevertheless, even though I "knew it all," I, in fact, *didn't know* that my mother and father *both knew* what I would do and whom I would reach out to before *I* did! Damned fool! They were right beside him when I called! And had already made the decision to turn me in themselves and not gives the pigs the opportunity to kill me! Whether it happened there in nashville, or Atlanta, or Louisville, or some other city, they knew that Death was on my head! And they wouldn't allow it, so they saved me from myself. When Punkin finally pulled up at Brian L's house (what was taking him so long anyway?!) and I came out the door, from the side of the house came my Pops and grabbed me from behind.

"*Son, I'm not gonna let them kill you, son! I'm not gonna let them kill you!*"

I could tell he was fighting back tears. But hell, what was *he* crying for? *I* was the one on my way to "Juvenile." Only later sitting in my cell at Woodland Hills Youth Development Center (the prison for Juveniles in west nashville) a few weeks later, did I recognize his tears as a mixture of relief, love, joy, sadness, and disappointment. And only then, did too, I cry…

(Not that it would have been smart to if I could anyway! Because the authorities were *looking for me*, remember?!)

"By the very nature of things in prison, you're forced to think a little more about yourself, about the meaning of your actions, about questions pertaining to your own Being..."
Disturbing the Peace by Vaclav Havel

TRIAL & TRIBULATIONS

Clink, CLINK. The sound of keys opening the holding cell door startled me awake.

"Verdict's back."

Damn, seems quick, I thought. Made me a little uneasy.

"What time is it?" I asked.

"A little after noon."

Less than two hours of deliberation – this *couldn't* be good.

A million thoughts and feelings filled my heart and mind during the short walk back to the kkkourtroom: My mother – she'd heard testimony that would've disturbed even the most loving and trusting parent – yet her kind eyes and reassuring smile were always there whenever I sought them throughout my trial. How could she be holding up with her oldest child maybe moments away from spending the rest of his life in prison?

And my son – not even three years old. How would he grow up without me to lead him, essentially his father, mother, and best friend all in one? I wonder if he'd ever forgive or respect his mother knowing that her vindictiveness and spite were the catalysts behind my case and incarceration? Equally – even knowing the situation and circumstances surrounding it – would he forever resent me for my actions and absence, much as I still resent my own father for his despite it not really being his fault? I hope 20 years from now he's not walking down this same path.

It took everything I had in me to fight back the tears. Yet not only for my son this time, but also for the son of Old School;

him angry and hurt, staring a hole through me throughout the trial with saddened, tear-filled, murderous eyes. Would he ever get over the loss of his father? Was that even possible? Or would anger, pain, and the streets push this 11-year-young child to grow into an angry young man that would take the life of another Black man like I was accused of – or even eventually seek to kill me out of vengeance? And hell, with the way I was portrayed in that kkkourtroom, could or would I even blame him if he did?

"*I'VE BEEN SHOT!!! I'VE BEEN SHOT!!!*"
"*Ok sir, ok sir, who shot you?*"
"*I DON'T KNOW!!! I DON'T KNOW!!!*"
"*Okay, sir, calm down. An ambulance is on its way.*"

No telling how long Old School's voice on that 911 tape would haunt me. To the rednekkk prosekkkutors, pigs, and so-called "judge," Old School was no more than another case, just another "vic," an excuse to rid the streets of another Black man and enslave him. I didn't see it that way, though; all I could think about was how our community lost another father, son, brother, uncle, cousin, and friend to the bullshit and violence of the streets. And here I was with my life on the line charged with his murder. What a damned shame. I was getting sick to my stomach…

"*All rise. The honorable judge seth norman, division four criminal court presiding.*"
"*You may be seated.*"
"*I understand the jury has reached a verdict?*"
"*We have, your honor.*"
"*Will the defendant please stand?*"

With every eye in the kkkourtroom seemingly burning a hole through my soul, I stood up.

"*To the first count of the indictment, Premeditated Murder in the*

First Degree, how do you find the Defendant?"

"Not guilty, your honor."

The kkkourtroom gave a quiet stir, but this meant nothing, of course. I was charged with two separate counts of murdering Old School,[57] along with a charge of the robbery of him thrown in for good measure. Two more counts to go.

"*To the second count of the indictment, First Degree Felony Murder, how do you find the Defendant?*" asked the so-called judge.

Suddenly, I witnessed a smile from an elderly lady on the jury! Fleeting though it may have been, I noticed it!!! Up until that point, everything in the kkkourtroom was one gigantic blur, just a hundred sets of accusing eyes. At that moment, however, everything came back into focus. And then, to my amazement, I noticed another smile, and another smile, and another smile on the faces of the jury members. So maybe these people *did* listen to the evidence!!![58]

---

[57] How one could be charged with murdering the same person twice, I could never figure out, but this is common practice in tennessee and other states in order to make it easier to convict a defendant. In essence, it allows the prosekkkution to present more than one theory (i.e. motive, means, modus operandi, etc.) of the crime and see whichever one "sticks."

[58] As trial was approaching, for some reason I wasn't nervous, afraid or anything. I always believed since I wasn't guilty, I would go free. Culminating in this over confidence, initially I didn't necessarily care to do my part fighting for my freedom – which is kind of a sad thing to say. As the date came closer, I realized, however, I had to get off my ass and research the law and help my attorney fight my case. Still, I was so sure I was going home. My mentality was if the trial starts on Monday, I'll be out Wednesday. I told my baby brother, "Be sure to get ready to pick me up."

Along with the indefatigable Ralph Newman, a young, extremely intelligent and passionate woman named Eileen Parrish was my lawyer. We collaborated a lot fighting the case. And although they really fought for me, they weren't nervous either. Once the trial started, the prosekkkutors, nonetheless, paraded witness after witness. However, none had anything really to do with me. Unbelievably, too, they brought the state's star witness, Paul Talley's brother Freddy Talley in. This fool was so stereotypically ghetto looking – he checked off all the boxes of what amerikkka's been made to be afraid of. He had an Afro a mile wide. His pants were off his ass. He was cursing throughout the testimony – that is, when he acted somewhat intelligent and you could actually understand what he was saying. The truth was, he knew nothing. All he knew was that I was prone to wear body armor. Other than that, he really didn't

"Not *guilty, your honor.*"

Not guilty!!! A noticeable gasp came from the prosekkkutor's table, temporarily startling the so-called judge, jury, and everyone else in the kkkourtroom. Everyone except me. I had been experiencing the a.d.a.'s hatred of me for over a year now, so her outburst wasn't really a surprise. Hell, I would have almost expected her to cum in her pants had they returned a guilty verdict. Devil bitch.

Allowing a smile to reach my eyes (but never cross my lips!) behind her reaction, I knew then that I had won my life back. At this point, I couldn't have even cared less about the bogus robbery charge, as it only carried 8-12 (years) anyway – meaning that eventually I would again go free. But no worries there, either. The so-called judge, now visibly perturbed:

"*And how do you find the Defendant on count three of the indictment, Aggravated Robbery?*"

"*Not guilty, your honor.*"

The kkkourtroom exploded!!! Not guilty on *all* counts!!! Cheers from the family and friends there to support me, tears from the family of Old School, and gasps of disbelief from the bailiffs and pig homicide detectives!!! The assistant district attorneys and so-called judge – now furiously banging the gavel shouting "ORDER! ORDER!" – were *pissed!!!* All of the nefarious work, time, effort, and lies told that went into finally charging me with something, *anything,* after all the years of investigation were for naught!!!

---

know me in any serious way. He and I had never hung out and I had only recently met him through Paul, his brother.
So besides Paul Talley's clearly untruthful and biased testimony, they had no real evidence linking me to the crime. Nor did I ever make any statement to anyone about *ANYTHING* regarding what I possibly knew concerning it. It simply was a case that never should have been charged. Furthermore, a friend testified in my defense and said she remembered where I was the day this crime happened. I was with her. I think we were either studying together in the dorm or in the university library. She was able to recall and prove it. And that's probably what saved me.

Trial & Tribulations

"General, is there anything, ANYTHING at all, that you have in order to keep the Defendant incarcerated?"

Unbeknownst to me, this would forebode things to come.

"No, your honor, we have nothing."

"Nothing at ALL???"

"Nothing at all, your honor."

I left the kkkourtroom that day once again a free man. Nevertheless, if some people had their way, I wouldn't be free for long...

Nashville's politics are mostly run by the descendants of hardcore former Confederates[59] – who even now, 150 years later, agonize over their cowardice, humiliation, and defeat in what is still referred to in the area as the "War Against Northern Aggression," seeking retribution in any way possible whenever their unfounded sense of pride and self-worth is affronted in any kind of way. And my acquittal was a direct affront to the

---

[59] Daily, in a quick ride around the city and surrounding counties, one can see numerous confederate flags displayed proudly on cars and houses, and even statues of kkk leaders along the interstates and upon the tennessee state capitol grounds. Disgustingly, prison slave labor was even used to clear trees to insure one statue – that of nathan bedford forrest, he of ku klux klan and the Fort Pillow Massacre of Black Union soldiers infamy – was able to be more easily displayed and viewed by passing vehicles. Insultingly, literally as I was fighting with prison and department of corrections officials for the return of this book's confiscated manuscript (which they deemed "racist against whites" and of "advocating violence against cops," in their words), tennessee's newly-elected governor signed a proclamation declaring July 31 (2019) "nathan bedford forrest day" as *required by tennessee state law.* State *law* not only *requires* this racist, traitorous slave-trading coward to be *honored every year,* but also the coward kkkonfederate general robert e. lee *every* January 19, and all the other racist traitors of the kkkonfederate *every* June 3 which the state deems "confederate memorial day."

This in a kkkountry that, only a day later, president Grab-em-by-the-pussy was demanding four duly-elected (unlike himself!) women-of-color to "go back to their own countries where they come from!" Please note that three of these beautiful spirits are native born *this* kkkountry, while the fourth is a *naturalized citizen!* Yet that orange bitch chose not to make any statements concerning the three separate incidents within ten days wherein young punkkk white supremacists killed at least 32 Hispanics and Blacks while leaving dozens more injured!!! How much more arrogantly and glaringly hypocritical can this kkkountry be, huh???

"southern sensibilities" of the "good white people" of nashville, tn. No way could that go on unabated for long. Of course, they had no clue how all of this affected me, the guy they unfairly tried to put away. They didn't know how I felt about almost losing my life; how I felt about not being there for my son and my siblings and cousins. I felt that I was a changed person, even if nobody else knew, or bothered to give a damn about it...

Following the verdict and my release, most of the people that feared me before my incarceration, feared me even more so tenfold. In fact, even some people that I never knew feared me *at all* would start acting very strange.[60] Everyone, mistakenly seemed to think that I would become even worse than I was before I went in – thought I would become even more dangerous than they already initially thought – and a lot of people really feared for their lives.

Especially Tsawa and her family. Because not only was she the one who put the pigs on me, she also was the one whom took the most important person in the world to me away – my son. The last few months prior to my trial, not only had she stopped him from coming to visit me, but she also kept him away from my family, too. And that was dangerous. If I was

---

[60] For example, I ran into an "Old Head" that, years before, used to pay me for my pistol play. And although we hadn't really crossed paths since my early teens, for some reason I got the sense that he was now wary of me. But we were "too cool" for that, in my opinion—hell, we both knew a lot of the other's dirt from the early '90s—so, of course, I had to ask him about it. And in essence he said that I was "all bite and no bark" and that could "really rattle some people." He even gave me an example where I had unnerved *him* for a time way back in the day, which *really* surprised me! And although he agreed with me that there was never really a secret of how I felt about someone or something (good or bad), he countered that, still, no one ever really knew what I was thinking or about to do until *after* I had made up my mind to do it. Towards the end of our conversation I helped him realize that he was at least *partly* responsible for the way I was/am by reminding him that he had always counseled me that "gangsters move in silence." However, even to that truism he responded that sometimes a person can be *too* silent. And although our conversation gave me a lot to consider, still I continued to harbor the opinion that my *actions* were always loud enough.

going to blow my newfound chance at life and kill anyone, believe me, she would have been the first on the list and most satisfying, indeed. But thank God, I had "changed." Just not in the way or for the reasons that everyone expected.

See, no one ever knew this, but every time I would close my eyes, or my mind would drift, I saw that little boy's eyes and tears. Every single time, it seemed. Furthermore, I saw my own son's. In fact, sometimes they were juxtaposed onto each other's. I would see Old School's son and my son as if they were one and the same. Which they were. I would close my eyes, see theirs, and then the softness would return to my own. Slowly, but surely, warmness also re-entered my heart. Both of these young men could have been fatherless; both could have fell victim to the same streets as myself; both could have potentially fell for the same traps that both Old School and I did. However, for some reason I didn't quite understand, I got a second chance to raise my son – and I would be damned before I blew it. My soul kept returning to the thought "What exactly am I doing out here in these streets to where I could've been mixed up in the spreading of pain to yet another Black family? What type of person *am* I?" Old School's son was the mirror put in my face that forced me to see myself clearly and I can't say I liked my reflection.[61] I had to go and see my son...

Seeing as how it had been almost six months since I had been able to hold or even speak to him, I just *knew* that his mother would have no problem with him visiting with me. Nevertheless, I was terribly wrong.

Calling over to Tsawa's mother's house to arrange in picking him up, I was informed that not only would I not be

---

[61] As said best by Brother Malcom in his autobiography, "The very enormity of my previous life's guilt prepared me to accept the truth." And although I take care not to liken myself to the great Brother Malcom, I can sympathize with his epiphany and the change he felt within himself when faced with a spiritually powerful truth.

allowed to visit with him without a *court order*, but also that I would not be allowed to even *speak* to him! Say the fuck *what*??? Just what kind of shit was *that*?!?, is what I was thinking! My *son*! To say that I was pissed doesn't describe a *tenth* of what I was feeling! As close as my son and I were, this woman would actually stoop so low in taking her hate out on me by keeping he and I apart?! I wanted to take and wring her fucking... – let's just say I was "extremely unhappy." Let's just leave it at that. And once my initial reaction of going over there subsided, I quickly came up with a plan so as not to fall into her trap.

 Thinking of something, not that it's "right," or justified in any way, but I can honestly understand how some men could up and just say "fuck it" when dealing with a vindictive woman that has your children. Her control over your kids is in essence her control over *you*, and no man wants to be pulled on a string by a malicious woman. Especially one with no compunction in putting "the white folkkks" in your business and sending you to jail when you bucked her control. I can see it. I can understand. Because even I sometimes felt like that, too. It's not about whether you love your children or not, but about the stress and strain of having to fight with someone you (more than likely at least) *used* to love whom is fighting you tooth and nail in an attempt to stop you from being involved in the life of someone you always will (your children), with every entity – the kkkourts, the kkkops, society in general – all in opposition to you. So, yeah, had I been a weaker man, I would have said "fuck it," too, and just tried to explain it all to my son when he was older. Nevertheless, I wasn't as weak as some other men, and I couldn't; Kyree meant the world to me. And as such, her control over him would always be my Achilles heel. Unless I was smart and beat her at her own game.

 Therefore I took out child support on *myself* and petitioned the court to acknowledge my visitation rights. If that was the game she wanted to play, then I would play it to the letter. And win. With the goal of always being a part of my son's life and as constant a presence as "the law" would "allow." It wasn't ideal, but it was the best scenario possible considering all of the bullshit between Tsawa and I.[62]

To set the amount of money I would owe, I worked for two days at a day labor place making $20 one day and $22 another, I think. I can't even remember what it was they had me doing or where it was, it was so inconsequential. Just as inconsequential as Tsawa felt I should be to my son's life. And I got my court order to be able to visit with my son every other weekend for overnight stays, and every Wednesday for a few hours in the evenings.

And as it turned out, I learned a valuable lesson from Tsawa via this experience – although it would still be awhile before it kicked in fully: I can't tolerate a romantic relationship with a woman whom didn't have a father or some other strong father figure – no matter if it was a stepfather, older brother, uncle, or family friend or even neighbor – in her life. Simply, there are profound differences between those women who have had that and those that didn't – and that's why I have mad love and respect for men like my brother John, my brother-in-law Perry, my cousins Juan, Mandingo, Punkin, Shotgun and Waldo and especially my own father that stuck it out and made sure they were *always* a part of their daughters' lives. (Even though that is what they were supposed to do anyway. There are enough men that don't do what they're "supposed to do" for this to be appreciated and acknowledged in some sense.) Because it's real easy to cut and run, send your child support and give a damn

---

[62] My attitude has always been that if someone really wants to do something, then they'll find a *way*; if they really don't, then they'll find an *excuse* as to why they cannot.

less about actually helping raise, protect and guide her to become a well-adjusted woman. Moreover, it truly makes all the difference in the world as to how much importance she puts on having a good man and a father in her *own* children's lives. Fathers *matter* – and not just financially but also emotionally, mentally, and spiritually for their guidance and protection.

Distressingly, a woman whom has grown up without a healthy love and respect for her father (or some other "father figure") will in turn usually teach that same disrespect and dislike/hate of a father to her children even if only subconsciously. I've witnessed it enough times in my own life to bring tears to my heart and I feel as if until this awfulness is rectified, then we'll never really get anywhere as a people in this kkkountry. Mothers are a child's first and most important teacher, so if the mother doesn't love and respect the man whom she *chose* to father her children, then why on earth would the children ever do so? Therefore, in my opinion, a lot of the discord in Black men/women's failed relationships can be traced back to a failed father - daughter relationship and therein also lies the "fix."

Telling you all you need to know about Tsawa's views on the importance of fathers: In all the years that Tsawa and I were involved in some way, I never *once* met her father. Not when she moved out of her mother's home at the age of seventeen-years-young to move in with me; not when she became pregnant a few months later or even at the birth of our son at age eighteen. Not when she and I were suffering numerous discords and contentious situations and fights; nor when she and I were going through our separate criminal trials. Compare that to my meeting Jannah's father within a month or so of us getting "serious" – although it *was* under somewhat less-than-ideal circumstances. Furthermore, when Jannah was in trouble, her father was *there*, right there *with her*, questioning me as to what was going on with his daughter, and letting me know in no uncertain terms that he would hold me responsible for any harm that befell her under my care. And I respected that. Furthermore, you could see the pride of having a protective father all in Jannah's demeanor and attitude. Most importantly, you could clearly see the love and respect she had for him. Every single time she spoke of him, every single time he was around us, it was clear, unequivocal, and undeniable. As opposed to Tsawa, whom only spoke of her father with disgust and detestment and disrespect; not to seem as though I'm piling on Tsawa, but these were/are clear-cut differences between these two women. That one instance of many says a lot to me personally about how much fathers count. Especially in how they profoundly impact their daughters and how their lives will ultimately unfold.

However, I couldn't articulate nor even understand this back then; I just knew that something was always "off" whenever Tsawa and I attempted a "relationship" – especially the other (usually older) men she always had lurking in the background, and I had no time for that bullshit in another one of my relationships again after Soyayya. So after I clearly "expressed my concerns" and noticed that it (the cats "in the cut") and other untoward shit would forever be a problem, I began to not take what we had and could have had as serious as I could have. This was in the near beginning of our getting together, yet we quickly became pregnant, and no matter our situation, I was the happiest man in the world to become a father. And I always knew it would be a son.

Furthermore, I don't say any of that to mean in any way that I didn't really "love" her – and at one time I was even "in love" with her. Yet, I'm not entirely sure that I loved her as I should have. There were just certain things that I couldn't get past at the time and after my son was born, I think I may have made this dearth of the love she wanted from me ever more apparent. Because there was no possible way to ever question that I loved my son, ya know? Even if it was two different kinds of love that we're talking about, it still may have seemed a slap in the face to her. I loved my son, he loved me, she loved our son and she, too, loved me (even if it wasn't in the way I felt it should have been), but did I, in fact, love her is what she always may have wondered? And that's a jarring thought.

And although I did at the time, I don't blame her now or at least not completely for the way she was reacting and acting towards me. Because far too early into our involvement I emotionally shut down to her as a way of dealing with my frustrations and fears of being made a fool again (long before I ever met Jannah) and in turn came more and more bullshit.

Therefore, I know the part I played in poisoning what Tsawa and I had and could have had; I realize now that there were numerous things I could have and should have done differently both before and after our son's birth to understand, support, comfort, communicate, and empathize more with her and maybe ease the fears I now know she was facing. Would our child be healthy? Would I even be there to be a true father to him, or would I be dead or behind bars somewhere when they really needed me most? Or even if I was physically available, would she and I even be capable of supporting and raising him in ways not just as well but even better than our parents did with us? And speaking of our parents, I doubted if we could or would; my mother, Tsawa's mother and my father were always there when Tsawa and I were tumultuously at odds, there when we needed a babysitter and/or place to stay or vehicle to drive during some hard times, and there as steadying presences when "street bullshit" almost led to us both being taken out of his life for good. So, it's very true that it does take a village to raise any child, because without the village of our parents (again, only the three aforementioned; her father has always been nonexistent in our and our sons' lives), our siblings, friends and other extended family members (especially on my side), I couldn't even imagine how life would have been for us. Because in spite of all the books I/we read about childrearing, birth, etc., we were still pretty clueless.

All in all, I can say that I learned from both my own and Tsawa's mistakes in our attempts at a relationship and a family and I vowed not to repeat them in the future. And, for the most part, I was successful. I would say that I was much more ready for, and comforting, understanding, communicative and empathetic in the pregnancy of my second son than I was during Tsawa's pregnancy with Kyree. I failed her in my inexperience and callousness and thus, I failed him (Kyree), too. Hurt people hurt people, as Tsawa and I both immaturely have done to each other far too many times in the past. But that doesn't excuse it. And, ironically, in my yearning to not make the same mistakes with my second child, I may have went from one extreme to the other, damn near to the point of being a pushover. Because I sure as hell went for far more bullshit (of a different kind) with Pasheni than I ever would have allowed Tsawa to dish out to me...

"They gave me all the tools to destroy myself – and I *fell* for it…"

Tupac Amaru Shakur

YOUNG & THUGGIN

Ro and I crept to the bathroom about ten minutes before closing time; every few minutes or so Mac would come in to check on us. Too often, in fact – he seemed somewhat nervous. But me? – I wasn't concerned; I *knew* our plan was foolproof: Giving Mac and the manager enough time to clean the front of the restaurant and kill most of the lights, no one would be able to see us creeping to the back through the front glass window. Spending more than enough time languishing in those cells in "Juvenile" and Woodland Hills reflecting on the mistakes I'd made in the past and how to avoid them if by some chance I had to "put it down" again, I knew this "easy lick" would go off without a hitch. Calm as the eye of a hurricane, breathing steadily, gun loaded and cocked, I awaited our agreed upon signal.

The lights went dark. Slowly counting to a hundred in my mind, I slowly but steadily led the creep from the bathroom, not seeing a soul in sight. Turning the corner to the back, I spied the manager sitting at his desk with his back turned to me – and money was everywhere. On the desk being counted and in the wide-open safe, I could feel the "fetti" in my hands already. Pistol drawn and pointed, silently stalking my prey like a panther, I covered the distance separating us in one serenely unconscious breath; I was so quiet that Mac even gave a startle of surprise at my sudden appearance – and he *knew* we were there!

Pistol now pressed to the back of the manager's head:

"Hey, Big Man... GET YO' MUTHAFUCKIN ASS ON THE GROUND!!!!!!! NOWWW FAT MUTHAFUCKA!!!!!!!

Mac was so spooked that he dropped the boxes he was loading on the shelf. I then pointed my strap at him:

"Hey, you, *muthafucka!!! Get yo muthafuckin ass on the ground and* don't move *goddamnit!!!"*

Turning to Ro:

"Cuz, if that muthafucka move even an inch, *put a bullet in his goddamn head!!!"*

Back to the manager – now shaking and whimpering on the ground, having soiled himself:

"Hey, Big Man, I see yo fat ass is counting a lot of money up in here, huh? Guess I'm right on time," I laughed, then kicked him in his ribs. *"Now stay the fuck still and I may not even kill yo ass!"*

After dumping all of the money from the safe and desk – cash, change, checks, and all – into a bag I brought along with me, I then interrogated the manager:

"Hey Fat Ass, any more money up in here?"

"N-N-N-No, Sir!"

"FAT BASTARD!" I kicked him in his ribs again, "DON'T *LIE TO ME!!!"*

Turning to Mac,

"Hey lil nigga – *anymore money up in here? I think y'all muthafuckas is holding out!"*

"I don't know man; I think that's everything."

Now either Mac's a really good actor, or this muthafucka was really scared. And *he* was the one who set it up! I threw a box on top of his head, and then turned back to Fatso:

"Fat Boy, you know if I find out you lied to me, I'm gonna kill you, right?"

"Ch-ch-check *my coat pockets,"* he stammered, *"I might have a few dollars in there."*

Emptying his coat of all its valuables, I then turned him on his back so that I could relieve him of whatever his pants pockets held, too. His eyes seemed almost glued shut he had them closed so tight – he was so terrified that he didn't even want to *look* at me.

"YOU FAT MUTHAFUCKA!!!," I screamed, snatching his pack of cigarettes out of his shirt pocket, *"don't you know cigarettes can* KILL YOU???" I kicked him in his ribs again. *"Now turn the fuck back over!"*

Let's go," I said turning to Ro, *"and both of y'all muthafuckas count to one hundred before you even* think *about coming up for air!"*

Removing our masks and gloves, leaving out the back emergency door, and walking calmly to the car, Ro seemed shaken.

"What the fuck is wrong with you?" I asked him.

"Cuz, you throwed off."

I started laughing. That was actually the funniest shit I had heard in a long time.

Spring of 1994, eleventh grade, finally released from DYD[63] custody into the care of my father, and honestly striving to live "right." But working a fast food job with the money not coming *fast enough,* wearing clothes that didn't fit, rocking kicks with holes in the toe – to go along with having a Pops that deemed me old enough to work for all the extra gear I wanted[64] – would soon help to reshape my views as to what was "right" or "wrong." An innocent high school joke session with a female I was digging "capping" on the holes I was trying to hide in my

---

[63] Department of Youth Development, i.e., the department of corrections for "juveniles" in the state of tennessee.
[64] In hindsight, I don't knock my Pops' views; in fact, I feel the same as he does. He provided me with food, shelter, and the clothing I *needed* as opposed to all the extra shit I *wanted,* ya dig? At that age, one should have learned by then to work for all the extra things you want out of life – helps teach the value of a dollar.

shoes would be the catalyst for my returning back to the path of destruction. With everyone laughing and no one really respecting that "work for what you want" shit, things really hit close to home and I fell weak to what would become my crutch: robbing people. Or more specifically, robbing *businesses*.

Wrongly, what I soon started to justify to myself as "right" was my getting out there and *taking what* I wanted, *when* I wanted, *how* I wanted – and never again allowing someone to get a laugh off of *my* appearance.[65] I would come back after that weekend "new down" (all new gear) for the entire week, my first few pieces of gold jewelry (which would soon turn into a semi-addiction), and well over a grand of cash in my pocket.[66] I felt the same as I had after I'd pulled my first store robbery at fourteen: damned good!

To say that I became dangerous during this time period would be the classic understatement – ashamedly, I became a one-man crime spree, pulling takeover robberies all over the city, at all times of day and night. Every few days, in every neighborhood, on every major road in nashville, every business with cash in it was a potential target. Sometimes I would even hit the same business two or three times over, a few weeks apart. And insanely, I must admit, it didn't even make a difference if a police station was just a block away – if you had the cash and I felt that there was some way for me to come and get it, then I was *coming!* That's how unbelievably bold I was.

Imagine that: 16-years-young, short, skinny, baby-faced to the point where I couldn't grow one whisker of facial hair (and

---

[65] I can't recall today what the final impetus for me learning this valuable lesson was, but I soon realized, understood, and accepted completely that I need neither the validation, acceptance, nor "stamp of approval" of *anyone* outside of myself. Yet those less humbly confident of themselves have sometimes taken this unmitigated truth as a personal affront. But to *hell* with them.

[66] Which, at the time, I thought was *a lot* of money. Plus, it was in mostly small bills, so to me that made it look and feel better. Idiotic, I know.

would need to have a mustache and goatee drawn in along with my eyebrows darkened in order to somewhat disguise myself), but with a sense of violent, yet cool calm to my aura where you could just *feel* the danger emanating from me. Sheer determination and confidence alone would carry me through all of the self-imposed turmoil of this time; as embarrassingly insane as it is for me to admit even now over two decades later, once committed to "making a move" an adrenaline surge would make me *invincible*.[67] Fearlessness would float me through the business's door – even in broad daylight:

"ANYBODY ELSE IN HERE???"

Drawing my weapon – usually a .357 magnum in those days – and pointing it directly at the clerk's face usually got my question answered pretty quickly. And even though more than likely I had already sent my female accomplices in on a reconnaissance mission a few minutes earlier to check for me, it never hurt to be sure.

"*No, no! No one else is here!*" he swore.

"*DON'T LIE TO ME GODDAMNIT!!! TAKE ME TO THE SAFE!!!*"

I would always make my way to the safe first – which was usually in the back somewhere; this was also another way for me to check that no one else was there. Instructing my hostage to place all of the money, jewelry, and anything else of value in the bag,[68] on this particular mission, both the clerk and I heard the chime of the door being opened which spelled trouble – and

---

[67] Unlike a lot of people that I knew personally, no drugs were ever wanted nor needed. In fact, I considered then – and still consider now – those whom needed weed or powder or alcohol or any other drugs to push them to do something/anything weak-minded cowards, and thus, untrustworthy. Those that know me "well" would go so far as to say that I despise "getting high" and *especially* those whom think they can do so "on my time or dime."

[68] Which I usually carried with me, although sometimes I would just use the bank bag that was a lot of times kept in most businesses' safe.

more so for him than I.

A customer had evidently walked in. Hid by the high counter as I crouched down walking the clerk back to the front of the business, I instructed my captive to help the customer pay her bill while I kept the .357 pointed to his side. I was also kind enough to warn him that if he "did anything wrong," I would "gun (his) ass down." With the interaction between the clerk and customer kept brief,[69] we got back down to business:

"*Let me get the rest of the money in the register,*" I said.

"*Wait, there's another customer here. Let me help him first.*"

Oddly enough, though, I hadn't heard the chime this time. But looking at how he played it cool the first time around, for some reason, I thought the fool was trying to help me. Boy, was *I* wrong.

Somehow, someway, before I had even noticed, the clerk had inched his way to the front of the store – I was *slipping!* Rising to my feet and quickly looking around, I then realized that there hadn't been a customer at all the second time around – and the clerk was now running out the front of the store screaming!

"*I'M BEING ROBBED! I'M BEING ROBBED! HELP! HELP!*"

"*Hey bitch!!!*"

I chased behind him, soon finding myself trapped inside the store with this six-foot something Black man holding the door! Now *I* was the hostage! I pointed my weapon at his face again and tried to talk some sense into him:

"*Bitch, if you don't get the fuck away from this door I'm finna gun yo' ass down!!!*"

"*HELP! HELPPP!!!!*" he continued to scream.

---

[69] Although, in hindsight, he *did* seem to try his damnedest to keep her in there, but can you really blame him?

"BITCH! YOU ABOUT TO DIE!!!"

I guess that snapped him back to what little sense he held in his head, because he finally backed away from the door, allowing me to get away. Stupid bastard. Why die for someone else's money trying to play "Hero," anyway?[70]

Anyway, I ran as if being chased by a pack of rabid dogs! I ran past the auto repair shop. I ran past the pharmacy. I ran and ran and ran – putting the shoe store, the furniture rental place, and *especially* the police substation a few blocks away, farther and farther behind me! I was running in broad daylight, gun in one hand, bank bag full of money and jewelry in the other, until I reached my get-away car. Ducked down in the backseat, at least a couple of cop cars passed right by us on our way to the interstate back home.

Having a great laugh at my narrow escape, experiences like that only seemed to embolden me more. I had no sense of mortality whatsoever – or should I say, I was so aware of the fragility of life that I chose to face my mortality head on by telling it to kiss my ass. There was absolutely nothing nor no one that I was afraid of, and my actions showed that at all times. Insanely, I took chances "just because" sometimes I felt that there was a good chance that things *could* go wrong. How idiotic was that?

Case in point: One way in the parking lot, one way out – and just a block or two down from the police substation.[71] Two

---

[70] During the time period when I was doing all this bullshit, my still developing mind, never – not once, that I can remember – even considered the trauma and suffering I was causing these unfortunate people. In fact, I couldn't even comprehend how/why some of the people would put up a fight for the money "when it wasn't even theirs" and the business "had so much of it." Ignorant, inconsiderate and indefensible of me.

[71] Not the same substation as previously discussed – this one was on another side of town. However, don't think that that would have discouraged me, anyway; I "hit" numerous businesses near *both* of these and all of the others numerous times even *after* the situations I am currently telling you about. As I've said previously, *nothing* would stop me when I was determined to come.

of us walked in, but it was I who did all of the talking to the young rednekkk sales clerk. Noticing that he seemed very suspicious of us anyway, for some strange reason I sensed that he also might have noticed the bulge of the .357 the shoulder holster held under my jacket. Moreover, strangely, my mind was uncharacteristically expressing reservations and giving me the signal to "abort mission" – however, fearlessness of the heart overrode all that. I *wanted* that money – so I pushed and *got it*.

Committing myself to pulling the move, I drew my weapon and pointed it at his face, but – can you believe – this fool reached out in an attempt to grab the strap??? The look of murder on my face and the sound of it in my voice saved him from going too far, however:

"*BITCH! YOU WANNA DIE FOR THIS SHIT?!?*"

I left no doubt that he would have, too. Making him take me to the safe and then the cash register and emptying all the contents into a bank bag, my accomplice then tied his legs together and hands behind his back with duct tape; we then made our way back outside to the get-away car. Caught up in stop-and-go rush hour traffic at a red light only a few feet in front of the store, we would soon learn that, evidently, the tape wasn't tied tight enough, though:

"*Dude just came out with a big ass gun in his hand!*" our driver said.

"*Yeah, right,*" I said in disbelief. "*You bullshitting!*"

"*Naw, I'm for real! Y'all just stay down! Stay down!*"

Shit. Here we are, ducked down in the back seat of the car, a bank bag bursting with looted money, jewelry, and other merchandise, held up at a fucking red light a block or so from the police station, with the sales clerk looking from car to car searching us out – how crazy is that? Nevertheless, the light finally turned from red to green and we were able to slowly inch away. So thanks to a guardian angel or something, perhaps, we got away. For then anyway...

I had far too numerous experiences such as the one above to even recount here – with each "mission" I survived only serving to embolden me more and more. And I quickly found that I somehow had an affinity for finding the vulnerabilities in most places' security, only abetting my success; where this came from, I'll never know. During the year 1994 I would say that I myself personally hit at least 30 or more "licks" in six months' time – sometimes alone, sometimes with a crew of confederates, sometimes before a business opened for that day's business, sometimes soon after it had closed. Fast food joints. Jewelry stores. Rent-to-own places. Hell, I even hit doughnut shops as a big "fuck you" to the police who were no doubt searching out my identity. Anyplace that had what I wanted was fair game. And the more challenges it presented me, the better. By the summertime, I was averaging 2-3 missions a week.

Symbolizing my metamorphosis to complete "thug" and "threat to society," I also became flashy for some reason – rocking not one but *two* gold and diamond rings on each of my fingers including my thumbs, a gold nugget watch and bracelet on *both* my left and right wrists, *five* thick herringbone chains and a thick "dookey rope" with a huge crescent and star medallion around my neck, and even gold earrings in my ears (two to the left, one to the right) all at the same fucking time! Flashier than any rapper you could possibly name. In retrospect, it was ridiculous and really didn't fit my (true) personality at that time. But it sure as hell fit my style. And also brought me the attention that I (evidently) was seeking – especially from the females.

Just as now today a man's clothing, job, home, or (more usually) the car he drives speaks as to what he's about to women, so did my baggy clothes and thousands of dollars' worth of jewelry. Everything about me spoke "thug" and "drug dealer." And made it extremely easy when it came to attracting women.

Leaving the drive from my Mom's house one evening with Ro and Mac on our way to go kick it somewhere, I had Ro stop the car – the most gorgeous face I had ever seen beckoned to me from behind one of the project buildings. Disrespectfully blocking traffic as we all stepped out to "holla at" the females I had peeped, I was instantly mesmerized by that same face that had initially caught my attention. Naturally beautiful with flawless, butter-pecan colored skin, a disarming smile, and intoxicating doe-like eyes, she also had a banging body that couldn't hide itself even in her feminine yet conservative dress. Oblivious to everything and everyone else around me, I can't honestly sit here today and tell you what it is I first said to her, but whatever it was, it worked: I left her with my cellphone number[72] along with a promise from her to call me soon. I also left with a smile in my heart. Her name was Soyayya.

Not even waiting, fifteen minutes or so before she called, we talked all the rest of the evening on my way *to* the club, and all that night as I was *supposed to be* enjoying myself *in* the club. And, to be honest, I was enjoying myself while there – just not with any of the "treats" that the club offered. Enchanting me as she had, I just had to see her again that night. And from that first kiss we shared on her porch as I readied myself to leave, it wouldn't be often more that we left each other's side after. I had found something that I never even knew I was missing in life: my soul mate. I was instantly, deeply in love.

Love is a wonderful thing once you've truly experienced it, and I can see why my mother is still in love with my father even to this day thirty years or more after they were broken up.

---

[72] This was back in the days when only "doctors and drug dealers" had them – neither cellphones nor "pagers" were as ubiquitous as the smartphones are of today; I think I was probably the first one of my age group in the city to cop one.

Because after experiencing the emotions and feelings and sensations that this 14-years-young woman brought to my 16-years-young mind, heart, and body, I knew that I would love her forever. And to this day, I still do...

Prior to Soyayya, I had never really experienced true romantic love – every young woman that had preceded her that I had caught "feelings" for I soon recognized as no more than "puppy love," infatuation, lust. But with Soyayya, it was something altogether different; she and I would become one another's everything; every single aspect of my life would become different after her.

How so? Well, my sex life, for instance; she and I *made love* and never "fucked" nor just had "sex" as I was used to. Our lovemaking sessions were *events*, lasting for hours it seemed, sometimes three, four, and even five times in one day. We explored each other's bodies as only two madly in love teenagers can, with every single one of our senses involved and in tune, every mysterious blessing of our bodies unmasked and conquered, and everyone and everything else about the outside world tuned out. I would lose myself in her lips for hours at a time – our breaths, our heartbeats, our orgasms, our souls were all in alignment, and I *knew* that this young woman, this young lady and her body and heart were meant for only *me*.

Soon, I was no longer going out with Ro, Mac, Dough, Hunk, or any other of my cousins and homeboys – each awakened moment I wanted to spend with Soyayya. My every breath, my every thought it seemed, my every wish, want, and dream were all in some way or another tied to her somehow. She was my universe, my joie de vivre, and making her happy made *me* happy. All that mattered to me was our love. For her, I would've done anything. Even killed...

Once fall came and my senior year started, I even stopped

attending school regularly. When I did go I was late – and hardly ever did I stay the entire day; as soon as Soyayya would page or call me, I would rush right home.[73] I couldn't stand to be away from her for even a few hours, nor could she tolerate not kissing my face, not holding my hand, or not making love to me for too long, either. We made people *sick* with our displays of affection, not caring *whom* was around – especially disgusting my cousins Dough, Ro, and Mac whom weren't used to me caring as much for a woman as I did for her.

Nonetheless, don't get it twisted because not all was entirely gravy in my world after meeting and falling in love with Soyayya; in fact, some things about me and my life became worse. As opposed to some people whom get soft when in love, I became *harder* in the sense that my love was reserved for her and my family and friends *only*. With others, I was horribly ruthless – doing things to innocent people back then that even today makes me cringe when I think about it. Locking robbery victims in walk-in freezers, hog-tying them in the backroom, just basically terrorizing the fuck out of them when I came through on a "jack move" – embarrassingly, I must admit that I was anything *but* nice. Furthermore, my growing arrogance and indifference towards others who were not a part of me in some way – from my family, from my "hood," from my side of town, whatever – made my enemies grow. Not that I particularly cared, however.

Yet, that wasn't the only thing that made me more enemies – when you're a walking jewelry store in the projects, chances are you'll become a target for a robbery or two no matter who you are.[74] Case in point: Visiting with some relatives of Soyayya's

---

[73] Looking back at it all now, I realize that even then as a young teen she already recognized her power as a woman. Or at least over me, I should say…
[74] Ironic, seeing as how *that* was how I acquired much of my own jewels – either through heists or from the proceeds of such. But seeing as how no one really knew

in some projects on the eastside, she and I decided to take her younger cousin out to the swings at the play park at the end of the row; this also happened to be where the "whole hood" hung out. No sweat from me, however – I was strapped with my .357, of course – plus, I felt like I was on some invincible shit, anyway. Despite my aura of danger and all of that other rigmarole, I would soon hear some little young cat around my age repeat something a few times that made me take notice:

"*HEY, ANYBODY WANNA BUY A HANDFUL OF RINGS??? AND A NECK FULL OF NECKLACES???*"

Now, was I hearing this motherfucker right? Was this fool talking about *me*? I adjusted the strap in my shorts pocket – letting it be known that I had it. I also let Soyayya take over pushing her lil cousin Beverly in the swing so as to keep my hands free and stay on my "Cs" and "Ts." I don't even think she (Soyayya) even peeped what was going on at that moment, and what's more, I didn't even know *which* cat had made the slick comment as he shut up like a bitch as soon as I turned to directly face the crowd. However, he soon revealed himself as he stood amongst six or seven other cats that I guess emboldened him:

"*YO!!! ANYBODY – ANYBODY AT ALL WANNA BUY A HANDFUL OF RINGS AND ABOUT FIVE OR SIX NECKLACES???*"

He was looking directly at me now, confirming that he was slick throwing a threat my way; Soyayya noticed it, too, this time, and started imploring for us to leave. No way in hell, though – now my *pride* was involved. Nonetheless, I told her to take Beverly in the house so as to get them out of harm's way; but no deal – she wasn't leaving me out there alone. My ride-or-die.

"*I GUESS SOME MOTHERFUCKAS OUT HERE*

---

how I was getting my money – nor that that would have stopped some cats, anyway – plus, seeing as how I really wasn't "from" any of the projects I boldly frequented, cats were bound to start plotting.

READY TO DIE TODAY," I said to her loud enough for every single one of them to hear, "BECAUSE AIN'T A MOTHERFUCKA TAKING SHIT FROM ME NOW OR NEVER!!!"

I then stood by the swing, never taking my eyes off the crowd of cats. After a couple of minutes of watching them converse under their breaths, I saw one of the older ones – maybe 21 or so – walk towards me; I put my hand on the grip of my steel, massaging the trigger as he got closer.

"*Hey young nigga, let me holla at you,*" he said. His face looked slightly familiar.

"*What's up?*" I said aggressively, never taking my eyes from him nor the cluster of motherfuckers he had just come from.

"*Ain't you from Out South?*" he continued.

"*Yeah, why what's up?*" I clutched my strap even tighter now. I didn't give a damn about being "out of bounds" and in "their" projects – I go where the fuck I want to go when I want to go, was my way of thinking.

"*Naw, 'cause I was just telling my lil young nigga to chill with that dumb shit 'cause I know you from Out South and'll put a hole in a nigga! You strapped?*"

"*Of course.*"

Stupidly, I pulled my gun out completely for him and everyone else to see. If he had been brave enough, he possibly could've got me because he had me slightly disarmed with that "I know you" shit along with the fact that I was focused primarily on his "young nigga" that had been running his mouth.

"*Well, homie, I got to let you know – you'll need more than six shots around here.*"

"*Naw, I'm cool. That's six niggas that got to die before they can get to me!*"

I had to let a motherfucker know. I wasn't saying that I

didn't recognize that I was outnumbered and could have possibly been overwhelmed had a shootout jumped off, but I let it be known that I wouldn't be the *only one* taking some serious lead! Soyayya, Beverly, and I stayed out there another 5-10 minutes longer until Soyayya's mother came outside and said she was ready to go – never even aware of what had almost jumped off.

It's crazy; shit like this would even happen close to home. Like, for instance, the time when Soyayya and I were walking hand-in-hand at the state fair being followed (unbeknownst to me) by some "plotters"; Soyayya never said anything at all about them until she saw that they were gone, as she *knew* how I would've confronted them – especially seeing as how I was strapped the entire time we were at the fair, on Ferris wheel and all.

What's more, unbelievably, I wasn't even immune to plotters in my "own projects" of Vine Hill. When information reached me that a particular group of cats were scheming on me, I at first didn't take the warning too seriously; those fools *knew* how I got down up close and personal, so I thought that Soyayya's friend who gave me the "heads up" could've possibly heard something wrong. Plus, we were cool, I thought – even though I really wasn't from "around there."

The second time, though – from another source, unrelated – I kept shit in mind. However that *third* time I heard something similar from yet another person (who didn't hang out with either of the other two), I decided to take action – get *them* before they got *me*.

See, what "trips me out" is that a lot of cats don't realize that *there are just some people that you shouldn't go around fucking with* and that you should *always* know the heart and mind of a person before transgressing against them. And these particular fools violated that rule almost to the death of themselves. I thought they had long knew that I wasn't a person to accept *any* disrespect – to me, I would rather die than allow it. And furthermore, I would rather kill than die myself.

Moreover, my unrighteous way of thinking during those days was if you put yourself in the situation where you even *thought* it was cool to do me harm or disrespect me in some kind of way, then *everything* and *everyone* you loved was "fair game." Your children. Your mother. Your father (if he was around). Your siblings. Your homeboys. Your old stanking ass *grandmammie* could have got it if you crossed me. Because I was looking at it like this: If I wasn't fucking with you and you chose to bother and fuck with me, then you just opened that door. Furthermore, I didn't give a fuck *who* you were, *what* "set," organization, or "gang" you claimed, *who* you had *with* you, or especially *what* color you were – fuck with me at *your own risk*.

So I took it to them in the only way I knew how to at that time. Something not to be discussed in these pages…

> Just got home, AINT Even been that long,
> A new day for me trying to right my wrongs,
> different year, same song,
> my past is catching up & I know it won't be long,
> how did my debt get so past due,
> it seems like yesterday I was innocent & didn't have a clue.
> Hands getting sweaty now, fate is in full view,
> blast on the run again, now AINT that the truth...
>
> *On the Run Again (4 – Delo) 5/25/01*
> by DeAndre Walker

RUNNING

So many times throughout my life people saw things in me long before I could foresee them in myself: I was a reputed killer long before I ever was charged in my first murder case, and a well-known drug dealer long before I got my hands on what *I* would consider my first "big pack." Sometimes this would push me to reach heights that myself maybe couldn't have seen; sometimes it, too, would push me to new lows. This was one of *those low* times – I was now hiding in the trunk of a car attempting to make it safely out of town.

But let me slow down a minute and explain to you how we got here....

My acquittal, although wholly expected, left me in an interesting place in life: Not necessarily "aimless" (because I was clear about a few things I needed to accomplish) but instead I would say "directionless," as I wasn't sure how to *achieve* my aims in light of my newly rediscovered conscience. Nevertheless, I was determined not to fall back into that false persona of "not-give-a-fuck-thug" that I (evidently) presented before I withered inside witnessing Old School's son's tears. And that's no matter *what* I was faced with. Because I *did* care – about him, about my own son, my brothers, nephews, and everyone else out there like them. So I resolved myself to getting Carvin home to his sons and the rest of our family where he belonged, to re-establishing a relationship with my own beloved son since it had been shattered by my enslavement, and to not causing any more fears or tears to any more innocent people (especially in my Black community) with my actions.[75] Because I doubt if my heart or spirit could bear the weight of any more responsibility than that which they already carried. Carvin was, perhaps, the only person able to perceive the subtle change in me when I went to visit him a couple of hours after my release from the same hell hole. But, of course, neither he nor I verbally discussed any of this, as all was understood without us ever saying a word...

In the immediate aftermath of my acquittal, those that were happy about my release invariably sought me out and I was constantly treated to brunches, lunches, and dinners (some even home-cooked!), thoughtful gifts, and numerous business opportunities, while those that weren't so happy avoided me like the mange, and seemed nervous or twitchy when I happened to somehow be/come around. Possibly it was the guilt and fear some felt thinking that I was aware (which I was!) of the slick comments made and shiesty moves taken after I was first arrested and "the streets" thought I would do "life" – what do you think? Nonetheless, I wasn't on any bullshit nor did I particularly want to associate myself with anyone that didn't want to associate themselves with me, so it was all good. But I

---

[75] And this meant directly *or* inadvertently because a lot of times our *direct* actions can cause *indirect* waves to form, drowning unintended victims! So although I didn't (and don't!) renounce "violence" completely, I resolved that it must be a last (and absolutely necessary) resort instead of a first inclination. Because I would (and will!) be *damned* if I sit idly by while I myself, my loved ones, or even some random innocent person were being directly threatened and/or harmed in some way! To hell with all that – I would have *helped* George Floyd!!!

kept shit in mind.

My Moms had imaginings of my going back to school and obtaining my degree, but if that happened at *all*, it would have to *wait* as I needed a recovery period from the stench that is "jail." So, with nothing really tethering my daily physical presence to nashville, I returned to a place where I had lain down deep roots years before, and re-established "home."[76] Yet, still nashville beckoned sometimes – for a multitude of reasons.

One of which being "Pasheni," a woman I had dug since we were kids living on opposite ends of the (Edgehill) projects. Notwithstanding the fact that I had spoken with her once when she was on a phone call with her cousin locked up with me at CJC, Pasheni and I had neither seen nor thought of one another in years (since at least high school), and only reconnected after I noticed her in the car with my cousin Jolonda stopping by my mother's house to visit me shortly after my release.[77] And like most of my eventual relationships, we flowed into it pretty freely as I had no intentions of getting serious with anyone (not even Jannah until/unless I could get my heart and mind properly together) after my release.[78] I would even go so far as to say that

---

[76] In a city and state that shall remain unnamed. Those that *know*, *know*, those that don't know, don't need to. I have and have always had family, friends, associates, and connections all over these united snakes, including aunts and uncles in Kentucky, Ohio, and all throughout tennessee among other places, and first and further distantly related cousins in those states along with Georgia, Florida, Texas, California and others. Furthermore, from the time of my early to mid-teens, my whims and sheer will would take me all around the kkkountry with nary a person aware besides those particular persons I may have been traveling with at that particular time and to that particular place for whatever particular reason I/we may have had. And everywhere I went I would meet and somehow connect with people, even though I was always my quiet, calm, and reserved self.

[77] Pasheni and Jolonda had, of course, known each other just as long as we all had, us all growing up together in Edgehill, but only recently had they gotten "super tight" with them both being single young women with young sons around the same age.

[78] Now that I think about it, maybe I should just start *planning* to get seriously involved so that I can trick my mind and heart into not doing so?! Maybe, *that'll* work?! Probably not, though, knowing me!

we *both* bucked "getting serious" in the beginning of what we had, because Pasheni was (rightly) reluctant to allow any random man into her and her son's lives,[79] and as for me (if I had been completely honest with myself) my heart still belonged to another: Jannah.

Jannah, simply put, is the most spiritually beautiful woman I've been blessed to know in this life. She allowed herself to be vulnerable, emotional, and open to me in every possible way I could ever imagine, and only too late did I realize that I did she and I both a great disservice by not allowing myself to do the same by being completely honest with her about my relationship, feelings, and dealings with Tsawa and my son with her (Tsawa). I wasn't fair to Jannah or our relationship, and for that I'll always carry regrets. And still to this day, over twenty years after we first laid eyes on one another, my love for her is never ending.

Nevertheless, I accepted the mistakes I had made, kept our (my and Jannah's) friendship intact, and went about the process of "moving on." Part of that moving on meant "talking to" and dating other women, and it was Pasheni whom I would grow closest to the most. It started with Pasheni, Jolonda, their sons and I going out to dinner a few times "chilling."[80] From there I stayed overnight a time or two (at her place) when her son was spending the weekend with one of her parents, and (as we all became more comfortable with one another) eventually that morphed into my staying overnight sometimes on the weeknights also. Nonetheless I always wanted to be respectful

---

[79] I would also learn later that at least part of her reluctance stemmed from the fact that she was still in love with her son's father (whom was in prison for murder) even if she didn't realize so herself. However, (as with my mother's undying love of my father), Pasheni's love of him manifested itself as intense hatred of him.

[80] I wouldn't even call these "dates" per se, but our interests were clear in one another, and these experiences allowed us to get to know the person each of us had become while "cooling" with no unnecessary pressure.

of their (Pasheni and her son's) space even as I was allowed more into it, and moreover, mindful of all that her son saw and heard between us as it was never far from my mind that my *own* son could be facing a similar situation. So, even though her son might notice that I was still there at the time he would go to his room to sleep and was "back" in the morning when he was awakened to get ready for daycare, it would be some time before either of us allowed him to see me take a shower over there or even walk into her bedroom.

Yet, in time that changed, with Pasheni telling me to just "rest in bed" instead of getting ready to leave at the same time as they did one morning (or even before). This was far from our usual routine the previous times I had stayed over, with her surprisingly instructing me to "take [my] time" with my morning routine.[81] As I wasn't necessarily all that comfortable being in her home when she wasn't there, I shortly thereafter took care of my hygiene and returned her key to her at her job.

I think this may have surprised her because she returned the same key to me under the exact same scenario a few days later. My reaction remained the same. After Pasheni gave me the key for a third time and I attempted to return it the same way to no avail (she told me to "just keep it"), I knew she and I would have to have a "serious" talk and we did. Still, I wanted to make no assumptions about our budding relationship, so even after accepting the key, I would call before coming over as I didn't want to be met by any "surprises." Soon, however, I had a closet full of clothes (not in her bedroom, but in the hallway closest to the door just in case either of us decided I should leave) and my own drawer in her bedroom, and we stopped pretending to her son as if I wasn't spending the night.

---

[81] By then, I had long had my own toothbrush in Pasheni's personal bathroom, and I even had a couple changes of clothes there.

Gradually, we took it even further than that (with neither of us consciously aware of doing so, in my opinion), morphing from friends and (sometimes) lovers into something akin to family. Not only was she right alongside me (for emotional support) in kkkourt as I was fighting for my son, but (since I didn't want to cause any unnecessary "drama" in taking him to another state) it was at her home in which he and I would eventually spend our (every other) weekend visits. Observing my son, her son, and my nephew (Carvin's oldest son) all love and kick it with one another (as only children can) during these times, we couldn't help for our affection for one another to grow. I witnessed how she loved her child, she recognized how I loved my own (and my nephews), so we *decided* to have a child together.[82]

Yet, Pasheni and I unconsciously carried the baggage of so many previous relationships that neither of us truly gave the other a chance. We were so young yet had lived so much – but in the alternate sense too young that we hadn't lived enough – that neither one of us saw each other in actuality as the unique and special persons that we were and could have been to one another. Only too late it seems, did we start to try.

But I have to say that, now as we've grown and gotten older, we honestly appreciate one another as friends and love and care for one another as the parents of the beautiful and handsome son we were blessed to bring into this world. She's a good woman and I'll forever have love in my heart for her.

Yet, Pasheni and I were never, at any point in time I think, "in love" with one another. True enough, we liked each other

---

[82] Both of our extended families had by then, gotten used to seeing us together (birthday parties, holidays, other family functions) and were happy when we got pregnant. Most (of the family members) had for years known their counterparts (even in some cases before she and I were even born), with some even having been involved in relationships at some point in time.

for the most part in the beginning, at least, but in love? – no. Our relationship was lacking in the affection and passion departments. Yet I'm a passionate person in every aspect of my life; whatever it is (or whomever it is) I may care about, I care about deeply and intensely down to my very core – those things, those ideals, those people, those places, I truly feel for. However it wasn't there with us – and more so on her part than mine (maybe because of fears stemming from previous relationships, I think now)83 which made me, in my opinion eventually pull and hold back from her after trying to elicit it (passion) from her end after so long. In fact, I would go so far as to say that I was so starved for love and affection in my and Pasheni's relationship that it set the stage for my falling quickly for someone in whom the passion, love, and affection was never lacking after we (Pasheni and I) finally, officially, "broke up."

But no "blame," ya know? Some people just don't "feel" you like that for one reason or another, so I'm not even tripping. It was just one of those situations where we ended up together ultimately for a few seasons and a great reason: to usher our son Kalii into the world.

Besides, we did care for one another. You know the cliché expression, "if you can't be with the one you love, then love the one you're with?" Well, I think there may have been a little bit of that on both sides with Pasheni and I; she couldn't be with her oldest son's father due to his incarceration, and I couldn't be with Jannah because she was generally tired of my "shit," stupidity, and indecisiveness in dealing with Tsawa.84 Furthermore, I can say that Pasheni did adore me somewhat,

---

[83] Also a possible contributing factor was the blatantly hypocritical, contradictorily prudish Christianity-based advice/pressure she sometimes received from her "single sisters in Christ."
[84] And I mean, how could I blame Jannah, right?! I had almost lost my life yet again because Tsawa and I couldn't figure out a way how not to be in a "relationship" while somehow still allowing me to be a daily part of my son Kyree's life. *Any* sane woman would have eventually gotten tired of that bullshit also.

just not as much as I would have hoped or was looking for. Additionally, I think as the birth of our son came nearer she even started to love me, yet still she never fell "head over heels in love with" me. But that's just the way it is in some relationships – not all of them involve "romantic" love – yet my knowing myself more now, my maturing as I have, I realize that that is what I'll always want and need. Romantic, passionate love...

"Let me just say: Peace to you, if you're willing to *fight* for it..."
Fred Hampton

I was starting to think that this world would/will *never* allow me peace: There I was, preparing for the birth of my second son, growing ever more closer to the type of relationship I remembered having with the first one (especially since his mother and I had somewhat repaired our friendship despite what she had done), building up my "war chest" to get my brother and other loved ones home, and *then* I was hit with *this* shit?! The *motherfucking feds*?! Fuck! I didn't know who or what or why someone "sicced" them on me, but once I found out... Damnit! Why couldn't they just leave me the fuck alone?! I hadn't even been free *10* months! These bastards wouldn't even allow me a *year* to breathe?! Here I was laying low, wasn't even "fucking with" nobody or dealing with that many people, and now here comes *this* shit?! What the hell?! Now I understand what they mean by not poking a hibernating bear! Because I *know* how ill-tempered I was feeling!

So here we go: back against the wall (well, actually, against the inside of the trunk I was hiding in!), gangster on the move, with the weight of the federal government stalking my ass! My initial thoughts were to head "home," but as I realized that I didn't know what (or where!) "they" knew about, I changed my mind and headed north and west. I knew that if I could make it to my good friend's "safe place" in the upper Midwest, no one would ever associate me with the area, and I would be allowed some time to get my mind together.

Because I had a lot to think about. Like *why* did they "hit" then? No one that I had been kicking it with had been acting "funny" in any way that I could tell. Furthermore, *why* hit in the way and at the place in which they did? Because it would have been easy to learn doing even the most routine surveillance (for as little as a week's time) that I didn't live with whom, nor *where* they had "bothered," so what exactly the fuck was *that* all about?! I know, just the age old bullshit amerikkkan gestapo tactic of harassing the community and/or loved ones (they think) closest to you in order to intimidate and force someone to "give you up." Yet I had long since been "hip" to that, so my own *mother* didn't even really know where I rested my head!

However, I *was* slipping, caught up in the city, as I had stayed overnight at Pasheni's. So without the warning I had received informing me that my loved one was in distress with "them boys" demanding information about me, then I wouldn't have had the time I needed to reach (relative) safety. Nevertheless the gods were with me, along with my guardian angel whom allowed me to catch my breath as I so sorely needed...

Yet and still resolving to witness my son's coming birth no matter the odds, I made my way back to tennessee the closer he was "due." Getting there just a few days before he came into this world, I couldn't have been a more blessed man despite the turmoil of my world outside of the birthing room. Now I had *two* beautiful sons to go along with two beautiful nephews and numerous new little cousins. A younger generation to love and teach and protect and give a better world to live in than I had received. I was motivated. They were all a part of my redemption. Even more so I was resolved to fight the bullshit that had come my way...

Speaking of which, can you believe that the people (attorneys, bondsmen, sheriff's deputies) I had check for me could find *no* record of a warrant out for my arrest? I couldn't figure it out, and at the time it was suggested that maybe I was "just the target of an investigation," so it was best to continue keeping my head low until I could get more information.[85] It didn't make any sense, however, but I was used to strange shit happening when going against them folkkks. Although it was "the feds" this time, they were just bigger bullies in a system/government full of them. And I knew how to deal with bullies; I had been doing so all my life...

So, I determined to "stay low," make my preparations to fight, and seek to acquire as much information as I possibly could about what and whom I was possibly facing. I reached out to "prominent" attorneys in Houston and New York among other places, wherein I was quoted exorbitant prices for representation. Yet, even if guaranteed their full retainer, no one seemed to want to "fight" but instead, wanted to lay down and "plea (me) out." Bullshit. So, I thereafter reached out to a nashville attorney that had a sterling reputation among a lot of the city's d-boys.

Coming into the city specifically to meet with this clown, can you believe that I wasn't there 5 minutes before I had to leave the meeting? We didn't even make it as far as discussing a retainer fee because as soon as I said "feds" he started talking about "you have to give someone up." Telling him to kiss my

---

[85] No one (or at least I) thought to check directly with the U.S. Marshal's service, ATF, FBI, or DEA to see what the deal was; I figured if a warrant was out for me, then *someone* in "the system" would be able to at least find it to tell me what I was being accused of, at the very minimum.

ass in the most respectful way possible, I left questioning *all* of those fools he had kept out of jail. Now a lot of funny shit happening around nashville's streets made much more sense to me,[86] and I wondered if I hadn't found myself in my current situation behind someone "giving me up?" Something to think about it...

Outside of the mental energy I had to devote to my assumed and expected legal woes, I also had to contend with the perceptible shift I noticed in my and Pasheni's relationship after I made it back in town. Likewise, as I was honestly confused about what I would be facing in the very near future, she in turn was in fear that she would be left with *two* sons to raise alone. Nothing I could say or do would assuage her fears and (now, years later) I can't even blame her for feeling the way she did. A storm was coming my way. At the time I sought in her shelter and support, yet she (rightly?) felt the need to get herself and the boys out of harm's way, and leave me (as a man) to weather it alone.[87]

So she "broke up" with me, which was probably inevitable anyway, as I doubt if either one of us would describe our relationship as "the best" that she or I have "ever had."

Tellingly, I used to catch glimpses of melancholy in Pasheni's eyes as she witnessed me fighting for, before, and interacting with Kyree after being granted, visitation and even sometimes when I was interacting with her own oldest son;

---

[86] Like how two cats could have similar cases and while one went to jail, the other kept his freedom but his homies would somehow get "caught up" weeks or months later. Shit should have been obvious.

[87] Pasheni always made it a point to never allow me to forget that my legal troubles "preceded [her]." True that. As did a lot of the things that came with *her* (or *any* person that *anyone* gets into a relationship with) that *I* wasn't aware of until it was somehow brought to my attention. Nevertheless, I took it all in stride. Because we *all* have the option to decide what we will and won't accept in our lives and/or from our "loved ones'" pasts. Nevertheless, I *did* (and do!) have a problem with her thinking I was being dishonest about my ignorance of my legal troubles.

watching me patiently help her son learn his numbers and/or how to read, no doubt that she sometimes wished it was his own father doing so. But also, I'm sure, she noticed unresolved sadness on my face, too. Because it never failed to hit me that there I was raising another man's son yet couldn't do so with my own as I wished. So, I cherished deeply my and Kyree's weekly two-hour visits on Wednesdays and lived for our every other weekend 48 hour home stays. He, I, Pasheni, Pasheni's oldest son (she was still pregnant with our own), and my oldest nephew Darieon (Carvin's son) would kick it all weekend visiting parks, the zoo, Chuck-E-Cheese, go shopping, etc., yet I never failed to fall into a slight depression every time I had to take him back home. Missing my son more every day (yet being with hers) was killing me, and I'm sure Pasheni noticed. So, maybe that's another reason why she never allowed herself to "fall for" me – she possibly could have thought that I would leave her to get back with Tsawa in order to be with Kyree more? I don't know; I never asked or even considered until now if she thought so, yet I would have never left her alone with our son like that. I wasn't raised, by my own father, to ever do something so evil and inconsiderate like that.

    Yet I did consider that Pasheni should have and would have been with her son's other parent had his (her oldest son's father) circumstances been different and he was getting out of prison sooner than 15 years. Because it was clear to me that even though she was pregnant with our child she was still in love with him (her oldest son's father), or the venom she always expressed for him wouldn't have been so intense.

    Yet, that's not even why we ultimately "broke up," however – it was more so because of her (justified, as it turned out) fear of my being taken away through prison or death and she being left with yet another child to raise by herself. Her fear grew larger and larger the closer our son's birth arrived, and ultimately reached its peak about six weeks after he was born, when she finally, forcefully pushed me away.88

Thinking about my and Pasheni's breakup brings me to a very important point, however: Far too many women89 look at her children as her children and hers *only* not our/their children, mother's *and* father's – and Pasheni had this mentality to the extreme! After Kalii's birth, whatever decision (no matter how mundane or how major) that she wanted to make she could because *she* was his *mother*. But me, his *father*, I gave constant push back on this because I wasn't an absentee father either physically, emotionally, nor financially at that time. I'm just not cut like that. I was *there*, I *wanted* to be there, and I planned to be there no matter my own circumstances and/or problems faced in life. Kalii is *my* son, too, ya know? Just as much as he is hers. And I knew that for us both to be the loving, caring, supportive and involved parents that he needed, then she and I would need to compromise and work together. But unfortunately, that wasn't her attitude at the time; Kalii was *her* child and ultimately, me as no more than his *father*, didn't really matter in the grand scheme of things.90

Need an example? Maybe a week or so before Pasheni and I finally "broke up," I learned via an argument that my son had a "godfather" that I'd never met let alone had chosen; now what

---

[88] All in all it was inevitable and necessary, however, because I was getting nowhere ducking and dodging the feds laying low in the house all of the time. I needed that kick in the ass our breakup brought to get me up off it (my ass!) so I could start making preparations (financial and otherwise) for the fight I suspected was ahead.
[89] Especially in the black community, but I surmise this stems directly from all the traumas experienced during slavery and even today.
[90] Tellingly, I had already witnessed this mentality in her dealings with her own father and the father of her oldest son, but me being the willfully ignorant idiot I can be sometimes, I chose to ignore it. However, I should have paid more attention as it's *always* a wise move to pay close attention to how someone you're dealing with treats other people. Because all of her dealings with her oldest son's father (coupled with her own as well) foretold our own.

kind of shit is that?! I was pissed to say the least, and from that point on our relationship was forever over in my eyes, hence even had she not have broken it off a few days later, I was mentally and emotionally, from there on, "checked out." I was done; I was through – I couldn't get hit with anymore blindsides like that, another lesson from Soyayya, ya know? Therefore, as Kalii's *father*, I was irrelevant and I strongly resented that. Even today, I'm still somewhat resentful of the fact that my son is not as close to my family and my other son[91] as he would be had I been allowed by life to be there to physically raise him. I'm resentful just the same that my nephews were denied the presence of my brother wrongly, but at least they were allowed to get to know him through visits. Kalii and I? We didn't have that luxury and we went at least a decade without being able to see and be around each other while his mother and I bickered over some bullshit that I still contend that she *always knew* wasn't true.[92] Even as I write this, Kalii and I have visited with each other only four times in the over eighteen years I've been enslaved with two of those four times when my family was allowed to bring him to me; once as a toddler when I was in nashville at the Justice Center, and once as a teenager when I was at turney center—despite the almost 12 years I was there only 45 minutes way. But I digress…

So, Pasheni and I were "broken up." Nonetheless, as I didn't want to leave yet another child in a "broken home," I held

---

[91] Whom Pasheni continues to want to look at as Kalii's "half" brother while *her* older child is somehow a "full" one because he came from *her*. When the reality is that either they're *both* Kalii's brothers as I see it, or they're both his "half" brothers because neither of the three share the same two parents, ya dig? It can't be one way and not the other just because she's the *mother* and I'm the *father*! That's bullshit!

[92] It had nothing whatsoever to do with my son but instead with the fact that she felt "disrespected" about something. But here's the kicker, that "disrespect" *never even happened* nor was it ever contemplated! Crazy, huh? Story of my life. The truth of the matter is I think it was a case of her mind needing an excuse to hate me so it came up with one – when it was all about my pending physical absence due to incarceration.

out hope for a while that she and I would get back together.[93] Yet Pasheni wasn't having *any* of that, so I "let it burn" after spending my birthday alone with nary of even an *acknowledgement* from her. Cool with me. So, I "let it go." As Pasheni *wanted* me to. That is, until she discovered I had found another woman...

Physically, Zara was, at that time, an absolutely gorgeous woman – there's no two doubts about that – and she would have probably been considered "beautiful" in almost every single culture and country in this world.[94] Yet, "beauty" entails so much more than just physical attractiveness. A "beautiful" woman is more so loving, caring, intelligent, passionate, loyal, humble, and full of soul than she is physically attractive. And most importantly, she has to *know* herself – what type of life she would like to lead; what type of character she has and wishes to have; what type of mistakes she's made in life and why; what morals she will forever hold dear in spite of the greatest of odds. That's what makes for a "beautiful" woman – the attractiveness of her heart, mind, and soul...

And Zara was no doubt a beautiful woman in those days.[95] I was drawn, initially, to her eyes: intelligent, forecasting a deep soul, a life that had been lived, a heart that had loved and been shattered a time or two, a passion buried, waiting to be unleashed. A look at her lips was instantly arousing – they were

---

[93] This in spite of our "passion problems" – therefore I understand clearly why others stay in loveless marriages because of their children. But, again, I digress...

[94] I can just imagine that she had the men and boys going *crazy* during the short time that she (and her mother's family) lived in europe, because she really *was* that attractive. She was like an "ethnic chameleon" able to naturally look the part of many different cultures, and most people would have been hard pressed to guess where she was "from" without her actually having to tell you. Because you sure as hell couldn't tell from her diction or appearance. I surmise that in another life with *her* physical attributes, combined with *her* intelligence, she would have made a great spy/secret agent for some government or organization.

[95] Or so I thought, at least.

full, delicious-looking, luscious, enticing, and tempting. And her hips? Good God! Curvy, full, *dangerous!*

Something outside of the physical, though, was telling me that I should *know* Zara – more so than any other man ever had. Our first conversations she came off as demure and shy, but I wasn't a man to be easily fooled. Not only had my homeboy put me up on game concerning some facts of her past, but I could also see past the beautiful face and banging body to glimpse the heart that she tried to keep concealed. Even more, I wasn't like most men – I was different – I wanted her *soul* uncovered to me. I needed that. Something was telling me that we were drawn to each other by fate.

See most men can't get past superficialities when dealing with women – a big butt and a smile could get the keys to most men's hearts, minds, and wallets. All the while she could be totally rotten inside, damaged goods because she had learned over the years that her mind, her heart, and her soul mattered little as long as she had an enticing enough pussy. Think about how much that would stunt a woman's mental, emotional, and spiritual growth.

Yet show a woman that you truly care about what she thinks, what she feels, what she believes, and be amazed at how she opens up to you. Be the man that listens, with no interruptions, no judgment, no solutions unless she specifically asks – and then see the type of woman you'll have by your side. Furthermore, spoil your women – and I don't mean necessarily materially,[96] but mentally, emotionally, spiritually, physically, sexually – aim to be the epitome of all that particular woman seeks in a man while still being yourself. Me, myself personally, I always had it in my mind that if by some chance myself and a

---

[96] Although that *can* be a part of it, but sometimes your individual circumstances at the time dictate that to be impossible.

woman, ever ended our relationship, she should always be a better woman for having been in it. More loving, more affectionate, classier, more ladylike, wiser, more sexual, more *woman* period. And in some way, with each relationship that I've been in, I think I've been successful at that. Even if the women in question can't initially see it as such.

At the time, however, I still hadn't opened my heart up to many women after Soyayya – and never to one completely – but for some reason I felt it totally possible with Zara. Meeting her was the shock to my spirit that I never realized it needed, and as her eyes and own spirit smiled my way, I stopped traffic as I knew (somehow) that I wouldn't have forgiven myself if I allowed her to drive away.[97] Try as I might at dinner a few hours later, I couldn't help but be captivated by her conversation, intelligence, laugh, and smile. I found myself wondering just where had this woman come *from*? And vowed to see her again once I returned to tennessee.

Which didn't take as long as I expected; I called her as I neared nashville late the very next night. Deciding that I should "come over" to her place, we talked and talked and talked, losing hours of time in what seemed to be only minutes. Late night soon turned to early morning, and at some point enchantment overwhelmed me.

"Am I ever going to be able to kiss those beautiful lips?"

Not meaning to, evidently I expressed my thoughts out loud.

Because we kissed; then kissed; then kissed, then made love; then kissed the rest of the dawn away. From that very first

---

[97] I just realized something as I write this: This was the *second* woman whom I would meet in this particular neighborhood who would turn out to be my wife. (It was the Vine Hill homes that had been turned from "projects" into mixed-income townhomes; I was leaving from visiting with my nephews as she was stopped at the gate waiting to enter.) Now that I've recognized this, I vow to stay the hell away! The women's spirits are too powerful for me! (I say this in jest.)

moment we had laid eyes on one another, from that very first kiss, Zara and I communicated on a much higher plane that I suspect could never be replicated. Our eyes, our lips, our hips spoke our capabilities of the great, good, bad and ugly, and foretold all the possibilities of our future to come. True enough, we might not have known each other's full names, but we knew everything we needed to know about the person we each held in our arms...[98]

Incredibly, (just as with Jannah) unexpected controversy with Tsawa would drive me deeper into Zara's embrace:

Running into each other by happenstance outside the contentious environs of (family) kkkourt and/or the daycare custody exchanges, Tsawa apologized for all of the unnecessary bullshit she had caused me to live through the previous few years; thereafter, foolishly, we again succumbed to the insidious love we share.[99] Nonetheless, *this* time I had a clearly defined role in her life, as she had a man (albeit locked up but a different one than the first a few years before!) with whom she had birthed a child after our own.

Cool. All was understood, right? No possible problems between us because of emotional greed and/or the need for "claims" or control entering the picture? Yeah, right! Eventually

---

[98] Zara and I may not have known each other, but we *knew* each other, if that makes any sense to you. Some people you can "know" your entire life but never *truly* know, and others you can truly know with only a glance. So, there may be other people (men she's been "involved with" included) that know more personal facts about Zara and her life than I ever could, but I seriously doubt that there's another person in this world that "knows" her (or *could* "know" her) as well as I do and probably vice versa. But she could only truly know me if she reminds herself of our first few days and nights together...

[99] You know, sometimes I really wish it was possible for me to "hate" other people. But no matter what someone has done, I'm just not capable of doing so; my spirit is too forgiving. "Teach a person a lesson" and/or prevent them from doing me or my loved ones any further harm, yeah, but to not see (at least some!) good in everyone or to do something out of "hate" for another? *Never!* That goes against the very nature I was born with. But I wish it didn't...

she wanted me to play the role that her man (admitted to, this time!) already held, but why in the hell would I?

Although it was "different with [me]" and I was her "one true love," as I sat (or lay!) next to her as she so easily lied to her son's father and/or his family, using the same phrases, inflections, and intonations she had used on me so many times before, I couldn't help but to trust her even less than I already did. (Hell, I didn't even consider that trusting her less was even *possible*!) She would make it a point to read this man's letters to me[100] (whether I wanted to hear them or not) as he expressed his love for her, their child, *my* son and all of their plans to be a family in the near future. Therefore how *could* I trust her? Especially considering that, in addition to lying to her "man," I witnessed her "blowing off" with lies the numerous other men she admitted she was already cheating on him with before I ever came back into the picture.[101]

Therefore I kept my guard up around my heart and feelings when near her, yet still Tsawa and I continued to "kick it" and "be there" for one another helping to deal with the difficulties we each faced. By then, some way or another, we had become each other's "crutch," so I helped her work through her postpartum depression, and she in turn helped me to think through a solution to my expected legal woes. Nevertheless, when her self-described "baby daddy" (oh, how I *hate* that term!)

---

[100] Yeah, his too!
[101] Although I resolved to be completely truthful when I set out to write this, I also resolve to be *fair*. Therefore, I don't want anyone to think that Tsawa is some type of "relationship monster" or harlot or whore or slut or "ho" or any other of the bullshit derogatory terms thrown at women when they do the same things that men (including myself *far* too many times in the past!) have done and do. Tsawa is like a lot of young women (especially Black women) that make certain decisions in an attempt to protect their hearts thereby emulating a lot of the bullshit they've witnessed. But this must change. And the first step towards that change for the better is being truthful with *ourselves* about our past mistakes, and – even more importantly – what type of lives and relationships we want and need and, *why* we want what we want? I recognize the mistakes I've made, and everyone in turn must recognize their own…

or his family called, Tsawa made sure I understood that I wasn't even supposed to *breathe* too loud. But I could dig it; I understood completely and played my position. Therefore I couldn't understand at all when she refused to play her own:

As I was already with Zara at the time, I simply informed Tsawa that I would "get with [her] tomorrow" when she called to come over. Never mind that Tsawa had suggested I put that particular spot in her name so as to not raise any red flags with those seeking me, but I was a happily single man whom made it no secret that, after my breakup with Pasheni, I kicked it with whatever women I chose to. Just as Tsawa made it no secret when other men called when she and I happened to be together[102] or when she couldn't find any time to kick it with me and/or spend the night when I was unexpectedly in town. Hell, I never "tripped," so why in the hell should she?!

Yet this night, she did more than a little "tripping" – coming up to the place where I was "ducked off" and caused a scene similar to the one she had a few years earlier at Fisk. And although this altercation didn't turn *physically* violent, it was so emotionally charged that I had no choice but to leave most of my things and flee the scene because of the noise, rising drama, and threats from Tsawa to "call the police" if I didn't "get out of [her] shit."[103]

---

[102] Coincidently, this is how I learned about her affair with the bondsman I (and the rest of the Southside) used. He had called more than a few times while she and I were together, and she let me know that they had been "fucking around for years." We both laughed at how stupid I had been.

[103] Some may consider it "disrespectful" or question the wisdom of having another woman over at a spot that was in Tsawa's name, so let me be clear about some things here: As I said earlier, I was a *happily single* man, so Zara was *far* from the first woman I had had over at the "spots" I used when in nashville, nor did Tsawa *ever* "stay there" with me (although she spent the night here and there, as did others), nor did she pay *one single penny* towards it! Furthermore, I could have and *should* have ignored *her* suggestion and just used someone less volatile – yet, I seriously doubt if that would have prevented what happened! (The only way to have prevented this incident was to have never gotten re-involved in the first place. So I place all of the blame on my *own*

Unbelievable, right? How could I have been anything *but* embarrassed and dumbfounded about all that had transpired? Zara had left as soon as the drama had started, but I owed her the biggest of apologies for that bullshit that had just gone down. Only minutes before we had been resting peacefully in one another's arms and then...and then...

"Come see me."

Can you believe that she actually turned around and headed to where I then was? Sitting in her car outside my friend's house the next county over, we communicated using no more than our eyes.

"Marry me."

We had neither thought about, let alone spoken of marriage before, but there was something between us that neither wanted to lose. It was powerful, amazing, terrifying, irrational, consuming, glorious, genuine, satisfying – so she said "yes."

---

shoulders for allowing us to get past the "cordial" stage.) But lesson learned; although I had previously been burnt by others when I "put shit in their name" like most other street cats, from that point forward never again will I in my *life*. Never again. No cars, no spots, no stashes, not even a goddamned purchase of a fucking toothbrush with a grocery rewards card! Never again! If *I* can't get it – or it would send the "wrong" signal or "look"if *I* had it – then *I* don't need it! Why put myself in that position again?!

"Prison will either bring out the very best in you or destroy you entirely. None is unaffected..."

George Jackson

JUVENILE

I had never – nor will probably I ever again – loved and trusted someone as completely as I did Soyayya. Whatever she said to me, whatever she expressed was "gospel." I had no reason to doubt her in any way – she loved me, I loved her, so why would she or I ever have a reason to be untruthful or unfaithful or disloyal to one another?

But of course, that was only the naïveté of a young man in love for the first time. Although I was completely honest and trusting of her, *she* was being untruthful to me all along: She had a boyfriend. The same man I was *sooo understanding* and trusting of her to talk to because he was her friend "in the hospital paralyzed after an accident," was in all actuality her boyfriend incarcerated soon to come home. Then he did – leaving me dumbstruck and heartbroken...

Ever seen the film *Talladega Nights* starring Will Ferrell? Remember the scene where he comes home to find out that his wife has left him because (and I'm paraphrasing here) their marriage "has been on the rocks for awhile" and he replies (and I'm paraphrasing again) "I didn't know"? Well hell, that's basically what happened to me. Soyayya and I would wake up that fateful day in each other's arms like any other, only for me to leave (for some reason or another to take care of something) just to come back to the news that our relationship was over and I had to move out.[104] To say I was stunned would be an

---

[104] By this time I had somehow or another found myself basically living with her over her Mother's home in Vine Hill Projects after at first being there later and later every

understatement of the worst kind. Dumbfounded, maybe? Lost? Crushed? Unaccepting of that news but having no choice *but* to accept it? Anyone who's lost a "first love" unexpectedly with no explanation will know exactly how I felt then.

Nothing about it made any sense and I wanted – no, I *needed*, some answers to the massive, crashing bricks dropped on my head and heart. Someone close to her – someone worried about my emotional and mental state but for some reason, I can't recall all these years later – said that I would learn all I needed to if I was at a certain movie theater at a certain time. Noticing she and he holding hands lovingly like she and I used to only a couple of days prior, I made sure she saw me before driving off with an even bigger break in my heart…

Want to know how I got over it? Well, who's to say that I ever did? Of course I got *past* it, but in some ways I've carried traces of that heartbreak in probably every relationship I've had afterwards. Which I admit was maybe – just maybe (because sometimes it's wise to be wary!) – unfair to every other woman that may have loved me after my relationship with her…

Unsurprisingly (to me, at least), she came back to me after a week or so. After (I'm assuming) her relationship ran its course with dude.[105] Which, as I said, wasn't necessarily unexpected by

---

night, then formally spending the night in the same room "with the door open," to everyone accepting the fact that we would sleep in the same bed, to all of my clothes being there after a few days straight of that being where I bathed. Both of our Mothers were initially against this arrangement – with mine more vocally adamantly opposed and keeping up her resistance the longest – but I think they eventually sensed somehow that there was nothing they could do to stop our relationship and the way we wanted to be/live together. We were both so headstrong – Soyayya even more so than I, I must admit – that either we lived together in a way that our parents could *somewhat* keep an eye on us, or we would move out on our own somehow. I had more than enough money for us to do so – and we both had more than enough wherewithal. This at the ages of 16 for myself and 14 for Soyayya. Unbelievable, huh?
[105] Even after seeing her with the other cat, I never really asked her about why she returned, if I'm remembering right. Nor did I tell her about how I cried – literal fucking tears! – on my father's shoulder after moving out my things. I can never thank my father enough for how he did his best to "help me get my mind back right."

me at the time. Somehow or another I had known with all of my being that no other man – not then and not ever – could ever love or take care of Soyayya or make love to her in the ways in which she had gotten used to with me. And for those very reasons, I always believed she would return to me. Or so I hoped. Foolishly, when she again showed interest in me I welcomed her back like the sick puppy I was.

Yet, she had damaged me and I afterwards recognized her capable of inflicting on me an immense amount of pain. Therefore my trust in her went from 100 percent and complete to nonexistent to the point where I didn't even trust her as far as I could *throw* her let alone as far as I could *see* her. Nothing she said to me after that added up. I started to re-evaluate our entire relationship, all of the love I thought we shared with one another, all of the experiences we had and lived through – was it all a lie? When she was with me, was her mind always on *him*? It was nerve wrecking, and wreck my nerves, I sure as hell allowed it to do. We were doomed from there…

Ironically, however, sometimes there's a blessing to be found in a betrayal: Soyayya broke my heart, true enough, yet she also taught me valuable lessons that would help prevent me from getting it broken again in the future. No more would I be so trusting of another person in this world, especially of another fickle woman. No more would I be so naïve as to believe that a "friend" of "my woman" was actually a friend only. No more would I ever allow my world, my entire universe and existence to be centered on any one person with the power to crush me at a moment's whim. No more would I be so quick to fall in love, and with such trust and faith. In many ways I became a cynic about these things, to protect myself; in effect, I made a solemn vow to never be fooled again…

After her deceitfulness was exposed, (as I've said) things

rightfully changed between us, but mostly in subtle, almost imperceptible ways. I was much less freely giving to her of my love, thoughts, feelings, and loving – and hell, I even started attending school more regularly. Amazingly too, I was still on pace to graduate (and still in "Honors" classes!) – as I had built up a lot of extra credits while I was in the Department of Youth Development.[106] But alas, school still didn't really have my focus; "the streets" still held sway.

So my "street campaign" continued, however soon it would all be over. And rightly so because I was wrongly and immorally causing too much havoc in the world. I *had* to be taken off the streets, if I'm being honest, because what little good I was doing out there was far outweighed by the bad. Far outweighed. And the "authorities" wouldn't have to look hard to find the ammunition they needed.

Remember that incident where my accomplices and I were stuck in rush hour traffic hiding in the backseat while the young redneKKK sales clerk was searching for us car to car with his gun out? Well, it was time to pay the piper for that one. An older cat (about 21 or 22) that I had taken on a mission or two (not that one) had gotten caught up and pointed the finger at me. Fantastic. He had made the mistake of telling his underage

---

[106] By my senior year of high school in 1994 (after my release from Woodland Hills Youth Development Center and the group home in Lebanon), I had transitioned (well, in school, at least, because I was still robbing businesses around town, no more coats/jackets or "pocket robbing") to selling marijuana and cocaine to the rich white kids who never failed to solicit either me or someone else in the clique – including as I sat in the honors classes. It never failed to surprise and stun me how a lot of the "best and brightest" of the white kids (especially the girls, again!) had by that age already acquired full-blown "weed and white (i.e., cocaine)" habits and spent hundreds of dollars in high school on their habits weekly! These were the sons and daughters of nashville's prominent judges, lawyers, doctors, educators, and businesspersons and very rarely, it seems, did the children hide their habits from their parents. In fact, more than a few times did some of my customers say they were purchasing *for* their parents and/or describe how they "got high" together! Unbelievable, right?

girlfriend[107] – despite repeated warning not to do so by me – his business and she called the pig police on him when he beat her up after catching her having sex with someone our *own* age. When confronted with the information she had given the kkkops – which, of course, the cat had given to his girlfriend – and subsequently charged with not only the shit he was involved in but, frankly, way more shit that he hadn't (I told you about how nashville's kkkops like to "clear the books"), well he thought to mitigate *his* punishment by putting them on *me*. So early one evening while Soyayya and I were out Christmas shopping for our siblings, the pigs raided her Mom's project looking for me; when not finding me there, they decided to then go a couple of rows over and raid my Mom's too! But, like I said, we were out shopping, and I quickly got the word to stay away from the projects because of what had just happened.

So I was, from that point, officially "on the run." And I can't honestly tell you that I was even *semi*-conscious of how the moves I would make in the coming weeks would affect me the rest of my entire adult life. Not in any shape, form, or fashion did I know – nor could *anyone* talk any sense to my 17 years young "know it all" mind. Both of my parents were in fear for my overall safety (with the kkkops activity searching for me regularly) and wanted me to turn myself in, but I wasn't trying to hear *any* of that bullshit – or at least until after the "holidays" and the New Year rolled around. For one, I wasn't trying to leave Soyayya – because I knew in my heart that I would somehow "lose" her again – yet I also wasn't quick to again be placed in DYD custody and incarcerated at Woodland Hills – with them able to keep me there for almost *4 years until I turned 21*, not to mention whatever time I would receive for my new

---

[107] Whom I had met him through as she was a good friend of Soyayya's. She had asked me to "look out for him" as he was "down" at the time. *Big* mistake on my part!

charges. That could have been 6, 8, or even 10 years or more that I could possibly be incarcerated, and hell, how long is that to someone who had only been on this earth for barely 17 years? So, yeah I wasn't with that *at all*, and had a more "catch me when and *if* they could" type of attitude. I mean what would any other reasonably minded person expect?

    I reconsidered after unexpectedly popping up at my Mom's house on Christmas to visit with her and my siblings. And although I had parked a good distance away and walked the rest of the way through the projects, I wasn't in the house a good 3-4 minutes before I answered the house phone to a detective greeting me by name. Now that told me either one of two things: Either I had some real shitty luck and the pig calling just as I got there was no more than a coincidence – or one of my Mama's neighbors was trying to earn some reward money to blow on more Christmas bullshit! Either way it goes, I didn't wait another 10-15 seconds to "kick up dust" the fuck out of there! Still to this day I don't know why they took the chance to even call, instead of just setting up a perimeter outside and apprehending my ass. Because with only one door in and out of the project, I would've had nowhere to run and nowhere to hide – and I sure as hell wouldn't have put my family in danger in some standoff.

    So I got away that day. But after receiving some clandestine legal advice, I decided to turn myself in the first Monday after the New Year rolled around. But even that – this being me – would not necessarily go off uneventfully:

    I changed my mind about the "turn myself in" part[108] as soon as we pulled into the parking lot of the newly built Juvenile Justice Center. After expressing to them my newly changed mind, my Mama and my Aunt Deborah Ann went inside to explain the situation to whomever they had worked out all the

---

[108] I mean, that's the most important – hell, *only* part of it all, right? Stupid!

arrangements with a few days before, while Soyayya stayed outside in the car with me trying to "talk some sense" into me. Didn't work. When I saw the plainclothes officer coming to the car with my Mom and Aunt, I had Soyayya get out and leave me in the back seat because "things [were] not about to end right."

Police Officer: *"Son, I understand you have a warrant out for your arrest?"*

Me: *"Yeah, and I've got a gun, too, so you're just gonna have to shoot me before I shoot you,"* I said, while reaching down towards the floorboard like I had a weapon.

Can you believe that this officer – a white man, at that – never, ever for one second went towards his gun on his hip?! In amerikkka?! After getting threatened by a young Black Man who seemed to be reaching for something?! Instead he stayed calm.

"Son, I'm not going to hurt you. And you're not going to hurt me. You're not going to do that. Not in front of your Mother and Aunt. And who is this, your girlfriend?"

All three of them had screamed in panic different variations of "he doesn't have a gun! He doesn't have a gun" after I had said what I had said; Soyayya had even started crying.

"You're not going to put them through that. Not these three beautiful young ladies that love you. And I don't think you have a gun anyway, but even if you do, you're not going to do that to them."

Could you believe this kind, caring, compassionate motherfucker?! Just who in the hell gave *him* a badge?! After recognizing that he saw right through me, I got out of the car, let him cuff me,[109] kissed all three of my ladies on their cheeks, and let him walk me inside to be "booked."

Unbelievable, right? A kind, caring, compassionate, considerate, sympathetic, and merciful police office – and white,

---

[109] He didn't even put them on so tight that they cut off my circulation! Just who *was* this motherfucker?!

at that! Not someone whom would gun down a 12-year-young little boy with a BB gun, or whom would choke a man to death for selling cigarettes; or whom would shoot a man five times in the back and plant evidence near his body, or whom would manhandle to the ground a young teen girl after being called about a simple argument at a pool or place his knee on a handcuffed non-resisting man's neck for 8 minutes and 46 seconds and kill him over a suspected counterfeit $20! – empathetic cops *do* exist! And this was the first time I can remember ever meeting one.

As part of my plan formulated with my "legal adviser" before turning myself in, I agreed to have my case tried in "adult court" so as to avoid a return to DYD custody in addition to having a bail bond set for me; the way it was all explained to me, I would have a reasonable bail set (no more than $50,000 tops) immediately after transfer to adult jail (the Criminal Justice Center, a.k.a. "CJC") which might take a week to ten days. However it didn't work out that way; after spending maybe a week at the Juvenile Justice Center, I was transferred a half mile up the road to CJC where I was informed during the booking process that I had something called an "Open Court" bond which meant that whatever judge was ultimately assigned my case would set whatever amount he or she deemed "reasonable" – and it was a 3-4 month process to have the hearing *after* I somehow or another figured out how to petition the kkkourt to start the process.

Do I even have to tell you how I was feeling after finding all of this out? Yeah, magnify that times ten.

In jail I noticed immediately that I was receiving some kind of "special treatment" – but not in a good way! Even though I was being tried as an "adult" in my case, I was barely 3 months past my 17th birthday which made me a "Juvenile" and by law

Juvenile

unable to be housed or even allowed around any "real adults" for my own safety.[110] So, after being moved to the front of the line for all booking processes, I was immediately moved to C-pod on the 2nd floor which was the "Juvenile Tank."

"Thunder Dome" was more like it. Out of six 2-man cells (to go along with two telephones at one end, a television bolted high up on a platform at the other, and at least one camera *supposedly* watching our "every move") in the cellblock, I think I was pretty much the only cat that didn't have a murder case and/or wasn't facing at least 50 years.

Unbelievably, however, I was also one of the oldest cats in the cellblock (with the youngest being, I think maybe 14 or so), yet nevertheless the scrawniest cat – with most of these cats built like bodybuilders.[111] I was moreover the only cat in there from the Southside and we all know what that means: *"Trying Season!"*[112] And "tried" I quickly was – with more than a few times, me being "tested" – however, I passed all tests with flying colors and soon I was accepted and embraced.

I also quickly fell in line with all of the foolishness of the Thunder Dome, and even found myself leading a lot of it eventually. Not only would we "test" every new cat in the pod just as I had been tested,[113] but we would also raise so much hell that a lot of officers would beg us for "peace" at the start of

---

[110] I think this was all put in place after too many incidents of adult on juvenile assault, rape, extortion, and/or murder throughout tennessee's jail/prison system – along with the too expensive corresponding lawsuits that no doubt came with them.

[111] I would find out soon enough that we were allowed to lift free weights at the gym for an hour or so every day, but usually I just shot basketball.

[112] At the time, the Southside was known more for "get money cats" as opposed to "gangsters" – and although they had some cats getting money, the Eastside and the Northside were the two sides where most of the robbers were from and where most of the murders occurred. Westside cats were usually about their money like on the Southside, but their hood was so small (only 2 sets of interconnected projects directly across from one another), that they usually fell in tight with the Northsiders that they attended school with.

[113] With some failing miserably – especially most, but not all, of the "whiteboys."

their shifts so that they wouldn't have to "do any paperwork" and/or have to tussle with one or more of us. That's how rambunctious we were back there – it was hell to pay if our food was cold or late, or the Kool Aid didn't have any sugar in it. Because not only were the majority of us facing a boatload of time causing us not to give a "fuck," but we were also juveniles which meant that although they could (and did, to a lot of us!) kick our young asses, they couldn't *kill* us and get away with it like they did with the adults! So that gave us a certain amount of leeway, which we unconsciously used to our (seriously slight!) advantage when confronted with bullshit, pushed and/or given the slightest reason.

Most of the pigs hated us of course. But I say "most" because I realize now that some of the officers that worked there used to love how we would stick together and stand up for ourselves when one of the rednekkk pigs tried their typical bully bullshit. More than a few times it would somehow be arranged for a newer young super kkkop rednekkk to have to work our pod for a few days.[114] Which invariably wouldn't work out well for them once their attitude – then cowardice – was exposed. I distinctly remember one particular rednekkk (whose "bitch" I brought out) being so unnerved that he would come back a week after our confrontation and announce through the bars at the head of the cellblock that he "would be waiting" for me at 12 midnight on September 26th – my 18th birthday and when I would be moved to the higher floor with the rest of the adults! Hilarious, right? This chump was still so pissed off about how I had called him out, that he had memorized my birthday which was still months away! When the day and time came, I was ready for him too. I had found and sharpened a screw real good, and

---

[114] Which really, only entailed coming in there for meals and to *try* to lock us down at the correct times; this could be much harder than it sounds.

kept it "locked up and loaded" for when and if he and/or his compatriots made a move! And even though he was there for my elevator ride to the 4th floor, all he gave me was a sheepish-assed smile and didn't make any moves. Sucker...

Sad to say, but I actually remember my time in the Juvenile Pod quite fondly; there I would connect and become lifelong friends with cats like Monster Loc and M Loco from the Eastside, and Labo from the Westside, among some other "thorough" cats that would come through on their way to "the pen."[115] And even though we were probably on some form of lockdown for various shit we did for roughly half of the 8 months I was in there, it seemed more a "Thug Summer Camp" than the jail it was for most of the time. Pitiful, isn't it? But, that's the way the "powers that be" ran it and allowed it to be run. Hell, they didn't even make an attempt at putting on a show like they were trying to "educate" us in any way; the only "education" we would receive was in whatever we learned in running wild like the criminals they thought we were. I mean, we were all on our way to prison anyway, so it's not like we didn't need the practice, right? Right.

Soyayya was, of course, lost to the wind shortly after we learned I wouldn't be receiving a bond any time soon; a few months later I found out she was pregnant by this "grown dude" with her belly growing bigger every day. After all those months of she and I failingly attempting to have a child together, I was crushed – but this time I was able to "deal" better as I found my

---

[115] Although this is when and where he and I became "super tight" like brothers, Monster Loc and I had previously met each other a couple of months before at the Juvenile Justice Center after I was arrested, along with a homie, for the possession of three guns out of Soyayya's Mother's house on Halloween. (My homie and I would stay locked up for 2-3 days before unexpectedly being granted – and making – a "juvenile bond" as the first two individuals in nashville to do so.) He and I like to lament the fact that we passed up a prime opportunity to beat the fake reverend jackson's ass (for lying to our face about some bullshit his "coalition" would take care of) when he visited the JJD on a photo op. Fake bitch.

comfort in the other young ladies I would visit with and talk to whom I knew had always "dug" me when I had attended all the various high schools and lived in all the hoods I had over the years. Plus jail/prison doesn't allow you the space to mourn any lost loved one – whether through desertion or even death – so I quickly got over that shit and put her ass behind me. Or so I thought.

    Foolishly, I accepted her back once again after she somehow got the word that I wouldn't be serving as much time as we initially feared; by then I was 18 (and now housed in and carrying on my "Thunder Dome-ish" type ways in the adult part of the jail) and she was seven or eight months pregnant. Nevertheless I moronically accepted her proposal of marriage anyway. Because what could go wrong, right?...

"To understand how any society functions you must understand the relationship between the men and women..."

Angela Davis

LOVING & LIVING

Life with Zara was tranquil, and serene. At least for a time. I knew going in that our marriage would need patience and understanding for us to survive and thrive. Because let's be honest, she knew nothing of me, and I knew almost nothing of her, besides the way we made one another feel and the love we felt we shared. Nevertheless, I felt that more than enough, so I was willing to accept whatever past she came with and whatever we had to face together in life...

Initially, our lives didn't change much, although I did move in with Zara and Maviya in a townhouse apartment in Madison. And since neither of us worked "official" jobs, I only left our home when I had to be away on business or when we went out to kick it. She, however, continued to "club" and receive calls at all hours of the night, of which I said nothing; I figured I would give her time to figure out that no man out in the streets could compare to me, and if so, then why marry me in the first place? And it didn't take her long. So days were filled with lovemaking, conversations to get to know one another, followed by even more lovemaking; our nights were filled with the same. Maviya was and *wasn't* around, in that we continued to take her to daycare every day, so as to give her some sense of normalcy even as we were trying to figure it all out the course of our new lives together...

My relationship with Tsawa was torn, but cordial. Even then, I knew that I couldn't blame her for her aloof attitude towards me after my sudden marriage to a woman that she never had an idea even existed. Crazily, though, I was still hurt, as I somewhat expected for nothing between us to change. I mean, why get upset with me over *my* situation, when I fell in line every time her youngest son's father or his family called when I was around? It wasn't as if I was still expecting her to have sex with me – I was determined to stay faithful to my new wife – but I didn't like the found again coldness that was directed my way. I felt the bullshit of the past coming all over again. Surprisingly, though, this time she didn't necessarily keep my son away from me, though she did take me off the allowed list to pick him up from daycare.[116]

Pasheni, however? – Pasheni was tripping! Every chance she got to make it hard on me, she took.[117] She was the typical scorned woman, it seemed, still unknowingly to me harboring illusions that she and I would get back together even though we were well broken up long before Zara and I got married. Soon, she would do whatever she could think of to undermine my new relationship.

And her mother was still right in the middle of things, of course – even going so far as to make up a vicious lie and cause

---

[116] Technically, she wasn't allowed "by law" to make this move seeing as how my visitation order specifically forbid it, however she knew that I wouldn't and couldn't "make any waves about it" considering the fact that I was ducking and dodging the feds at the time. Rotten ass woman...

[117] History is, indeed, prologue. Just as, in my opinion, a woman should consider it a glaring red flag whenever a man mistreats and/or speaks negatively about the women in his life that were there before her (i.e., mother, sister, aunts, the mother(s) of his children, even coworkers), I, too, should have taken heed to Pasheni's negative attitude towards her oldest son's father and even her own father after witnessing them going above and beyond to try to get along with her. (Especially her own father — a good-hearted man whom was even supportive of *me* in a time of great strife.) Yet, I ignored these warning signs, and thus I was destined to go through some of the same bullshit with her that I attempted to counsel her through with them.
However, again, lesson now learned: It's *always* a wise move to play close attention to how someone you're dealing with treats other people. (And this goes for in your business *and* personal lives!) Because that same honesty or dishonesty, respect or lack thereof, kindness or cruelty, courtesy or discourteousness, loyalty or disloyalty could soon be coming *your* way. Can you dig it?

my marriage's first serious test. Nevertheless, I was determined that no matter the obstacle and bullshit I was up against, my son wouldn't want for anything and would always know that his father loved and cared for him as long as I had breath in my lungs.

At times, however, I *did* get frustrated – as I think any reasonable man would have in the same situation – but I still made it to *every* checkup, still came *whenever* there was even the *possibility* of something being wrong, and still made sure Kalii had *every* essential need fulfilled (and even *most* of his mother's *wants!*). Still nothing was ever good enough; I was accused of doing more for a child that "wasn't even [mine]" – although of course, neither of my children wanted for anything; of not "having him enough" – even though before I married Zara, Pasheni didn't even want me around him for fear that "something might happen" when the feds finally found me; and of even not coming fast enough whenever she called me for something. I quickly got hip to her tricks – Tsawa, had of course, taught me so much in that regard – and attempted to counteract them: I bought Kalii way more than I knew would be enough for those time periods when I knew I wouldn't be in town; I asked for him way more than I knew she would be comfortable being away from him; and I started telling her I wouldn't be able to come whenever she called for something frivolous, yet I *still showed up – every single time!* Nonetheless, still the complaints came, and I quickly became exasperated.

However, all in all, though, this time in my life was one which I consider one of my most peaceful periods, yet darkest all the same because both of my brothers were locked up and I knew somewhere in the recesses of my mind that my relationship peace probably wouldn't last. Before long, Pasheni would become more disingenuous in her demands; once, she called as Zara and I were on our way home from a late evening date, demanding that Kalii needed diapers; mind you, I had just bought a couple of the biggest bags possible a day before, instructing her to get *any and everything he needed* as I expected to be out of town on business for up to a week. I had even offered her money – which she refused to accept, of course – just in case something came up unexpectedly. Yet when I conveyed to her to drive the 5 minutes from her home to the store to get the diapers, she informed me that she didn't have any money; I knew then that she was again playing some type of game. Flatly telling her that I wasn't coming out again until the following morning, I eventually had to hang up on her curses.

Zara then gave me the strangest look I had ever seen from her up to that point, and then *instructed* me that *"[I would] be going out again to get his diapers."* What??? *Fuck that!*

"I'm not going anywhere *or doing* shit *because she's bullshitting,"* was the calmest way I could respond.

Again, I got that strange look,[118] with her then picking up the phone to inform Pasheni that I was on my way. I snapped:

"Don't you ever *in your life again go behind me and against my word to someone else! And I don't give a fuck* who *it is!"*

"Naw, Delo, you're wrong; you're not about to deny that baby what he needs," she said.

I was frustrated as hell.

"What??? Fuck that!!! Have I ever *denied him what he needs??? Have you* ever *seen me deny anything,* any *of what you muthafuckas even want??? She's playing games! You were with me a couple of days ago when I just bought the shit!!! Fuck that!!! Fuck you* and *her!!!*

"Fuck me? Fuck *me?* Okay, cool, fuck me. *It's cool. Remember that.* Fuck me."

Our very first argument. All over some bullshit which

---

[118] As a matter of fact, unbelievingly it was even stranger this time around!

Pasheni would later admit to me was a ploy she was using in an attempt to get me alone over to her house. And I was pissed. I couldn't stomach my own wife going against me no matter what the reason. This, however, would forebode things soon to come.[119]

Soon, however, Zara and I got past that — or so I thought — and I thought it wise of me to no longer have direct dealings with Pasheni (or at least without Zara being present) so as to no longer give her or her mother the chance to lie on me again and cause discord in my relationship. Furthermore, since Pasheni and Zara were such *good friends* now, I might as well allow them all the dealings with each other when it came to arrangements on me seeing and providing for my son. So some days when I came home from a business trip Kalii was there, giving me a chance to spend time with all three of my children at once. However, of course, this wasn't all that often...

Nor was this arrangement easy to transition to, because I'm just fundamentally opposed to needing a mediator — no matter whom it may be — to help dictate how and when and where I provide for and visit with my children. That mediator wasn't there when the mother and I made them were they? I submit that parents should be able to put bullshit differences aside to work out what needs to be worked out, however I've learned to understand that this is not always possible. Yet, I still don't have to like it. Nonetheless I quickly recognized its necessity as Pasheni was relentless with her bullshit: After causing its first argument, she wouldn't even allow my marriage two hours of peace and possible reconciliation without hitting it with a diabolical lie. And even though I'm getting pissed off all over again as I think about it, here's the complete and

---

[119] I was also upset at myself for hurting her feelings in the way I spoke to her, but it's taken me a little while longer to admit to *that*. Even to myself...

embarrassingly ugly truth as to what happened:

After Zara and I had reached home, I left out again on an aimless drive in order to allow us both the space we may have needed to "cool down" – I didn't want either of us to say or do anything more that we might later regret.[120] Yet I wouldn't be allowed peace – my phones kept ringing and ringing and ringing and ringing. Finally, I answered the "family phone" without ever looking at the caller ID:

"*What. The. Fuck is it?*"

"*Damn! What's wrong with* you?!" the voice on the other end said. It was Pasheni's cousin Rana.

"*Oh, my bad. I didn't know it was you. Your crazy ass cousin got me frustrated, bullshitting. But what's up, though?*"

It wasn't unusual for her to call me sometimes as she and I had grown into having somewhat of a big brother - little sister type of relationship when her cousin and I were involved. Although the frequency of communication slowed down no doubt, that friendship didn't end after her cousin's and my relationship did. Nor did any of my friendships with all of her other family members – male *and* female.

"*Nothing. I was just trying to see if you was ever gonna let me braid your hair?*"

I had been growing my hair out the last few months as a "throw off" to the feds, and braiding was her "side hustle." Cool.

"*Hell, you can do it now. I ain't doing nothing.*"

"*Alright, I got one person's hair I'm doing now, but I'm almost halfway done.*"

"*Cool. I'll be there in about 20 minutes.*"

Simple and innocent as that – but shit was about to get a

---

[120] Ironic, huh, that I would drive around aimlessly instead of just heading over to Pasheni's house after her request that had started it all, right? Wrong! I knew instinctually that night that she was just "on some bullshit" – which she years later inadvertently admitted to me!

lot more complicated...

Arriving to her home, I greeted her father and brother as I did all the other untold amount of times I had been over there – both with Pasheni and when Pasheni sent me over there to pick up Rana so she could babysit for us; I then awaited my turn to get my hair done. As she was finishing my last few braids, Rana asked if I "minded taking [her] to get something to eat?" Cool with me if it was cool with her father, and after obtaining his permission, we headed off towards the McDonald's. Simple 10-15 minute trip right? Until we ran into the Devil. Or to be fair – because I still somehow have love for her despite all that she would go on to put me through – someone who had "devilishment" on her mind: Pasheni's mother.

Stopping for gas on the way to the McDonald's, after coming out from paying, I noticed her a couple of stalls away appearing as if she was trying to see who was behind my tints. I didn't think anything of it at the time and greeted her. Then we had a conversation.

Therein she informed me that she was aware that Pasheni and I were "into it again" and advised me to "just go over there and fuck her" as "[we hadn't] fucked since before [my son] was born" and "that [was] the problem." And although shocking to some who may be reading this, this conversation didn't *at all, in any way*, surprise me in that Pasheni considered/considers her mother her best friend – seemingly apprising her mother of every orgasm (or lack thereof!) I had given her, along with everything else that went on in our relationship. Notwithstanding the fact that I never ceased being uncomfortable with her mother "all up in our business" in that way, I had long since ceased to be amazed at it. All the same however – no matter what Pasheni's mother said – I still wasn't going to "fuck" her daughter. Not only was I faithfully married,

I knew (somehow) inherently, that messing around with her in any kind of way like that would come back to haunt me in some terrible way. I just knew it.[121]

Anyway, I ended the conversation by telling her I would "think about it" and then made sure – after noticing she was still trying to see behind my tints – that Pasheni's mother and her niece had greeted one another. Not thinking anything of it, Rana said she "wish [I] wouldn't have [did] that" as her aunt "always keeps up some stupid shit." I thought Rana was maybe overreacting. My mistake.

A few minutes later, as we awaited food in the drive-thru, I answered Pasheni's call – I understood better now how she was possibly feeling after my conversation with her mother. Or so I thought:

"*So you fucking my 16 year old cousin?!?*"

"*Huh? Say the fuck what? Huh?*" I said confused.

"*So you fucking my cousin now?! So you fucking my cousin now? You got me fucked up!*" she screamed.

"*Huh? Are you fucking crazy or something?*" I asked calmly.

"*My Mama just told me she seen you with Rana! You knew she was gonna tell me! You got me fucked up!!!*"

"*Man, you tripping and ain't nobody got time for this. I'm just taking her to get something to eat.*"

"*You got me fucked up!!!*"

I hung up on her, and that settled it for me – she sure as hell wouldn't be getting any "dick" from me that night…

Rana had only heard my end of the conversation (although she, of course, did hear all of Pasheni's shouting) and said "I told you so"; after I told her what was actually said, she said "Oh,

---

[121] Hell, she had never – not once that I could remember – wanted to have sex with me so bad when we were actually in our relationship together! But maybe I should have just went over there and fucked her and I *might* not have went through all the bullshit that was to soon come. But I digress…

here we go." It's a damned shame that she was wise enough to know more of what was coming than I was. Or maybe she just knew her aunt and cousin a whole hell of a lot better than I did? Either way, Zara called before we had even made it out of the drive-thru good:

"*So you fucking lil' 16 year old girls now?*"

Not her too.

"*Come on now! What type of shit y'all on? I'm not fucking* nobody! Let alone a 16 year old child! *I don't fuck* children!"

"*Well that's not what Pasheni said. She said her Mama caught you with her cousin.*"

Caught me?! *Caught* me! Nobody *caught* me doing a goddamned thing and I was starting to get really pissed!!! *Hell, I* was the one that made sure they spoke to one another – let alone had I done anything wrong nor had I been trying to "hide" anyone or anything to be "caught" doing shit!!! Therefore, I explained to Zara what *really* happened – what *really* was going on – and told her I was on my way home.[122]

Dropping Rana off, as she got out of the car she again said, "I told you so," and all I could do was shake my head.

At home, Zara recognized the truth for what it was. Hell, she knew that I was a *protector* of women and children instead of a *violator* – and to be honest, I know that motherfucker Pasheni has always known the goddamned same! Come on now – Zara and I shared a two years young daughter, and I had young sisters and female cousins at that time – just what does anyone think I would have done to the 24 year old *man* that tried to have sex with them at 16?!? What would I have done??? Come on now – motherfuckers *know*!!!

And for the record, I don't mess around with any "out of

---

[122] Besides even just my telling her so, she would see the proof of the truth in my for-the-first-time newly braided hair.

bounds" women. Never, not once in my life, has a "homeboy" or friend or family member had to worry about leaving their wives, girlfriends, mothers of their children, etc. around me – that's not my style. Furthermore I'm not about to "hit on" your sister, your mother, your cousin or aunt or nothing. For me to even *consider* the possibility of kicking it like that with one of my homie's/friend's family members (and no matter what I could never entertain the idea of messing with a friend's mother!) then *she* would have to come on to me and *he* would have to approve beforehand! And *still* I'm reluctant – because I just foresee too many potential problems.[123] And I *sure* as hell don't mess around with children!!! Who does that?!!! Not Fucking Me!!!

Furthermore, let me be clear by saying that just as much as I detest the acts of forcing yourself on a woman, or taking advantage sexually of a child, I abhor just the same the knowingly false accusation of someone of doing so. They're *all* equally reprehensible in my eyes – as they all usually cause lifelong scars. I know it did me – making me angry even to this day, and making me a whole lot more suspecting and wary of putting myself in even the most innocuous and innocent situations now.

This lie really damaged Rana too – doing an unimaginable number on the young girl's psyche. Can you believe that she was still a virgin throughout all of this? I'm not sure if she had even *kissed* a boy until weeks/months after this, yet with her own "family" accusing her of such unspeakable bullshit?! I damn near came to tears as she was telling me this (of her virginity) all those years later, and all those of her family that didn't believe and/or support her can possibly never imagine the harm they caused

---

[123] However, I do admit to there being at least a couple of women who got past my natural aversion to "too close for comfort" relationships – but you'd better believe their brothers (my homeboys) approved it if not downright supported it. If not, we never would have become involved.

her. They should be on their knees begging this (now) young woman to accept their apologies. Pitiful.[124] Anyway, (like I said) Zara recognized the truth so she and I would have no more drama about it – until Pasheni started blowing up my phone early the next morning with more of the same bullshit.

"*You got me fucked up fucking my cousin, Delo! You got me fucked up!*" she screamed.

I was a fool to even answer the phone, but (stupidly!) I thought, somehow or another, that she had come to her senses. Instead, evidently, her mind had been in overdrive flipping itself out.

"*Man, you tripping early in the morning – you need to miss me with that bullshit.*"

"*You got me fucked up, Delo! You got me fucked up!*"

I hung up the goddamned phone and quit answering every number I knew to be associated with her. But she still found a way to get through – including by calling Zara's phone. But I wasn't trying to "rap" (talk to her) – and I was really getting kind of offended that Zara kept hearing her out.

---

[124] Especially the aunts and female cousins because they *know* how it feels to be a 16-year-young girl trying to come into your own as a woman! This incident occurred sometime in late November or early December of 2001, and after months of false accusations of being a "slut" that "fucked her cousin's baby's daddy," Rana would go on to actually *lose* her willing virginity and become pregnant with her first child. And although I was locked up in federal custody (in the Cincinnati area of Northern Kentucky) on January 4, 2002, I was accused by Pasheni of sending someone to "look at [Rana's baby] to see if it was (mine)" after she gave birth to him sometime in *mid-December* of *2002*.
Did you catch that? Did you catch it? Now, one thing I've never been accused of is not being able to count – so that means that I would have had to be so foolish as to believe that a child could be mine that was born 11 ½ months *after* possible conception *if* Rana and I had sex, right? What am I? The carrier of "Magical Super Sperm"? Or maybe I have a "Magical Super Penis" – able to travel through bars, walls, hundreds of miles and state to state to impregnate young girls/women with the U.S. Marshals never having been the wiser?!
Or maybe, someone perpetrated yet another lie to perpetuate the one previously told – with some goddamned fools actually believing her?! I'll let you decide what the truth is…

Nevertheless, there was one call I did accept from a number I knew to be associated with Pasheni: from her aunt whom was Rana's mom. Now this woman had "some sense" from what I remembered; *she* would be able to get down to the bottom of the bullshit. Plus, it was a respect thing; had it been my daughter I would have wanted some answers too! So I heard her out.

And she explained what her sister and niece had brought to her and told me she would have me prosecuted "if [I had] touched [her] daughter." I said I "respect[ed] that to the fullest," and then told her the truth as to what happened. And I know she knew it to be true – I could tell in the way she was listening. Still I told her not to take my word for it, but instead "talk to your daughter, talk to your husband, talk to your son, and then talk to your sister and niece and try to find out why they're lying to you." She ended our conversation saying that she was "going to have a doctor check Rana out,"[125] which I fully supported; and I ended on how I would appreciate apologies after it was all said and done.

So that was that – right? Or have you actually been listening as I've explained the irony that is my life? Because nothing is ever settled so easy when it comes to me. Whether due to karma, my own misguided actions, or even just happenstance – I am forever faced with a struggle even in dealing with the simplest situations. And this would be no different; even though we all – every single party involved – always knew what the truth to be…

So Rana's Mom evidently investigated and then (evidently) had a conversation with her sister and/or niece. Because even more evident was the fact that somehow – unbelievable as that

---

[125] Which I'm assuming that she never did for some reason, because how embarrassing would *that* have been for some people?! Boy, I'm wishing she would have!

Loving & Living

is – Pasheni was even more pissed than before:

"*I don't give a fuck how you convinced everybody else – you know what the fuck you did!!!!*"

Goddamnit – just where in the fuck is she getting all these phones?!

"*Look, man, you trippin – you know I ain't on that bullshit.*"

"*I know you fucked my cousin, Delo! I know you fucked her! You got me fucked up!!!*"

"*Look, I'm not about to keep arguing with you, but you know I didn't fuck that girl. You tripping,*" I said calmly.

Why in the hell do I even keep wasting my time repeating myself? It sounds like she's almost even convinced her *damned self* of the lie that she and/or her Mother *made up*!

"*I know you fucked her!!!! I know you fucked her!!!!!!*" she shrilled.

You know, I used to criticize the hell out of those fools that – after enduring hours of police interrogation – "confessed" to some shit that they honestly were/are innocent of. But now I can totally dig it because I would have said anything to shut her shrilling ass up!

"*Yeah, I fucked her! I fucked her!*" I said sarcastically in the most hateful way I could possibly ever speak – and then added "*and her pussy was better than yours too!*" (or something to that effect) for good measure, being hanging up and tossing my phone.[126]

But wouldn't you know? – the day's just getting started – and I'm about to have some more "fun" that ain't even funny at

---

[126] You know, I hate that I've even had to address this bullshit in this way – but for far too long Pasheni and/or her mother have been allowed to propagate this despicable lie to her/their family members and others. For far too long my son has had to grow up under the whispers that he has a cousin who's "also his brother." For far too long a young lady's reputation has been besmirched simply because someone didn't get what they wanted that night. The shit has to stop now!!! The shit has to stop… (And keep your fucking apologies – I don't even want them now. That shit was/is indefensible. No matter what your motives may have been…).

all! Although she had sat up in bed beside me as I had every conversation that morning; although she knew the entire truth as to what really happened and why, Zara took great offense at the last couple of statements I had made:

"*So you* fucked *her, huh*?! *So you* fucked *her*?! *And the pussy was good*?!"

Not *you* again? This can't be happening, *right*? Not *again*. *Impossible*. Im – fucking – *possible*! Well, I'll be goddamned – got to go through *this* shit again! We exploded in argument...

Absurdly, Zara seemed to expect me to hit or harm her physically in some kind of way, but that has never been my style; my motto was "I don't hit women." So I walked out.

See, if you or I feel as if we have to put our hands on one another in a harmful way, then something is terribly wrong in our relationship; anytime things are close to getting physical in that kind of way, then it's time for me to leave.

I had already gone through the "fuck and fight and fuck once more" stage with Tsawa, and never again would I put myself or any other person through that for a second time. Not that *I* was the one doing the *physical* fighting with Tsawa, mind you, but *I* allowed the cycle to go on for far too long. That was our thing, though: she would smack me, sometimes even punch me, in the privacy of our home, out in public, no matter who was around including my homeboys (How embarrassing was that, right?), then invariably she would "make it all up to me."

No matter the warnings I constantly gave her to "not put [her] fucking hands on me," and that I would finally get tired of that shit, but still she continued. She liked that; that's what she was used to in her former relationships.

But me, my path was different; I had seen my mother and father fighting a time or two when I was younger and I vowed to "never put my hands on a woman." Tsawa would push this vow of mine to the brink time and time again. Until, finally, my patience was extinguished, and I exploded, hitting her ass *back*:

Spring of 1998, she and Jannah were once again fed up with the lies I was telling and the games I was playing and caught me up in a trap: Some way or another, they acquired each other's phone numbers and had been talking all day, comparing what and how I was doing for one the same I was doing for the other. I mean, this conversing of theirs was amazing in and of itself – seeing as how Tsawa had stabbed Jannah and I both only months before. But like I said they were "fed up" – and little did I know, I was too, myself. Shit was about to get hectic…

However let me be clear about something first: I've never felt that the love I hold for one person in any way diminishes my love for another; love can take many forms, hold different intensities, have various bases, and be expressed in multiple ways. I only feel that love must be "true" – that is its *only* requirement. I say all of that to say this: The love I felt/feel for Jannah doesn't discount what I had/have with Tsawa, it was just different, you know? Furthermore, I could never completely trust Tsawa after all the bullshit and all of the "friends"[127] she kept lurking in the shadows, so really, in my eyes, there was no comparison between the two; I trusted Jannah in ways that I could never (in good conscience) trust Tsawa. Still, Tsawa and I had our son together, so we would always have some type of bond. Whether I liked it or not sometimes.

Frankly, however, Jannah was whom I wanted to be (in a relationship) with – yet Tsawa was someone that I (at the time) wouldn't let (completely) go. If only I had the courage to be completely honest and candid.

But lacking that bravery (at the time), here comes the "fun": *My* plan was to get off work, stop by campus to kick it

---

[127] That usually I found out were also former and/or future lovers far too often.

with Jannah for a few minutes on my way to making a "run" on the Northside anyway, head to Tsawa's Mom's house to help bathe and feed my son, then put him to sleep and afterwards head back up to campus to spend the rest of most of the night with Jannah. *Their* plan was different – they were about to make me choose one or the other once and for all!! Well, shit, *this* is not about to turn out good!

So I pull up on campus (actually *enjoying* my life at the time!) and Jannah and I sat outside her dorm in the parking lot – windows down, sunroof open, music bumping, enjoying the night. But when it was time for me to leave to make my run, she kept stalling me for some reason. Hell, I didn't think anything of it – it always took a Herculean effort for us to not want to spend every second together anyway – until I noticed a familiar car pull up in my periphery and my mind flashed "DANGER!"

My door opened.

"*Un huh! You're caught!*"

Well, I'll be goddamned. I looked at her, I looked at Jannah. I looked at her again, then again looked at Jannah (who by now had her arms folded across her chest).

"*Y'all set me up,*" I said more so to Jannah. "*I can't believe y'all set me up.*"

Can you believe that *I* was the one that was offended? Fucking idiot. I started shaking my head, I was so disappointed. And needless to say, I was no longer enjoying my night.

"*Man, shut my shit, man,*" and, "*Get the fuck out,*" I said to one then the other – but more so as pleas than demands of any kind. I was *not* in a position to demand shit.

"*Nope!*" returned one and, "*I'm not going anywhere,*" returned the other. "*You about to tell us which one you fucking with.*"

Shit, I wasn't about to do that! Not then. Not there. Not in those circumstances! Forced to choose, one of them would *not* have liked what I had to say – and I was deathly afraid of what her reaction might be! So I pleaded again:

"Please just shut my door, man," I said to one and, *"Please just let me go,"* to the other.

"Nope!" said one defiantly – and no answer at all from the other. Shit!

As I was pleading with Jannah to let me leave, somehow or another Tsawa had pushed her way past me to my backseat. Now I was feeling crowded. And she was the primary reason why.

"Come on, man, let me leave. I ain't fucking with neither one of y'all," I said while attempting to pull her out of my truck.

Pop!!! She gave me a nice "solid" to the face.

"Don't hit me a-fucking again!!!" I warned. I tried to get her out again.

Pop!!! Pop!!! – this time, a "two-piece" to the face!

"Quit fucking hitting *me!!!*

Pop!!! Pop!!! Pop!!! That was a sweet combination, I've got to give it to her – but that shit made me *snap*!

Before I even realized it, I had snatched and thrown her out of my SUV, pounced on her, and given her a few blows to the face and body! I quickly realized what I had done, and turned away from her, walking back to go and sit in my truck, still in a fog. Until she stopped me.

"Ah, you done fucked up now!"

I turned back to see her digging in her pocket for something – and no way in hell was I about to allow her to shoot at or stab me again! Who knows if she'll miss with the gun again, being up so close? Or even be satisfied with a *little* of my blood this time if it's only another knife?! So I rushed her – pinning her up against the nearby building while I kept her hand from coming out of her pocket! Grabbing myself what she was attempting to retrieve, I found no more than her phone and tossed it into the nearby grass. Safe – *this* time!

By then, the other students and their guests outside attempting to enjoy the nice night were screaming variations of "Stop"; "He's beating her!"; "Call the police!"; and "Call Security! Call Security!" and I knew I had to get out of there. Back in those days, it was never really ever a good time for me to submit to a police search, but doubly so seeing as how I never had a chance to make my "run." Climbing into the driver's seat, I go to turn the ignition and (wouldn't you know it!) my keys were gone!

"*Where are my keys?!*"

Jannah hadn't seemingly moved at all, and was still sitting in my passenger seat and I paid no attention to my music no longer playing.

"*I don't know.*"

"*What the hell? They were just right here!! What the fuck?!!!*"

I couldn't even comprehend at the time that she must have had them, because everything kept coming at me so fast. To avoid a (not so!) nice, long "federally sponsored vacation," I would have to think even faster! So I grabbed my gym bag, stuffed it with everything that made me "dirty," and took off on campus towards the nearby projects. Hastily stashing what I needed to stash without anyone (miraculously) seeing me, I headed back to unbelievably find my keys somehow dangly in the ignition! What the hell!!! Seeing my chance to drive away, I started to reverse out of my parking space (with Jannah still sitting in the passenger seat, I might add!), only to be stopped by two Metro police officers blocking the way! Shit!!!

Since this was a campus incident and I was a student and the two Metro officers were "moonlighting" as campus security, I was marched off (embarrassingly in handcuffs) to the Campus

Security Office to allow them to investigate before carting me off to jail. Left alone was myself, Tsawa, and a Black woman Metro police officer whom I could quickly tell hated my guts. I couldn't even blame her.

"*So you like beating up women, huh!?*"

I know what this looks like; I'm the "animal" in handcuffs and Tsawa's face is already showing signs of swelling and blackening.

"*It ain't even like that. I was just protecting myself. I* ain't *no woman beater.*"

"*You ain't no woman beater?!* Look *at her! Ain't nothing she could've done to hurt you!*"

If the officer only knew. But it's cool, I wasn't even tripping. And I wasn't expecting sympathy considering what it looked like anyway. Plus, Tsawa was milking her he-beat-me-please-protect-me-from-this-animal face for all it was worth. So, what would I expect for anyone to think or feel about me?

As I was thinking about everything that had happened – and everything that was soon about to – I realized that I would have to make bond fast before they found out I was on parole. So I reached out to Carvin.

"*Bro!...Man, just listen 'cause I got to talk fast!...Nah, this police officer is letting me use the phone to call you...Nah, just be cool – nothing like that!...Nah, done got into it with Tsawa again and they taking me to jail...Nah, just call Trina and y'all meet me downtown to make my bond!...Just bring a thousand, no, bring two thousand, no, just meet me downtown and bring about $5,000. Alright, bet, good looking! Love you too...*"

"*Wow!... it's that easy to just call and get $5,000 in cash???!*" the police officer said.

This set Tsawa off.

"*Oh, that Dairy Queen job and shit he got on is just a* front*! He* *sells dope! He robs people! He's paying like $900 a month on his truck out there! You think he can afford that on a Dairy Queen job?!!! Y'all need to search his house* and *his car! Ain't no telling what y'all find in* there*!!!"*

What in the hell, right?! Like, *what in the hell?*! Tsawa just escalated this shit to a whole other level! Was she even *thinking*! I mean, I'm the *father* of her *son*! What happens to *him* if something happens to *me*?! Does she even give a fuck? Is she thinking straight? I'm pleading with my eyes for her to *shut the hell up*!!!

"*She's lying! She's lying!!!"* was about all I could muster out.

"*That's all right. And you might think you're 'slick,' but if you're doing any of what she says you're doing, we're gonna catch you! We'll get you! Yeah, we'll get you.*"

Motherfucker! This night was going from bad to worse! And about to get even stranger...

After about a half hour or so, another police officer came to transport me downtown to the jail; he was a young Black man about 5 or 6 years my senior and, I guess, he had done some investigating and witness interviews because he "snapped off" after he had me in the back of his car:

"*This is some bullshit! What man* doesn't *have more than one woman?!... You sitting here minding your own* goddamned *business and a motherfucker confront* you *and* you *going to jail?*!! *This is some goddamned bullshit! Motherfucker put they goddamned hands on* you *first but* you *going to jail?*! *Goddamned bullshit!... Goddamned women just think they can do anything to a goddamned man and we supposed to* take *it?*"

Now understand – I hadn't said one single word. Not one. You think *I* was about to interrupt him while he was so pissed off? And *I* was the one going to jail. He continued:

"*And I don't give a fuck what you're doing in the streets – you think I didn't hustle to put myself through school and the academy? Man, fuck that! Keep doing what you doing but don't fuck with that bitch no mo! She trying to see you done in, man! Matter of fact, don't even say shit when we get in front of the commissioner – just let me talk!"*

He talked the entire short ride down to the jail. And again, I didn't say even one word.

Skipping ahead of the line and taking me in front of the commissioner, the officer went on to explain the incident (generally) in the same way that I just explained it to you: How I was a student at Fisk sitting with my girlfriend in my own vehicle on campus, then confronted by the mother of my child, assaulted, and then arrested after defending myself. The Night Court Commissioner looked confused as to what he was hearing, as did everyone else in the courtroom besides Tsawa there to press charges. So he (the commissioner) wanted to hear from me.

So, I explained more in detail all he had just heard from the officer – and how I just wanted Tsawa to stay away from me. I imparted how I was tired of getting stabbed and shot at and kicked and punched and slapped and forced to watch my girlfriends get hurt by this same young "innocent looking" woman, and that from there on out I was going to protect myself no matter who it was if they were trying to do me harm. I said I was just tired of it all.

The courtroom was completely silent as the commissioner stared at me for a few seconds to discern if I was telling the truth. Then he turned to Tsawa:

"Young lady, did you hit this young man first?"

"Yeah, but he shouldn't think he can just keep fuck-"

"Young lady, if you ever put your hands on this young man again, you will be arrested for assault. And if you ever step foot on Fisk University's campus again, you will be arrested for criminal trespass!" Turning then to the officer and I, he said, *"I will not be granting*

this warrant and young man, you are free to go!"

Free to, *huh*?! Free to *what*? Free to *go*!?! What the hell just happened here?!

The officer immediately took me out of the handcuffs and escorted me safely out of the jail; and after not seeing Carvin or Trina, I decided to accept the officer's offer of a ride because, hell, why wouldn't I trust him at this point? Somewhat.

Pulling up to my Mom's house, I was completely surprised to see my truck in the driveway behind Carvin's car and find he and Jannah sitting inside. Needless to say, they were both just as surprised, seeing me walking through the door…

Tsawa, however, was not through with her vendetta against me by a long shot! Not only had I audaciously hit her ass back, but I also hadn't chosen her when pushed to decide between her and Jannah – for these things I had to be punished. So early the next morning I received a page from my answering service informing me of a message from my parole officer; I was instantly on alert because all of my fees were paid up months in advance and I wasn't scheduled to see him again until the next month. Returning his call,[128] he was pissed informing me that his supervisor had come down hard on him about my still being free; he said it was bad enough that he had homicide detectives consistently informing him that I was a suspect in numerous murders,[129] but now he had this young lady saying I was "beating on women, robbing people, selling drugs" and that I didn't even live where [I] told him [I] lived. He gave me "24 hours to get an order of protection and stay away from the woman" or he was "locking [my] ass back up!" So I did – at least the order of

---

[128] This was a new parole officer – a young Black dude about 5 years older than me who was also a grad student at Vanderbilt University.
[129] We used to argue about this a lot – I told him that all I did was "go to school fulltime, go to work fulltime, and fuck hoes fulltime" and if I was really out there like they said I was, wouldn't I be locked up already?!

protection part...

After that, there was no more of her punching, smacking, shooting at, or stabbing me; she knew that there would be consequences if she did.

Which is what I think every person – women included – should understand: you can't physically do harm to another and not expect them to fight back. Fuck that turning the other cheek shit because she's a woman. Had that woman at the college in Oklahoma pushed then choked *me*, I would have (rightly) hit her harder than that pilloried young football player that broke her jaw and other bones in her face did. Had my fiancée spit in *my* face after repeatedly punching me as the professional football player's did, before he knocked her ass out, shiddd, she would probably *still* be in a coma now. Because that shit is not cool in any shape, form, or fashion. As I mentioned earlier, I vowed to never put my hands on a woman to do her any harm ... but that is if she *also* upholds that vow *to me*. Don't do harm to me and I won't do harm to you, but harm me and I will be *damned* if I don't teach you to be more careful next time. It's as simple as that. And I don't care who likes it.

And that goes for the "authorities," too: you can't expect for us as a Black and Brown people to continue to be oppressed and killed in the streets without that same harm being returned your way. To hell with amerikkka; even the meekest and weakest person has a breaking point where they'll finally stand up to a bully. And ours as a people is soon coming.

Then this kkkountry will pay for the deaths of Sandra Bland, Eric Garner, Trayvon Martin, Oscar Grant III, George Floyd, Ahmaud Arbery, Breonna Taylor, etc.; then it will pay for the unjust enslavements of my brother, Glenn Ford, John Edward Smith, all the others, and myself. We will rage *undamned*...

"The moving force of history lies in the determination of the oppressed classes to free themselves from their condition. If that condition is intolerable and humanly admissible, the rebellious conscience becomes revolutionary..."

Cheik Anta Diop

On April 7, 2001, Timothy Thomas,[130] a nineteen-year-young unarmed Black man was shot and killed while running from police in Cincinnati, Ohio; Thomas was wanted for driving without a license and some other misdemeanor of like gravity. As the Cincinnati pig police force had killed at least fifteen other Blacks since 1995 – with four having been murdered within four months of Thomas' killing alone – the city's Blacks blew up in uprising. Two days of "rioting" followed, with shop windows broken, drivers pulled out of their cars and beaten, and – for the first time in amerikkkan history – Black "rioters" focused their attacks on an upscale predominantly white neighborhood. Hearing of this on the news at the time but really paying it no mind, less than nine months later I would find myself in this racially charged atmosphere "breaking the law."

However before I get into what led to my being convicted of five federal counts of "aiding and abetting bank fraud," let me say this while it's on my mind: For hundreds of year now – long before the election of the current narcissistic racist hypocritical coward sexual-assaulting piece of shit, the united snakes has put itself out to the world as the paragon of "human rights." Even in light of the genocide of the Natives, (continuing) enslavement and mal-abuse of Blacks,

---

[130] Of no relation (that I know of) to my family; "Thomas" is evidently just the name of the barbarian motherfukkker that claimed to "own" this young man's ancestors as one also claimed to own my own!

demonization of an entire religion (with over a billion worldwide adherents!), and its dehumanization of all the peoples that come from south of its border and other "shit hole" countries, the world has somehow continued to eat up this crock full of shit! But no more. Grab-em-by-the-pussy, his "supporters," and all those of his regime no longer even make a base attempt to mask their bigotry, brutality, callousness, white supremacist mentalities, or the blatant hypocrisy inherent in their brand of kkkristianity. The fact that the Fifth Ave Fuhrer clearly puts out to the world what amerikkka has *always* been has the "liberal" demokkkrats and more-decorum-minded republikkkans constantly "clutching their pearls" mouths agape in utter shame! Yet *not* at his actual underlying actions, but in the fact that he doesn't have the "decency" to mask them! President Bone Spur is an unapologetic "grab 'em by the pussy" type of guy. And I love it – let the world see it all!...

Furthermore, I hope/pray/wish/beg of the World to take this opportunity to witness even more what the united snakes is and always *has* been: send United Nations "Observers" to the Southern border and the I.C.E. "holding facilities" ("privately-owned" concentration camps!!!) to observe the human rights abuses there; send Observers to any random prison or jail (again, *more* concentration camps!) to witness the beatings, government-sanctioned and/or covered-up killings, and all-around dehumanization that occurs *daily*; send Observers to any one of the next few police shootings (because, let's be real – we *all* know more are coming!) of *un*armed *un*aggressive Blacks and Browns to witness these 21st-century public executions (crucifixions!); send Observers to look into the details of the enslavement of my brother and/or myself – or to witness any one of the thousands of kkkangaroo kkkourt proceedings that happen *daily* across this kkkountry that have resulted in the enslavement of more people in this land than a lot of countries have citizens! Please – I *beg* of The World – *please* take this opportunity to make a conscious effort to address the human rights abuses that occur consistently and constantly tens of thousands of times daily in the same land in which the United Nations has its headquarters!!!

Moreover, to all these whom believe in true justice, I say this: After Trayvon Martin, after Walter Scott, after Philando Castile, after Sandra Bland, after Sean Bell, after Alton Sterling and so many others in just recent memory, *none*, no one at all can be blind to or ignore what's happening to Black and Brown men, women, and children in this kkkountry![131] So, it's time to "put up or shut up" – to flee or to fight for our Creator-given rights as *human fucking beings*! As the Fifth Ave Fuhrer[132] said, "what exactly do we have to lose?!" No more "woe is me" whining, no more *begging* for "justice and equality," we have to *demand* what should have *always* been ours with no "compromises" and/nor *waiting* for our declared[133] enemies to all of a sudden find some *actual morality* and follow the "Golden Rule" that is *supposed* to be the foundation of their faith and/or laws! To *hell* with waiting any longer! I say shut this kkkountry *down*! No more participating in its military dominance and oppression of others; no more participation in its entertainment through music, sports, acting, etc.; no more participating in its ekkkonomy and/or kkkonsumerism that has led us *nowhere* in at least two generations since the so-called Civil Rights movement! Shut this motherfukkker *down* or continue to die and be exterminated like we are now!

---

[131] I, of course, wrote this before the murder of George Floyd and the subsequent uprisings.
[132] In my estimation, the perfect personification of what amerikkka truly thinks, feels, and does!
[133] Through it/their actions...

Or just leave. Just leave and get out of here if we're not willing to fight and we're not willing to continue dying and/or so-called "living" in oppression as we are now. Instead of a mass exodus from the South to the North of this kkkountry again (where "justice" *still* couldn't be found, we foolishly, quickly discovered!), how about a mass exodus to some land, some place, some people, some country(ies) that will *appreciate* our talents, our imaginations, our creativity, our tenacity in the face of centuries of brutality and oppression never known before in history, and, most importantly, recognize and respect our humanity?! And just let "them" have this kkkountry to themselves.[134] Because this kkkountry never has been "great" to *or* for us, nor will it ever be unless something fundamentally changes and soon! And when I say "soon," I don't mean within the next two or three generations but within the next two or three years because a couple more generations we do not have![135]

Think it's a "game," right? Think I'm over-exaggerating the problem/threat? Well tell that to what's left of the Natives of this land whom have to endure daily onslaughts of racist sports nicknames, desecration of what's left of "their land," and a yearly celebration of the genocide of their people every fourth Thursday in November! Ask them if the threat is real!

Ask every person like me that rots in prison for something that it's easy to see that they're innocent of! I wish we could've asked Glenn Ford before he died 15 months after finally being freed after enduring 30 years on Louisiana's death row suffering for something he didn't do, yet Alfred Woodfox is still around, ask him! Geronimo Ji Jaga Pratt, the Exonerated Five (whom Grab-em-by-the-pussy said should have been executed!),

---

[134] I mean, because – as an avowed aryan once asserted to me in a political/history discussion – they *did* "take it 'fair and square,'" right?!
[135] Again, I wrote this passage years before the current George Floyd uprisings sweeping the planet.

Amerikkka

Mumia Abu Jamal, the 15 wrongfully convicted men out of Chicago whom were released just late last year after they were found to have been set up by just one punkkk pig!136 The names go on and on and on...

So, put up or shut up, fight or flee, and whatever is decided, please don't forget about us souls and souljas trapped in these cages within cages waiting to join you in either a promised land of our own or a paradise in the beyond...

But back to what I was saying; where was I? Oh yeah – convicted of the five counts of "aiding and abetting bank fraud" in federal court in the Eastern District of Kentucky.[137] And (not that I would ever attempt to do so!) there's no getting around or dressing up the fact that I was guilty. And as such, I was convicted within 45 minutes from the start of deliberations on all five counts by an all-white jury.[138]

Nevertheless, I won't get into the details of my "crime."[139]

---

[136] And think about what the case of just that one pig says about how great the problem is! See, also, how just one pig decimated an entire community of Black people in Tulia, TX through imprisonment by lying (accusing them of being "drug dealers") a few short years ago.

[137] Although the case originated out of Cincinnati, Ohio, I was arrested across the Ohio River in Northern Kentucky, and since the case was linked to another set of charges out of Louisville and Lexington, Kentucky, the kkkourt with jurisdiction over where I was arrested handled the case.

[138] Notwithstanding one super honest "gentleman" being excused during voir dire (jury selection) after referring to me as a "nigger" when the judge referenced my being the only Black face in the kkkourtroom at that time. Like, who can make this shit up?

[139] Although, this is all public record – so for any interested parties you can check the trial transcripts, newscasts, and newspaper articles from January – April (?) 2002. Believe me, I have nothing to hide, baby! So, as to avoid damaging some (uncharged) others whom, at first sought me out to finance a venture of theirs, and then ultimately taught me the ways of the united snakes' banking system (that I would have never ever considered or suspected!) after they repaid my investment with a nice interest. Just understand that (at the time) I saw nothing wrong with what I was participating in, as it was explained to me that I should consider it "reparations" from the same people/companies/systems that had kept myself and my ancestors wallowing in enslavement and/or oppression since we were kkkidnapped to these shores. Not that I needed much convincing, mind you, as my back was against the wall anyway, in trying not only to keep myself free, but in also trying to figure out a safe way to purchase my brother's and others freedoms as well. So, I was "with it" with eyes wide

As I must now ask you: Is something inherently "criminal" about us (the Blacks and Browns of this kkkountry)? Or is it that this *system* is inherently set *against* us forcing us to rebel in ways now deemed "criminal"? The question is long past due and *must* be asked and *honestly* answered by us all.

Because politicians such as pantsuit kkklinton would have you believe that people such as I are "super predators" and just out-and-out socio-and/or-psychopaths. That we are the incorrigible, the unredeemable. Yet she/they have probably never taken into account that all that Blacks have *ever* had in this kkkountry is somewhat of a "conditional citizenship." Conditional being that we're only citizens when and how they (the ruling whites such as pantsuit!) *want* us to be! When they want to be entertained. When they want us to help defend them against some other people they've pissed off and/or oppressed. When they want us to sacrifice *our* lives for them in some type of weird and/or never-reciprocated way. Yet the color of our very skin has been "criminalized" from the very beginning. Think about what that would *do* to a people.

Therefore I opine that most, if not all, of we Blacks in this kkkountry unconsciously suffer from PTSD. However *our* PTSD doesn't stand for "post traumatic stress disorder," but instead *perpetually traumatic* stress and *despair*.[140] Because our traumas are incessant, endless, unceasing – and a lot of us, even if only subconsciously, have given up hope of things ever getting better in this life.

Therefore it's wild to me how, in this last national election, a majority of the Blacks and Browns that voted in this kkkountry

---

open – and it worked in my favor for a while. Until I (temporarily) lost my (laser) focus of what was and wasn't (but not *who* was and wasn't!) important – thrown off by the kkkonsumerism of a "holiday" that I don't even believe in – and (rightly so!) I was punished by "the game" with everything going "sideways" for me with my arrest.
[140] This despair is manifested in our alcoholism, drug use, "convenient-and-contradictory" religious views, and/or just overall self-destructiveness.

seemingly blindly followed pantsuit, her husband slick willie, and other demokkkrats when more Blacks and Browns were enslaved under *their* watch than at any other time in amerikkkan history.[141] Amazing. As if our lives would have actually been better somehow with *her* in power! Demokkkrats have promised that our lives would be changed for the better if they were re-elected my entire life, yet shit never changes for the better, only worse. Reminds me of a legal maxim I've learned over the years: *Adjuvari quipped nos, non decipi, beneficio oportet* – Surely we ought to be *helped* by a benefit, not be *entrapped* by it. I mean, just look at the lives of the everyday Black or Brown person; have things actually gotten better under the demokkkrats – especially the kkklintons – or worse? At least republikkkans don't make it a secret how they hold us in disregard and think we are the scum of the earth. That's why I'm actually happy that Putin's bitch won; his candidacy exposed that there's already a major social confrontation brewing in this kkkountry and I expect that crazy fucker to start some type of war with another country within the first year of his presidency[142] that will leave amerikkka with its ass kicked and us – the Black, the Brown, and the Natives – finally with the chance for some fundamental change in our lives.[143] Fuhrer Fifth Ave is the perfect representation of what the united snakes is now and has always been – arrogant, schizophrenic, delusional, hypocritical, and most important, dangerous to all others in the world

---

[141] And now – considering the choice between devil #1 and devil #2 – will soon vote to elect the very *architect* of our current predicament! Good grief!
[142] Sadly, this never happened as all other countries in the world quickly realized that Mr. Bone Spur was all bluff and no *bite*.
[143] Although a war with another country never jumped off, (Because of Grab-em-by-the-pussy's inherent cowardice in my opinion! I've met his type many times throughout my life – talk all of that bluster and bullshit yet back down like a bitch when it's time to throw down!) the George Floyd uprisings still gives us the chance to foment some fundamental change! I'm *very* encouraged!

"Black young men in American cities today are the primary targets for destruction – not only from drugs and police brutality, but from each other..."
Toward Black Empowerment by Manning Marable

HUSTLING

Exposed dirty white brick walls, windows with tattered covers over them, and a door leading to the hallway with four different locks and chains on it – less than 24 hours after my release from CCA and I was already in a dope house with a pack and pistol in my hands. Money Mac and Lil Man had left me alone to answer the door while they went out to pick up more "work." My release on parole had been granted 3 weeks to the day after I had turned 19 – October 17, 1996. By then I was closing in on six feet but still weighed a scrawny 140-150 lbs. However, I was strong of mind, and more importantly, I had a *plan*.

Picked up by my cousin Trina while walking away from the county prison, I can't even recall how she knew I had been released; I didn't know what day it would be myself, nor do I remember calling anyone that morning when they hurriedly told me to pack it up. At any rate, she was there, and I sure as hell appreciated her saving me the long ass walk to the hood.

Which at first I didn't think I would make. When that sweet ass white 70s model Nova with the deep-tinted windows, chrome pipes and rims, and slap[144] banging "FBI" by Top Authority crept up alongside me out of nowhere my first thoughts were "FUCK!!! ENEMIES!!!" My mind instantly raced as to whom I could have possibly pissed off to the point where they would try to smoke me right outside the prison???

---

[144] Loud ass music.

Moreover, how in the fuck did they even know I was being released??? FUCK!!! The window rolled down.

"*Get in, fool.*"

"*Damn, who this? This you, cuz???*"

"*Yeah, nigga, whose you think it is?*"

"*Pops said that you and Lennie was getting it, but I didn't know y'all was doing it like this!*"

She started laughing.

"*Aw, shit, this ain't nothing. You coming home at the right time. You'll see. We got ya.*"

"*Man, that's what's up!*"

I had no idea at the time that she wasn't bullshitting as to how they were getting money – and feeding me full of shit as to how they "had me" all at the same time. I would soon find out that neither her, Lennie, nor anyone else would be giving me shit. Which is not what I ever expected nor wanted from anyone anyway. Anything that came my way would have to be earned or *took*, which was one and the same to me anyway. But hell, that all fit into my plan.

"*So where you wanna go first?*"

"*Man, I need to see my Mama and then my Daddy.*"

"*That's a bet.*"

Pulling into Vine Hill with my mind, of course, on high alert, somehow things didn't look or feel the way I remembered them. The dumpsters were still full and smelly as hell, broken glass still littered the streets threatening flat tires, and the zombies were still out in full force on "tweek" mode (high as a cloud), but *something* was different. Maybe it was just my older eyes.

As always, my Mama's door was unlocked and the house was loud from the television; I walked right in – it taking a second for anyone to even notice me.

"I see y'all still don't keep the door locked, huh? Slipping!"

"DELOOOOO!!!"

My brothers and sister all ran and gave me a tight hug. It took everything I had in me not to cry; it had been awhile since I had seen them all.

"Where Mama at?"

"She still at work; she be here in a minute."

I took a seat and peeped how everything in the house still looked the same, but for some reason strange to me. I soon figured out what it was, though – I could no longer be satisfied with us living the way we had been living before I left. It was cool, however – just made me even more determined to put my plans into effect.

Observing everything and everybody, I couldn't help but to be impressed with Carvin; now 16-years-young, he seemed to be a whole hell of a lot smarter and mature than I was at that age. At sixteen, I was robbing and shooting people, selling dope, and was already living with what became my first wife; I could tell that he wasn't into any of that bullshit. That I could see at first glance, anyway. At the least, he was keeping whatever dirt he may have been doing hid well. I'd have to have a private talk with him later.[145]

My Mom was greeted to unexpected hugs and kisses from her visibly now older son.[146] Her newly-released "prodigal son." We let the tears flow freely and I visited with her for an hour or so before the whole scene replayed itself at my father's home with him (my Pops) now the joyous parent. Throughout my homecoming celebration(s) I could tell that they both had a

---

[145] Despite how I grew up and the path I took, I've never wanted either one of my brothers in the streets; not only was it hard for me to imagine them going through all that I have throughout my own travails, but a major part of what I was doing was to keep them from it. But of course it had the opposite effect, and they would inevitably follow my path.

[146] I now had somewhat of a *mustache*! And even a few chin hairs!

searing pride of me (why? – I don't know) and expectations as to how I would from then on live my life that they couldn't quite put into words...

But it wasn't my homecoming alone – it was also the weekend of TSU's[147] and the celebrations were in full-swing citywide in all the Black haunts, clubs, and neighborhoods. I would kick it that weekend with numerous cousins and friends that were excited that I was home – from Trina to Jolonda (whose birthday was the day I was released) and (Money) Mac, among others – who would take me shopping, take me out to eat, take me clubbing, and take me to "spend some time" with more than a couple "female companions" that expressed an eagerness to see me. The excitement of the weekend had me hyper as well – and I'm positive that I never shut my eyes for even 60 seconds while running off pure adrenaline alone.

Contributing to my adrenaline surge was the fact that I witnessed – along with maybe a couple of hundred other people including the metro police officers working crowd control – two cats get gunned down outside what I thought was a respectable "older folks" club near downtown; I would thereafter have to take over the wheel of the Nova to get away from the scene, as Trina was too "tipsy" to drive. Hours later I found myself in the dope house I earlier referenced "serving" for a couple hours, with customers coming as if we were giving the coke away for free. Later still, leaving yet another club because of a girl shooting this cat I knew from doing time, I found out the club was burned down seemingly as soon as the ambulances and kkkops left! This all in my first few days home! Hell, the city

---

[147] Tennessee State University – one of three HBCUs (historically Black Colleges and Universities) in nashville, along with Fisk University and Meharry Medical College. Fisk has historically been world renowned in a multitude of ways while Meharry, even to this day, continues to graduate more Black doctors than any college in this nation. TSU by comparison has all my lifetime been known as "the party school" in town, despite being the alma mater of Oprah Winfrey.

seemed even more "live" than I left it! And I would have to stay on my toes if I wanted to not only survive but thrive in it!...

That Monday I went, for the first time, to visit with my parole officer – who let me know in no uncertain terms that he generally didn't give a fuck; all he said was to "make sure [I] didn't get arrested," to always make sure [I] had a check stub for [him], and to not embarrass [him] in any kind of way" (whatever the hell that meant), which was all cool to me. He also admonished me to keep my parole "fees" paid up "at all times" – as falling behind on those would be "the quickest thing to send [me] back to prison." Cool on that, too. No problem at all...

I didn't waste any time in getting "about my hustle" – and I was coming home at a unique time in history: the availability of cocaine throughout the nation was at a seemingly all-time high due to the kkklinton regime being in power,[148] which allowed kkklinton to not only boost (if not underpin!) the uptick of the amerikkkan ekkkonomy, but to also bolster slikkk willie's image as a "good ol' true blue hard-on-crime Southern demokkkrat" by giving him the excuse/pretext to enslave more Black and Brown people since the amerikkkan "Civil War." And I fell right into the trap – going full-speed at coming up on the 5-10 cakes I felt it would take me to "maintain" how I wanted, and make the moves I had planned.

Instead of sharing with me a percentage of profit, Mac gifted me with all of the proceeds from my "holding it down" at the dope house while he and Lil' Man were away. It was only a few hundred dollars, but I reinvested $100 of it into a 3-gram "pack" (3 grams of what we called "ready" – i.e. crack cocaine

---

[148] I could purchase wholesale a "cake" (kilo) of coke for between $16,000-$20,000, dependent upon whom I was purchasing from, what city/state I was purchasing, and how many I was "copping." Florida and Texas, for me personally, had the highest quality coke for the best (cheapest) "tickets" at the time but I could still find some decent product in tennessee or Georgia for around $18,000 or $18,500.

– for its readiness to smoke and instantaneously get "high" off of), and, from there, I would jumpstart my plans.

I hit the projects on the Southside of which I was most familiar and commenced to "piecing out" my pack – selling "dime rocks" ($10) and "twenties" at roughly $50 a gram. However, "selling" may be too generous of a word as to what I was faced with – because in the open-air drug markets that were in the majority of "inner-city" Black neighborhoods all throughout this kkkountry at that time, all I had to do was be available by making myself seen and the crack would sell itself.[149] So after selling 2 of the 3 grams I started with, as soon as I made $100 I bought another 3 gram pack, leaving me with 4 grams; after banging (selling) all of that out, I was now able to purchase a "quarter-zip" (quarter ounce = 7 grams) for $200.[150]

Using the same concept with the quarter that I used with the 3 grams, I sold about 4, bought another quarter, so now I had 10 (grams). I would use this same concept – not spending a *penny* of my "hustle money" (profit or principal) for even food or clothing – to flip that first $100 into a "four and a split" (four and a half ounces), a little over a grand ($1,000) in the "stash," my own "duck off" (low key) apartment, and a couple of "Pack

---

[149] Just as I had to endure the constant and consistent solicitation from my white classmates in high school which finally pushed me to start selling powder cocaine and marijuana, the average Black male over the age of 10 would (at least in those days) endure multiple solicitations for crack cocaine daily just by being anywhere out and about in his neighborhood. What would that do to the psyche of even the most moralistic young man struggling to feed, clothe, and/or shelter himself? He would fall victim to "the game," too!. But I digress…

[150] At the time, almost anyone could easily purchase – just the same as buying groceries at Walmart – 3 grams for $100; a quarter zip (7 grams) for $200; a half-ounce (14 grams) for $375; a whole zip (ounce, i.e., 28 grams) for $700 - $725; 2 and a quarter (2 ¼) ounces for $1,500; four and a half (4 ½) ounces – known to us in my hood as a "four and a split" – for $2,750; 9 ounces (known to us as a "quarter bird") or a "quarter cake" for $5,000; a "half a bird" (18 ounces) for $9,500, a "whole cake" (a kilo, i.e. 1,000 grams or roughly 36 ounces) for $18,500, and so on and so forth.

Runners"[151] within a couple of months' time after my release. I primarily "copped" from three people in the city: a Northsider I dealt with through Mac; a Southsider, a few years my senior, that I knew from Edgehill and whom I dealt with directly, and another Southsider: known as "Big Al" whom was a family friend (and the best friend of my cousin Duck) – whom I sometimes used to deal with when putting my money together with my cousin Ca-Carl so that we could both take advantage of cheaper "tickets."

It wasn't before long, however, that I would transition completely out of the crack cocaine business and move primarily into powder cocaine and marijuana. For one, in 1996, after my release at the age of 19 from the CCA county prison, I was too soft-hearted to continue selling "crack" after a couple of months or so. Or at least to be successful at it. I was a sucker for a sad story or song when a "junkie" owed me money and I was always curious to hear the hows and whys and whats that led that person to smoking dope when it was easy to see how it had taken so many others down before them. And invariably, the commonalities were always undealt-with pain, abject depression, and extreme disappointment with what life offered and/or served them. Yet listening to the stories would invariably depress *me* as I couldn't help but consider the plight of my people. Ironic, huh? Selling crack to others wasn't healthy for *my* mental state...

To add to my reservations of dealing with the "smokers" anyway, my oldest cousin Raymond called from the feds to

---

[151] Dope Boy cars used to take me on my "runs" to "serve" my "bites." In the cities and states I frequented in the South and Midwest, these were typically mid-70s to late 80s amerikkkan-made metal that some fools would even be so silly as to fix-up with "bang" (booming stereo systems), rims, candy-colored paint jobs, and/or lush interiors that foolishly drew the wrong kind of attention to themselves! Me, I just kept it low key with a late 70s "True Blue" Chevy Malibu and an early 80s two-tone Blue Oldsmobile Delta 88.

inform me of a rumor he had heard that I was "walking the projects with an Uzi"[152] and to be careful not to get "caught up" because the feds were "flooding" the federal prisons with young Black men just like me on "convicted felon in possession of a weapon" charges that carried a mandatory minimum 5 years for every felony on a person's record. (That meant 15 years minimum for me – as I had violent felony convictions from the ages of 14, 15, and 17 respectively – and your juvenile record *does* count!) He also counseled me to be even more careful in my "hustle" – as there was a 100-to-1 ratio for crack as opposed to powder cocaine, meaning a person getting caught with a quarter-zip (7 grams) of "crack" would by law have to serve more time than someone who got caught with a half a cake of powder (500 grams)! For the same drug! As he went on to explain to me how it was a law targeted at Black folks (since we aren't the ones bringing it into kkkountry nor are we more likely to have larger quantities of it), and how it was also being used to flood the prisons with an entire generation of Black men like myself for decades of their lives, I knew then and there that my days of "crack dealing" were not too much longer in the making!

As the final nail in the coffin, I quickly peeped that "piecing crack" didn't serve my ambitions, anyway – as it was too slow[153] for the money I needed[154] in that most cats (that had been out there for the entire time I was "away") had regular customers that dealt with them exclusively, and they could afford to give customers more dope than I since they had "bigger packs." But I soon saw my "lane." Since most hustling

---

[152] It wasn't an Uzi, however, but instead a Glock 17 9mm with an extended 30-round clip – and it wasn't even mine! I only had it in my possession for a week or so, and it's not like I was walking around brandishing it, so how he had even heard about it in the feds, I have no idea. But he always had connections and kept his "ears to the streets" in some way.
[153] Too many individual sales required!
[154] *Wanted*, if I'm being completely honest here!

cats (at least 90%, in my observation) in the city had habits themselves of either powder cocaine and/or marijuana, I would start serving *them*! And that's what I did. I didn't have a "weed" and/or "white" habit, but I sure as hell didn't mind servicing *theirs*! So, after quickly relieving myself of the rest of the "ready" I possessed after Raymond's conversation with me, I invested all of my money into marijuana and powder cocaine and set myself up as the "weed and white" man. Let *those* fools serve all of the "smokers," and I, in turn, would serve all of the fools! Soon some of the older cats – some that had been selling drugs in the hood since before I was even a teen – would be buying their packs from me! I didn't even have to make a profit, initially, when I first started selling "weight," in that I was just making cats comfortable with purchasing their "work" from me! Then, after a business trip or two as near to "the source" as I could get in this kkkountry, my profit margin would be *enormou*s as I had already built up my clientele! That's how I "came up!"

And to clarify my thoughts, in my opinion, there's nothing inherently wrong with the selling of drugs nor with the using[155] of drugs themselves; all that this kkkountry calls "drugs" can be considered in the alternative as medicine or poison, dependent upon its use and dosage. Think about it. It's the same with food – in just the right amounts, it's a life-sustaining sustenance, yet if you overdo it, it's called gluttony and could even cause you cancer and kill you.

Same with tobacco and alcohol. Think about why those two "drugs" are legal, while others such as marijuana, cocaine, and heroin are not. Could it be because the "powers that be" understand that not only have they found ways to regulate their commerce (tobacco and alcohol), but also that it can be grown

---

[155] Although I've never been one to indulge in "drug use" personally because I think "getting high" is utterly pointless. At least it is for me.

and produced in this kkkountry as opposed to the poppy plants that only grow primarily in Afghanistan or Russia, or the coca leaves that are native to South America. So it's a win-win-win for this kkkountry by opposing the legalization of such products: demonization of a "developing" country's native crops, thereby making it even harder for it to rise out of poverty; the raising of revenues by this kkkountry actually being the one to import the drugs surreptitiously; and then, the incarceration and ultimately eradication of an entire group of undesirables for selling the same "illegal drugs" that it imported into the kkkountry in the first place! So it's not the *selling* of drugs that's wrong to me, but the way that we've allowed them to be used against us.

We've allowed this kkkountry to demonize an entire generation of our youth with the now derisive term "drug dealer." "Drug dealer" is tossed around to justify the harassment of our youth, the beating of our youth, the incarceration of our youth, even the murder of our youth. All of this is unwarranted and we've fallen for it. Just like the false cries of "rape of a white woman" in the not-so-distant past, now it's "drug dealer" and to a growing extent, "gang member." However, we've got to realize that these same "drug dealers" and "gang members" are our sons, fathers, brothers, uncles, cousins, and friends and we should *never* allow this kkkountry to turn us against them.

And another thing, no one forces anyone else to use drugs in my experience. Fuck what you see in the movies. More importantly, though, no one forces another to *abuse* drugs. Just as no one else forces a person to eat fast food day-after-day so that you catch heart disease or colon cancer; and no one is putting a gun to your head to smoke pack after pack of cigarettes and catch lung cancer, using "drugs" is something one does of their *own* free will, and if one abuses it, then you know, that falls on the shoulders of personal responsibility to me. It was *your* choice to smoke the blunt, to hit the powder, to shoot the dog food into your veins, to smoke the rock. As such, it's up to no one else to deal with the consequences or repercussions of *your* actions. And you can take that how you want to take it.

You know, it truly amazes me, how time and time again, we've allowed this kkkountry to scapegoat the Black and/or Browns for the ills that it (this kkkountry) has so clearly caused *itself*! Not once in my lifetime – not even one time in either the streets or prisons where I've either "hustled" or watched others do so – have I observed *one* person try to push or force or pressure some "dope" off on another! Not *once*! *That* shit only happens on television and/or in the movies! Or maybe that's a "white community thing" or something?! Because what I *have* observed time and time again, what I *have* noticed, what I *have* experienced are *white* people – young *and* old, male *and* female – solicit almost any and every young Black male to sell them some type of drug! Pick any 5 random Black men who's ever lived in any "inner-city" neighborhood in this kkkountry, and I can almost guarantee you that at least *4* have stories (*multiple* – not just one!) of being approached *unsolicited* by a random white person to sell them some drugs! And after one or two instances, what do you expect a "starving" man to do?! Hell, even I myself, had *never* sold cocaine or marijuana until *after* I was repeatedly approached by my white classmates in Honors Classes to buy some! Think about that shit. Just *think* about it! Now back to what I was saying!...

Jumping "head first" into the weed-and-white game, it didn't take me long either to notice that most cats had "the game" twisted – in it for the fame and not the "fetti." But me? – I was on a paper chase – and the fame I let the "suckas" chase.[156]

Because I look at it like this: if you're involved in something that you know can send you to prison for years, even decades out of your life, just *why* would you want to broadcast that fact to the world? Makes no sense, does it? Why make yourself a target for the women out "sack chasing" looking for a man to save them?[157] Or the jackers looking for a nice lick to hit? Or even the pigs looking for a bust to justify their slave patrols?

---

[156] Outside of picking up from work a dancer friend of mine from one of the city's well-known strip clubs a few times here or there when she and I wanted to "kick it" for the night, that first weekend after my release would be the last time anyone would see me in any clubs. Nor was I flashy with my cars or clothing, as I considered all that "highsiding" (showoff) bullshit for "new money" cats anyway. And even though I may have "gone broke" a time or two, relative to what I had grown accustomed to over the years, by then I hadn't been "new" money for quite some time. Leave that "stunt on" (impress) the hood shit to everybody else.

As far as my cars, I was much more concerned with "runners" (vehicles that ran strong, comfortably drove, and "kept up" well) than I was having the most expensive car with the most expensive rims and paint jobs and music systems – that type of attention would actually be a detriment to my safely reaching my goals. Same with my clothing: my usual daily attire was long- or- short sleeve "Dickie" shirts and khaki-type pants; "Gangster" Nikes (in the spring and summer) or Timberland-types boots (in the fall and winter), and a full-body "snowsuit" when the winter hit. The whole point of my "uniform" was that my mind and focus were completely on getting to work accomplishing my goals. Fuck wasting my money on the (get-me-nowhere!) newest fashions! (And when I did "dress up" – say, for instance, for a date or something – then it was in a lowkey "understated elegance" pretty boy/preppy type style. If that makes any sense to you.) And as far as jewelry, I wore none besides a simple watch and earrings – all of that flashy bullshit I had left alone (shortly before getting locked up in the Juvenile tank at CJC) after my Aunt Carlene passed away and I embarrassingly couldn't make it through the hospital's metal detectors to be with my family until after taking all my diamonds and gold off.

[157] Any man, it doesn't even really matter who. Sack chasers don't give a damn what a man looks like, what his dreams and nightmares are, who he's been with before her, how many kids he already has that he doesn't take care of, nothing; all a sack chaser cares about it that sack and how much she can benefit from the profits of it. Reminds me of a quote by the author (and former Harlem "hustler") Azie Faison: "There are two types of women. Those who recognize the qualities a man brings to the table, like being honest and hardworking, and those who judge a man by his finances." That says a lot, doesn't it? I say we can heal our community from this way of thinking – Men and Women, both – by adopting a lot of the techniques/strategies espoused in the book, *Black Love is a Revolutionary Act* by the authors Umoja.

So I was determined to play the game and not let the game play me. Support myself while I was going to school, make sure my mother, father, and little brothers, sisters, and cousins didn't want for any pressing need, and stack me a little money to get my business up and running when I graduated, and I was cool.

Yet even though I loved the fact how some other cats loved playing front street, the fame found me anyway. Or should I say the infamy?

One day, out and about in Vine Hill, Mac hit me up stating that he needed to rap with me about something; for some strange reason he wouldn't tell me what it was over the phone. When he made it over my Mom's house, he informed me that some cats (that I had grown up with, I should mention!) over in The Village thought that I had robbed them. *What???* Any fool that knew me knew that I would never rob anyone on the Southside, where I lay my own head, where I was even *related* to most of the people in some way or another, the side that *made* me, and which I considered "*home*."

How did these idiots even conclude that it was I that had robbed them? Ironically, during the robbery one of the jackers dropped a beeper. Once a page came through, Boo and Hershel – the cats that had gotten jacked – called the number back asking the caller whom she was trying to reach? Why the bitch said "Delo," I'll never know, but say it she did. And unbeknownst to me, these fools were planning a retaliatory hit when Mac overheard them plotting. Still around them when he had called me, that's why he couldn't tell me what it was over the phone. (The idiots didn't even realize that they were talking around a family member of mine; people would be surprised how often this happens when you have a family as large as my own.)

Mac, myself, and Trina – who was on her way to hook up with me, anyway – rode up to The Village to clear the air; and even though they were there themselves, Frog spoke on behalf of Boo and Hershel, as we got down to the bottom of not only why I was suspected, but also more importantly, whom had actually pulled the move in the first place. Because now I was down to ride on *them* for putting me in the mix – even if it was inadvertent.

"*D, I know how you get down,*" Frog said, "*I know you bar none. If you say you didn't have nothing to do wit' it, then that's just what it is.*"

They all knew what the deal was; first of all, Hershel and Boo both knew who I was, and more importantly for this situation, what I looked, walked, and talked like. Hell, we all used to play together when we were younger. Nevertheless, we hadn't seen each other in years, since at least before I had to go off and do those two years. Plus, whoever that bitch was, *had* put my name in the mix.

So I really couldn't knock them for trying to see what was up with me; good thing for them, though, is that I caught the word before they made any aggressive moves. Because then – mistake or not – I would've struck back ten times *harder.* That's just my nature. Hit me, I hit you back harder with enough force to deter not only *you* from ever fucking with me again, but *also any other motherfucker that may have been watching, also.* Fuck turning the other cheek – you shouldn't have struck me in the first place. I'm not quick to instigate or bully someone,[158] but if you fucked with me, the last thing I would do is back down. And I've been that way my entire life.

So, like I said, *they* knew what was up. Because again, if I *had* done it, I sure as hell wouldn't be coming to "clear the air" – I stand on *every* move I make. They knew that much, at least. So, I left The Village that day thinking all was cool, surprised a few months later as to how this particular accusation would set

---

[158] Ironic, isn't it? Seeing as how I used to *rob* people, huh?

my already infamous reputation ablaze; shit would soon revisit me in ways I never would have imagined.

Later I found out who the bitch was whom had thrown my name in the mix and asked her ass why she erroneously said she had paged *me* on that pager? After receiving nothing but evasive non-answers, I could only conclude that she was either: A), protecting the real robbers and just threw my name out there to deflect the blame (and given my reputation at the time this wouldn't have been *too* much of a stretch!); or B), paging both I *and* the robbers at the same time, and made an honest mistake when those fools that got jacked called. Either way, the dirty bitch never would tell me what the truth was, although I would've liked no more than to give her the benefit of the doubt as I *thought* that she and I were on the road to becoming good friends. Since the incident she's gone on to give birth to twins by this cat that I used to somewhat hang with at that time; matter of fact, now that I think about it, he and I met her at the same time, however they took it to another level while she and I kept it friendly seeing as how I and a cousin of hers used to "kick it." And as far as her man, well we naturally drifted apart once I was able to see that he was still on that same bullshit we were on as 15-year-olds while I got on my grind with the greenery and coke. Last I saw of him was on the news with a warrant out for his arrest for robbing a pizza man – at the age of *35!*...

Even the best laid plans can be derailed or altered by necessity when the Universe throws you one of life's "curveballs." My life was no different – as I had no intention whatsoever of involving myself in any serious relationships for quite some time after I made up my mind to divorce Soyayya.[159]

---

[159] I didn't even seek her out after my release on parole; only after running into my older homeboy Kerry P. at a gas station or something during (TSU's) Homecoming weekend did I unexpectedly receive a call from her while over my father's house. Her

Yet the Universe had other plans, and I soon found myself "falling" for a young lady named Tsawa.

We had met shortly before my campaign of craziness in '94, when Mac had driven the wrong way down a one way residential street,[160] which resulted in our receiving a "cussing out" by two beautiful young ladies with mouths even fouler than ours. Crazy enough, that was somehow attractive, and I started "talking to" Tsawa, while Mac kicked it with her "cousin," Trecie. Although she and I shared a few kisses before I met Soyayya, once I did, (meet Soyayya) our contact faded away. Until we started school that fall, when she and I became really "cool" while she and Mac then started "talking" themselves. (Even she and Soyayya became cool, as she used to come over to our house with Mac sometimes.) After I got locked up in '95 in the Juvenile Tank, she and I started somewhat "talking" again with me calling her regularly, us writing each other numerous times, and even her coming to visit me a couple of times.[161] And after I came home, she was one of the young ladies "eager" to see me.

Yet I don't think she expected us to get "serious" any more or less than I did; for one, she had not one but *two* other men she was involved with in some way,[162] on top of her "indulging

---

receiving the "cold shoulder" over the phone, she wouldn't understand that she no longer held any sway over me until she received an even colder shoulder in person. I spurned all of her advances, her offer to take me shopping, her wish for me to meet her child, and even for her to come inside to sit and "talk." I told her that all I wanted from her was her signature on the divorce papers once I got the money up to file them.

[160] Isn't that odd?! It was actually one street split down the middle by trees with some apartments on one side and houses on the other. She lived in one of the houses.

[161] Despite her being underage (almost 2 years younger than me) as I was myself. She had a grownup "aunt" whom brought her to see me – and also to see who in the hell I was and why did Tsawa have so much interest in me!

[162] One from the neighborhood whom she had "broken up with" only a couple of days before I came home, and another cat – an Eastsider a few years older than I – whom I had just left at the county prison.

in" some shit that I made clear that I "wasn't with" nor did I consider "ladylike." Nevertheless with her not "indulging" when she was around me – and eventually leaving it alone completely[163] – along with her statements that she didn't "go with" either of the two cats any longer, I decided to go with "the flow" and let things go as they may.

So we went with "the flow" – with the flow ending up being her mom dropping her off to me over my Pop's house every morning before she went to work; after a couple of weeks of this, eventually Tsawa started dropping her mom off (at work – not to me!) and keeping the car herself. With that, she would drive me around allowing me to take care of random business I had to take care of and this really allowed me to hasten the process of "getting myself together." Tsawa would even be the one to take me to get my driver's license in her mother's car.

Soon she was spending the night with me over my Pop's house and/or in hotels, more times a week than she was actually staying at home. Much like Soyayya and I, Tsawa and I eventually started spending more of our time together than apart, and her mother offered no objections (that I knew of) when she moved with me to our first apartment together on Decatur Street.[164] This is where she would become pregnant – with both of us instantly feeling something "unusual" when a little of my life force left me and entered her.[165]

But want to hear something crazy? Until we found out she was pregnant, she and I were not "officially in a relationship."

---

[163] Although I never really believed she ever stopped some of what I disagreed with!
[164] She was still only 17, so her name wasn't on the lease – but she stayed there every day that I did.
[165] Neither she nor I ever took any precautions against her getting pregnant, nor do I remember us ever talking about birth control despite having sex numerous times every day. I honestly didn't think I could have any children after not being able to get Soyayya pregnant (and her subsequently getting pregnant soon after I was locked up!) – and I'm sure *that* discussion came up – but I really just think that Tsawa and I "didn't care" in "going with the flow."

Why not? For a multitude of reasons – with most of those reasons centering around my distrust of her and/or her actions.

For one, again, she and Mac had "talked" for a while after she and I faded away from each other our first time around, and no way in hell was I claiming as "mine" a woman whom had been sexually with a cousin or homeboy of mine – that shit was/is too close for comfort. A woman's past is a woman's past – as long as that past doesn't involve someone so close to me. But after reassurances (separately) from both she and he that they never did anything more than kiss a few times, I continued to let what she and I had "flow."[166]

Much more of a hindrance to our getting together, however, was the narrative of how she claimed to have broken up with her (Eastside) boyfriend: She said that she had warned him that if he "was ever locked up again, then it was over between [them]"; after he, in fact, did get re-incarcerated shortly thereafter, then "he [knew] what it [was]" so there was no need to have any further discussion about it. Evidently, he didn't get the memo, however, since he continued to claim her to everyone as "[his] girl." I can understand his confusion, still and all, since she continued to write him and accept his collect calls, send him money, keep in touch (at least weekly) with his mother and sister, and visit him (after she turned 18) periodically throughout his entire incarceration. Therefore I knew what the deal was with that.

The thing about her (Eastside) boyfriend is this, though: He's the one that inadvertently brought she and I closer together. With his *words*. Because had she not shown me the coward's letter where he was talking about "popping on" me even though I was "cool as hell," then maybe she and I would

---

[166] Although I was very much aware that she would/could possibly lie to me about the situation, Mac had no reason at all to do so. He and I never lied to each other – and especially about something like that.

have "kicked it" only a few times instead of every chance I got after I read what he said.[167] In hindsight, maybe that (us "kicking it tougher") was the whole point in her showing me his letter — as I can think of no other good reason as to why she did it.

Nonetheless, even more of an obstruction to us "being together," in my eyes, was her "overly enthusiastic excitement" at the appearance of her numerous male "friends." After asking her "what the fuck was that?!" following her flagging down a car full of cats I didn't necessarily "get along with" as she and I were hanging out in the drive in Edgehill – and her seeing no problem with it even after I explained it – then I just knew that there was no way in hell I could ever trust her completely with my heart. No way in hell.

Yet still she and I continued to "kick it" – with her growing more and more possessive the more we did so. She would never fail to make a show of me being "hers" when she and I were out and would even slap the hell out of me when she thought I was "looking at" another woman. I would "express my concerns" in a "threating tone," yet all that ever did was seem to "turn her on." She would inevitably "make it all up to" me and explained (more than a few times) that she acted that way because she was "catching feelings" for me. As I was (surprisingly) "catching

---

[167] Although she had informed me of having a "dude" when she and I reconnected when I was in the Juvenile Tank, she always referred to him by his "government" name instead of his "street" name. So after I met him at the CCA county prison, I never associated the two of them together until after he and I got somewhat "cool" after hooping together a few times, and he thereafter asked me if I knew "[his] gal Tsawa" since I was from Out South. I did. Well. I then (naively) showed him some recent pictures of her that *he* didn't have and then went to the phones to call her since he didn't have her new number and couldn't get in touch with her that way (over the phone). After letting him converse with her for a couple of minutes, I then finished the rest of the 30-minute phone call conversing with her myself. In hindsight, I can see how he (evidently) was offended by the entire episode, yet he should have just "brought it to me" when he was right there with me in the same pod in the same prison instead of cowardly going to write her a letter threatening harm to me yet *never saying anything sideways to my face.*

feelings" also, I was "all confused" as I had never been in a situation like that before.

Additionally, I let go of most (but not all) of my apprehensions after we became pregnant – and even more so after she informed her (Eastside) boyfriend (in front of me, over the phone) of our coming child. Nonetheless the pregnancy caused her to become even more possessive, with a corresponding increase in irrationality and violence.

For the record, I've always liked intelligent and headstrong women; a woman who not only challenged me be a better man in some way, but also whom I can have decent conversations with outside of the bedroom, too. And Tsawa was, no doubt, a young woman in that mold; a young woman whose intellect was probably unmatched by any other up until that point. Yet her propensity for violence (when angered, upset, or feeling "disrespected" in some kind of way) and vengeance was unrivaled, also – far outmatching my own, in my opinion – and never something I would have expected in a beautiful young woman. Check it:

Shortly after we moved in on Decatur, my homeboy Tonio was finally coming home from prison. Tonio was one of my oldest and best friends and I'd already discussed with Tsawa how I would pick him up from prison and help him get himself settled. So, no problems, right? Wrong! After picking him up as we had previously discussed – and calling her every hour or so to "check on" her and update her as to when I would be home – she still had it in her head that I was "out fucking off" after I turned her down for sex! (No bullshit! This is my life!) I admit that that was a first for she and I – and probably a first in my entire life with any woman – but I was generally tired after I came home and knew I had to get up early in the morning for work.[168] No way was I about to let down Todd and Peggy (whom had just promoted me to "assistant manager") by being late to work, plus Tsawa and I had already made love a couple of times that day, so I didn't see what the problem was.

Besides, she and I *always* had our morning showers together – all it was was that I was really fucking tired! Not to mention a little depressed: with Tonio being released on parole he had to "register" at the downtown jail – and that shit was more than a little "let down" noticing all of those people looking just like him and me being marched through in handcuffs to start the process of enslavement that he and I both were still struggling to fully complete! The sight of that shit drained my spirit. Besides, while I'm thinking about it, let me be clear about something here: No one – men *nor* women – has the right to force a person to have sex with them! No one! Period! Each body is our *own* to do as *we* please! And that means saying "no," no matter how much it might hurt a motherfucker's feelings!

So, I said "no" by telling her I just wanted to "get some sleep." But that wasn't to be allowed, so every time I found myself "drifting off," I was shaken or elbowed awake. After repeatedly explaining (because of her interrogation) that I hadn't been "fucking off" yet still disbelieved and kept awake, I decided that the only way I would be getting any sleep that night would be somewhere else.

"*Where the fuck you think you going?*"

I had already moved from our bedroom to the living room,

---

[168] After a few weeks where I had filled out at least 20-30 applications for employment, my parole officer threatened me with re-incarceration if I didn't come to our next visit having verifiable employment. So, I changed my strategy on finding a job – now I would no longer admit on the applications that I was a "convicted felon" and I would also accept any job that I could get – even "fast food." I also badgered family and friends to "get me on" where they worked. This culminated in my homie Sin getting me an interview at the Dairy Queen where he worked in the mall. I aced the interview and the two owners, Todd and Peggy, gave me a chance and would subsequently end up becoming some of my biggest supporters in life.

but she wouldn't allow me sleep there either.

"Well, you won't be taking one of the cars," she said snatching my keys.

"Man, I just want to get some sleep, man! Goddamn!"

I guess she thought that would keep me there or make me fight, but I just said "fuck it" and walked out the door.

By now it's maybe 2 a.m. and I had no earthly idea where I was going. As I neared J.C Napier projects, I thought about the fact that I was unarmed and contemplated going back. (Yeah, that's what I'm going to do and just go ahead and "fuck" her – and she can't even blame me if I fall asleep mid-act). Then she pulled up alongside me.

"Delo, baby, I'm sorry," she said rolling the passenger window down, *"I'mma let you get some sleep."*

"Man, fuck you – you tripping!"

"Baby, just get in the car and come on home. I promise I'll let you sleep!"

"Fuck you!"

Now why in the hell did I say that? Why in the hell didn't I just get in the car if I was about to turn around anyway?! Stupid. Just fucking stupid!

"Delo! You get three seconds to get in the motherfuckin car before I start shooting!"

Well, goddamn. Didn't expect that.

"One!...Two!...Three-"

I broke out around the side of a building – and shortly thereafter heard shots.[169]

Running across the streets and entering the projects, I

---

[169] Now, I'm going to be completely fair to Tsawa here, and admit that I never actually *saw* her shooting at me – I was too busy running for my life! And out of the numerous times over the years we've discussed (and even laughed about) this night, only *once* has she slipped up and ever even admitted that she had one of my guns. So, I'll give her the benefit of the doubt, and admit that it's *possible* that someone else fired off shots that night. Yeah, it's "possible."

jumped fence after fence trying to get away from her. And she was *coming* too! – with the cats posted up on the block warning me as she circled through the drive at least a couple of times. I found myself hiding behind buildings, on the side of waste dumpsters, behind bushes, and even in bus shelters – all in an effort to keep her from (at worst) killing or (at least) maiming me somehow. By the time I somehow made it to my cousin Renee's project in University Court without getting shot or run over, it was almost 4 a.m. and I collapsed on her couch.

But want to know something crazy? Although I was "cautiously scared," I wasn't "*scared* scared," do you know what I mean? True enough, I felt she would have hurt me somehow had she caught me that night, but I doubt if she would have *purposely* killed me. Am I making any sense? Because she *loved* me, she wouldn't have wanted to *lose* me in killing me, so she only wanted to "teach me a lesson." Or so I foolishly and egotistically thought then. Because let's reverse the roles and see how it plays out then: ... What if *I* had demanded sex from *her* in order to prove that *she* hadn't been "fucking around"? What if *I* then snatched her keys from *her* because I didn't want her to leave?! What if *I* had demanded for *her* to get in my car after she left anyway – and then threatened to shoot her when she refused?! What if I was the one constantly smacking and hitting *her* then apologizing and "making it up to her"?! I would be excoriated as a "woman beater," wouldn't I? The absolute scum of the earth! But because she's a *woman* and I'm a big, bad, thuggish *man* (who albeit, had vowed long before meeting her to "never hit a woman"), this entire situation and others similar to it were met only with hilarity by all those who came to know about it. Hell, even *I* laughed about it at the time – excusing all of her actions because she was "drove to it" because she "loved me so much." Insane, huh?

So, it was that I found myself later that morning about 6 a.m. greeted at my door with a smile and a kiss and a face that acted as if nothing had ever happened.

"Man, you fucking crazy," I said, involuntarily returning her smile and kiss.

"Boyyy, you know I love yo' ass – you just keep driving me to do shit," she returned.

"Yeah, alright – I'm gonna get tired of that bullshit and fuck you up one day."

"Yeah, right – you ain't gonna hurt me," she said, and all I could do was smile.

What a few hours, right? She had my clothes out for work, food for me ready to eat, and she soon joined me in the shower. Up until I knew she was satiated, I still thought she was plotting to kill me, but after that, my only thought was "she loves me to death." That says it all, huh?...

My relationship with Tsawa was the most tumultuous I could ever possibly imagine having with someone in this life. It's hard to believe all of the twists and turns we've taken, all of the bullshit we thrust upon each other and endured, and had it not all happened between she and I, I wouldn't believe a tenth of the story if it was someone else telling it to me about their life. Yet she's a woman whom I'll always love and care for even if it's only safe for me to do so at a distance. Furthermore, she's more spiritually beautiful than she allows herself to ever show. Her painful past[170] causes her to hide it all, however. But underneath that "don't give a damn," nonchalant attitude and exterior lies a good woman if only she'd allow herself to be more vulnerable sometimes. *That* woman beneath all the bullshit, drama, and vindictiveness is the young woman I fell in love with oh so long ago for as short a period of time as she allowed me to see *that*

---

[170] of growing up without a father in her life, in my opinion.

woman and whom I still love and appreciate for giving me one of my most treasured gifts in life: my first-born son Kyree...

Messing around with Tsawa wouldn't be the only time I would come under gunfire in what I felt was a relatively mundane situation: Getting a page from Vell, I returned his call to find out that he "needed to holler at" me after I got off work. Making my way to the apartments where he and his Moms lived shortly thereafter, I pulled up to find him and his partner Jay posted up on the curve.

"*What's good?*"

"*I think I might have an issue with some niggas (on the other side of the apartments).*"

"*An issue? What kind of issue?*" I said.

Jay started talking, explaining that there was "some bitch" that had "been going back and forth" between Vell and one of the other cats "on some bullshit"; the more he talked, the more it seemed to me that he was the "bitch" that had "been going back and forth."

"*Look, cuz – we ain't got time for none of that he-say she-say bullshit! We supposed to be out here getting money! Didn't you say you and the nigga used to be cool?! Let's just go holla at the nigga and squash that dumb shit!*"

Silly as hell not knowing how to handle a simple situation! I understand that, as men, we may sometimes have "disagreements" with other men, but not every disagreement need be dealt with violently. *Firmly*, yes – but violently? – not *all* the time. Because once violence is introduced, "all bets are off" – I'm a firm believer in returning violence tenfold when it was served upon me unrighteously.[171] So thinking in that vein, I

---

[171] The only exceptions to this rule were women and those "I had love for" such as family and "innocent children." But this way of thinking would leave my brain and heart "scrambled" like eggs (not knowing how to function or respond) in the very near future when some very serious violence and betrayal would be served upon me

believe in dealing with problems when they're *small* problems – and effectively enough to avoid them growing larger. No sense fighting a grown grizzly in the future if you can kill it as a cub.

So, I drove Vell and Jay to the other side of the apartments where they said the cats were usually hanging out; it was damn near as quiet as a ghost town, but at the time I didn't think anything of it.

"Where are they?" I asked, as I was turning around to return the way we came.

"I don't know; they usually out here all the time."

Then I noticed about 7-8 cats come from either the side or behind a building I had already passed.

"Is that them?" I asked, watching in my rearview and slowing down even more than the speed bumps already had me.

"Yeah, that's them," said Vell, and I completely stopped halfway over a speed bump.

But wouldn't you know? – shit started to get hectic:

"What the fuck is he – Is he pulling out a…?"

I couldn't even get it all the way out. BOOM! BOOM! Well, I'll be damned – right about now is when I start to think that the situation is a little bit more serious than the way Vell and Jay had explained it – because these goddamned gunshots were starting to ruin my day! And I hadn't even *noticed* myself bleeding yet! BOOM! BOOM!

"They shooting! They shooting!" one of the motherfuckers in the car with me said.

Can you believe that both of them were "strapped" – yet trying to disappear into the floorboards?!

"I know they shooting, motherfucka! Hell, shoot the fuck back!!!"

I had slowly started to drive off by then (goddamned

---

by some people I loved more than my very life. Shit is still a "mindfuck" even over 20 years later.

speedbumps!), but do you think either one of those bastards shot back? Within seconds, I pulled up in front of Vell's house.

"*Man, y'all get the fuck out!*"

"*What you 'bout to do?!*"

"*Man, just get the fuck out!!!*"

I was fucking furious! But then I noticed something sticky flowing down my ear and neck, so then I became fucking enraged!!! These! Mother! Fuckers!!! These motherfuckers had drawn blood! Whether from glass, shrapnel, or buckshot? – I didn't know, didn't give a fuck, didn't take the time to find out – I'm about to get their asses back!!!

That's all I was thinking as I rode back and forth on a (somewhat busy) side street flanking the apartment complex[172]– fuck if the police were on their way or anything! Finding the bastards I was seeking my second or third time up and down the street, I hit the brakes, emptied the clips, then drove the fuck off...

What happened after that? Well, I made my way safely to a nearby friend's house and let her put her nursing skills to work cleaning and sanitizing my superficial wounds. And after a couple of hours of not hearing anything "hectic" from Vell, I made my way where I needed to go and "ducked off" that particular vehicle.

How many of them had to visit the hospital for a time to nurse their injuries, I honestly don't know – and the fact that none of us went to jail (that I know of) behind this incident, I have no idea how that was possible. And at the time, shiddd, I couldn't have cared less about going to jail behind this clash, anyway. These fools violated *me* of all people, my prideful arrogance thought. And for that they had to be punished.

---

[172] No way would I drive right back into another trap through the apartments, of course!

Amerikkka

Consequences be damned…

"Only one-fourth of the sorrow in each man's life is caused by outside uncontrollable elements; the rest is self-imposed by failing to analyze and act with calmness..."

George Jackson

BODY BLOW

"THOMAS! ATTORNEY VISIT!" the overseer called.

Attorney visit? I wonder what the hell this was about? Couldn't be good news. Hell, it had only been a couple of days since I was convicted at trial, and both I and my attorney knew that there was no hope of an appeal. So what the fuck was up *now*? Having no idea of what was in store as I walked the hall leading to the visitation room, I opened the door to an unwelcome surprise:

"Hello, Delo."

AL-FUCKING-GRAY!!! WHAT THE FUCK??? AND SOME WHITE WOMAN!!! WHAT THE FUCK WAS THIS???

"WHAT THE FUCK YOU WANT???" I said.

"Oh, I just want to serve you with these two sealed indictments," he said with a smirk, *"one for a count of criminal homicide and the other for two counts of attempted criminal homicide."*

Say the fuck *what???*

I snatched the papers from his hand as he stood there with a devious smile on his face, waiting for my reaction; the FBI agent just observed it all, saying nothing. In fact, I don't remember her ever saying a word. As I finished reading, my face turned from a look of confusion to fury.

"Well, you got anything to say?" he said, nervous now.

What he was expecting, I don't know, but yeah, I had something to say:

"FUCK YOU!!!" I disdained and stormed out.

As the overseer was escorting me back to the cellblock, my mind was racing, particularly as to the two attempted murders – who in the fuck could *that* be? As far as the murder charge, that had been rumored from the time I had started pressing the feds to give me a bond; I had always just thought that was a pretext to hold me. Guess not.

Back in the cellblock – although I wouldn't allow my face to show it to the other captives – I was *crushed!* I lay in the bunk for at least two days, not eating, not speaking, just balled up under the covers not even asleep. And I guess they had to have known that something was wrong, because no one even said a word to bother me; they just let me be. It had to be obvious that I had heard something fucked up when I went up there.

But I soon had to snap up out of that bullshit. However not before I wrote individual letters to most of my loved ones expressing all that was on my mind and in my heart. As I torturously poured out each word, however, my will got stronger and I thought about how my sons, brothers, nephews and father would feel if I went out like a punk and gave up fighting? Which of them would have been proud to have me as a father, son, brother, or uncle if all I was, was a coward whom conceded the fate my enemies wanted me to have? I mean, they would still love me, I'm sure, but being proud of me – why be proud of me when clearly I had no pride in myself if I chose to lay down and accept the role my enemies had written for me?

Pinning a murder on me that I'm sure "they" *know* I'm innocent of and I just let the train run me over? How is *that* my being a man? Or even allowing that coward Terrence Freeman[173]

---

[173] The cat whom I was charged with the attempted murders of. Our families had peripheral ties in that everyone knew each other in living on the Southside, and he had (by the time I was charged) conceived a daughter with Renee (my cousin Duck's sister and Aunt Nancy's daughter). Keep up – because this note is important!

to do bodily harm to my teen age sister and brother[174] and then have me locked up after I had a couple of "conversations" with him about it? – Why in the world should I let that bitch win? If anything, make that bitch get on the stand and testify in front of the entire world as to what *really* happened (and more importantly, why!) and I'd be satisfied with whatever time the jury said I deserved – so get up out of this bunk and *get ready!*

Any other course of action (or inaction) and everyone whom I loved and thought mattered would've been disappointed in me. Yet no more than I would've been disappointed in myself. How would I have ever been able to look at myself in the mirror again had I continued to cower under the covers? So slowly my resolve grew – aided along greatly by thoughts of the love shown – and sacrifices made by – all those whom there was/is no doubt have always truly loved me. Those whom I wrote the letters.

Speaking of sacrifice, I want to make clear that even with the things I've said that weren't necessarily "normal" or "mainstream" about my childhood, I wouldn't change one thing about either one of my parents or the way I was raised because I always knew even as I witnessed them struggle to "make it" and/or make mistakes that *both* of my parents loved me and *both* of them were doing the best they knew how under the circumstances in which they and I and all of my siblings were thrust into the world. They loved each other, they loved us children, and even after the separation they worked hard and strove to make things better for us all.[175]

---

[174] When "the hood" thought I was "gone," of course!
[175] So many times throughout my life my mother and father *both* broke their necks and sacrificed to show how much they loved and cared for me. Yet I was a spoiled (in the projects at that! How ironic, huh? A "spoiled" Project Kid!), unappreciative and inconsiderate idiot. Never thinking how my mother had to scrape up her money somehow and save or put things on lay-away so that I could wear "name brand" shoes and clothes and "Starter" jackets to school like everyone else. Or when she sacrificed

So, no way in hell was I letting my *true* loved ones down by "giving up." And let backstabbing fake "christians" like my Aunt Nancy win?! Why would I ever do that?! You think it escaped my notice as to why al-bitchass crackhead-gray was the one whom served me with the sealed indictments?! He was her "*good friend*," so it was just another play in an attempt to rattle me because Nancy was still "on that bullshit." Amazing! In fact, I wasn't so sure that I wasn't at least in *part* charged with the bogus murder case because of my aunt's poison infecting others![176]

Which brings me to something: I was forced to learn from an unspeakable amount of personal trauma and drama that not everyone that shares my skin color is of "my people." And on the flip side, someone of a different ethnicity/race can be my greatest friend. Even more jarringly – not everyone that shares a blood tie with me is of my "family." "Family" is similar to "love" and "community" in my eyes in that – even though they are nouns – they are still *action* words in *all* instances, in that they require *action* by us in order to give them true meaning. You can't

---

her and my siblings' weekends and extra money to come visit me at Woodland Hills, the county jail, and eventually state prison. Or when I was in the group home in Lebanon, she still made it a point to visit me until I finally "earned home passes," and saved enough money to buy me the boombox I wanted for Christmas. I did but I didn't appreciate these sacrifices she and they made for me repeatedly – not nearly enough did I...

And my father, too, sacrificed repeatedly for my siblings and I without our (or even my mother's) true appreciation and/or acknowledgement. He made it a point to be very involved in my probation when I thought I knew it all at fourteen; allowed me to parole to his home a few years later; was present at every one of my trials (state and federal) in kentucky and tennessee; and has visited me regularly throughout my various incarcerations.

[176] I wonder if Nancy (or any of the other sisters or nieces or nephews) ever took the time to consider – or if she even cared – how all of the bullshit she was on affected her younger sister? I know for a *fact* that my Mother loves her oldest sister yet continues to be brokenhearted having been chained to the emotional roller coaster of her *sibling* making false accusations of her *son* murdering her *nephew*! It's like Nancy has always had something against my Mother, or something – long before *I* was ever born – and Duck's death was the excuse for it coming to the surface.

"love" me or be considered my "friend" or a part of my "family" if your conscious actions of disloyalty or backstabbing or desertion or outright malice constantly and consistently show otherwise; just as well, how can/could we be a "community" if we don't/never take the necessary steps to build, maintain, and sustain communal ties? The cliché is true: *Actions* (and *in*actions!) speak louder than words and in our failure to *act* as a family, *act* as a community, *act* as if we truly love and care for one another, then our *true* beliefs are betrayed…

So, regarding those that drank from Nancy's poisoned well? – I can dig it; I'm cool now that I know where we stand. Will I always love those family members, "friends," and other loved ones that betrayed and/or deserted me in some way after Duck's death? Yes, of course, even though I wish to hell sometimes that I was somehow "built" differently and I could somehow dismiss my love much like they dismissed me in times of strife and/or when it was convenient/expedient. But will I ever trust or respect[177] those like my Aunt Nancy (Duck's mom) again? I just don't see how that would ever be possible, so I seriously, seriously doubt it. I mean, what did/do they see in me that made them think I was/am capable of murdering my own flesh and blood? I guess, a better question would be, what did/do they see in *themselves* that would have made them react and retaliate the way they *thought* I did?!

But who knows what this life may bring. I've been hit with so many twists and turns that I've learned to never say never.

Yet, I just can't for the life of me understand the stupidity of some motherfuckers in this world – especially those in "my family" that should have *always* known better!

Who else but the police or a police-sanctioned hit could get away with *murdering four people* in a heavily populated high

---

[177] I've already forgiven them, whether they know it or not.

density residential neighborhood late at night when even *one shot* would've awakened the prying eyes of neighbors, let alone the (I assume) dozens of shots that transpired?! Come on now! But people want to scapegoat *me*?! Kiss my ass! Isn't it amazing how, still to this day, no one has ever been arrested and/or charged in the murders? And even more amazing, how another unsolved quadruple homicide that went down eerily similar to my cousin's in a hood on the opposite side of the city happened *years after* I was already in prison — couldn't blame me for that one, huh?[178] It wasn't until years later that my mind would be emotionally clear enough about Duck's death to think about the implications of all of this.

So, I replayed in my mind a conversation I had with Duck where he mentioned that their[179] "people" would love to fuck with me because I "wasn't going,"[180] I was "getting [my] money," I didn't "get high or drink or anything," and I was "smart as hell," too![181] He went on to mention how Al was "plugged in" with a prominent white nashville businessman I had vaguely heard of before and how the "police or nobody" – not even S.K.[182] would fuck with them, and that he and Al were getting more money out there than anybody! He went on to mention "Willie Stones"[183] and a couple of other cats the police never fucked with and let get their money, and how they were "plugged in" also, and how it "couldn't get no better than that

---

[178] Although, ironically, I was associates with (I wouldn't necessarily say we were "good friends," but we were "cool") two of the victims in that one, too!
[179] Al's and his, I surmised.
[180] Meaning that I didn't take any "shit."
[181] "Smarter than any of those other niggas out here!"
[182] A well-known assistant United States attorney whom had a reputation of coming after/prosecuting all the "big dope boys" but not *some*, as Duck would go on to tell me.
[183] Who's *still* a reputed "Upper Echelon" informant out there to this day. In the years since then, I've been informed of at least one federal trial where Willie Stones (government name initials J.M.M.) and his close compadre "Sweet T." testified for the prosecution resulting in the defendants receiving life imprisonment.

in the streets." Duck – exaggerating, probably – promised I could have not only "protection from the pigs fuckin with" me, but also delivery by them (the pigs) to me if that's what I wanted! That's how serious it was!

Yet I've always had what some people consider a "problem." I'm nobody's "nigga." I've always been independent-minded, an independent thinker, and you could/can never force anything on me or get me to believe anything whether it be your religion, your politics, your philosophy, your mores, your traditions. If it made/makes sense to me, then I was/am "with it"; if it didn't/doesn't, then to hell with it and with you also, if you felt/feel determined to attempt forcing it on me! My thing is, the truth is always easy to either see, feel and/or think, and doesn't have to be forced ever! Only lies have to be forced down people's throats and/or into their minds; the truth can easily be seen from example, and I feel like I'm a walking example of my truth and what I believe in.

But, you know, to not be "owned" or "claimed" or "protected" by someone in this kkkountry, preferably someone "white" or "mainstream" is a kkkapital crime for Blacks. Blacks are not supposed to be independently working for themselves even in the "the dope game." And I quickly peeped game and saw that Duck, Al, Stones and all of those fools that I thought were "independent" hustlers like I was, were in fact working for the white man/the pigs instead, when you really got down to it! And I ain't/wasn't the one! No way in hell was I working for or "with" some white man "plugged in" with the pig police! To hell with that! I was doing me! And who was to say that the white man/the pigs wouldn't sell them (the Blacks) out in the end anyway, like what always seems to happen?! Furthermore, what were those fools offering the white man/the pigs in return for their "protection" besides money, because the pigs and the prosekkkutors had to have someone to go after in order to justify keeping their jobs! Shit just immediately didn't sound or feel right to me, so I diplomatically let him know I wasn't "with it," put it out of my mind, and continued doing my own thing independently.

In hindsight, I guess Duck took what I expressed in our conversation back to whom he needed to, whom I assume was Al. Because I can't see Duck having that conversation with me without already having had a conversation with someone else about me concerning the subject. I just thought the whole thing "weird," but, of course, I couldn't articulate that at the time and to be honest, I don't even think I would have wanted to had I even been able. Moreover, I don't think my nineteen years young mind was ready to deal with the implications of all he had told me. Including the loss of respect I feel, even to this day, for all those fools he mentioned working "with" the "white man" and, thus, our (Black community) pig enemies…

Yet after our conversation,[184] it was probably no more than a few weeks later that Duck and Al were accusing me of "robbing Al's spot." Crazy, huh? Come to think of it, how do I even know that that (Al's spot getting "jacked") ever really even happened? Looking at it now, it could have all been a ploy to draw me in somehow, for all I know. That makes just as much sense as anything/everything else about that/this entire situation.

And I realize that some people reading this may think that I'm just being overly paranoid or possibly even making shit up and all I can say to them is take a quick look at mnpd[185] and how in just the last 20 years alone [1997-2017] far too many of "nashville's finest" have been caught selling drugs; jacking cats

---

[184] Which really couldn't have taken more than 3-5minutes to have while Duck and I were standing out in the projects "chilling."
[185] metropolitan nashville police department

for their coke, their weed, their heroin, and/or their money; stealing money and/or drugs out of "evidence"; and/or perjuring themselves in kkkourt and/or setting people up amongst other things! Just look at it. Then tell me I'm lying, bullshitting, or overly paranoid! Because I sure as hell know that I wasn't capable of pulling off the murder of four people and getting away with it back then! Sounds like someone powerful got rid of some people they no longer had any use for, doesn't it? And then tried to scapegoat and pillory me for it.

But like I said, it's cool. Someone once pointed out to me that maybe I've been "targeted" not necessarily because of what I am, or even what I've ever been, but more so because of what I have the potential to become. Just like every Black man before and after me. And as I think about the person I used to be, the person I am today, and the person I want to become – I think that, hey! – she just might have been right!....

"Unchallenged, a lie often becomes history…"
Author Unknown

DUCK

Duck was a bitch – although at the time my heart wouldn't allow me to recognize that. All my mind's eyes could see was the cousin whom I'd looked up to my entire life, the person I wanted to be, someone whom I proudly bragged on being related to. So him calling me that spring day in 1997 asking me to meet with him and Al after I got off work, of course I'd be there – with no hesitation nor second thoughts.[186] Usually, I would head home first to check on Tsawa whose stomach was growing larger every day with my son inside, but on this day I found myself in the Projects per Duck's request. Maybe five minutes or so after I got there, Al and two other cats pulled up in a money green sedan – Duck hopped in the passenger seat with some guy I didn't know behind the wheel, Al in the back with another. Four deep.

"*Get in for a minute,*" Duck said, "*Al wanna holla at ya.*"

I hopped in with naïveté having me convinced that Al was about to pay me for "putting in some work" – I thought nothing of the cat in the back seat hopping out and hopping back in placing me in the middle, surrounded. I felt safe, unawares – I was with my big cousin Duck and Al! – and still had no idea as to what was actually going on when they pulled away from the curve. Until Duck and the cat sitting beside me pulled weapons.

"*Where that money at, nigga?*"

What??? I don't owe these motherfuckers *any money*, I'm thinking confusedly. Hell, I don't owe *anybody* any fucking money, in fact.

---

[186] Hell, if Duck and Al wanted to see me, then it *had* to be about making some money!

"*What fucking money?*" I said clueless.

"*Nigga, you know what fucking money,*" said the cat to my right with a gun now to my side, "*somebody came up in Al spot last night and took $92,000!!!*"

Fuck! Not *this* type of bullshit again!!!

"*Man, what the fuck that got to do with* me?"

The cat to my right – who I later learned to be Reggie M. – took over the conversation, his voice rising and falling with each accusation. This bitch should have won an Oscar for his performance. Ironically, Al was totally silent to my left, just observing it all, yet it was *his* money that evidently had come up missing. Duck, it seemed, had fallen mute, too, but with a gun pointed at me, also; I looked him in his eye:

"*You set me up,*" I said, still not believing what was really happening.

"*Man, Al just want his money,*" was his reply, turning his eyes away from me.

"*I can't believe you set me up.*"

All I could do was shake my head, trying to awaken myself from the nightmare of *one of my favorite people in the world* setting me up for a *killing – for some bullshit I had nothing to do with!!!* I couldn't believe this shit!!! I *had* to have been dreaming!!!

Driving down 12th Ave., I came to understand that in the course of this robbery of Al's spot, a blue Chevy Malibu – the same type of car I was sitting on the hood of when they pulled up – was seen leaving the alley behind Al's house; unfortunately for me, I not only *owned* a blue Malibu, but also had a "dick-dragging"[187] cousin who knew of this fact and volunteered the fucking information!!! See Duck was no ordinary bitch, he was *Al's* bitch. So much so, that he now sat with a gun pointed at

---

[187] Ass-kissing; brown-nosing. We used to say that a brownnoser was "all on a [person's] nuts" or "dragging [their] dick."

me – his first cousin who up to that point thought he could do no wrong – ready to open fire at Al's command!!! What the fuck???

I was crushed. Not so much with the fact that I was about to die – I had, of course, been resigned to death since at least the age of 14 – but with the fact that I had loved and revered this man my entire life and he was now the one at whose hands I would fall. Hell, I had even left my gun in my car, I felt so safe with him. I felt like such a fool. No woman has even broken my heart so bad. All I could do was keep shaking my head and repeating "you set me up, you set me up." There was just no way for me to believe it.

Finally making our way to "the spot" in the alley behind 11th Ave. – somewhere I'd never been inside before *or* since then – I was escorted out of the car and into the duplex at gunpoint; I quickly noticed that we weren't alone. At least six other cats came out of back rooms – all strapped, all ready for war, it appeared – and added their three cents on how the robbery had went down the night before.[188] Every single one of them expressed some variation of me not looking like "one of the ones who did it." After a few minutes, Al finally spoke up for the first time:

"Somebody needs to be coming up with my money," he said, looking my way.

"Man, I ain't had shit to do with your money coming up missing," I replied exasperatingly, *"hell, I didn't even know this spot was* here!*"*

Reggie again began with his theatrics; I tuned his bitch ass out. Al again:

"Well, you might as well get comfortable 'cause ain't nobody *leaving here until my money comes up,"* he menaced out.

---

[188] Some I recognized, most I didn't. I wasn't really paying attention to them anyway; I was still in disbelief on how Duck had betrayed me.

Everybody – including Reggie's bitch ass – got quiet. And I could tell by the atmosphere that someone in that room knew more than they were letting on about that missing money; although they were now seeking to use me as their scapegoat, I think Al knew what was up and their plan was falling apart. Hell, he probably already even knew the deal before they snatched me. Whether you choose to acknowledge it or not, the truth is easy to see when it's right there in front of your eyes.

"*I ain't have shit to do with your money coming up missing,*" I said, "*but if you want some money, I'll call and get you some money and* then I'll help you find out who *really* took it."

"*Naw, I don't want* any *money, I want* my *money.*"

He wasn't even looking at me when he said it, but instead seemed to be off inside his own head and world somewhere where he was facing an awful truth. Because he knew; he knew. He knew I could come up with the money if pressed for it; yeah, it might've broken my stash, and I'd also have to make a couple of phone calls, but he knew that I could get it. Him saying he wanted *his* money and *only* his money let us all know that he wanted the snake within his midst more than anything else.

"*Well,* I *don't have it.*"

So there it was; resigned to my fate. If he felt it necessary to kill me to find the traitor in his circle, then I was dead.

It all felt like a fucked up dream. Me, myself, I was there but not there, also – I had lost all sense of time, space, direction, feeling – everything. All I could see was Duck – my own flesh and blood. I'm surrounded by motherfuckers with straps blaming me for something I didn't do, with my own cousin at the center of it all. Shit was fucked up. My disbelief wouldn't allow me to be afraid, angry – nothing. All I felt was numb. Everybody and everything else became fuzzy background noise. I kept repeating over and over again – more to myself than to my cousin, by this point – "you set me up; I can't believe you set me up." And that's probably what kept me alive.

For some reason, after a few minutes, Al decided for us same five to go for a ride again; why? – I don't know, but at the time I figured it was to take me to my grave. And, honestly, I didn't even care. Whether I lived for a hundred more years or not, I knew that I would never completely recover from what I was feeling. My own cousin. My own cousin. I still couldn't believe it. My only request was to Duck that he "look me in the eye when them niggas shoot me in the head." To that, Duck didn't even have the courage to respond, even after Al replied that they were "going to kill him, too." Duck just sat there, mute, gun in hand. Unbelievable.

I soon noticed that we were crossing the railroad tracks to the "other part of south" where I currently lived; my thoughts instantly went to the safety of Tsawa and my unborn son as I thought that maybe they were taking me home to search my spot or something.[189] But as we neared the projects – J.C. Napier and University Court – the driver kept straight, at almost cruising speed, through the drive "Up Top." Al carried the conversation now:

"Well look – even if you wasn't the one who got my money, you probably know who did."

What??? How in the fuck was *I* supposed to know who took his money? What type of game was this cat playing???

"How am I supposed to know who got your money? Let me know who you think got it and I'll kill 'em my goddamned self!" I replied.

"You a robber, so you probably know all the robbers and which one it was that done it," this idiot replied, going on to name off a host of "robbers" from that side of town and others whom I guess it

---

[189] At the time I never even considered the fact that no one should have known about my "low-key" spot anyway; but indeed, I found out startlingly the next morning that Duck had indeed shown Al and Reggie M. where I lay my head.

could've possibly been.

"*Well*, I *don't know; all I know is* I *didn't have anything to do with it.*"

This fool was stupid; how he made it as far as he did in the dope game, I'll never know. Here he was, riding me around in broad daylight, speaking to what seemed like everyone we passed in the projects – including my cousin (and Duck's brother, I might add!) Reggie L. (who I swear saw me in distress sitting in the backseat!)[190] – telling me that not only did he *know* that I wasn't the one who took his money, but also that he wanted only *his* money back with the very person who set him up more than likely sitting with him in the same car! Idiot! Made me wish that I *had* been the one to have jacked his bitch ass!!!

After riding around for what seemed to me like hours (but which couldn't have been no more than 20-30 minutes, tops), the driver – who I later found out to be "Mumbles" – turned back towards Edgehill off of some signal from Al. Al again seemed to be in deep thought, rapping a couple of times to himself the Notorious B.I.G. verse "nigga, you should, too, if you knew, what this game'll do to you." I'm sitting here thinking to myself that no other statement has ever been truer – look at what my own cousin had done to *me* in "the game!"

Crossing the railroad tracks separating one part of south from the other, Al instructed Mumbles to drop me off in The Village to "those lil niggas he robbed a month ago" so they could "kill" me. I guess he didn't have the nuts to do it himself, or maybe thought better of it since so many people had seen me getting in the car and riding around with them that day. Then he thought better of that, also, and told Mumbles to drop me back

---

[190] But hey, maybe he didn't. Maybe his mind was too preoccupied on the prowl for more children to molest!

Duck

off to my car.[191] Then he warned me:

"*You lucky your auntie is like my mama. But if I find out that you had* anything *to do with my money coming up missing, I'mma kill you. I don't care if it's a week from now, a month from now, or a year from now, don't let me find out you got any money.* And don't tell your auntie or mama what happened either."

Ain't this a bitch??? Just *who* did this motherfucker think he was??? Well he had *me* fucked up!!!

Pulling up to my car, I was still in disbelief as to all that had happened and that I was still alive – not to mention the fact of how this fool really felt he was untouchable, or something, leaving me breathing like that. Duck got out of the front seat, then Reggie let me out of the back moving up front, and Al stayed in the back being chauffeured. Watching shockingly as they pulled away, I hurriedly opened my door and retrieved the .45 I kept under the driver's side seat. Grabbing it, I raced to catch up with them going around the drive to no avail. Making my way back to my car, I noticed Duck staring at me with a glossy, pitiful look in his eyes; I stared back at him, furious, biting my lip, tears involuntarily falling from my own eyes, gun in my hand at my side.

"*Man, Al wasn't gonna do nothing to you, he was just tryna scare you.*"

Pathetic. I continued to stare at him, my vision evermore getting cloudier, trying to find the person whom I used to hold in such high regard; I didn't see him. I turned my back to him, got in my car, and drove away.

What transpired in the next few hours – who I talked to?, where I went?, what I did? – I'll take that to my grave; but know

---

[191] Again, how smart was this idiot? Allowing so many people to witness me getting in the car with them, topped off by riding me around in three different sets of projects for all to see? If you're going to kill someone, then *kill* them! Don't leave any unnecessary witnesses or allow chances for escape. Stupid motherfucker.

that I made sure that those I loved and cared for were secure and safe, out of harm's way. And I changed – in ways that I never would have thought imaginable. My trust for people soon dissipated – whether you were "family" or not – and I vowed to never again get caught slipping, by *anyone*, at *any* time *ever* again. The next few months I threw myself fully into the streets, grinding hard, taking trips down south, determined to get my money up, gearing up for war. It was unavoidable....

The family came down hard on Duck – well, at first, anyway – especially his mother Nancy and "our Granddaddy," Bay Walden. These two were also some of the first ones to flip the script, making excuses for him, justifying what he did, forcing a rift in our family's dynamics. Within days, Nancy would call my mom to accuse and argue – in addition to trying to convince some of the other sisters that somehow *I* was wrong and that *"Delo probably did take that money; you can't fault Al for trying to get his money."* Nancy equally tried to convince the family that they were "only trying to scare" me; however, *she* wasn't there, and I *know* how close they came to taking my life.[192] My oldest aunt; I soon clearly saw that Duck got his snake-mentality honestly.

Unfortunately, that was just the start of all the bullshit and drama to come from my Aunt Nancy's way – and it seemed to me that my family and entire world was falling apart with people I had loved all my life for some reason turning against me. I just couldn't understand. At the time, I couldn't foresee or fathom that my kidnapping would be the catalyst for animosities long-older-than-I coming to the surface. But it quickly became clear.

Attempting to salvage some type of relationship between myself and Duck, Shot called a family meeting of us cousins:

---

[192] I have no doubts whatsoever that *her* son would have been the first one to pull the trigger, too! Anything to prove his loyalty to his "Daddy" Al.

him, Duck, Ca-Carl, my brother Carvin[193] and I met up at the spot in the Projects. Duck tried unconvincingly to make us believe that he "wouldn't have let anything happen" to me and that all they were trying to do was "scare me."[194] All I could do was express my love, anger, disappointment, and hurt. We left each other that night both feeling sadness – myself sad at the hero I had lost, him sad at how he had lost me forever. My heart was heavy. I accepted it for what it was.[195]

---

[193] Carvin was actually there in the Projects that day when they dropped me off to my car; he instantly could tell something was wrong and after learning what happened, was instantly ready for whatever like always.
[194] "Scare me," for what? – even he didn't have the answer to that bullshit he was trying to feed us. After he said that, my memory resurfaced of him pulling a pistol on Putt shortly before he died; Duck had nothing to say to that transgression against the family, either.
[195] Ironically, our "family meeting" was broken up by Ca-Carl's sister bursting up the stairs crying that some dude had "smacked" her and we all broke outside together to confront him. The cat in question was then smacked *himself* by Ca-Carl after the fool compounded his disrespect by calling her a "bitch." Where the fool then got the strap he pulled on us, I *still* can't figure out because I was looking right at him when it suddenly appeared in his hand. Attempting to get to my own .45 in my jacket side-pocket, the cat noticed my movement and pointed his pistol in my direction. (The second time that week I had been drawn down on! What kind of luck was *I* having, right?!) Ca-Carl then distracted him for a split second screaming about how he was "gonna get the Tech!," and dude foolishly took his eyes off me; I pulled my strap and opened fire.
Forgetting, I guess, the gun he already held in hand, he and the cat along with him (I knew him and we were cool, but this was *family beef!*) broke out, trying unsuccessfully to get away from the heat. Metal puncturing flesh reminded him of the pistol he had, I guess, so he finally turned around in an attempt to return fire. I can still see it in my nightmares sometimes, the way he took aim at me until his body jerked around the side of the building from the absorption of another one of my cannon's shells. In the heat of the moment, Ca-Carl – who by then somehow now had the Tech-9 in hand – and I stalked around the building aiming to finish him off; we ran headfirst, guns drawn, into a police car coming through the drive. Everyone scattering to different directions, we somehow escaped.
Again, ironically, Duck somehow ended up in the car with *me* on the way to a low-key spot Out East; thinking better of trusting him in the same car with me again (he *had*, of course, just set me up for a kidnapping a couple of days before!), I made the young lady I had driving pull over at a payphone so that I could check to see how hot it was in the Bricks; come to find out, a good friend of mine wanted to speak to me from next door to "the spot" where dude had been.
Calling her, I was informed that the cat I'd shot was "drunk," "fresh out the penitentiary," "sorry," "didn't want any more trouble," and so on and so forth – hell,

The last I saw of Duck alive was a few months later at a backyard cookout – him seeking me out to finally apologize. He didn't look the same, seemed like something was bothering him.

"*Delo, man... I love you. You my lil cousin. Man... I haven't even been able to get on my grind lately, for thinking about that shit, man, and I don't even fuck with Al like that no mo.*"

Interestingly enough, I found out a few minutes later that Al was there at the party with him; no matter to me, though – I had by then accepted the fact that he would always be Al's whore. I continued to listen:

"*You been on my mind a lot lately and I know shit won't ever be the same, but you need to try to let me make it up to you.*"

My Pops noticed us talking and tried to pull me away; I told him I was cool and that I'd continue to hear Duck out:

"*Look, here's my number, man; just call me tomorrow sometime so we can go out to eat and talk, just me and you.*"

He seemed sincere; I took his number. No matter what, I still loved my cousin, still wanted to try to understand how he could have done me like that. Unfortunately, though, it wasn't to be: The next morning found him along with Al, Mumbles, and a fourth person all shot and killed inside the same duplex where they had taken me during the kidnapping; I would soon

---

I was just happy that he didn't *die!* Although I knew that he had pulled the strap on us first, I also knew that this was the projects so no one would tell *that* part when the story was told – nor was I convinced that the pigs would find or even *look for* his weapon. The story would, more than likely, just be "Delo killed him." And here I was gearing up for war on the fools that had just pulled a move on me, yet I'm caught up shooting some cat that I wouldn't even recognize if he was right in my face today! Shit! How crazy was *that!* Goes to show how fast something can jump off in the streets – anytime, anywhere, and for any reason.

Anyway, the last I heard of the cat that I'd shot, he had "found his calling" and become a preacher – guess he saw the light when he thought about how close he'd come to dying. My cousin whom he had violated ran into him one day on the streets (I'm not the only one that didn't recognize him; he had to remind her of who he was!), and he reminded her of how her "brother" had "shot [him] in the projects." She replied "un unh! My brother didn't shoot you; *my favorite cousin Delo shot you!*" Hilarious. But I'm truly happy that I was able to help him turn his life around... ☺

be one of the primary suspects.

But I didn't kill my cousin; I had nothing to do with the death of any of them. Fate and karma just came calling from all that fake ass gangster shit they called themselves pulling in the streets; I wasn't the only enemy they'd made.

True enough, I would have gladly and eventually killed Al – *when* I was ready – but Duck?, never; I wasn't the person *he* was. I couldn't have looked *my* aunt in the face knowing that I had something to do with the death of *her* son. I'm not that coldhearted. But, of course, some will never believe that. Let's me know what type of heart *they* have.

Never have I felt comfortable enough, though, of discussing with anyone the way I felt about Duck's death; this book will be the first and *only* time. And to be honest, *who* could I have talked to about it? Who could have even understood? Who could I have trusted? Where could I have turned to for a shoulder?

Even more so than normal, I found myself withdrawing within; not even the closest people around me had any idea the swirl of emotions raging my heart and mind. Thinking of the way he likely died – alone, in fear, in pain, not realizing I accepted his apology – almost threw me over the edge. It's taken me years, even, to accept the fact that he's gone. Sometimes I still can't believe it.

But the only tears I allowed myself to shed were in the shower, *alone*. The only emotion I showed was *none*. A lot of people at the time may have took me as being cold, calculating, and capable of murdering my own flesh and blood, but in truth, it was because I was consumed reliving the moments I last saw him alive. Could I have saved him somehow? Was that which I noticed about him not "looking the same" actually him feeling Death breathing down his neck? I've always wondered, was there anything I could have done so that things could've turned out differently? If I had been more forgiving of him that night, would he still be here?? What if — instead of the next day — we had decided to kick it *then???*

Because I *loved* Duck; I *still* do. And although I'll never forget how he betrayed me and broke my heart, I forgive him. And I pray that wherever his soul may rest, he knows that...

> It is our duty to fight for freedom.
> It is our duty to win.
> We must love each other and support each other.
> We have nothing to lose but our chains…
>
> Assata Shakur

FIGHTING

After sentencing, I was booked into the Fayette County Detention Center in Lexington, Kentucky – *a lot* different from my last trip to the city, to say the least. Still under the custody of the U.S. Marshals, I was fingerprinted, had my picture taken, and they even did an iris scan – a first for me. Yet, that wasn't the only unusual booking experience that I had at that time: I noticed the Marshal who signed me over to the jail writing on my booking sheet "Murder x 4." Not giving it much thought at that very moment, I would soon see how it would affect the rest of my incarceration.

Taken to the holding area along with all of the other newly jailed captives, I noticed that people were being called out one by one to meet some type of classification officer. However, when it came time for *my* classification, *I* was met by two officers who *escorted* me to the classification office. Furthermore, although there was a seat (that I assume was) for prisoners to sit in in front of the officer's desk, it wasn't offered to *me*; *I* was left to languish standing – *with* my escorts behind me, of course. Oblivious to exactly what was up at that time, I knew that it had to be something serious.

Strangely, the pig sitting at the desk looked up at me from the papers in front of him, looked back at the papers as in disbelief, and then back at me once more again. Finally, as curiosity was clearly winning over the both of us, he couldn't help himself any longer:

"I have got to know – how in the hell does one get four federal murder cases?" he asked.

"Murder x 4" – that motherfukkking bastard!

"Four?" I said, *"as far as I know, I've only had two."*

"Well," he responded, *"maybe a couple of other people have died."*

Murder x 4 – now I can see why those bastards were acting strange towards me! They considered me some type of mass murderer or something!

Speaking of which – did you know that there were three main classifications of murderers? The first is your regular run-of-the-mill murderer[196] whom kills when backed into a corner somehow (whether in business or their personal lives), who usually gets caught soon after, and even if he or she doesn't get locked away for it, doesn't kill again. These people usually live out the rest of their lives – whether free or not, regretful of the killing.

Then there are your mass murderers, who kill two or more people at one time;[197] they, too, usually stop after that one incident. A lot of times this is because they plan and then succeed in taking their own lives in the incident, or because they're soon caught and imprisoned in a mental hospital or sometimes even an actual prison.[198]

Then, finally, you have the serial murderer, who kills, then

---

[196] As if murder could ever be run-of-the-mill!
[197] For instance, the typical crazy suburban kid – usually white – who kills his entire family for complaining about playing his music too loud or not allowing his strange Goth friends over.
[198] Interestingly enough, however, these deranged (more often than not) white kids usually achieve their goals of at least local if not national fame/infamy with numerous write-ups in the papers and/or stories done in the newscasts in an attempt to "understand how things went so terribly wrong" with Little Johnny (who was *such a good boy*, ya know?). Yet, this is never done in the case of Black victims and/or murderers. No one cares. Not even in our own communities. Black murderers are almost always demonized universally.

Fighting

kills, then kills, then kills, then kills, and kills until finally stopped by incarceration and/or death. These are your Ted Bundys, Walter Williams, John Muhammads, Jeffrey Dahmers, and the like.

Well, come to find out, I was considered by at least the U.S. Marshals, the F.B.I., and the Metro Murder Squad to be a *serial mass murderer* – a killer of multiple people in one series after the next! What in the fuck, right?![199] Apparently because of my being such a heinous and savage killer, I was classified to what I can only guess was the high-security wing of the jail; if memory serves me correctly, the front of the cells besides the door were entirely made of Plexiglas, allowing for your observation 24 hours of every single day – eating, sleeping, or shitting; the cells were all single-man, of course – couldn't put anyone in danger by housing them with me; and it was either entirely underground or dug into the side of one of Kentucky's rolling hills – in order to see any sunlight you had to go "outside" in the rec cage and look what seemed to me 50 feet in the air. In essence, I was constructively placed in a dungeon. Reflecting upon it now, though, I can see how the gods were preparing me for the oncoming onslaught I had up ahead.

Another way I was unknowingly prepared for the drama soon to come came courtesy of an unexpected visit from Zara:

"Delo," she said, *"I read the letters."*

Huh? *What* letters? *What* now?? The bizarre look on her

---

[199] The FBI defines "mass murderers" as persons who murder at least four people in a single incident, while "serial killers" are defined as those who kill at least two people in separate incidents. The "authorities" considered me both: a "serial mass murderer." "Experts," however, say it is highly unusual for a serial killer to begin with a mass murder as I was (wrongly, albeit!) alleged to have. These same experts go on to say that "many serial killers appear so normal (that) they don't raise suspicions and sometimes cultivate that appearance in what amounts to be dual lives… In fact, most people are shocked when they find the person who is finally arrested because they will say he is a very nice person, he didn't cause any trouble. They (serial killers) are able to be chameleons." Wednesday, November 9, 2016 USA Today.

face should have told me all. She continued:

"*And I can't believe that you would express your love for another woman when* I'm *your* wife!"

Come to find out, Zara had went through the meager belongings I was allowed at Newport (Kentucky) when I had to mail them home when transported to Frankfort[200] for sentencing; stumbling across unmailed letters I had written to those I cared about when I was thinking about giving up, she took great offense when I expressed to Tsawa how much I had really loved and cared for her. But seeing as how I expressed my love in all of the letters I chose to write to people, I knew that Zara was just looking for an excuse[201] to justify leaving me after I received that time. I could dig it, though; not only was I already sentenced to serve 32 months in federal prison for the aiding and abetting bank fraud, but I was also facing life plus an additional 135 years in pending cases! There was the possibility of life imprisonment (if convicted) on the murder charge wherein I wouldn't even become *eligible* for parole until after I served 51 years in a tennessee state prison (And that only if I received all possible "good time"!); another probable 120 years in state prison on the two attempted murders (60 years apiece, because I would no doubt be considered a "violent career criminal."); then there would be another 15 years-mandatory minimum on charges of being a convicted felon in possession of a weapon – which was the original reason the feds were seeking me in tennessee![202] So, my enemies really had it all lined

---

[200] Also in Kentucky.
[201] To herself – I didn't need one; the results were the same to me – fuck whatever the reason, ya know?
[202] Come to find out, the gun taken off me when I was arrested in the first murder case was turned over to the feds for prosecution since the statute of limitations had run out to do so by the state of tennessee. I suspect that initial thoughts were that it had been used in some type of crime they could link me to (preferably murder), but of course, it hadn't, and the state authorities simply dropped the ball in charging me

up for me; lose any one of my pending cases and Zara and I would be separated for at least a decade and a half! Compare that to the less than three short months she and I had been together while I was free — intruded upon by the bullshit wrought from Pasheni and her mother – yet doubled by the six months I had already been enslaved at the time of my sentencing, and what could I have honestly expected?

Not to mention that assassination of my character came her way from the moment of my inopportune arrest. As Zara had served as a sheriff's deputy in nashville only weeks before we met and married, she quickly faced questions of why she was married to a guy like me!

Coming from a law enforcement/corrections background, outsiders couldn't understand how and why she fell in love with such a despicable man. Did she know what I was capable of?, they asked. Well let me inform you as to who your husband really is!, they answered. They made me seem like Hannibal Lecter in the flesh to Zara – and did all they could to break up our marriage even before my federal trial.[203] Eventually the pressure from outside agitation took its toll and unbeknownst to me she started "looking for a reason."

However, had I even considered that we wouldn't be together "till death do us part" then we would have never married in the first place. I mean, what would be the point? Neither of us needed the piece of paper, so my understanding was that it was "all about love" and never losing one another; before we actually had the ceremony Zara and I had talked and

---

with it since they felt they had me for at least one murder anyway. I wouldn't learn any of this (for sure) until after I was arrested in Kentucky.
[203] In fact, Zara was the one that informed me (well, accused me actually) that I was "charged with murder" as I was fighting for a bond. Someone in authority informed her that I would "never be a free man again" because of that and she and I argued over it more than a few times because she (wrongly) felt as if I was lying about my charges. At the unsealing of those indictments, finally both of us were proved right.

agreed to accept whatever each of us came with for the rest of our lives. Yet I held up my end of the bargain; however I can dig why what came my way ended up being too unbearable for her. Disappointed, yeah, but I can't say that I didn't/don't understand.

So, in essence, due to life circumstances, Zara and I were never really given a fair chance, it seems. Yet due to those same life circumstances she and I were loving and loved and emotional and vulnerable and open with each other in intense ways one wouldn't believe, and I've always been curious as to how things would have turned out had I not been snatched away so suddenly, so soon. But I'll always remember my time (free) with her favorably, and our lovemaking simultaneously passionate and serene, one and the same.

Yet although I understand why she had to leave, that still doesn't excuse the foul moves she made while she was making her slow but sure exit. First being, not only accepting prosekkkutor lisa naylor's card (against my protests) and offer to call after the devil introduced herself to Zara in kkkourt, but also allowing her head to be filled with all manner of bullshit! From my *enemy*! The prosekkkutor whom vowed to "make her career off [me]" even before charging me in three separate state cases (2 murders and 2 counts of attempted murder) or heading up the joint state-federal task force which led to the federal gun charges! Even though the morally kkkorrupt bitch knew from jump that the cases were bogus (at least in regards to the murders), I was just another "throwaway nigger" so who cared? And *this* was the bitch Zara chose to believe over *me*!? Her *husband*? Come on now! Zara even supplied naylor with a letter Tsawa had written (while I was in Kentucky) where she made reference to a couple of abortions she had over the years[204] that naylor used at trial to make it look like I ordered the "murders" of the babies! (Believe me I can't make this shit up!) And *this* (Zara) was the woman *my* dumb ass had married!!!...

Zara helped me face an awful fact about myself: I "love" too easily and far too hard. I'm much too quick to give and show my love and far too slow to ever take it away. No matter the bullshit or mud I may have to wade through, I always seem to find and see the "best part" that lives in everyone. Simply put, my heart is stronger than my mind and this character flaw of mine has proven detrimental and/or dangerous to me time and time again in that it makes me (sometimes) not able to recognize "bad intentions" quickly enough. I wish I was wired differently; I wish I could change this about myself. But I can't.

Yet what I can change are the safeguards I put around my heart. For instance, I realize that "marriage" (as constituted in *this* kkkountry!) is *not* an institution for me, therefore I vow "never again." I would like to love and trust and depend on someone completely and them the same with me,[205] but that is just unrealistic in this day and age. So, in any and all future "relationships" I vow to make adjustments.

Or maybe I should just be more careful about the women I accept in my life? I've always felt that women are the most beautiful of God's creations, but that doesn't mean I should partake of every enticing fruit available to me.

---

[204] Of which in at least one I refuse to believe that I was the father. But that's another story.
[205] Telling you all you need to know about me. My favorite song was *Can you Stand the Rain* by (my favorite group) New Edition, until it was (somewhat) supplanted by (one of my top two favorite singers, along with India.Arie) Alicia Keys's *Diary*. Rounding out my top five are Tupac's *Keep Ya Head Up* and *Dear Mama*, followed by Maxwell's *Lifetime*. Hell, even my top two favorite movies are *Love & Basketball* and *Boomerang*! (But don't get it too twisted – they're closely followed by *Menace II Society*, *Django Unchained* and *Get Out* so it's *still* all the way Intelligent and Revolutionary *Gangsta* with me baby!)

Furthermore, it's not like I can say that I haven't been blessed with at least *one* great woman in my life; *that* woman I'm sure would have made a great wife and mother but *I* blew that. Who knows? – With the way she encouraged me to be a better man in every way, maybe a lot about my life would have turned out different had I realized what/whom I had. Being with Jannah, making love to her, kissing her, feeling her heart beat to the tune of my own, is the closest I've ever been to heaven here on earth – our bodies and souls felt that connected. Our love and lovemaking was peaceful, intense, passionate, and comforting all at the same time. I don't even know how I would have *survived* the period of my life following the intense scrutiny that came after Duck's death without her, to be completely honest; my troubles would go away with simply a smile, a kiss, or a laugh from her, and I felt like I could face whatever came my way simply because I knew I had her love in my life. That's what the love of a good woman can do for you…

Therefore I recognize that fleeting pleasure and the storms in my world caused for me to choose the wrong woman for a wife. Had I been thinking clearer, had I not had the "do or die, live every day as my last" attitude, Zara wouldn't have been even a one-time *mistake*, let alone someone I dedicated myself to before the Creator and my baby sister. But that just goes to show how much my thinking was messed up at the time in which we met and married.

Although I had lain with this woman, given her my last name, and given her my heart, she didn't even care enough nor have respect enough for me, herself, or our marriage to keep her affairs discreet. At least then I could've acted as if I didn't know what was going on right before my very eyes. Even more important to me with all that I was already dealing with, at least it wouldn't have been all out in the streets. No man –

Fighting

incarcerated or not – wants to hear about his "wife" being paraded around town with another man; I sure as hell didn't want to receive all of the letters, visits, or phone conversations from others bringing to my attention her indiscretions. Unfortunately, I did, though. Hell, I think I would have been better off if she had had enough respect for what we had to at least keep her pussy out of my immediate circle. Or at least not get pregnant by one of my "closest friends," ya dig? Especially one that had confided in me years before (his and Zara's affair) that he was stricken with not one but *two* incurable sexually transmitted viruses that he had passed on to the mother of his children. Simply put, Zara played *herself, not me*. If I didn't know if before, I knew it then that I was through with her ass. And him, too, for the most part. Fuck them both...[206]

I had to somehow force Zara and my "friend's" betrayal to the recesses of my mind, and keep on pushing on. I still had an epic war on the horizon whether I had connubial support or not. And with my having three separate cases to fight simultaneously, it would take all that I had in me to focus on all three battle fronts the energy they needed for me to win.

---

[206] This incident makes me extremely reluctant (in the future) to expose anyone other than my *tried* and *tested* relatives and/or *true* friends to any relationship I hold dear. In essence, not everything – nor everyone – is for everybody to know. As said best by Sista Souljah, "When a man allows you into the inner circle of his life, the unspoken agreement is that you don't abuse the proximity," yet not only did this sucker "violate," he inadvertently helped me out by forcing me to consider how far too many supposed-to-be-cool cats have followed "too closely behind" me with a lot of the women I've been "involved with" in my past. Yet I never would have *ever* considered doing the same. A couple of these relationships (after me) have resulted in children being born and one even in an enduring marriage, but situations like that always made me wonder whether "glances" were being exchanged while the woman and I were together. And that makes me question a person's loyalty (specifically, the cats that "followed" behind me") – which has never been a good thing. Would you believe, however, that a couple of those fools have thereafter felt as if *I* was the one that couldn't be trusted around "their" (used-to-be-my) women?! Un-fucking-believable! Yet, I've never – *not once in my life* – considered for a *moment* "involving" myself again with the women after they've "been with" these fools! It may be *those* cats' styles, but it's sure as hell not *mine*! But I digress...

Nor would I have time to rest between any one battle before the other. I was first, in early August of 2002, transferred to the Middle District of Tennessee (based out of nashville, but I was under the custody of the U.S. Marshals in Leitchfield, Kentucky) for arraignment in federal kkkourt on the gun charges, then a couple of weeks thereafter transferred to the custody of Davidson County Sheriff's office for arraignment on the murder and attempted murder charges.

But check it (because this is *very* important!), I was transferred to DCSO in nashville pursuant to something called the Interstate Agreement on Detainers (or "IAD") which mandated that I be tried within 120 *days* of my arrival in nashville. "Mandated" as in, if my trial – on every single case I was arraigned on – didn't begin (or "commence" in the language of the IAD) by the time that 120 days flipped over to 121, then *all* of my charges would be *dismissed* never to haunt me again! I mean, this IAD was something serious; a compact between 48 different states and the federal government that had been used to order the dismissal of (double, sometimes!) murder cases, bank robberies, attempted murders, and any-and-everything else you can possibly think of! And (this is not a "pat on the back!") I knew this law probably as well as anyone in the kkkountry, having researched every case and application of it I could find after getting served with those sealed indictments.

As such, I made it clear (in *no uncertain* terms!) to the "attorney" appointed by the kkkourt to represent me in my (unexpected, so soon!) arraignment that I *demanded* to be tried on both cases (the murder and the attempted murders) "within 120 days as mandated by the IAD" and that I would "waive *no* right under it!" I informed this "attorney" – c. leann smith – also that "failure to try me on either or both the cases would *mandate* dismissal" so the kkkourt, prosekkkution, and her (if she wanted

Fighting

to represent me) all "better get on the ball!" I let them all know (and especially leann in particular) that I "wasn't playing any games," but it seems as if they took me as the typical "stupid uninformed defendant" because the state authorities started violating the IAD within a matter of a couple of weeks, if not just only a few days.

See, another section of the IAD mandating dismissal of all charges says a defendant can't be "shuttled" back and forth between jurisdictions (say, for instance, the feds to tennessee and/or tennessee to the feds) without the *resolution* of any and *all* charges. And I was constantly being transferred to federal custody for kkkourt in the feds one day, only to face kkkourt in the state a few days later under the state of tennessee's custody. This was the very situation the IAD was enacted to prevent, but back and forth I went, back and forth. And I protested to all hell to anyone who was listening[207] that they were "violating my rights! Breaking the law!" with the repeated transfers of custody. But still no one would take me serious or listen, because "what did I know?" I was just another "dumb nigger" who had only the rights "they" chose to give me.

Cool with me. Guess I'll just have to show "them" how much of a "dumb nigger" I am...

---

[207] U.S. Marshals, leann, my federal attorney, kkkourtroom bailiffs whom wouldn't let me enter the kkkourtroom to raise hell directly to the face of prosekkkutor lisa naylor and/or "judge" seth norman!

There was never a time in my youth, no matter how dark and discouraging the days might be, when one resolve did not continually remain with me, and that was a determination to secure an education at any cost..."
Up From Slavery by Booker T. Washington

FISK

Sadness, tension, and fear all helped to suffocate the funeral; the police presence – both visible *and* unseen, local *and* federal – didn't help either. I could dig the pigs' reasoning behind it all, though – no one yet knew who was responsible for the murders (nor who might be next!), plus a veritable *Who's Who of Nashville's Streets* would be walking through the church's doors to pay their respects.

And see and be seen. As Duck, Al, and Johnny had their services held together,[208] seemingly everyone with even the remotest connection to these three made it a point to file past one or all the caskets at the front of the church. I imagine the pigs must have had a field day filling up their intelligence files, as damn near every cat getting any decent money in the 'Ville took a walk down those aisles. There's no telling how many investigations were started or updated that day.

Due to an article in the local rag newspaper – in addition to the added speculations of the "ghetto media" – rumors the morning of the service were already rampant concerning my alleged involvement in the murders. They ran the gamut from Duck & Al having kidnapped me the *night before* their deaths and my somehow gaining control of one of their straps and

---

[208] Mumbles' funeral was held separately – I don't think the other families deemed him "worthy" of being buried with Big Al and Duck.

knocking them all off,[209] to my commissioning hitmen from either my down south or west coast ties, to even my calling in some cousins from my father's side of the family[210] in some convoluted murder plot.

Furthermore, in addition to all of the various rumors already flying, my aunt Nancy was keeping the tension among the family strong behind the scenes – supporting me to my face, yet blaming me for her son's murder behind my back.[211] Ironically, I can still hear clearly my aunt's voice as she hugged me, crying, as we all met up at her house to ride to the funeral: "Delo, *please* find out who did that to my baby!" It was no secret as to what she was asking – she wanted the motherfuckers dead just as much as I did. So for her to blame *me*, or for *anyone* to allow the *thought* into their heads that *I* was somehow responsible for his death, I'll never understand.

Nancy's vindictiveness even went so far as to convince a couple of my other aunts – Virga and Charlene – to join in turning against me; their children, grown ones included, were soon instructed not to "hang with" me. Truly loving Virga and Charlene, and being what I thought was real close to their children, I assumed that at least these aunts would be able to see through the bullshit and would defend me. But no luck there. Shit was crazy. Not only was I hurt and confused, but offended

---

[209] I guess I'm some type of "Ghetto Green Beret," or something, even though I've never had any "formal" military training.
[210] Since Duck was a cousin on my mother's side, I guess. What's ironic, though, is that the main "cousins" attributed to this particular plot were some I hadn't seen or talked to in *years*, if *at all!* Hell, to tell the truth, I'm not even sure if I would recognize them upon seeing them, we're so distantly related! Hilarious! How people sit around and come up with this type of shit, I'll never know.
[211] For the longest while I was in the dark about my aunt's maliciousness in regards to me, but my siblings and a few loyal cousins soon informed me of all she was saying and doing behind my back. My mother continued to keep it from me for as long as she could; I don't blame her. How dreadful did it have to be with your oldest sister blaming your child for her child's death?

and disappointed on top of it all.[212] Initially assuming that Duck's funeral would again pull us all together, it wouldn't soon be long before I finally accepted that everything "family-wise" was irreparably damaged and had forever changed.

Out of all my cousins it was Raymond — my very favorite — who was the most loyal and supportive during this time. *He* knew my heart and the love I held for our family. Raymond was, in fact, the *only* person who I remember that even considered how hard I was taking Duck's death. Crying on his shoulders visiting FCI-Memphis sometime shortly after the funeral, it was he who finally and truly opened my eyes to his mother's viciousness and ways:

"Delo, that's my mama, but my mama don't love nobody but herself!"

Coming from her oldest child, how could that not speak volumes? Moreover, considering the fact that she virtually left him for dead during his 27 years spent in the feds, I can now see where he was coming from.

Yet and still, even with all of the backstabbing bullshit going on around me, I was there at the funeral to support my family and see my cousin for the last time. In fact, not only was I there,[213] but Duck and I were dressed *exactly* the same. Same white suit, same gold tie, same gators; the only visible difference was that I styled mine with a white brim.[214] An unseen difference

---

[212] I mean, let's look at it all the way real — *Duck* was the traitor to our family, *not I*! Hell, I wasn't even the first one in the family that he had done some lowdown, despicable shit to — there was Putt *years* before there was me! Furthermore, only the Creator knows how many times I've visited Duck's grave to mourn him and converse with his spirit — all the while having to endure him, even in death, at the side of the man whom he betrayed me for!...

[213] One of the strangest rumors floating around is that I didn't show up and attend the funeral. Hundreds of people there know the truth, so I can only guess that this comes from 4th, 5th, or 6th hand information through the ghetto media.

[214] My aunt Nancy had advised me as to where to buy my clothes and had the salesman waiting on me when I got there – *she* wanted Duck and I to be dressed alike.

between my and Duck's stylings, however, was the .45 I carried in my shoulder holster – along with the extra seven-round clip in my pocket. As I said earlier, *never again* would I get caught slipping – *anytime* nor *anywhere*. If something happened to have went down in that church, I was protecting my family and myself to the *death*.

Moreover, judging by some of the looks I received, I was more likely to need the strap than not. Not only were most people surprised that I had shown up it seems – in fact, even dressed the same as one of the men in the caskets – a lot seemed to be downright *angry*. However, I could have given a fuck less – I was there for my cousin and my family. I returned stare for stare, frown for frown, *daring* a motherfucker to make a move on me.

Watching my surroundings, I soon spied my cousin Renee (who was doing a little time for boosting again) being escorted in shackles by two CCA officers; I met her at her brother's casket:

"What's up, cuz?" I said awkwardly, hugging her, not really knowing quite what to say.

"Delo," she choked out, *"please get whoever did this to my brother!"*

All I could do was look her in her eyes and nod, but really, there was no need to ask; she already knew what was up. Hugging me back, I noticed she gave an imperceptible jolt as she felt the steel under my arm; soon, the COs hurriedly walked her out of the church. I found out later that she'd requested to leave after thinking about *why* I was armed and then really taking gauge of the atmosphere. Danger was lurking.

Returning to my seat, my eyes and ears were alert for any

I had no ill thoughts on her suggestion back then, but now I'm starting to think it was so she could imagine that it was *I* inside of that casket instead of him.

moves made my way; no worries, though – plus my security was quietly on scene, too: a cat a few rows directly behind me, one each in the far back to my left and right sides – all trusted gunmen, all ready for war, all watching everyone and everything that moved. The services soon started:

"*Everybody here can remember something that Al did for* them, *but who here can remember something that* you *did for* Al?" the Muslim brother speaking asked.

If I were to guess, I'd say, almost no one. Most of the people there seemed more consumed with how *they* would lose the material things that Al *provided them* rather than with losing Al *himself*. It was pitiful. Moreover, I could almost guarantee that most of those cats that he was feeding wouldn't lift a finger to find his killers. Hell, a lot of them thought *I* was the one who smoked him and there I was a few feet away, yet they would do no more than stare if and when they thought I wouldn't notice. Bitches, the whole gang of them. But I digress.

"Who *here has offered to take* Al *out for dinner? To buy* Al *or* his children *some school clothes, shoes, or supplies?? Called* Al *to inquire as to* his *health, or to* his *children's grades?* Who???" the brother continued.

Damn. That touched me and I thought about it; I guess dude really was halfway decent in looking out for the hood – but that still wouldn't have stopped me from putting a hole in him for that move he made, though. Fuck all of that other shit; his day was coming anyway. Just wish my cousin hadn't fell victim, too. The other three I couldn't have given a fuck less about...

Soon after, Security hit my cell informing me of some cats that had been staring at me since I returned to my seat: "Stones" and Al's brother M.J. No threat, really – they were both bitch made suckers in my eyes – and I soon let them know with my returning glare that they could get *whatever* they wanted *whenever* they wanted it. I had a strong feeling that they didn't want to die and join their brother and homeboys, though. Still, never really being able to anticipate the moves of a coward because I didn't think like one, I would keep an eye on them. Who knew what could turn them brave and suicidal?

The Nation brother finished speaking, seemingly having moved the entire church; I know he touched me, putting a lot on my mind to think about. Was I spreading smiles and touching hearts, or spreading tears and breaking them out here running these streets? Moreover, when my own funeral came around, who would be there to mourn my death and who would be there just to make sure I was *dead*? Would people actually be celebrating my demise like I thought? Or would most actually be distraught? Makes you think about what effect you're having on people and the world. Listening to the brother speak sincerely from his heart, I really took stock of how my life was and how I wished it to be.

The longer I sat there, seeing my cousin lifeless in that casket, hearing the anguished cries of my family, being smothered by the ever-growing tension and fear in the air, the more I realized I needed to leave and just allow my family to grieve; I made a call, and soon a car with three more of my "trusted" pulled up to the front of the church, myself walking out with my three guns trailing me. All those that took notice – pigs and other cowards, alike – made no attempt to stop or confront me.

Driving away the sky seemingly darkened, matching the mood I held in the backseat. My cousin was dead; Duck was really gone. Sadness weighing a thousand pounds on my chest, anger ever growing thinking of my family's tears and broken hearts, I wouldn't dare look back at the church.

Later that night, lying in wait atop the roof of my Pop's

duplex to ambush the supposed drive-by that "the streets" rumored, I contemplated how great my world had changed in so little time: Duck dead; my family fractured; and soon I was to become a father. Having no idea whatsoever where my life was headed, I knew it was time for some type of change. Directionless, distraught, and murderously angry, I knew that that could soon be me next lying in a casket, my family in tears yet again...

Duck and Al's death wouldn't be the only ones I was mistakenly suspected of during that time; as 1997 still holds the record for number of homicides in nashville, my name would come up as a suspect in at least one other murder investigation. A few weeks after the funeral, the fools that had gotten jacked earlier that year in The Village – putting my name on blast – would get jacked again, this time with fatal consequences.

One evening in mid-late September, a knock at their dopehouse door[215] would be followed by a gunshot to the head of 15-year-young Keith Stevenson; disregarding the fact that Keith was my little cousin Juan's best friend at the time, the "ghetto media" quickly placed my name in the mix of the ensuing investigation. Ironically, yet luckily for me, I was at the exact time of the murder embroiled in a brawl with some cats from another side of town beefing with my brother Carvin; during the melee, I would get hit upside my head with a two-by-four, resulting in my needing a CAT scan later that night. Fighting our way out of the scrum,[216] my brother would overhear a comment from a pig police called to the scene that

---

[215] Yep! The *same* spot as last time! How smart of them to keep hustling out of the same spot, huh?
[216] And I must say that we *got down*, outnumbered at least 3 to 1, with some cats I didn't expect to get down with me doing so, and a cat I *did* expect to ride nutting up like a little bitch! This particular coward even had *my* gun in *his* waistband, yet didn't throw *one* punch, pull a trigger, or even move *a finger* to help!

shows how much my name was ringing at the time:

"*Hold up! Hold up! Where my brother at? Where Delo?*" my brother hollered above the fray.

He was speaking to a friend "getting down" with us; in the chaos, he didn't realize the pig was close enough to overhear him. The response he heard was shocking:

"*Delo!!!*" said the pig, "Kenneth Deangelo Thomas??? *He is a very dangerous individual! Stay away from him!!!*"

Wow, right? This from just some random pig in a uniform, overhearing my family-given nickname, yet that being enough to quote my entire "government" and tell people to stay away from me! Unbelievable. I thought about the implications of it all as I shot up the other cats' neighborhood later that night after I left the hospital...

Furthermore, it wasn't as if my attitude discouraged the thoughts that people were having about me; after that funeral, those looks I received, and all of the rumors that consistently involved me, I basically took the attitude of "fuck it" in regards to the street shit and just embraced whatever label – "killer," "the Reaper," "Toe-tag-em," "not-to-be-crossed" – that it gave me. My whole thing was if you *thought* I did it – whatever the fuck "it" was – then come and *act* like I did and *do* something about it! Because I refused to bow down or run from anyone! And that went for the pigs, the streets, cats' families, *who-the-fuck-ever!* I was ready for *whatever, whenever, however!*

Perfect example: One day shortly after the funeral, while paying for gas near my Pop's spot, Vell had me to take notice of some cats he peeped staring at me when I walked into the station; it was Cletie and another Acklen cat in Al's minivan. Them pulling off before I realized who they were, I hurriedly followed the fools[217] down 8th Ave in an attempt to confront

---

[217] Or was *I* the foolish one?

their stares. Catching up to them at the Kroger's,[218] my hand caressed the 9mm in my lap just *itching* for a reason to open fire. Circling the van, staring a hole through him a couple of times at three-miles-an-hour or so, I pulled off once I realized that he wasn't as suicidal as I first suspected.

Leaning on my car in front of my Pop's house a couple of days later rapping with Trina, lo and behold whom did I see pulling up in the same minivan?[219] After giving him a chance to make a move if he wanted to, I pushed everything to a head:

"Cuz, why don't you tell your friend to step up out the car and talk to me like a man? I said to Trina.

I was staring directly at him as I said it. I was also leaning on my car with my arms folded across my chest; he could tell I was "strapped." Surprisingly, though, he hopped out to talk to me!

"Man, how the fuck y'all fools gonna think I killed my own cousin?!" I exploded after a few moments of tense quiet.

"Man, we know you didn't have nothing to do with that."

What? Now I was confused! He was even looking me in the eyes when he said it! And to top it all off, this fool wasn't even flinching or nervous at all!

"Well, what's all this bullshit I keep hearing in the streets about y'all motherfuckers supposed to be doing this, y'all motherfuckers supposed to be doing that?!" I countered. It was easy to see that I was prepared for a confrontation.

"Man, that's just that bullshit – you know how the streets is. We know you didn't do that shit."

What the hell? I had heard so many rumors and warnings

---

[218] Well, catching up to Cletie, anyway – the other cat had made it into the grocery store by the time I made it through the light.
[219] He was coming to see Trina – and although I know her loyalty to me, a lot of the lines were blurred between friend and foe during this time. Hell, up until a few months before, *I* would've rode myself with most of the Acklen cats in any beefs they had.

concerning Al's homeboys supposedly trying to retaliate on me, that I didn't halfway know which way was up sometimes. I was on hyper-alert, ready to fight for my life and kill every second of every single day since my kidnapping. Moreover, I didn't trust anyone I knew he ran with. Including this motherfucker.

"*Well, what was that shit at the gas station the other day then?*" I said.

"*Man, I didn't know* what *was going on – dude that was riding with me said 'there go Delo,' I looked over at you then drove off. I didn't think nothing of it until I noticed you following me. I kept thinking to myself:* 'Damn, I hope this young nigga don't try nothing."

Huh??? The way he was explaining it, I almost smoked his ass for nothing! I damn near even *believed* him! Either way, though, good thing for him that he didn't make any stupid, sudden moves that day. Because I sure as fuck wouldn't have hesitated to send him to rest with his homeboys.

Talking a little while longer, we discussed a few other things that gave me an understanding as to a lot that had been happening and/or rumored in the streets. He even let me know his thoughts as to who he thought was responsible, and his reason for thinking so; I wasn't surprised, as they were similar to my own. It was clear to us both that at least part of the blame lay with someone with close access and information concerning Al's whereabouts and movements – just as in the robbery from a few months before. We parted with what I felt was a clear understanding of each other's perspectives on things, but I still didn't trust him, though. There was just too much going on, too many rumors being circulated in the streets, and too many loose ends as to what happened the night they were killed for me to trust no more than a limited few...

Incidents of a similar nature during this time period were too numerous to even mention now; most of it was behind my

Fisk

highly sensitive nature and refusal to not show my face in all the haunts where I knew possible trouble lay. In fact, I may have been hanging out even more than usual in a show to all that *I wasn't going!* People were seeing my presence in the hoods of south nashville more than at any time since when I was a teen. No way in hell was I going to allow anyone to feel like I was ducking and dodging anyone or anything that the streets were screaming. If anybody or anything was coming my way then I wanted it to come *then*, while I was ready.

Likewise, I can't honestly sit here and say that I wasn't abrasive sometimes, too. Even though I've never been a "shit starter," instigator, or bully, I never failed to let it be known when given the chance that I felt as if a *motherfucker wouldn't dare fuck with me!* And they didn't either. So soon all the plotting and rumors would turn into stopped conversations when I appeared and whispers when I left. Everyone became too afraid to say something to me directly. Sometimes even people I had been cool with for years. I was miserable inside. I really found no solace anywhere...

One night, attempting to escape the turmoil surrounding me for at least a little while, I agreed to kick it with a coworker from Dairy Queen;[220] at his direction we ended up at 88.1 FM – Fisk University's radio station.

Formerly the site of the amerikkkan "union" army's Fort Gillem during the amerikkkan "civil war," Fisk University was established in 1867 shortly after the South's humiliating defeat.

Fisk is most famously known as the alma mater of alumnus W.E.B. DuBois and the Fisk Jubilee Singers, but also served as

---

[220] You'd better believe I still worked there – I was still on parole, wasn't I?!? Not having a job would have been the quickest excuse to violate me and lock me up when there was no reason or evidence otherwise to have done so. Plus Todd and Peggy were both cool as a cloud, and working with them gave me some grounding and an escape from the bullshit of the streets.

the intellectual breeding ground of thinkers and activists such as Diane Nash, (former mayor of Washington, D.C.) Marion Barry, (Georgia Congressman) John Lewis, in addition to music mogul Matthew Knowles, renowned poet and Professor Nikki Giovanni, and filmmaker Antoine Fuqua among others. Home to the four-week meeting of "the generals" of the Civil Rights Movement in the summer of 1961, revolutionary luminaries such as Ms. Ella Baker, Kwame Ture (then known as Stokely Carmichael), John Lewis, the Rev. James Lawson, Ms. Diane Nash, Ms. Lucretia Collins, Julian Bond and others walked these same grounds plotting their impacts on the nation. I had no idea the role this beautiful and inviting place would play in my geopolitical development and my growing sense of serving a positive and constructive purpose in my Black and Brown peoples' lives.

Fiskites made me proud by raising hell just recently the day after Fuhrer Grab-em-by-the-pussy's election by protesting and blocking off the streets in downtown nashville. Although I myself would advocate even more radical tactics than stopping traffic, I have to admit, the spontaneous student protest *was* newsworthy and an effective way of showing displeasure with the results of the election of the Russian dupe. But let me be clear by saying that not only do I advocate the use of marches, boycotts, blocking off streets, etc., I feel that we have not only the clear right but the *duty* to use *all* means available to us to fight back against our oppressors and oppression. Including armed "insurrection." But I digress...

To take it back to my story, to say 88.1 blew my mind away – hell, the entire campus – is an understatement! Brothers were sitting around vibing and chilling, politicking, and just plain old kicking it with no worries of one another shooting, backstabbing, or otherwise harming each other! These brothers didn't know me from the man in the moon, yet embraced me instantly as one of their own in intelligence and brotherhood! I felt *safe* and *secure* letting my guard down for one of the few times in my life! I didn't even realize places like this *existed* outside of fairytales or the movies! Fisk was the shit! This was the first time in my life actually being around progressive and positive people – progressive and positive *Black people* – all trying to make a way in the world and succeed! I could've almost smacked myself thinking of all the times I had rode past this jewel in north nashville never giving it more than a fleeting glance! I instantly felt *home!*

Within days, I applied for admission – writing an essay expressing my desire to leave the streets in the past – and I was accepted rather quickly, but still leaving me only a few days before the start of classes. With no time really to prepare, for a while there, to be honest, I was somewhat lost and confused as to what to do and how to do it. This wasn't like high school (or jail, for that matter) where everything was structured and people always told you where to go and what to do – here you were on your own to make your own decisions and do your own thing. I had no ideas *what* to do, *where* to start, *who* to talk to concerning my ignorance – which was in fact *everything* concerning the "college life."

Who knows how many faux pas I committed my first semester there? A major one was wearing a white suit to Convocation – when all men were supposed to wear *black*.[221]

---

[221] In my defense, I only learned of the welcoming ceremony a few hours before its start, with the young lady that inquired as to whether I would attend only advising me to "wear a suit." Highlighting my ignorance, however, the *ladies* were supposed to wear white – dresses, I think – while the men were supposed to rock *black*. I mistakenly thought all of the stares that I received from the other men were ones of jealousy over how suave I looked, but after being seated – men to one side of the chapel, women to the other – I soon realized how flashy I had to seem, with my appearing a salt speck in a sea of pepper suits. Got my picture in the yearbook, though!

Another glaring faux pas was my consistent referring to my professors as "Miss" or "Mister" instead of their more proper titles of "Doctor" or "Professor." An egregious example was my repeated calling of one of my favorite professors "Miss Bracks" instead of the proper "Dr. Bracks." After not understanding at the time the strange look I used to receive in return, I can only hope these years later she knows that my misspeak was by no means any form of disrespect of her or her gender or any sign of male chauvinism; all I can hope is that she was smarter than I was and knew that I meant nothing derogatory by it. Equally, in my defense, I ask you, how was *I* supposed to know of my blunder since no one ever told me or even corrected me? I think my professors could all tell that I meant no disrespect by it – I just didn't *know*. And as with other mistakes I've made throughout my life, I corrected it once I realized the error. All I can hope is that they all knew that in no way did I mean any disrespect.

So in other words, I was out of my element, yet totally where I belonged all at the same time. No one I was close to had ever been to college of any kind, so they, of course, couldn't or wouldn't have been of any help. Not that I would've sought any, anyway – hell, I was used to everybody always looking to *me* for the answers. Even my friend Lisa, who was already a sophomore there, I dared not lean on too much because I was too embarrassed for her to know all that I *didn't* know. All I knew was that whatever needed to be done to be a successful student, I would figure out and do. And I did.

Of course, all of the extremely beautiful women at Fisk made my desire to get it together even easier and faster. The Bay Area, Philadelphia, St. Louis, Pittsburgh, Memphis, Knoxville, Birmingham, Atlanta, Chicago, New York, Indianapolis, Louisville, Cleveland, Houston – even The Bahamas – all supplied the campus with gorgeous women! I mean these women were not only from all over the country, but they were, in fact, from all over *the world!* Outnumbering us men *8-1!* I was in Young Black Man Heaven!

And Tsawa knew me well, making what I thought at the time was the oddest request: "Don't start fucking off with all those pretty girls!" Yeah, right. Attempting to keep the little peace amongst us we did share, I agreed, but come on – I knew it to be a lie before the words even formed in my throat![222] And she did, too. I mean, I was already "fucking off" when things were somewhat cool between us, so *why* exactly would I stop when things were rocky as hell, anyway? It was never far from my mind how she'd never let her boyfriend go and that he'd soon be getting out of CCA anyway – no way was I going to sit around just waiting for *that* to happen! Take care of my responsibilities concerning my coming son, and enjoy my time with her as much as possible *while* it lasted, yeah, but continue to do *what* I felt *whenever* I felt like it, *that* was my thinking. No way was I going to just leave my heart completely in *her* hands again. Or any other woman's for that matter. Women couldn't be trusted with your heart. I learned that painful lesson first with Soyayya – which was then reinforced by Tsawa herself. So fuck that – I was living my life. If it worked out with her, cool, and if not? – well, I wasn't about to wait around just in case it didn't.

Used to "enjoying the company" of numerous women while running the streets, I had no doubt that I would enjoy the company of more than a few ladies on campus, also. I took my homeboy "Tee" with me to Registration, cracking him up as I

---

[222] It may seem a fucked up thing to say, but the typical man doesn't lie to women that he cares *nothing* about. Lying takes effort, consideration and thought — even if only a little; lying is sometimes done to protect a woman's feelings, to protect her from her fears, her worries, her insecurities—so to take the time out to lie to a woman is sometimes the clearest sign that a man actually cares. Ironic, isn't it? Nonetheless, I no longer have the patience to do so…

pointed out all the women I would soon "make acquaintance" of:

"*See her?*" I pointed to a caramel-colored, longhaired, Pocahontas look-alike, "*she'll be pregnant before the end of the semester.*"

He almost hit the floor laughing, having just as much confidence in me as I had in myself – he knew the deal. I continued:

"*And see her?*" I pointed to a short, extremely beautiful, deep dark chocolate, edible-and-luscious-looking, human Coke bottle standing beside who I assumed to be her father, *"Her Pops is going to be pissed at me!"*

We both shared a nice laugh, but I was just bullshitting around. Somewhat, anyway. Tee would soon see me with her and most of the other women I pointed out that day, also.

At first, I thought I would have to quit my job, but Todd and Peggy were completely supportive, accommodating my work hours around my class schedule. In some ways, in fact, they were more like an aunt and uncle, giving me raises regularly and paying me all of my hours even when the rush hour traffic from school had me running late. I'll never be able to completely thank those two enough.

My life quickly turned into one of a full course load of classes, federal work-study in the campus library and then kicking it in the dorms with all the young ladies I was meeting after that – this was my typical day. I'm trying to remember now, how was it that I even made any time for hustling *or* studying? It's hard to believe, but somehow I did. I had one foot in the streets, and one foot in school. Not realizing it at the time, I was actually neglecting both, however.

Fisk also became kind of the nail in the coffin in my relationship with Tsawa. Especially after she more than once found me with my newfound friend "Jannah" – the woman with whom I would soon fall in love. Not only did I become neglectful of Tsawa, but also blatantly disrespectful by being seen around the city with Jannah, and even going so far as to introduce her to my family and friends. In fact, Jannah was the reason behind Tsawa (and ultimately, myself) moving out of the apartment we shared.[223] Thinking I was being slick one day, I left the home in one car, only quickly to go to my Pop's house to trade vehicles. Now in the Astrovan, I headed up to Fisk to pick up Jannah and another friend to show them around the city. Still making my business runs,[224] I received a call from Tsawa's cell phone – which was strange because I *knew* I left her at home; why not use the house phone?

"What are you doing?"

She sounded strange, possibly even suspicious of me, but maybe I was just being paranoid because I knew I was creeping.

"Nothing. Just riding around taking care of some business."

"Aw, ok. Who with you?"

Oh shit.

"Who with me? Who the hell did I leave the house with? Nobody's with me! I'm with my motherfucking self!"

Overreacting to the question – a dead giveaway that I was doing something wrong.

"Oh, ok. No reason to get upset. I was just asking."

She tried keeping me on the phone but I made up some excuse to hang up and got back to attending to my friends. Not even a couple of minutes later, she soon called back:

"What car are you in?"

Huh?

---

[223] This was the new apartment; we had, by then, moved out of the one that Duck had tipped off to Al a couple of days after my kidnapping.
[224] Discreetly, I thought; but I found out later that they knew what I was up to all along.

"What fucking car did I leave the house in?? You stay asking me some weird ass questions," I snapped off.

I have to ashamedly admit now that I wasn't the nicest person to her at all around that time. No excuses, but our relationship had been for months on a quick downward spiral after we took a trip down south that had ended in an argument,[225] and I had finally accepted the fact in my mind that she would always in some type of way have ties to dude. So my attitude was really like "fuck it" and "fuck her." But we still had a child soon to come.

"Oh. I thought I saw you in the minivan. My mama came by to pick me up a lil while ago and now I'm in her car."

What??? Saw me??? Shit!!! Fuck!!! Who has time to deal with the bullshit I know is coming???

"Naw, you didn't see me. Maybe it was my brother, or something. Anyway, I gotta go. Let me call you back later."

Ironically, the woman was following me the entire time. Pulling up at the gas station to fill up, a few seconds later she pulled up in the stall right next beside me. Busted!

"Un huh, you caught! I thought you said you was by yo'self?!"

Embarrassed, and yeah, I admit, even a little afraid of her reaction, I was tongue-tied and on stuck feeling stupid.

"So you not gonna introduce me to your friends?" she said.

As I saw that she wasn't really trying to cause a scene by getting violent – to my much-appreciated relief, of course – I quickly recovered:

"Ok, Friend Number One, Friend Number Two, this is my baby mama. Baby mama, these are my friends."

"Baby mama." Such a derogatory, dismissive and belittling term in my eyes and so disrespectful to her. I wish even now I

---

[225] I realized later that she was completely right in her expressed concerns on our "business trip," but at the time I wasn't trying to hear it.

could somehow take that back. Furthermore, I no longer use that term when referring to the mothers of my children or others.

Anyway, Jannah and my other friend started laughing and I quickly pulled Tsawa to the side so we could talk. I somehow convinced her (or at least I thought I did) that I was only giving them a ride to get something to eat (or some other bullshit like that) and that the only reason I lied was because I knew how she would "trip." Acting as if she believed me, I quickly dropped Jannah and my other friend back off to campus, and met back up with Tsawa – whom I guess by then had finished with her own "creep session."

A couple of weeks later in what can only be described ironically as one of my "smartest" moments in life, I agreed to give Jannah and the same friend a ride to the mall; for some dumbass reason, I decided it best to go to the same mall at which Tsawa worked. Being what I thought was careful, I parked at an entranceway away from the one near where she worked, going one way while my friends went the other. Delightfully surprising her by popping up at her job "just to express my love,"[226] she thought it strange when I left the store and walked in the opposite direction in which she thought my car should have normally been parked.[227] Taking her break minutes later, I was soon surprised to see her 7 or 8 months pregnant ass running through the mall, catching me again with the same two women as last time! Caught! No way out of this one. Agreeing to go ahead and "take a break," we decided she would move out of our apartment and back in with her mother until at least after

---

[226] Tsawa and I did love one another, but I forever had issues with the ties she kept to other men, and – can you believe – she forever had issues with the fact that I didn't like being sexually tied down to one woman. The nerve of that woman, right? (I say this in jest!)

[227] This woman somehow always knew when I was up to something – even before *I* did!

our son was born. She also made me agree to "not fuck anyone."

To that end, she still came over every day, and the only thing that changed between us was the fact that she went home to her mother at night. In fact, I honestly think things were better between us while we were living apart because we seemed to have a better appreciation for one another. Moreover, I liked the freedom of not always having someone question my every move and whereabouts. Within a week, though, I would too even fuck this up.

One day after making love, I would ask Tsawa to take the sheets off the bed so that I could change them. Nothing unusual – or so I thought – as we were at the time also doing the laundry, anyway. Nevertheless, *her* mind told her that I was "up to something." "Up to something?" – hell, I honestly had no intentions whatsoever at the time of being "up to" any more than my usual. However, her woman's intuition[228] inspired her to unlock my backdoor and its screen door when I wasn't paying attention.[229] She knew that I never came in or out of the backdoor, and as long as my alarm engaged indicating that everything was locked up and secured the way I left it, I wouldn't check. Big mistake on my part. When later that night I had Jannah over for the first time ever and spending the night, we would both be awakened in the morning first by the doorbell, then knocks at the front door, and finally by the alarm going off indicating a security breach. I reached for the gun I kept beside my bed as the bedroom door flew open.

"*Un huh, I knew you had a bitch in here!*"

I lowered my pistol; I honestly did love her and she was pregnant with my child.

---

[228] Which I think the Creator was totally unfair to give to the already smarter sex, by the way!
[229] When Tsawa had moved out, she gave me her house keys; she did, however, keep the extra sets of keys to the cars.

"Man, what are you doing here? We don't even go together no more!"

The alarm was still blaring, waking up the entire neighborhood; I knew the alarm monitoring company would soon be calling. More important to my immediate concerns, though, I had an enraged and pregnant woman in my face that seemed to have murder in her eyes! Strangely, though, the look didn't seem to be for me:

"And you been fucking this bitch in our bed! You been fucking this bitch in our bed!!!"

Technically that wasn't true; by the time Jannah and I had made it *to* the bedroom we *both* were in need of some blissful sleep in one another's arms, but I had enough sense not to argue the point at the time. Jannah let out a laugh as Tsawa had screamed the last statement, causing me to have to hold Tsawa back from attacking her. Can you imagine the scene? – Jannah lying in bed as naked as she came into this world, as I'm completely nude myself, all while I'm trying to force out of my bedroom door an enormously pregnant and dangerously pissed woman! Not one of my finest moments, I should say. Anyway, it would get worse.

Somehow holding Tsawa back as I turned off the alarm and gave the proper code when the monitoring company called, I did my best to diffuse the situation. I brought up the fact that we were "officially broken up," that I knew she was still communicating with and even going to visit her supposed-to-be-ex-boyfriend, and all other kinds of things better left unsaid until another time. Needless to say, I was not successful at diffusing the situation at all! I doubt if she heard a word I said, anyway.

Distracting me with a knee to the groin, I was thereafter stabbed in the hand with a chef's knife grabbed off my kitchen counter.[230] Bleeding and trailing her to my bedroom, I watched horrifically as she pulled back the covers and slashed Jannah across both her legs! I couldn't believe this shit! This woman was fucking crazy! The entire apartment turned into one big scream fest, as Jannah was screaming in pain and shock over being stabbed, I was screaming at Tsawa at how she was "fucking crazy," and she was screaming as to how she was going to "kill" us both!

"*Fuck man, FUCK! I got to get this girl to the hospital!*"

Jannah was bleeding everywhere! I couldn't believe how much blood was coming out of her legs!

"*Fuck that bitch! Let her die! Both of y'all gon' die!*"

Tsawa was being completely irrational – all the while she's swinging the knife erratically, not really at myself or Jannah, but still coming dangerously close! Plus, of course, she'd already stabbed us both. I got in between her and Jannah, as it seemed like she wanted to strike at her again. And I tried to talk some sense into her:

"*Man, fuck, man, FUCK! You* tripping, *man! You going to* jail *if she die!*"

"*I don't give a fuck!*"

"*Please, just let me take her to the hospital!*"

By then, Jannah had somehow put on her clothes, but the blood was soaking profusely through her pants' legs. Noticing it, I was getting even more nervous and afraid that she would die from the loss of blood. Strangely, though, she was calmer than I was; I guess it was the shock and adrenaline pulling her through....

How did we all three make it outside without Jannah or I stabbed seriously again? – I don't know, but somehow, we did.

---

[230] That's where we had made it by then, with my guiding her away from the bedroom and Jannah; this is when I noticed my backdoor wide open.

Yet and still Tsawa wouldn't let me get Jannah to the hospital; in fact, it was hard enough just being able to shield Jannah into my car. Moreover, every time I would attempt to make my way inside so that I could drive to the hospital, Tsawa would slash murderously close to my face and chest.

"*Look, man!...Goddamn, man!... SHIT!!! – I'm not about to keep letting you fucking cut me!!!*"

"*FUCK YOU!!! I'm finna KILL y'all asses!!!... Both of y'all about to die!!!*" she replied.

"*Goddamned, man!...You bullshitting!...I got to get this girl to the hospital!!!*"

"*FUCK HER!!!*" she said, slashing at me again, and then I remembered the gun I kept in my trunk.[231]

"*Look, man. You fucking tripping… Please, just calm the fuck down!...Look, I'm about to get the goddamned gun out the trunk and you know I'm not about to let you keep cutting me!*"

By then, of course, Jannah was safely secured in the passenger seat with both doors locked, but with Tsawa not letting me get in myself, I went for the trunk. However, before I could get it open, again Tsawa came slashing at me with the knife. Thinking then (I'm assuming) to go for the gun herself with her extra set of keys,[232] she was distracted enough that I was able to rush up on her, push her down knocking the knife out of her hands and tossing it in the bushes, and then finally make it in the car to drive off without getting cut again!

What a relief, right? Of course not! Just what could I possibly say or do to comfort and/or console this young lady who was horribly harmed under my care? No matter *what*

---

[231] This was an extra gun; I had locked the other strap in my bedroom safe somehow before Tsawa had stabbed us.
[232] She, in fact, did admit to me later that her first thought was to get that extra gun *before* she ever came into my apartment. Think about how this could have turned out had she done so!

happened – no matter *how* it all went down – there is *no excuse* for harm befalling her when she was with me! Call it "old fashioned" all you want, but men are supposed to be the protectors of women, children, and the elderly, and in this, I miserably failed! Pathetic. I don't even think I was man enough to look at her for too long or too hard and instead I concentrated on making it to the nearest hospital as quickly as I could. And to Jannah's credit, she stayed calm throughout this entire ordeal, and, in turn, that helped to calm me…

 Why Jannah didn't completely cut me out of her life after this horrible incident — even over two decades later I can't entirely say or comprehend. I know that I wouldn't have blamed her even a *fraction* of a little, had she no longer acknowledged even my very presence. Instead, she allowed me to love her; she allowed herself to love me; and in turn we both allowed ourselves to shortly fall in love with one another. I grew on to recognize Jannah as the most empathetic and understanding person that I've been blessed to know in this life.

 Yet, I don't want to mischaracterize or oversimplify things as if Jannah was/is "perfect" or something – no person that has ever walked this earth ever has been nor ever *will* be, in my estimation – however, she was/is "beauty personified." Nonetheless, I'm not referring to her physical attributes (although she *is* stunningly attractive!), but to the fact that her inherent character of that of a woman who's caring, comforting, supportive, understanding, empathetic, loyal, protective, passionate, and – at least in regard to me – forgiving of my (numerous! I'm ashamed to admit) faults. And let's be honest here – how rare is she in this day and age of callous, selfish, and overly materialistic people?

 Jannah even understood me as a man in ways that I probably didn't even understand myself at the time: (without prompting nor a request from me) she naturally gave me space whenever I needed room to think or feel or vent; gave me attention when-and-however I needed to feel it; and even respectfully and coyly (because most of the time I never even realized it was happening!) put me "back in my place" when I was getting too "out of line." Compare that to Tsawa, whom to this day I feel has never really understood me as a man – nor especially understood and/or respected me as a *Black* man struggling every single moment of every single day just to *survive* in this kkkountry.

For example, I remember an instance when – months before I had even enrolled at Fisk, let alone *met* Jannah – I had called Tsawa at home to inform her I was wrapping up some business and would be there "in 15 minutes at the latest." Well, it actually took about *45* minutes or more – because I was harassed, pulled over, and searched by a rednekkk pig for "recklessly eye-balling" him (not even a mile or so from my home) when we were *going in opposite directions at a STOP sign!* I mean, I was supposed to look directly in front of me at *a STOP sign* in addition to my left and right, right?! Well, evidently, not to this pig! Because no sooner than we had both made it through the STOP sign did this pig make a U-turn, hit the lights, and ask me "What the fuck [was I] looking at?" I instantly took offense yet still calmly answered, "I'm looking at what the fuck is in front of me like *I'm supposed to!"*

Well, my matching "obscenity" for obscenity and disrespect for disrespect didn't go over all that well, so within seconds – after being instructed to "get the fuck out of the car!" – I'm (tightly) cuffed behind my back, (roughly!) put in the back of the police car, and forced to watch (fuming!) as this pig (unlawfully!) searched and tossed the inside of my car and trunk a couple of times over. Only after not finding – nor planting –

anything did the rednekkk inform me that I was "going to jail for driving without a license and [that my vehicle] would be towed." Not this night, motherfukkker – in his angry haste to enslave me in the cage known as his back seat, the bastard hadn't really searched my person and my *valid driver's license* was in my wallet in my back pocket! Stupid racist motherfukkker. After being informed of my license and the pig checking himself to confirm I indeed had it, I was let completely out the car, uncuffed, and instructed to "watch who the fuck [I'm] looking at next time!" before he quickly pulled off in the direction he had come. The bastard drove away so fast and I was so pissed and dumbfounded about what had just happened, that I didn't even notice the few hundred dollars missing out of my wallet until a couple of hours later...

But the drama wasn't over yet for the night: I was "late" – and being "late" was the farthest thing on my mind. But not for long. Although all I wanted and needed was to take a shower, make love, and lay my head down and rest away my frustration, anger, and fury, I wasn't a few steps in our apartment before I heard "What happened to 15 minutes?!! Your bitch didn't wanna let you leave, did she?!?!" And even though I heard the venom clearly in her tone, I still found myself silently searching her face for *some* sign that she was just fucking playing with me somehow. But she was clearly serious – and actually seemingly waiting for an answer – so I just turned and walked back out the door without ever speaking one word.

Crazy, right? Even crazier is up until that point – after we had become pregnant and actually "officially" decided to "be together" – I had been *faithful and loyal* to her while she was still writing, talking to, and sneakily visiting her *supposed-to-be-ex* boyfriend in the C.C.A. county prison. Hell, she was even stealing from me to provide for him! How did/do I know this to be true? Well, he couldn't keep his mouth shut, cats and kittens in his circle weren't as loyal as he thought, and I set up more than a couple of traps (for Tsawa) to confirm what kept getting back to me. And it was all true.

But like a fool, *I* continued to keep it "true" and faithful for a time – partly out of a thought (wish perhaps) that she would "come to her senses" – the closer we grew together, but mostly out of anticipation for our soon-to-come son – until this evening when I had had enough. And from there – because of the constant and consistent disrespectfulness (including that which I had perceived at a recent trip we had taken), disloyalty, unsupportiveness, and not understanding of what kind of man I was and could be – I gave up on our "relationship" and my entire attitude towards her changed. Yet, I doubt if she ever even realized why any of this happened, as I admit to (and regret) being an extremely reticently incommunicative man...

Therefore, a "wise" man would have let Tsawa "go" after she cut me and Jannah, right? I mean notwithstanding that she attempted to murder me (for at least the *second* time that I *knew* of!) and an innocent young woman, yet also I knew and felt in my heart and mind that she and I were not destined to "work" for a multitude of reasons. Right? But *who* was a "wise" man back then? Because surely the hell you can see that *I* wasn't.[233]

So unfairly to us all (myself, Jannah, Tsawa, our coming son) – despite Tsawa stabbing us; despite my growing love of Jannah and increasing resentment of Tsawa; despite her (Tsawa's) boyfriend still being in her life and soon coming home; despite my *knowing as deeply as I've ever known anything in this lifetime* that she and I couldn't "work" being who we were at that time, I soon "forgave" Tsawa of the stabbing and agreed to

---

[233] A fool learns from his own mistakes while a wise man learns from the mistakes of not only himself but also others. Yet a *damned fool* just doesn't learn at all, it seems! And clearly, without a doubt, I was a damned fool back then...

"work on us" (mostly) for the benefit of our coming son. Yet I was wrong, and all I did was serve to prolong all of our pains...

Therefore, we were "together" again, but always in the back of my mind, still she wasn't *my* girl, you know? How could she be? She had so many ties to former boyfriends and other men that no way was I falling for *that* type of trick again. So I enjoyed the time we spent together and fun we had as best as I could, but I knew that realistically that there was no chance of us ever really "being together." Or at least not for long. I just didn't trust her. Which made me untrustworthy to her myself.

So in hindsight, how smart was it of me to impregnate a woman I knew to be the next man's anyway? Whether he was in jail or not, he still had her heart. I was just a placeholder until he came home. And you reap what you sow.[234] But try telling that to a 19-year-old fresh out of prison with a ready, willing and dangerously attractive woman right there in front of you, however. Besides, as I explained earlier, before she became pregnant, I wasn't necessarily planning on her being around forever anyway. So what did I care that she kept ties to other men and ethically belonged to someone else? Never mess with another man's women, money, or property, though. I would learn this the hard way...

---

[234] With that being said, never will I allow myself again to be involved in the disrespect of someone's marriage or "committed" relationship. Relationships are hard enough in and of themselves, so how unrighteous and unwise would I be to again interject myself into one? I've already *learned* that lesson. Besides, who needs the added drama and/or potential for a violent outcome?? I know *I* the hell don't. There are far too many "unhitched" women out there in the world for me to seek out *that* type of "excitement." Nor do I need the karma...

"There was nothing outside of self-destruction that could stop my progression. I discovered time and again while reading Black history that regardless of a person's background, when one's mind, behavior, circumstances, and spirit are aligned with destiny, the impossible can be achieved…
Ajamu Niamke Kamara (b.k.a. Stanley "Tookie" Williams)

CONVICTED

Hearing Youngsta's father and his testimony up there on the stand created craters in my heart; the love and loss he felt over losing his son hit me savagely, deeply, having no mercy on my spirit and the guilt I felt over the person I used to be. Regardless of the fact that I take to my grave that I wasn't the person who killed Youngsta, his father's words and tears caused tears in my own heart that will never subside.

I often wonder, who *was* Youngsta? What type of person was he? What type of son? What type of brother? Was he a good friend? A good boyfriend to his female companions? Was he a father?

What were his dreams? His wants? His wishes? His fears? His secrets? His regrets?

Was he someone whom I would have liked had I had the chance to ever meet and get to know him? Would he have even liked me as a person if we were ever given that chance?

I think about all of the cats that I've met over the years (in the streets and incarcerated, both) from different hoods, different cities, different states, different walks of life, different affiliations that I've gotten to know and like and even have love for who – had we possibly met under different circumstances than we had – we would have both been eyeing each other as enemies. Isn't that pathetic?

All of us have families and/or loved ones that love and care for us, people that worry about getting that phone call saying something awful has happened or we're in trouble somehow. All of us have dreams, wishes, wants, fears, loves, and the like that make us all human and in essence one and the same. There isn't much difference between us, but somehow, some way, those small differences we have, have been played up to the point where we are killing one another. "Sad" doesn't even begin to describe it all.

And what of Youngsta's parents, especially his father? No parent should have to bury his or her child. Yet look at how often this occurs in our Black and Brown communities – and usually due to our *own* hands. Why is it that we're so able to be compassionate and understanding and empathetic of others, but not of ourselves? Why do we as a people so love other races, but seemingly not our own? What is *wrong* with us? What is/was *wrong* with me???

How could I be angered at the unjust deaths of Trayvon, Tamir, Sandra, Alton, Laquan, Jordan, Philando, Michael, Freddie, George, Breonna, Ahmaud, etc., without also be angered at the deaths of Zavieon Dobson, Treyonta Burleson, Hadiya Pendleton, Youngsta *and* Old School, too? How could I not be?! Every single one of their unwarranted premature deaths were/are symptomatic of the oppressive system in which we Black, Brown, and Native peoples are forced to live in this kkkountry. Some may consider that as unfairly transferring of *personal* blame onto the shoulders of amerikkkan society in general, but I see it as placing it exactly where it should lay: if the USA was actually — or even *strived* to be — the meritorious libertarian democracy for all that it propagates to the world that it is, then we/I would have no complaints. But it's not – Blacks have never really been universally allowed to vote[235] — and the oppressive hypocrisy that it constantly dishes to people like me serves as a daily slap in the face. Then, sadly, the unwise among us take our frustrations out on one another — often with deadly consequences.

More so than anything else, I feel that we, as a community, as a race, as a family, as a potential nation have to *care* about and for one another more. We have to *care*. And until we do, *why* should anyone else?!!!

If I didn't realize so entirely with Old School's son, I knew so with Youngsta's father that the "old Delo" was dead, never to be revived. Because I couldn't (can't) deny that I care – Youngsta's father could have very much been my own (had some bullets not missed their mark), in far too many instances. Damn...

You know, I wonder sometimes if I wore the distress of the person I used to be on my face and some took that as a sign of my guilt or something? Because if so, they were only *partially* right. I was guilty (true enough) of living far too long of my life in *exactly* the way it was set up for "my kind" to live in order for us to destroy one another, but of Youngsta's death I held no culpability so I just *knew* I would win an acquittal, yet the jury convicted me anyway.

You know what? I take some of that back because in the back of my mind I *did* feel like "they" wouldn't let me leave that kkkourtroom without some type of conviction. The atmosphere didn't feel right, didn't smell right, didn't sound right – just wasn't "right." Nor was it "righteous" — as my charges should've been dismissed (mandated" by law, remember!) months before and it was illegal to hold the trial anyway.

---

[235] Don't believe me — check for yourself how many of us have been "duly convicted" of "crimes" since the passage of 13th Amendment so as to have a pretext to keep us from the voting booth.

Amerikkka

And you know what's ironic to me? The fact that I have *never* shot a shotgun even *one time* in *my life*, yet that's what Youngsta was murdered with. Hard to believe, huh? Out of all the weapons I've owned and fired, not one of them – not one – was a shotgun. True, I've held one in my hand, contemplated buying one a time or two, and even caught my first robbery charge at the age of 14 with a *borrowed* single-shot one, but *never* in my life have I *owned* or even *shot* one. And I've thought about this fact, too – many times wracking my brain trying to find a memory, *any* memory (however long suppressed), of me *shooting* a shotgun. And there is *none!* Not a .410, a 12-gauge, or 20-gauge. Neither! And you want to know why? Because I've been *afraid* of the ferocity and power of a shotgun ever since I helped save the life of this young lady shot in the face with one when I was 16 or 17 and skipping school in Vine Hill.[236] I've been *afraid*. Of the possible kickback; of the possible damage that could have been done to not only my targeted victim, but also to *me*! Pitiful and ironic, huh? "Big Bad Murderer Delo" afraid of shooting a shotgun! Yet convicted of killing someone murdered by one and sentenced to "life imprisonment."

And another thing that still has me confused to this day – just how in the hell did the evidence of my staying at the motel on the day and night of Youngsta's murder just up and disappear? Because I'm pretty sure the pig police investigated every aspect of my whereabouts when I was initially arrested for Old School's death in 1999. And in that investigation they would have easily and clearly seen surveillance video of my *never leaving my motel room at all during the hours preceding, during, or after Youngsta's death*. I mean, shit was clear as rain. So no way would I get convicted of this crime, right?

---

[236] She, along with her new boyfriend, were both shot in the head and face by her preacher stepfather who had been molesting her for years — yet another reason that I'm suspicious of "preachers."

A grave mistake I made actually *believing* in the issue of "fairness" and that the pig police would do a good job of investigating Youngsta's death and would clearly see that I was no way involved in it. I mean, you can't be in two places at the same time, right? And as long as I was innocent of this crime, I would never actually get convicted of it, right? *Right?*

However, I was monumentally wrong; justice nor fairness nor the truth had anything to do with it when there I sat as Black man having had the audacity to take a previous case to trial (and win!) in nashville, tennessee. This – this was entirely too much! Vengeance and revenge would be the order of the day – innocence of the crime I was on trial for be *damned*!

Me being a Black man, I must be taught a lesson to teach others a lesson, too – don't ever try to fight "us" back and you'd better be "happy" with whatever plea bargain table scraps we offer you! So then comes evidence "lost" or manufactured, witnesses cajoled to get their "stories straight," and myself saddled with an "attorney" that was in on the fix from the get-go.[237] Still, I was naïve and blind. Actually believing that "truth" and "justice" would prevail? – such an idiot, I was!

This brings to mind a theorem I read in prison attributed to a famous Fifth-Ave.-Fuhrer-supporting-supposedly-"liberal" attorney called "The Rules of the Justice Game":

- *Rule 1* – Almost all criminal defendants are, in fact, "guilty."
- *Rule 2* – All criminal defense lawyers, prosekkkutors and judges understand and believe Rule 1.
- *Rule 3* – It is easier to kkkonvict "guilty" defendants by *violating* the kkkonstitution than by complying with it, and in some cases it is *impossible* to kkkonvict the guilty

---

[237] Her first question upon meeting me was, "How did you beat the Ransom murder?" In hindsight, that was a BIG warning sign that I missed!

Amerikkka

without violating the kkkonstitution.

- *Rule 4* – Almost all police lie about whether they violated the kkkonstitution in order to kkkonvict "guilty" defendants.
- *Rule 5* – All prosekkkutors, judges and defense attorneys are aware of Rule 4.
- *Rule 6* – Many prosekkkutors implicitly encourage police to lie about their violation of the kkkonstitution in order to kkkonvict "guilty" defendants.
- *Rule 7* – All judges are aware of Rule 6.
- *Rule 8* – Most judges pretend to believe police officers who they *know* are lying.
- *Rule 9* – All appellate judges are aware of Rule 8, yet many *pretend* to believe trial judges, who *pretend* to believe lying police.
- *Rule 10* – Most judges disbelieve defendants about whether their supposed "kkkonstitutional rights" have been violated, even if they *know* they are telling the truth.
- *Rule 11* – *Most* judges and prosekkkutors would not kkkonvict a defendant who they believe to be innocent of the crime charged (or a closely related crime).[238]
- *Rule 12* – Rule 11 does not apply to members of organized crime or "gangs," "drug dealers," career "criminals," potential informants that can be used to ensnare others, or just all-around "thugs."
- *Rule 13* – The reality of "justice" is merely an attempt to pretend there can be law and order in a hungry and greedy kkkapitalistic society. Nobody really wants or cares about justice.

---

[238] With all that I've witnessed, lived, and experienced in this kkkountry, I vehemently disagree with this supposition!

So true, huh?

I mean it absolutely amazes me the blatant hypokkkrisy of those devils in that kkkourtroom! There I sat kkkonvicted of a crime even Ray Charles could see I was innocent of, albeit a full 13 ½ months after I was *first* transferred to tennessee! Remember the IAD? The law that said I *had* to be tried within 120 days or my charges *had* to be dismissed?!! Well fuck that, *my* trial didn't start until over *410* days in my case – to *hell* with me! Remember the provision against "shuttling" (again, mandating dismissal of *all* charges) between jurisdictions, (state and federal, federal and state)? Well, not only did it *never* stop, but I had a trial in the feds the very next week! Back to back, week to week fuckery, and "they" just think they can get away with it??? Of course they do. Because they did…

I feel like Dred Scott. It doesn't matter that I'm innocent, it doesn't matter that I'm suffering, it doesn't matter that I have the evidence to prove my innocence and that the "law" is supposedly in my favor and equal to all. All that matters is that my Black ass is considered somehow "threatening" and/or "dangerous," so amerikkka wants to keep me in a cage! Blatant hypokkkrisy — *that's* why so many people worldwide hate amerikkka! I know that's why *I* do!

And the *way* they "secured" my conviction? I mean, Damn! I always knew that Paul had no integrity and would say whatever the prosekkkutors wanted him to, but Vell?! *This* motherfucker?! Out of all people, *him*! Unbelievable! Their made up bullshit lies were diametrically opposed to one another and people actually *believed* that shit!? And I got to give it to that motherfucker Vell; he knew me so well that he knew he could get up there and blatantly lie on me and I still would *never* tell the *real* deal as it was told to me a few days after it happened! Bitch-made motherfucker! But it's cool! It's *all* cool! Sucker saw his way out in sacrificing *me*!!!? The whole world would've been better off had it been him leaking on that floor instead of his brother! Motherfucker! But it's cool! It's cool. Just let me calm my ass down and fight my way through this...

My mind was a jumble of all of the preceding thoughts, but never did I give the devils the satisfaction of knowing they'd got to me. Taking the verdict so much in stride, within minutes of my return to jail from kkkourt I was placed in the "hole" for "security reasons" on maximum custody. Even still, no reaction from me...

During my time in the hole, I had nothing more to do but think, and I started to replay the scenes of my life. I thought about the mistakes I'd made, the women that I had loved, the smiles and frowns and tears I had caused others, and slowly I changed. I changed. No more in good conscience could I continue being the person I was...

All the same, if I can change, then all those of a similar upbringing can, also. We just have to be compelled through our *own* understandings and empathy. No *law* can make us better men nor women; no prison nor jail either. *We* have to make ourselves better. *We* have to care enough about *ourselves* to do things differently under this system of inequality, injustice, and oppression in which we live. And if *we* choose not to in light of what *we* face, well, then, who can *we* blame other than *ourselves* if we don't survive?...

"Anyone compelled to choose between love and fear will find greater security in being feared than in being loved... Love endures by a bond which man, being scoundrels, may break whenever it serves their advantage to do so; but *fear* is supported by the dread of *pain*, which is ever present..."

Niccolo Machiavelli

SURVIVING

"You know we gotta kill him, right?"

I pressed my ear to the phone even tighter, as if I could somehow hear the voices on the other end even clearer and louder than I could with the volume already set at sky high. Because this shit was important – this was *my life* they were discussing!

"Yeah, man, I know. 'Cause you see what he did to them other niggas that let him live."

SNIFFHH!!! He took what sounded like another snort of cocaine.

"Yeah, you right. We just gone haf'ta kill him. Let me beep him again to make sure he on his way."

I hurriedly hung up the phone so that "E" didn't know that I had been listening. Needless to say, I was in somewhat of a state of shock.

"E" was a cat that I had run around with here and there during my middle and early high school years whom I had lost contact with a few years back when I had to do those two years at CCA. Last I knew until I ran into him in U.C. earlier that day, he'd moved to California ducking some shit he'd pulled in tennessee that had the pigs hot on his ass. He came back repping "Blood."

Lost in my thoughts and disbelief, a few seconds later his

page came through. I took a few minutes to collect myself, and then returned his call.

"*What's good?*"

"*You still coming through, homie?*"

Now I could notice how fake his voice sounded, and how keyed up he seemed to be.

"*Yeah, I'm coming through. I told you I had to put my son to sleep then I'd be heading out so we can chop it up. Where you say you were at?*"

He gave me directions to a house in Woodbine, a working class section of south nashville that I was very familiar with, yet I told him that I probably wouldn't be able to find it – there was no way in hell I would be walking into *that* type of trap again.

"*How about you just meet me at the gas station, cuz? I know where that is.*" I purposely called him "Cuz" to irk him.

"*Aiight, cool. How long before you be there, homie?*" he responded, with extra emphasis on the B.

"*Give me thirty more minutes. I'll call you when I'm five minutes away.*"

"*Bet.*"

I pushed mute on my phone, and luckily, the gods were still with me as he attempted to hang up the phone once more again unsuccessfully. Either this fool was just high as a cloud, or that was just one raggedy ass old phone. Matter of fact, probably both. I continued to listen.

"*Yeah, he on his way Blood. Man, we gone do that nigga! Hitting me up with that crab shit and shit! He know I ain't on that!*"

I listened for maybe another five minutes as "E" and whomever it was in the background[239] plotted my kidnapping, robbery, and death. As my disbelief swelled to anger, and my anger swelled to murderous intent, I hung up the phone and quickly formulated a plan. I couldn't believe that when I saw this

---

[239] Luckily, for them, I couldn't catch their voice and never found out their identities!

bitch-made sucker earlier that day that I had intentions on throwing him a pack to help him get up on his feet – and all the while he was probably plotting my death from the beginning! Now this chump was about to feel what fucking with me was all about!!!

Pushing a different vehicle than the one he'd seen me in earlier, I pulled into the shadows of a building with a direct line of sight of the gas station and called "E" telling him that I'd be pulling up in a few minutes. And although some may question the wisdom of my even heading anywhere near where someone was plotting my abduction and death, I still had to see with my own eyes that this cat would be foolish enough to try to cross me. I just kept telling myself that there was just *no way* for this cat to be *that* stupid – he knew me up close, and more importantly, *dangerously!* This fool *knew* what it was! My ears, my gut, my heart, ALL had to be wrong!

But, of course, they weren't. I soon saw "E" walking down the street dressed in all black wearing gloves on a warm spring night.[240] I watched as he waited by the payphones, nervously looking back and forth from the direction he thought I'd be coming from, and from that in which he came. After about ten minutes or so, he started "blowing up" my pager.[241] As I continued watching him, it was easy to sense his growing frustration at my not showing up or returning his pages; I also couldn't help but to notice the same nondescript car passing by the gas station. After about 15-20 minutes of my not showing up nor getting any answer from me, he finally flagged down that

---

[240] This fool seriously had to have been crazy out of his mind on coke, or something. If I *was* unawares about what was about to go down, did he not think I would notice and wonder about how he was dressed? We weren't on a mission to "put in work" on that tip.
[241] He couldn't call my cell back, of course; I'd learned by then to never trust but those closest to you with a direct line to reach you so I always called associates "private," whether from my home or mobile.

same car and hopped in. That confirmed it. I'd specifically told this fool not to bring anyone with him to meet me.

The next evening I popped up over his mom's house; it was a crapshoot, but I figured that there was no better place in which to start looking for him. Plus, even if he wasn't there, it would make him realize that I remembered where she lived. Blowing the horn after pulling into the driveway, "E" soon opened the door.

"What's good homie? Ride with me."

"Bet. Hold tight."

He came back out within a couple of minutes after having changed clothes back into the same black shorts, black shirt, and even the black gloves he had on the night before. Hopping into my passenger seat, neither one of us brought up the fact that I never showed up the night before, and I guess he didn't notice how while I kept my right hand on the steering wheel, I kept my left underneath my thigh on the trigger of my pistol. I didn't know when or what type of move this fool would try to make, but I was ready. A couple of streets over, I stopped the car.

"What's up, homie?"

He wasn't nervous, just curious as to why we had stopped so soon.

"Aw, shit, instead of me putting you down with a few zips,[242] *I thought I'd hook you up with big cuz that could front you a cake or so."*

"Bet."

Hopping out of my car, this idiot still seemed not to notice the pistol I now held in hand down the side of my leg – guess he was too lost in trying to figure out how to make what I was exposing him to work for him; knowing him, he probably would've abandoned my kidnapping for the time being to plot on robbing the house he thought I was taking him to. He did

---

[242] Ounces. "Cake," "slab," or "bird" were the terms we used for kilos.

take notice, however, of a couple of people walking towards us and finally sensed that something was wrong:

"*Who is* that?"

"*Aw, you straight, homie. That's just my cousin and them.*"

Suddenly, no more than a few feet away now to where we could both see the masks they wore, one of them reached onto a lawn and grabbed an assault rifle and pointed it at "E's" face – which he now noticed my 9mm pointed at, also!

"*BITCH!!! YOU WERE GOING TO KILL ME, HUH???*"

CRACK!!! I hit him in the side of the head with my strap, instantly drawing blood.

"*OWW!!! MAN THOSE NIGGAS LYING!!!*"

CRACK!!! I hit his bitch ass even harder this time.

"*BITCH!!! I DIDN'T EVEN SAY NOTHING ABOUT THOSE NIGGAS!!!*"

CRACK – CRACK!!! He hit the ground where we beat him mercilessly and stripped him searching for a pistol – which the stupid motherfucker didn't even have! I beat and beat and beat and beat his ass – barely leaving him with just enough breath and blood left to live. *If* he fought for it. As I thought about how he so callously plotted ending my life, it took everything I had in me not to kill his stupid ass. But something, someone watching over us both, kept me from doing so.

An hour or so after leaving him no longer moving, I received a "911" page from an unknown number; when I called it back from a payphone, the caller on the other end of the line snapped:

"*DELO, IF "E" DOESN'T LIVE, YOU GOING TO JAIL!!! WE KNOW HE LEFT WITH YOU!!!,*" some woman screamed.

"*Bitch, I don't know* who *or* what *the fuck you talking about. Lose my number."*

Hanging up, I thanked my instincts for being alive and well and kicking; something in my gut had stopped me from killing "E," and luckily so, as he had the wherewithal to tell someone who he was leaving with. Hell, probably some of the same ones that were in on the plot on my life. And although I would never see "E" again, a couple of months later he would see a cousin of mine in U.C. and try to explain:

"I don't know why Delo believed those niggas man. Me and him too tight for that. I wouldn't do something like that."

Bullshit. He never knew that I actually had *heard* his bitch ass with my own ears! And to this day sometimes I regret not toe-tagging[243] that snake motherfucker: less than a year later he would again go on the run, but this time for robbing and killing some distant relatives of mine...

It's funny how life can turn you into a person you never thought you'd – or maybe never even wanted to – be. After that experience with "E," my trust in people was nonexistent. I never knew when and where the next strike against my life would come. I didn't like anyone to know where I lay my head at night, nor to know even what I would be doing an hour ahead of time. I looked at everyone with a wary eye, not knowing if they were related to or friends with someone whom the streets held me responsible for robbing and/or killing. Or even just someone looking for a come-up. All I knew was, considering my reputation, anyone that *would* have the nuts to come would of course come *correct*, ready to kill or die. So I had that attitude, also – always ready to kill, always ready to die, broad daylight, in the middle of the darkest night, traveling the streets, shopping

---

[243] Killing him. Ashamedly, I heard from various sources back then that one of the nicknames "the streets" bestowed on me was "Mr. Toe-Tag-em." This is not something to be proud of...

for groceries, on the toilet, or even in the shower – I was always armed, always on the alert, determined to survive. Paranoid doesn't even begin to describe the way I was feeling.

In spite of it all I kept my ready smile and cool, laidback demeanor; no one, I felt, though, could appreciate all that was happening beneath the surface. All they saw was a "thug intellectual," a vegetarian who rocked furs, a "killer" with a heart of gold, a gangster who cared too much. I was a walking contradiction.

Tsawa wasn't an option as someone to turn to – who knew the next time she'd be lying calling the pigs on me, or stealing my money and dope to share with the next man, or sharing my secrets with her boyfriend again? What little peace and solace I was able to steal from the world, I found only between the arms, lips, and legs of Jannah; what little intellectual stimulation and comfort I found, I found walking the campus and halls of Fisk. I found myself falling deeper and deeper in love with them both – Fisk and Jannah; in the classrooms, in the library studying and reading, in the dorm with Jannah laid up, I felt safe and peaceful, no need for my vest or a strap. Nevertheless, believe me, those were the *only* places I felt comfortable enough not to have them.

Jannah was good for me. Although I can't necessarily say that I was good for *her*. Not with all of the turmoil surrounding my life. A lot of bullshit and drama came with dealing with me. To her credit, she stayed strong and supportive by my side – even as I didn't necessarily deserve it.

Even so, I still loved Tsawa; shit, being completely honest with myself I have to say that I loved Tsawa and Jannah both, yet for far different reasons. With Tsawa, I was *drawn* to her – for reasons I still can't quite explain even today, never being able to get her completely off my mind even when I deathly wanted to be through with her; it was/is just something that was meant to happen in the grand scheme of things. But with Jannah? – Jannah was peace and serenity and comfort and safety and passion and intense love to me – all of the things I felt whenever she was around. I was always at ease in her presence, and I could lose myself in her love; more times than I can remember, friends of mine that saw us together would tell me that she was the one I should be with and put my all into. But they couldn't understand – even though I honestly and truly was in love with Jannah, my heart, also, wouldn't allow me at the time to give Tsawa up. Ironically, losing both would soon break my heart almost beyond repair.

To add to the stresses of my heart, my financial situation wasn't quite what I had become accustomed to, either. With the way I was being surveilled, and my limiting now who I dealt with, money wasn't coming in as fast as I would have liked. Plus, the "ticket" I was used to paying went up due to my slowing down of the trips south. Although I desperately (felt like I) needed the money, I chilled for a lil minute with good reason: On the way back from one of those trips, the young woman accompanying me awakened me from a snooze; no problem, I thought, just time for me to switch over to the driver's seat. No such luck.

"Hey," she said as she shook me awake, *"the police are behind us."*

No worries really; the car was mine, registered in my name, we all had licenses, everything was legit.

"Ok. Cool. Were you speeding?"

"No."

"Then we're cool, then. They ain't got any reason to pull us over; we're straight. Matter of fact, though, I need to use the bathroom anyway so get off at the next exit."

I still didn't feel as if anything was wrong, but just as we pulled off the exit, the pig put the lights on us. I spoke up from the passenger seat as he sought her license and the registration:

"*Excuse me, officer, what did you pull us over for?*"

"*A light is out over the license plate*" was the weak-assed excuse the rednekkk Georgia highway patrolman offered. "*Where are you coming from?*"

Where we were coming from had nothing to do with a fucking light out over a license plate, but I answered the question anyway because I knew we were "dirty."

"*My aunt just got married in West Palm; we're on our way back to tennessee so I can make it to work on time.*"

Of course, no reason I gave would have actually mattered to this rednekkk chump; he stopped our Black asses with the intent of making an arrest for "something" that night.

"*May I search the vehicle?*"

There it was. I wonder how many white families not speeding and otherwise following all rules of the rode he had stopped under some bullshit pretext and requested to search the vehicle?

"*No, you may not search the vehicle; you have no reason to. My registration is in order, her license is straight, and like I said, we'd like to be on our way.*"

Stepping away from the car, we all heard the rednekkk pig calling for the k-9 on his radio – and of course, I knew we couldn't possibly get past the mutt. You see as opposed to other cats that would go to great lengths in order to conceal their dope, I on the other hand put most of my effort into not getting pulled over in the first place: We always drove nondescript, well-maintained vehicles; we always rode with the flow of traffic; and we never did anything so foolish as to allow one person or another to drive so long as to get tired and fall asleep at the wheel. Big mistake, though, that in my naïveté, I didn't consider *enough* the phenomena known as "racial profiling."

However, I *did* have a contingency plan in place just for times like this: the other passenger; he was there expressively for these types of moments. Because although I planned to not get pulled over by the cops, I planned for the chance that it could still possibly happen. But that was what my guy was there for; this was what I had paid him for all those other times: do whatever he had to do to get away or to get rid of the dope. This was where he earned his pay, in my eyes. So remaining calm, I gave him "the look" through the rearview mirror and let him know what was up – we would allow the pig to search before reinforcements got there. And starting with my driver and I first should distract the pig enough to give my guy a chance to do whatever he had to do.

Calling the rednekkk back to the car, he began his search: first frisking the driver, secondly frisking me, then frisking my guy. While he was frisking the driver and myself, I kept making eye contact with my guy waiting on him to make his move; it never came. At this point I'm wondering exactly when my get-away-guy is going to make a break for it, but as Pig Rednekkk neared him, he still didn't budge! What the hell? He frisked him also, but still *nothing!*

After patting us all down, he commenced to searching my car with a vigor! First the driver's side, then the passenger's side, then the backseat! He even pulled out the backseat somehow away from its hinges! Still nothing, however! Pig Rednekkk must not have been able to believe it either as he extended his search to include popping my hood and searching my carburetor, searching my wheel wells, and even popping my trunk and searching my speaker box! All the typical spots where drugs are hidden and transported he could think of, he hit – my rims, dashboard, everywhere, nothing! By this time, I'm thinking even to my damned self, *where in the hell is it?!* Finally, the search came to an end and despite a call having been placed earlier, it turned out that the k-9 unit was too far away to engage in the stop; he had to let us go. We pulled on over to the convenience store, waiting until we got inside to talk:

"*What did you do with all that dope??*" I asked.

"*Shidd, I didn't have nowhere to hide it so I just put in on the floor and put some newspaper over it,*" was the unbelievable response.

"*Yeah-fucking-right!*" I said.

"*I swear.*"

"*Man, you* bullshitting!" I said, astounded at his answer. I still thought he had it on him somehow, someway.

"*I swear; it's back there.*"

And, unbelievably, it was. Pig Rednekkk had searched all the typical spots just to overlook the obvious spots! This fool had really put all that coke on the fucking ground and covered it with all the newspapers and magazines I read during the drive! I thought to myself, this *has* to be a set-up on the part of the pig – no way in hell could he have missed *all that yola!* He must just be waiting on us to cross the state-line or something into tennessee so as to make it a federal case! That *had* to be it!

Finding my packages exactly where he said he had put them – and finding that same pig following us again when we hopped back on the exit – I instructed the driver to again get off at the very next exit maybe 5 miles up ahead; I had her to take the coke and put it in the ceiling of another convenience store's bathroom. If we were to get stopped again once we crossed the tennessee state line, we would be entirely clean, and able to file a harassment charge. Later on that day, while I was at work frantically replaying all of the events of the last few hours, she and a couple of others went back in another car to retrieve it. I wouldn't feel safe for either her or myself until she safely got back. And when she did make it back to me an hour or so before I had to close the store, I remember thinking that somebody somewhere must have been praying for us all...

Surprisingly even to myself, I took that close-call as a warning sign from the Universe (or something) and slowed down to a crawl my trips and started copping from a couple of cats intown. However, this greatly dug into my profit margins – I was barely paying less than what I was wholesaling it myself for – and money started being tighter than I had ever been used to before. And once you start having financial woes, all others intensify in my experience.

Case in point: My relationships with *both* of the women in my life deteriorated as I became stressed beyond stressed over the constant surveillance, empty pockets, and justifiable paranoia. Yet I learned long ago that if the man in the relationship is in any way weak or submissive, a woman will automatically lose respect for him and try to flip shit and dominate, fucking up the natural order of things. And I must say that I wasn't "up on my shit" at this time, causing myself avoidable problems.

First there was Tsawa: I noticed the frequency of our lovemaking changed, along with her general attitude; she always seemed to pick a fight to get out of spending time with me, seemed to be unavailable at the oddest times of day and night, and just could never get her stories for the day straight – you know, the same bullshit that *I* used to do! On top of that, the way she dressed changed, the way she smelled, *everything* just shifted dramatically. And I myself taking *her* advice when she was trying to understand what was going on when *I* was fucking off,[244] I attempted time and time again to talk to her and find

---

[244] Not that I ever stopped being involved with Jannah; I did, however, leave all of my other women alone, and in my mind, this was enough.

out what was wrong. But no deal there – it was already too late; although the cat I had always known about was still locked up, she was fed up and fucking around on me with at least two other dudes including an older cat that she worked with.[245] I found out through one of her "friends" that was living with her at the time and wanted me to herself. Attempting to ingratiate herself to me by spilling the beans on her friend – as if I would ever trust anyone that betrayed the person that had given them a place to stay when they had nowhere else to go – she let me know that all those late nights when Tsawa was incommunicado she was actually out with dude. Hell, the friend even gave me his pager number and Tsawa's special "code" to reach him.[246] Confronted with the evidence her "friend" supplied me, she crushed me with her callousness over my (surprisingly!) broken heart. The wetness in my eyes and heaviness in my heart shocked even me myself. I knew it was over. I could never erase the mental picture of yet another man inside the mother of my child, nor could I anymore tolerate her sexual recklessness putting us all (herself, me and our son) in danger.[247] The possibility of me ever "committing" myself to her ever again was forever dead…

Which reminds me of something: Women – without fail it seems – always have that one cat "in the cut" ready to step in when she's ready to step out. Whether she calls him her "play

---

[245] Tsawa's (supposed-to-be-ex) boyfriend had long-by-then been released from county prison, yet lasted on the streets just long enough to catch another petty robbery charge (resulting in a much longer *state* prison sentence that trip!) and impregnate Tsawa as he so proudly informed his inner circle. Yet I doubt if Tsawa *ever* suspected that I was aware of any of this, as she informed me that she was pregnant (purportedly with *our* second child) *weeks after* I had heard so from "the streets." After informing her that I wanted a DNA test, Tsawa unilaterally terminated the pregnancy.
[246] Lesson learned: Be careful what you expose to someone else – even a "friend."
[247] And yes, I do recognize the irony in all of this, considering how she and Jannah *both* were the "women in my life" at the time. Although I'm sure this hypocrisy on my part escaped my notice and/or eclipsed my emotional understanding and awareness back then.

brother" or "play cousin" or just plain old "friend," he's *always* there. Biding his time. Just waiting in the wings to make his move and show her everything she wants to see in another man besides her own. And the reason why I say "want" to see is because what he *shows* her is not necessarily who he truly is. A woman in search of something will tell a man all that she wants him to show her in her complaints about who/what she has at home. The treasonously unwise and disloyal woman will usually confide in this "cut buddy" all the secrets of – and complaints she has about – her man, leaving her significant other at a distinct advantage and precarious position especially if he's in "the streets" as I was. Hell, a lot of times I've *been* the "cut buddy," and now I was faced with the fact that this disloyal woman I chose to be the mother of my first child had left me at the mercy of one.[248]

---

[248] Even amidst all of the turmoil of our relationship, I refused to not be an active and daily part of my son's life somehow, but neither I nor Tsawa were mature enough to know how to make that a reality without being in some type of "relationship" together – as it was clear by both of our actions that that wasn't what either of us really needed nor wanted. Still, her "infidelity" stung but not in ways that most people may think. What hurt most about her indiscretions was how she time and again so callously put all three of our lives (my own, hers, and our sons) in danger. She knew I had enemies, yet she consistently and repeatedly allowed other men, potential grave threats, into her world, and thus, all of ours. I know of at least two instances where street cats got "close to" her just as a way of getting close to me. Yet she never "believed" and/or admitted that that some men would use a man's woman or family as a way of getting next to a person or to have something to hold over a person's head. Furthermore, she held taking our son away from me over my head in almost every argument it seems. And I was too immature and too ignorant to have figured out any other way to deal with the situation besides giving into her demands somewhat. Because my love for my son was my kryptonite.
My complete distrust of her and my growing resentment caused me to feed her as much disinformation and misinformation as I could. I wanted for everything she exposed to the next man (or the police) to be as wrong as possible. Besides her not knowing where I really lay my head at night when I wasn't with her and my son (I didn't want her to know beforehand when/if I was coming!), I also misled her on who my associates were I was "kicking it" with, how, when, and where I got my money and how much I ever had, and just basically everything other than the bare minimum of what I had to directly expose to her. Tsawa had taught me painfully well not to trust her further than she could be thrown. But my mother had also taught me painfully well how a mother could poison a child against his or her father, so even in

I took Tsawa's embarrassingly reckless indiscretions as the last and most clear sign that I should have been with Jannah in the first place. Unbeknownst to me, however, she had been slipping away from me, also. I can't even remember now why she said that she and I should "take a break," all I can remember is that she did. So there I was in love with and loving two women for two very different reasons – nonetheless, neither woman any longer wanted to be with me. I was heartsick.

In hindsight, I wish I would have just been completely honest with both of the women I loved about how I cared for them and the other. Maybe then we could have maturely confronted at least *some* of the issues we shared in a practical and adult manner. Nevertheless, opportunity missed and mourned...

Yet even through all of my heartache, I still wasn't taking any shit in the streets. In fact, I probably was a little quicker to shoot my pistol than even before. I can recall one instance of catching a cat that had robbed a dice game that my brother was a participant in before he had gotten locked up; even though he wasn't directly targeting Carvin, he *did* make him cough up his ends along with everyone else thus making him a target of *me*. All of the rest of the fools accepted the jacking because the robber had a notorious reputation for being a killer, but fuck that – his rep didn't mean shit to me and to be honest wasn't half as bad as my own even though he was ten years older or so. Plus, he had violated my *family*, so no doubt that I would come gunning – for the very first time the same night of the robbery after I got the call about what happened. Upset with myself that he had survived the shootout we all had facing each other from

---

trying to protect my life, I'd be damned before I allowed that to happen with me and Kyree. So, I was stuck between the proverbial "rock and a hard place" unable to leave for a multitude of reasons, but also unable to fully trust or be comfortable with the person life's circumstances dictated that I be around.

opposite ends of 12th Avenue, I started to stalk all of his known haunts and his hood.[249] However, with him catching the word of whom he had unwittingly offended, he started laying low and being hard to catch. But I knew I would get him eventually. And I did.

Ironically, on the same day that we were able to get Carvin out on bond after they reduced it to under $100,000, this cat's reckoning would catch up with him. Leaving the bondsman's office, my brother would first want to stop in the projects to holler at this lil gal that had held him down while he was in there. Pulling up in the drive, stepping out of the car, and who was the first face that we saw? *This* motherfucker! And the idiot wasn't even paying attention to his surroundings while on a "flake chase."[250]

Deciding in that moment to go around the side of the project building and then come around and gun him down, I changed my mind and instead went straight towards him; I wanted to look him in his eyes as I shot him instead of ambushing him. Distracted still with his nose, I guess, itching in the search for some powder cocaine, he actually asked *me* if I had "any flake?" Damned fool.

"Yeah, I got you right here homie."

This idiot didn't even notice the strap I clearly held to my side. He soon felt it, however. PAT! PAT!! PAT!!! He hit the ground, leaking. Thinking of no more than the fact that he had threatened my brother's life in robbing him, I pointed the gun at his dome as he was struggling in pain attempting to crawl away from me on the concrete. Barrel of the pistol now only a few feet away from his head, a presence I felt told me to look up.

Turning behind me I saw a lady halfway in halfway out of

---

[249] He wasn't from "Out South," he just came out there to rob and fuck around with a couple of women.
[250] Search for powder cocaine to either snort or "lace" your cigarettes or weed with.

her doorway with eyes wide open watching in shock as she witnessed what was going on. Plus, it wasn't like there weren't other people around as it *was* broad daylight and the projects were "dunked." I knew but didn't actually care that there would be witnesses when I shot him, but something about the way she was looking at me brought my conscience to the forefront and made me think about what I was doing. Looking at her and the way she looked deeply through me, I backed up off of him and started to walk away. And I'm glad I did. What I was doing was wrong. No matter what he had done. Even if not wrong to retaliate against him for his actions, it was wrong to put that lady (and any others that were watching) through the nightmares undoubtedly to come from witnessing what I was doing. She had nothing to do with what was happening and shouldn't have been made to feel unsafe in her own neighborhood. I mean think about it – neither I nor my victim were residents of the projects at that time, but there we were bringing our beef and problems to it. That's not right.

Furthermore, it's not as easy or as simple as you see in the movies or read in the "street novels" to shoot someone (especially in broad daylight) and get away with it – and multiply the likelihood of getting caught a hundredfold if that person dies. Because a murder investigation is a-whole-nother ball game – with people coming out of the woodworks to share their side of the story and get your dangerous ass off the streets. People seem (and rightly so!) to think that killing someone in broad daylight (as opposed to trying to conceal it in the dark hours of night, I guess) is especially heinous, and they want your ass *gone!* But can you really blame them?

I think that if most of us that are in the world "thugging" actually took an honest look at all the hurt we cause in our worlds then things would be drastically different. There wouldn't be as many tears shed over the loss of a son to an early grave or prison; there wouldn't be as many worry lines on our mothers' or fathers' faces; and shit, we could actually *be* fathers to the children we've made and *men* to our wives and/or girlfriends. Hell, our own people wouldn't be as afraid to walk and live in our communities as they are today either! Can you imagine?

Nevertheless, that wasn't necessarily what was on my mind as I turned and walked away leaving him bleeding in the street; wouldn't you know it, though? – I felt and then heard gunshots coming my way as we turned the corner of the building. I quickly turned around aiming to see this motherfucker actually holding in his guts unable to aim but shooting wildly in our direction! My instincts kicked in as I heard the first shot and I emptied the rest of the clip with him catching at least one more bullet to the torso. As we were dipping off, we heard sirens coming from not far away. Good thing, too, because even though he was eventually charged for the pistol they found on him, they *did* make it there in time to save his life. Furthermore, I've got to give it to him, too – he kept it all the way "Gangsta" and never told the pigs that I was the one whom had shot him.[251]

So I guess it's true what they say: hurt people hurt people. Because I sure as hell made people feel my pain when they gave me an excuse to do so. But I tell you here today that none of that makes the things I did right or righteous in any kind of way. We all go through pain in life, we all experience heartbreak a

---

[251] I found out later that he was out that way again evidently on some more "jack shit" and I just happened to be the first person he ran into once he made it out to that side of town. Doesn't the Universe have a sick sense of humor? Because, I mean, what are the odds of that? Coupled with the fact that he just happened to be the first person my brother and I saw less than 30 minutes after we had gotten him out of jail. Crazy, huh? Last I heard, though, that particular incident convinced him to finally retire from the "street shit." He realized that more and more of us were just as wild and dangerous – if not more so – than he was.

time or two if we're lucky; however, our own individual hurts don't justify us spreading that to others. And why would you want to anyway? If anything, we should want to help prevent others that we care about from unnecessarily going through that which we've already learned from.

And all the while that I "wasn't having it" in the streets, unbeknownst to me, the "authorities" and certain "family members" of mine like my aunt Nancy were steadily plotting and facilitating what they thought would be my ultimate downfall; this would soon culminate in my being persecuted as "Target Number One" on some new "Persistent Offenders List" that the metro-nashville police department had formed in an effort to get "dangerous persons" such as myself off of the streets. In essence, it was a "hit squad" – take the others and me on the list down by any means necessary. Legally or illegally, didn't really even matter much how they accomplished it. All that mattered was they were coming for us. And my dumb ass had no idea of what was brewing outside of the normal bullshit I was going through.

Case in point: Tsawa, my son and I were out eating dinner when Vell called for me to pick him up; he was in Old Hickory – on the same side of town that we had recently moved to in Donelson, and only a few miles away from where we currently were in Hermitage. We experienced no problems Tsawa driving to pick him up and heading back towards home, but once my son started crying and "fussing" (as I assume his coming-in teeth were bothering him), she and I switched positions after pulling over and now I was driving. Well, here comes the drama: her tags on the car were expired.[252] Had *she* been driving after the

---

[252] It wasn't a matter of lack of funds or any bullshit like that; she had just procrastinated in getting them. I know for a fact that I had reminded her to do so at least a couple of times before this day, but with her being in school full time and working full time in addition to us having a toddler, I guess she just didn't find the

pig got behind us, I doubt if we would have even been pulled over, let alone what happened next. But after the rednekkk came to the car and was greeted with my I.D. instead of a driver's license,[253] I had the not-so-unusual feeling that there was about to be "some bullshit." And of course, my feelings were right.

Within minutes, another pig car pulled up. Then another. And another. And another. And another. Yeah, something definitely was up. Five cop cars for a little traffic stop? Come on, now. So my already heightened alert level went up to hyper-vigilant. I warned Tsawa and Vell to get ready.

"Friendly Pig" finally came back to the vehicle after conferring with his compadres:

"Can you step out of the car please?"

"Why? Can you just write me my citation so we can be on our way? We're trying to get our son home and in the bed."

"Step out of the car please."

So, I step out of the car and he asks me to place my hands on the trunk to be frisked; as I walk towards the back of the vehicle, I notice that every single pig out there seems to be on edge, hands on their holsters ready to draw and open fire. Friendly Pig starts to pat me down; within a mini-second he sets off the alarm bell:

"He's got a vest! He's got a vest!"

Weapons are instantaneously drawn and menacingly pointed at me and the car.

"Where's your gun?! Where's your gun?!"

"What gun? I don't have one," I say calmly.

"Well, why are you wearing this vest?!"

"For the same reason you're wearing yours."

The pigs placed me in tight cuffs behind my back and put

---

time. However, neither did she tell me either until *after* I was hit with the blue light special.
[253] Wherein he was actually ostensibly friendly when he first approached.

me in the back of one of the police cars. And then they start to search Tsawa's car and the rest of its occupants, starting with the biggest threat of course: Vell – the other grown Black male. Luckily he was clean. Then they pat down Tsawa and check my son's baby bag before she's questioned alongside the car while they ransack it looking for my-assumed weapon and/or other "contraband."[254]

What did they ask her? "Where [was my] gun? Why [was I] wearing a bulletproof vest? Why [was I] on [something they kept referring to as] the "Persistent Offenders" list? Why [did she] have a child by someone as despicable as [me]?" And so on, and so forth. However, I guess she wasn't being as forthcoming as they would have liked with her answers because I could sense the pigs' frustration level rising by the second. And as they had found nothing in the car nor had anything to arrest them for, Tsawa, my son and Vell were soon let go (to arrange my soon-to-come bail, I assumed) and I was transported to the new police precinct in Harding Place across from the CCA prison. Friendly Pig had the nerve to try to slick question me on the way:

"Why are you on this Persistent Offenders list?"

"Say what? That's something you need tell me; I had no idea about any list y'all got. I'm tripping off of how I'm going to jail on something that I thought people are only issued citations for."

"Well, we have the discretion[255] to either issue the citation or take

---

[254] Anything a "nigger" shouldn't have. Could be something deemed illegal for everyone, but that which only Blacks or Browns are usually charged with (i.e. marijuana), or it could be something not actually "illegal" but just looks bad for *us* to have. You know, like a nice watch, ring, or chain, a nice jacket, or even too much cash.

[255] This "discretion" is a hell of a thing when it is applied to Black and Brown people; "discretion" on the part of the police authorities, judges, district attorneys, prison officials, etc. is always invariably used to the detriment of us "minorities." "Discretion" allows for you and a white guy to have the same set of facts, same "crime," etc., but him to be let go and you to get fucked in all kind of ways. So we would be wise to be wary of all of the new laws passed around the kkkountry like the marijuana ordinances in nashville that will allow for us to be harmed even as white

you in for booking, but once I ran your name through the system it popped up to call Lieutenant (I-forget-the-pig's-name-right-now) anytime there is police contact with you – whether you're pulled over, arrested, questioned, whatever; hell, even if your name just comes up in an investigation we're supposed to contact the Lieutenant. And after calling him he told me to make sure to search you and the vehicle for weapons and to take you to jail no matter what we found."

Damn. That's interesting. So whoever this Lieutenant was I guess had to be actively investigating me. I wonder if this pig was even supposed to tell me all that he just did or did he slip up or something? Because he actually seemed somewhat surprised at whatever it was that he found in his computer and/or what was said to him by the Lieutenant. Or he was trying to play me on that "good cop" shit. Like I would fall for that. By the time we made it to booking, the "good cop" Friendly Pig was joined by a pig now there to play "bad cop" to furthermore question me as to why I was on that list.

"You've gotta know why they have you on this list; this is for the worst of the worst and my understanding is that you're damn near at the top of it."

"Man, how the hell am I supposed to know why I'm on a fucking list, I didn't even know this so-called list existed. But you better believe it's something I'll be asking my attorney about. Speaking of which, do I need to call him now?"

That question was totally ignored, of course, but it put them on notice that I knew I had the right to not be questioned and to call my lawyer.

"Well, we just want to help you get down to the bottom of why they have you on this list and if it's a mistake to help you get taken off of it. Because it could really hurt you whenever you get pulled over. Especially if

---

folks get rich "legally" off of the shit that so many of us languish in jail and prison for.

you don't get your license straightened out," said Friendly Pig.

I played right along with him:

"Thanks for your concern; I'll be sure to have my lawyer check into it in the morning as soon as I get up out of here."

"Bad cop" couldn't take it anymore and really got dramatic then:

"You know why you're on this list; you know! That's alright; we'll *get you! You'll slip up and* we'll *get you!"*

I laughed at that fool and shut down after asking "what was taking so long with the booking process, anyway?" I was trying to hurry up and make bond and get back to Tsawa and my son. And as the pigs knew that they would be getting *no* information from *me* and that they couldn't stall me for too much longer, I was finally taken in front of a video screen for the formal reading of my charge and bail setting by a magistrate. Here came yet another surprise:

"Kenneth Deangelo Thomas, you are charged with 'Driving on a Suspended License,' a violation of tennessee code annotated 55-50-504, bond set at $750. In regards to the charge of 'Possession of Body Armor,' a violation of tennessee code annotated 39-17-1323, bond will be set at..."

I cut him off right then and there.

"Excuse me. But you can't charge me with 'possession of body armor.' Tennessee code annotated 39-17-1323 only prohibits a person from wearing body armor during the commission of a felony, *and driving on suspended license is not a felony. I can't be charged with this."*

You should have seen the look on not only the magistrate's face, but also both of the punkkk ass pigs – "good" *and* "bad" cop – whom all were absolutely amazed that not only did I *know* the law by *memory,* but knew *how* and *when* and *why* I could and *could not be* charged with breaking it. I mean they seemed *astounded* that a young Black man not only would not fall for that lame-assed "good pig – bad pig" routine, but that I wouldn't be an easy "fuck" for them in any shape, form, or fashion with a bogus charge.

There's a lesson to learn in that. From the time I caught my first cases at the ages of fourteen and fifteen I always made it a point to know the ins and outs – penalties and defenses included – of *any* law that I may potentially be breaking. Furthermore, I read the local and a national newspaper every day, with an eye out for any legal or economic issues that may have affected me or the people closest to me. As they say, knowledge is power, so even before the "bulletproof vest" law went into effect I had already researched its ramifications in regards to me and those I loved, along with discussing how and when I could be hit with it with an attorney as soon as it was first approved in late-May of 1997. Because, like I said earlier, I would be damned if I was caught without it, ya dig? And I'd also be damned if I allowed them to run roughshod over my supposed rights to wear one and protect myself.

So they had to rewrite their paperwork and take that particular charge off. And after finally making it to a holding cell with a phone, I called Marcus the bondsman (through Tsawa) and asked how much longer it would take to come get me. However, as it was by then almost 3:00 in the morning and I could easily tell that he was "laid up" with some little young thing that he didn't really want to leave, he and I agreed that he would just come bond me out later on that morning about 7 or 8:00. So I lay my head down and rested a bit.

Want to hear something wild, though? The "little young thing" he was laid up with was *Tsawa*. Yeah, *crazy*, huh? Come to find out a few years later that she and he had been disrespectfully sneaking around behind my back for *months* while all the while laughing in my face. So of course he and she would try to postpone for a few hours my getting out of jail so they could "creep" a little while longer. I had no idea, obviously, or I sure as hell wouldn't have reached out to *him* to come bond me out; I could have called another bondsman and went on a "creep mission" myself. And hell, besides, I wouldn't have had *any* business dealings with him whatsoever had I known. I may have even smacked him up a couple of times for the blatant disrespect he had shown me. It wasn't about him getting the pussy – hell, that was *hers*; Tsawa, of course, can share with whom she chooses, her own body – but for him to be all up in my face like we were cool while thinking they were pulling one over on me, well, hell, let's just say I've learned not to deal with those type of shiesty motherfuckers. Because they'll do anything to stab you in the back when given the slightest opportunity. And as far as her, well hell, what does that tell you that she'd have me looking like a fool while all the while fucking around with *this* dude? So disrespectful. But it's cool. It's cool.[256] Taught me a lot about to whom and in what way I would expose my relationships to others. Some people – because of their inherent disloyalty, betrayal, shiestyness, etc. – are just not worthy of being seen with and/or "claimed." Sorry if that hurts any feelings, but that's just a sad truth…

But anyway, after making bond and being released, the pigs tried to stall me out about receiving my property (my vest) back. First they told me that they had already transported it to the "main police property room downtown," and that they didn't even know if I *could* receive it back. After threatening to sue over

---

[256] Although in all fairness, I recognize that the onus was on *myself* in that I should have realized then — as I do now — that Tsawa was/is *not* a woman to be contented with having only one man in her romantic/sexual life. Not passing judgment on whether that is "right" or "wrong" in the grand scheme of things, I just know that that kind of woman is wrong for *me* as I don't need the extra security risk. And that, ultimately is the issue I had/have with her fucking off with that particular cat – what did he learn (or what did he *attempt* to learn?) about *me* in fucking around with *her*? Because — not exposing how I know this — it's deeper than him just coming up on a "piece of pussy." Believe that.

my property, I was given a number to call to arrange for me to pick it up. Calling all that day (Thursday), after my repeated threats of just getting my lawyer involved because of the run-around I was receiving, I was finally informed that I could pick it up the next day on that Friday.

  I was there at 8:00 a.m. sharp. I presented the same I.D. I had when I had first gotten pulled over and the bullshit started, waited about five minutes along with a gawking pig that was placing a confiscated gun into evidence, signed the necessary documents before putting my vest on under one of my T-shirts in front of the pigs and leaving, driving off to their stares…

> I am a black man
> An Afrikan man
> Detained
> But not destroyed
> Enslaved
> But not extinct
> Conquered and
> Oppressed
> But not for long...
>
> *I Am a Black Man*
> by George Edward Tait

DETAINER

Lisa naylor blatantly lied in that kkkourtroom and we all knew it. As the devil bitch argued to the so-called judge that "neither [she] nor anyone in [her] office ever filed a detainer against [me]." We all knew this to be untrue. But that was just the lip service – the boldfaced lie that the so-called "judge" needed to hear for public record in order for him to rule "the IAD didn't apply [to me]" so as to proceed with the illegal trial. I guess they never expected me to find the evidence to expose them...

Thinking of something, you know what astounds me the most about amerikkkans? Their unmitigated arrogance, gall, and hypokkkrisy! These devils (seemingly!) sincerely expect *you* (the entire rest of the world and especially those of us they hold in enslavement and/or oppression) to believe everything that comes out of *their* mouths just because *they* say so! Bullshit! When has amerikkka *ever* – at *any* point in the kkkountry's wikkked history – righteously held the moral high ground!? Yet, they'll piss all over your face and actually get *offended* if you don't take their word that it's rain! It could stench and sting like piss – hell the devils could even still have their proverbial dicks out shaking them off – and they'll *still* get irrationally angry that you just didn't "take their word for it" and just be cool with having been pissed on! Now tell me that I'm wrong!?"

So, although I didn't know how I would prove it, I knew in my heart somehow that I would be able to prove to the world how I was railroaded into life imprisonment for something "they" always *knew* I was innocent of. I *knew* I would find evidence of the detainer that would then mandate that bogus case's dismissal. "They" couldn't have covered up *everything*, right?! Right??? I was determined...

After spending a month or so more at CJC on "Max" – during which my federal gun charges were dismissed on very much the same grounds as my state cases *should* have been,[257] the state had me go to kkkourt on the legally should-have-been-dismissed attempted murder charges, and I was thereafter put on a bus, then a couple of planes, then (another) bus eventually winding up at FCI (Federal Correctional Institution) Beckley in Beaver, West Virginia. Greeted with open arms by a few cats that I knew from the streets – to go along with the more than a few that "knew of" me, in addition to those that respected "how I got down" – I quickly fell into getting done what I needed to do.

Which was work on my cases[258] and get home as soon as

---

[257] One thing I can say about the federal government from my personal experience: It *seems* much more receptive to actually following the law when it comes to protecting defendant's rights. What an interesting concept, right? Not saying that they're above reproach – I mean, this *is* the united snakes government, after all! – but it just seems as if they just take the attitude of "Touché! We'll get his ass *next* time!" and just wait for you to fall into a hole of your own digging. But that's just my personal observation; I wouldn't put it past them to have repeatedly done the same shit to others that the state of tennessee did to me...

[258] Specifically the murder charge wherein I had already received a "life" sentence, and the two attempted murders where I was still facing another 120 years.

Detainer

possible to my family. So I got a "job" in the library allowing me the time I needed to read, research, and battle on the chessboard to keep my mind fresh.[259] However, the most important piece of paper I needed to find and read would fall into my hands through no efforts of my own.

Called into the counselor's office one day, I was greeted with a copy of some papers and introduced to him with his warning:

"Look, you'd better not get into any *shit at this prison,"* he sternly began.

Well, hell, where in the fuck is *this* coming from?! I *hadn't* been getting into "any shit" at the prison – I was trying to fight my way home!

"You're not even supposed to be *here, you should be at a USP."*

United States Penitentiary – high security – but I was there at the FCI which was officially designated for "medium security" kkkaptives. Only after reading Demeco Boothe's book *"Why Are So Many Black Men in Prison"* over a decade later (on Max in state prison) would I realize why he had so much trepidation: There had been an uprising at the prison a few months before I got there in which hostages were taken and "prison property" was damaged. The irony wouldn't escape me as I was then on Max myself for something altogether similar.

"No one else is here with a life sentence, and if you had any more federal time to serve than you do, I'd get you on the first thing smoking out of here!"

Well, damn. Uhhh, okay, I guess! I assured him that getting into "any shit" was the last thing on my mind and walked out of

---

[259] Speaking of chess battles, I had some *great* ones here – although I can't remember losing a match. (A battle?, yes – but a match?!, no. And believe me, I *would* remember!) Almost every day it seems a different cat would come up in the library or sneak into the unit (or invite me to sneak into theirs) challenging me because my homeboy Rome was bragging that they "couldn't fuck with [me]!" I could dig it, though – Rome and I both won more than a few dollars on him hyping me up.

his office without even a glance at the papers.

But man, oh man, when I read them! Wouldn't you believe that out of the 3-5 sheets one was labeled "Detainer" and signed by *lisa naylor*?! From *May 31, 2002* – less than *three months* before I was ever transferred to the state of tennessee?!

But, hey, devils don't lie, amerikkkans won't piss on your head and tell you it's rain so maybe she just *forgot* that only *81 days* before I got there and started raising hell about it that *her* office sent a *detainer signed by her* that specifically instructed the institution where I was held to "lodge this against defendant as a detainer under the *Interstate Agreement on* Detainers." Maybe the bitch just forgot? Yeah, fucking right! The bitch blatantly lied to the "honorable" kkkourt in order to proceed with my illegal trial, but you think she was ever censured, admonished, warned or charged with perjury by the kkkourt?! Yeah, fucking right – this is amerikkka, isn't it? So we *all* know the answer to *that* one!

Anyway, I thereafter turned back around and went back in the counselor's office and demanded any and all other papers he or the prison had in relation to my detainers. I explained that he wouldn't have to worry about putting me on the "first thing smoking" because I would be leaving to fight those charges just as fast as he could get me the paperwork to sign. A few weeks after signing everything that was required of me to (again) invoke my rights, I was picked up by two davidson county sheriff's officers and headed back to bumfukkk nashville, tennessee…

Only the *strong* go crazy
The *weak just go along...*

Assata Shakur

EILEEN

Coming from the Federal prison in West Virginia back to the Criminal Justice Center in nashville was comparable to a move from a penthouse suite to a rat-and-roach-infested motel room; that's how extreme the living conditions differed. Before it was – at last – demolished in December of 2016, CJC had to be one of the worst possible places any human being could be. Maggots were breeding, climbing out of the (usually clogged) shower drains; the walls were all thick with mold; the cells reeked of the ammonias stench of a thousand men's piss – to describe this place as a hell hole is actually making light of the situation. It was disgusting, inhumane; in some ways, Guantanamo probably would have been an improvement.

Upon arrival I was immediately placed on maximum security again; this meant handcuffs and shackles every moment I was out of the cell; fifteen minutes a day to shower;[260] fifteen minutes a day to read the newspaper; fifteen minutes allowed to make one collect phone call; and another fifteen minutes to shuffle up and down the tiny cellblock that housed myself and my fellow neighbors in misery land. Outside of our screaming to one another through the glass covering the cell bars that was in place to keep us from grabbing or throwing shit or piss at the officers and PCs that passed, or under/through the cracks in the door, there was no contact allowed with most of the other captives as I was considered a "security risk" and a "danger" to

---

[260] The handcuffs and shackles came off here, of course – but *only after* I was placed in the separate cage that housed the showers.

other people. Though I had been on "Max" before being transferred the initial time around to serve my time in the Feds, this time, of course, things were worse and would last a whole hell of a lot longer.

I survived – barely – on a diet consisting of rice and commissary – chips, candy bars, and sodas. And needless to say, my body suffered tremendously from lack of nutrition causing me to lose a lot of weight. By my being a vegetarian – and because I had "connections" at the jail – I was given peanut butter and/or extra rice to supplement every meal; still it wasn't enough. Those types of circumstances call for one to become creative with what was given, so crunching my chips into my rice is what made my meals tolerable – somewhat; however, my drastic weight loss was still easily noticeable. Nevertheless, things were even more dreadful for those that didn't have the resources I did.

Honestly, too, I don't think that any of the environment of CJC was by happenstance, either; the way things were set up, after a couple of months, the typical man clamored for the chance to plea bargain and go off to prison. Or committed suicide. An out-of-town cat that I befriended was trying to make bond; although his bond was sky-high,[261] I hooked him up with this bondsman I knew who suggested he seek a bond reduction. He did, and of course they denied him as the kkkourts are want to do. Not only that, however, they increased the amount of his bond, thereby making it even harder to come up with the money to pay it.[262]

---

[261] Murder case; no ties to the community; Black on a Friday night (which is, of course, the most serious charge of all, it seems!), etc.

[262] Denying a defendant a reasonable bond – especially a poor (of any race), Black, or Hispanic defendant – is a common practice of the amerikkkan "justice" system to destroy all manner of hope of adequately fighting your charges; raising one's bond is a method used to psychologically deter one from asking for a bond reduction in the first place. Obviously, if someone cannot meet the demands of the initial exorbitant

Eileen

You know the saying "when it rains it pours?" Well, this cat knew the reality of such a statement to the extreme: Besides trying to cope in the foul ass living conditions we were in, and being denied a bond reduction and separated from those he loved and cared for, come to find out his girlfriend *had spent all of the money he already had saved up!* Talk about stressed! All I could do was express some generic run-of-the-mill bullshit about "keep your head up" and to "keep fighting." Not surprisingly, it didn't make him feel any better about his situation.

Later on that night of the failed bond reduction hearing, I overheard the 3rd shift officer break out into a panic, calling a "code" requesting other officers and a nurse immediately; as they all ran towards the back of the cellblock, I asked my partner what the deal was:

"Damn, cuz, what up? One of those PC bitches kill themselves or something???"

No answer; guess he didn't hear me through all of the commotion. I wasn't serious anyway, as I honestly thought someone may have just been having a seizure or something. The way the officers and nurses were acting, though, it had to be a serious one. A few minutes later I called out to him again; still no response. I hoped it wasn't *him* with the medical condition.

Finally, the paramedics made it in with the stretcher. Passing by my cell as they left shortly thereafter, I was shocked to see the hole in his neck,[263] his arm dangling limply off the side, life extinguished. He had given up, and hung himself...

Those of us that survived Max did so by relieving our

---

bond in place, the malicious act of raising it is like adding insult to injury and as well a form of chastisement: *How dare you take up this "Honorable" Court's time by objecting to the kidnapping fee we were so gracious as to set for you???*
[263] Some vain attempt to resuscitate him, perhaps?

stress causing it to others. The PCs[264] on the other side of the gate were easy targets, especially if they made the mistake somehow of doing something to piss one of us off. This could have been almost anything such as turning the television provided them off of videos,[265] or even just looking the wrong way when passing by our cells on the way to the shower or something. Always prepared for such an occasion, they would get "pissed down" – urine thrown in their faces that we'd saved in cups for that express purpose – as soon as they came to the gate to get their meals or walked by going to the rec yard or showers.[266] A lot of times, too, the COs would even set them up for a "pissing" by leaving our pie flaps[267] open "by mistake" – they hated the little dick-sucking child molesters and rapists just as much as we did. Hearing them whine, scream, and otherwise bitch over what we did to them always gave us a good laugh lasting for a couple of hours or so, in so doing making our lives a little bit less miserable by making theirs' more so.[268]

Sometimes, too, we got a "live one" on Max *with* us, and with those, we *really* had some "fun." One particular cat that I myself had a lot of enjoyment fucking with came in late one night about 3 a.m. and if I remember correctly, I don't believe he quit screaming and kicking his cell door until breakfast came a few hours later at 6. And what was he screaming? What wasn't he screaming is more like it. Whatever language he was speaking,

---

[264] PC – short for "protective custody" – were housed separately away from the dangers of "general population," but *especially* from those of us on Max deemed too dangerous to others.
[265] Although we couldn't *see* the television because of being locked in our cells all day, in addition to the gate separating PC from Max, we could hear it. A lot of times listening to the television is what got me through the day.
[266] This was yet another reason for our having glass over the bars of our doors – an attempt to prevent this. Didn't work, though.
[267] Holes cut in the door to receive our meals, mail, and commissary without officers having to experience the danger of opening our doors.
[268] To even them, now I apologize. Bullying others is not cool in any shape, form, or fashion and it's bullshit to feel better in making others feel worse.

whatever words he was expressing, I've never heard before or since then. Matted gray hair tightly coiled all over his head and face, it was easy to see that this 50-ish military veteran was mentally insane by a long shot. Whether it was Vietnam that pushed him over the edge, or just the trauma of being birthed Black, this dude was absolutely nuts! And considering all that I've witnessed and done myself, that's saying a lot!

Yet the cat was hilarious as hell, too. The main thing that I can remember about this dude was how funny he was. Whether it was smearing feces completely over his front and back windows so the officers couldn't see in, doing naked martial arts (killing a gang of "crackas" in the process, his mind told him), or just arguing in his special language with whatever imaginary person was with him in the cell that day, this guy kept us cracking up laughing. The dude was totally "throwed off."

For some reason, however, I was able to completely understand him – sometimes spending my entire 15 minutes allowed in the cellblock standing in front of his cell observing his crazed expressions and movements (he never seemed to sleep, for some reason) and sometimes even attempting to converse with him.[269] The little time he was there before being transferred to the mental hospital, his lunacy really helped me to pass my own time...

Nonetheless, though, I must be honest and say that it was a misery pit back there in that dungeon; for most people it would've been hard to survive it with most of their mental faculties intact. The sheer tediousness of it all – even with all of the bizarre shit that went on here and there – was enough to make the average man insane. But I made it – or so I think – with my visits and visitors having a large part with my doing so.

---

[269] In addition to his own language, he also understood English – although he only spoke in short sentences the rare occasions that he did so.

Twice a week, an hour or so each time, different female friends of mine would take the time out of their lives to visit with me behind that grimy ass glass. I perhaps didn't miss five or so visits the entire time I was there – and then only because of unexpected car troubles or scheduling conflicts. I could above all count on my friend Nasiha like clockwork.[270] As well as my female friends, needless to say, my family came also – particularly my younger brother John and my sister Devonne.

I also took advantage of every opportunity to visit the roof for an hour of "recreation" – again, in handcuffs and shackles – whenever it was offered. We were allowed to shoot basketball and walk around an even larger cage up there – *and* in the *fresh air* to boot! So unless it was pouring down rain or absolutely freezing cold, I was there.[271]

One such trip to the roof one morning would for a second time result in me running into my lifesaver: Scheduled for trial on the attempted murder charges of Terrence Freeman, my "attorney" leann smith was again nowhere to be found. Calls, messages, and letters – again – all went unanswered. In addition, I wasn't stupid – I knew another setup was in the works. I mean, I hadn't even *seen* the woman since my extradition back to tennessee until trial was scheduled to start in less than two weeks. As well, all of my petitions to the "honorable court" of so-called "judge" seth norman seeking permission to fire her also went unanswered. I was planning to raise hell from the

---

[270] Furthermore, since I wasn't "in a relationship" at the time, there was no drama over my telling a friend that she would have to "come the next time" or when two or more people showed up unexpectedly. Sometimes, life in some ways seems a little easier when you're not "committed" to anyone in that way. Especially when incarcerated.

[271] And with the shackles and handcuffs a part of the uniform, you wouldn't believe how sweet my already sugary jumper and footwork became. Because believe me, flicking your wrist the wrong way or moving too fast in those chains would have you regretting it for *days!*

moment I stepped foot in that kkkourtroom.²⁷²

Sitting on the bench awaiting my turn to get shackled, my attention was captured by a confident and captivating strut, awe-inspiring statuesque shape, and breathtakingly stunning naturally-beautiful face approaching the gate to the hole; now *this* was an unusual sight. Wait a minute, that's – that's – *Eileen!??*

"Kenneth!?"

She gave me a hug; the first time another human being – besides when I was being cuffed, shackled, and escorted somewhere – had touched me in months! There's just no way possible for me, even today, to describe how magnificent it felt!

"What are you doing here?" she asked.

The last time we had spoken, I had asked her for an attorney referral on my federal gun case; I guess she didn't remember.

"It's a long story. What are you doing here, though? I thought you were still only working with juveniles?"

"Well, that was only for a little while. Now I'm back to criminal law."

She was there to see a client.

"Good! Because I've got trial coming up soon and I need a new attorney."

"When's the trial and who's your attorney now?"

"LeAnn Smith, but it doesn't even matter; she's getting fired. And trial starts Monday."

It was Thursday or Friday or something by then – trial was only a few days away.

"What?! The judge won't let you do that! You've waited too late!"

"Watch. Don't worry about it. Just give me a way to get in touch with you."

---

²⁷² Doing what? – I had no idea. All I knew was that I wouldn't willingly participate in my own demise in that kkkangaroo kkkourt as I did the first time around!

She gave me her card – along with another hug to my absolute happiness – and my heart was filled to the brim with hope as I played ball on the roof. After seeing Eileen, I felt like my life was improving already.

Informed that I had an attorney visit later that evening, I told the officer to tell LeAnn "fuck her." I mean, come on – this bitch wanted to wait until a few days before my trial to come visit me and *then* investigate my case??? How in the hell could a proper investigation be done with less than 72 hours to go??? So fuck that; no way in hell was I about to stand silently by as I got railroaded again.

As the officer told her exactly what I said and in the way I said it, I could hear LeAnn as she came to the gate (shocked perhaps?), hollering down the cellblock for all to hear:

"Delo! Come on out so we can get ready for your trial."

"FUCK YOU, BITCH!"

That was the only response she warranted from me – how else could I have felt any other way?

Coming back once more that Sunday night and getting the same response, she would try again as I awaited transport from the holding cell to the kkkourtroom to somehow convince me to participate in the trial; no luck there – what kind of fool did this bitch think I was? I didn't say even one word to her – nor would I put on my "trial clothes." The so-called "judge" called me into the kkkourtroom in an attempt to admonish me:

"Delo Thomas."

To my chagrin, the rotten motherfukkker always used the name given to me by my family; it sounded sickening coming out of this bigoted bastard's mouth.

"You will not disrupt my courtroom today! We are having this trial! And you will participate!"

Yeah, fucking right. This rednekkk motherfukkker had to

have known that he couldn't put any fear in my heart, so he was doing little more than wasting his breath. How he expected me to have any respect for him after he led the charge of my railroading, I'll never know. Ignoring him as he said a few other things that made no difference whatsoever to me, I asked for a chance to speak after he finally shut the hell taking a breath before passing out.

Making a case for my firing LeAnn, I brought up the fact that I had the evidence of all the letters and motions I had written to the "honorable court," to LeAnn herself, and even the Board of Professional Responsibility that was charged with policing such issues. He knew just as I did, that if he didn't allow me to fire her, then this case was more likely than not coming back on appeal. Begrudgingly giving me two weeks to hire an attorney under the threat that he would appoint me another one (like I'd fall for that trick again!), I was on the phone with Eileen that evening after being transported back to the cellblock.

Back in kkkourt a couple of weeks later, the plea bargain offered me magically went down to a 2-year sentence after the threats of 120 years (60 on each count, to run consecutive to one another) when LeAnn was my attorney; amazing the respect that having an attorney who'll fight for you instead of setting you up affords you, huh?

Still, I told Eileen, I would refuse to take it; I explained to her why: Although most people wouldn't think that it really mattered that I added two years to an already given life sentence, I saw how fighting this case would help me in the appeal of my other one; I knew that the statutory violations of the IAD mandated dismissal of my cases – both the attempted murders and the murder. Seeing as how the facts of both this attempted murder case and the murder case were exactly the same regarding my transfer to tennessee pursuant to the detainer, I knew that a ruling in my favor on this one could only serve to show the appeals courts the violation in the other. Thus – in my mind – my release would be forthcoming shortly. Or so I thought. So thinking along that vein, Eileen convinced me to hire another attorney friend of hers named Jeffrey Powell, who would concentrate strictly on my detainer issue while she concentrated on the trial.[273]

So we got on it. I gave Jeff all that I had researched concerning the IAD, the specific facts of my case in regards to it, and also what I expected to happen. And to his credit, the more he read and painstakingly researched it himself, the more he was convinced that I was right, and the more passion he put into helping me fight it. Moreover, Jeff was good, too. In fact, to both his and Eileen's credit, they both would hear me out and consider my views (though never coddle me as so many defendants seem to want) even when we had slight disagreements on strategy, tactics, or how hard to press the State. In other words, they were the perfect attorneys. My trepidations at going to trial in that bigot's kkkourtroom disappeared. Still, I knew it wouldn't be easy considering the evil we were up against; I knew full well the devils we had to face...

Those of this world whom illegitimately hold on to power, for eternity want those to whom they hold dominion over to ignore or forget how they *came* to power; this is especially true of the amerikkkans. Blacks in this kkkountry are always asked to "put the past in the past," to "get over slavery," and to "quit

---

[273] Even though I right away took a liking to Jeff and his passion in regards to the law, I to some extent had to convince him of the veracity of my IAD issues also. It seems as though this law was so seldom used that even talented legal minds such as Jeff and Eileen weren't even knowledgeable of its procedures, issues, and sanctions. Hell, it seems that lisa naylor was the lone person familiar with the IAD's 120-day rules and procedures – besides myself, of course – and even she dropped the ball blinded by her own maliciousness. Nevertheless, I was determined to win on this issue alone.

complaining" about racial profiling, police brutality, and all of the unjust and biased laws that detrimentally affect us. Yet, the very reasons we are in the positions we are in this kkkountry are a direct result of those horrific crimes perpetrated against us during the Black Holocaust called "Slavery" and its aftermath that is still ongoing. My own mother and father were born during the very heights of the "Civil Rights" movement, and during my lifetime alone I have witnessed the white crimes against Rodney King, Amadou Diallo, James Byrd, Timothy Thomas, Sean Bell, Trayvon Martin, Leon Fisher, Michael Brown, Tamir Rice, Sandra Bland, Oscar Grant III, Eric Garner, Walter Scott, the Charleston Church Nine, Malissa Williams, Kalief Browder, Rekia Boyd, Natasha McKenna, Laquan McDonald, Alton Sterling, Terence Crutcher, Philando Castile, Keith Lamont Scott, Jocques Clemmons, Daniel Hambrick, Freddie Gray, the Move Members in Philadelphia, Ahmaud Arbery, George Floyd, Breonna Taylor, and countless others. How can we "get over" something that is still unending?

This kkkountry is the only one in the world's history that was built upon two great crimes: the genocide of its Natives, and the enslavement of my ancestors, the Alkebu-lanians – better known as (yet derisively to me)[274] the "Africans." I say that instead of us "getting over" slavery, we should finally, once and for all, have a political, financial, social, and more importantly, moral "correction" in this united snakes of amerikkka to right the wrongs that slavery and Native genocide perpetrated. As the Blacks were held in bondage for centuries, as the Natives were constantly robbed, killed, and pushed off their land, so too should the invaders of this soil be. No longer can any of us justify giving "the system" the benefit of the doubt; how many

---

[274] How in the hell could the Motherland of all of this world's peoples be known by a european's name??? I think it's pathetic that so many of us – myself included before I became the wiser – have accepted this.

more times do we have to be abused, ill-used, and betrayed before we get the message? There is no "justice" for us under the present kkkapitalist united snakes system; never have we – the Natives, the Blacks, the Browns, and other "minorities" – been able to rely on the "laws" to protect *us*. And I think it's both logical and perfectly justified in our demanding of positive and progressive change by *any means necessary*. *Justice* needs to be served *finally*, and a legal maxim comes to mind when I think of what that justice looks like: *Sublato fundamento cadit opus* – When the foundation is removed the superstructure falls. What that means to me is that *no* amerikkkan should be allowed to hold political office; serve as a judge, a member of a jury, on any public school boards; or work as police officers, in the military, as correctional overseers, as prosekkkutors, or at any other position that was "legally" or factually unavailable to the Blacks, Natives, women or other "minorities" at any time in this wikkked kkkountry's history. Fifty years – two generations – should be enough to rectify the historikkkal injustices. Call it a racial revolution if you may. I just call it righteous and necessary.[275]

And in this day and age of Fuhrer Bone Spurs, if we don't do something *now* to fundamentally change things for the better for ourselves, then *when* will we? If not now, then please someone tell me when? Isn't it each one of our responsibilities

---

[275] I would be remiss if I didn't clarify what I mean by "amerikkkan." I am talking about anyone – white, Black, Hispanic, of Asian or Native descent – that feels as if they can impose their will and the historikkkally hypokkkritical "amerikkkan values" on any other peoples around the world, including in this land. True enough, with the state of this kkkountry, most of these individuals would no doubt identify as "white," however, far too many Blacks have the same mentality in that they have been successfully indoctrinated with this mindset from the days of slavery and Jim Crow. (This brings to mind the character "Snow Ball" (Head House Negro Stephen) from the movie *Django Unchained* and the Black pig that pulled over "Tre" on *Boyz in da Hood*.) My personal observation is that to a lesser extent this will involve Natives, Hispanics, or those of Asian descent.

not only to ourselves, but for those that come behind us to do *something* to foment righteous change? And if not *our* responsibility, then *whose* is it? I say that if you can look within your own self, your own character, and with a clear conscience then continue to say that "nothing is wrong" with this kkkountry or "nothing should change," then you are the personification of delusional. And my enemy…

Nevertheless, I feel encouraged by the fighting spirit that I witness in the generation of my sons, goddaughters, nieces and nephews – yet *dis*couraged by the fact that I feel their fighting spirit is still too often misdirected at one another and not our true enemy: this amerikkkan system of injustice, inequality, enslavement, oppression and even murder of us "undesirable" Black, Brown and Native "minorities" which has served as this kkkountry's foundation since the very beginning. Furthermore, my discouragement comes from us "Forgotten Souls" behind bars that have been ignored as a vital part of the struggle.

"The way men *live* is so far from the way men *ought* to live that anyone whom abandons what *is* for what *should be* brings about his *downfall* rather than his *preservation*…"
Niccolo Machiavelli

"Every time I went to the projects, he would come out and start shooting at me."

The words of Terrence Freeman. Eileen had brought his documented interviews as part of my case discovery and the content was mind-blowing, to say the least; unbeknownst to me, a joint federal-local task force had been formed to capture or kill me – headed by lisa naylor, of course. Soon as I thought I had heard it all, she surprised me yet again with just how far she'd go to get me. I mean, I had heard she was supposed to have vowed to "make her career off me," but damn! And no doubt in my mind that finally within the devils' grasp, their intent was more so to kill me than to capture. I guess this would have been her legacy.

Terrence's dumbass would thereafter agree to become the bait to lure me to my death with that statement. Foolishly, the task force figured the Bricks were where they might find me so the plan involved them setting a perimeter around Edgehill with U.S. Marshals along with metro murder squad detectives; idiotically, Terrence would drive around in circles under their safety and surveillance. Once I reared my head to get him, I guess, they would in fact get *me*! Tellingly about Terrence, he trusted them well enough to where he felt fine being cannon fodder.

And speaking of Terrence, this idiot has got to be one of the stupidest people I've ever known in my life; I mean come on – did this fool not consider all of the family ties we shared and how easy it would be to find him when he did what he did??? Did he not think I was coming for him??? He *knew* me – up close and personal! So for him to put his hands on my sister and later still put an AK-47 in my little brother's face and rob him, this fool must have had a *death wish!* That powder must have really had what little mind he was born with *gone!*

Furthermore, he couldn't run from me. Not only did our mothers and aunts grow up together as friends, but he had just recently had a child (and was living!) with my first cousin Renee! Not only did I know where he lay his own head, but I could also touch his *family* if I wanted to – the idiot's grandmother had lived in the same home since we were kids! And topping all of that off, by the time trial rolled around his sister and my own would share an apartment as *roommates!* This fool couldn't have hid from me anywhere in the city – I would always be able to find him! Nor did I need to be present to make my presence felt! Idiot should have just been happy that I was only shooting to *wound* him and talk some sense into him with what he did…

Yet, Terrence wasn't the only one in on the plot to get me – so was my cousin Renee. Yep – Nancy's daughter and Duck's sister! The same person who asked me to "find out who did that to [her] brother" and kill them! She was doing her part to see lisa naylor's vision of my demise come to fruition by going to my father's house jotting down the license plate numbers of any cars that could have been mine or somehow associated with me. In addition, she began frequenting my mother's house all of a sudden. Her mother taught her well, I guess.

Anyway, none of that bullshit worked. Moreover, the pigs probably now feel as if they gave up on the plan too soon. Because they soon showed signs of panic and their typical incompetence: Before long I would get calls saying the pigs had the "hood hot" looking for me.[276] One such call I received while kicking it with some partners in St. Louis informed me that they had pulled over and detained a cat I grew up with (but have never really been close to like that) and a friend of his because they thought his *passenger* was me. Not believing either of them when they informed the pigs that not only was the passenger – whose name was, ironically, "Lucky" – *not* me, but they had no idea where to find me, they would both only be released after Lucky's identification was verified by being taken to the police station. Asking my caller if the Lucky cat even looked like me,[277] I got one of the biggest laughs of my life being told that he looked more like a "midget Mike Tyson" than like me.

---

[276] Like I would actually show my face – had I even been *in town* – in the very same place where they were asking for information as to my whereabouts. I guess lisa naylor forgot to remember the one thing that no one has ever called me was an "idiot."

[277] I didn't know him, nor had I ever heard of him, and only by happenstance did I, years later, meet him in prison.

Another more serious call obliged me to call the father of one of my partners, whom was an old family friend:

"Son, I don't know what you've done, but you better be careful 'cause those white folks is out to get you!" he informed me.

Mistakenly, his home had been surrounded earlier that evening by the same task force who forced their way inside thoroughly searching it in some odd belief that I was there. In fact, I don't think I had been to his home in years – if at all if my memory serves me correctly. Hell, I know I hadn't been there anytime recently – I had been going back and forth between Georgia and Florida on business the couple of weeks prior so I hadn't even been in tennessee! Supposedly, though, a task force member had followed me directly to his home. And because we "all look like Tyson" I guess, his home was raided.[278]

All of these instances and more I attributed to the pigs' stupidity and lack of information at the time; I didn't realize how sinister all of the plotting was that was going on behind the scenes though. Only by the grace of God (or the protection of the Devil, depending upon whom you're asking) was I able to survive these deadly traps…

Anyway, we pressed on – myself and Eileen preparing for the trial, myself and Jeff preparing to get the case dismissed before it ever *reached* trial. A couple of weeks before the trial date, we had a hearing on my motion to dismiss the case, with the so-called "judge" so clueless as to not even realize what *his* job was at the hearing *he* had set:

"JUDGE" NORMAN: *All right. State of Tennessee versus Deangelo Thomas as a Motion to Rehear and a Motion to Dismiss.*

---

[278] Although, of course, in no way was his home getting raided my fault in any shape, form, or fashion, I apologized to this family friend anyway. However, I even then recognized the age-old tactic of the amerikkkans harassing the entire Black community to compel it to give up one of our own to quell the harassment. They knew this man had nothing to do with me and my issues with them, yet they brought my troubles to bare down on him anyway. Bastards.

You ready, Ms. Parrish?
EILEEN: *Yes, Your Honor.*
NORMAN: *All right. You ready, General?*
LISA NAYLOR: *I'm ready, Your Honor.*
JUDGE: *I'll hear you.*
NAYLOR: *I believe Mr. Powell will probably argue this motion.*
NORMAN: *All right. Mr. Powell, are you ready?*
JEFF: *Am I up first, Your Honor?*
NORMAN: *Yeah, going to put you up first.*
JEFF: *I thought the State was going to go first.*
NORMAN: *I think it's probably your motion, isn't it?*
JEFF: *Well, I already argued it.*
NORMAN: *I know you have. That's why I'm wondering why I am here?*

Stupid, right? Jeff had to explain to this so-called "judge" why he was there in his own kkkourtroom:

JEFF: *Well, the State wanted to set this, as Your Honor knows, Your Honor was going to rule on our motion. We took it under advisement and was going to rule on the motion on the day of trial. We reset the, continued the trial to January 31. And Lisa, General Naylor thought that it was better for Your Honor to hear, I guess her argument because she filed a brief.*
NORMAN: *Is that where we are, General?*
NAYLOR: *I think that's pretty accurate, Your Honor. As I recall, also, I think I had noted to the Court that the continuances in this case, the attempted homicide charge were based upon Mr. Thomas' request. And I think Your Honor had requested that we go ahead and get the transcripts from those dates and madam court reporter was kind enough to do that for us. So we have all that information. So we would like to make that part of the record and I actually have a little bit of proof that I'd like to put on.*

Lisa naylor thereafter put on a lot of inconsequential

"proof" that meant nothing whatsoever in the grand scheme of things – all it was, was an attempt to "muddy up the waters" of them having no choice but to dismiss my charges as warranted. She would even make another "money play" at me in attempting to bring up the fact that I was represented not by a public defender or appointed attorney as they would like, but by retained attorneys:

> *My understanding is that the Defendant is represented by two retained attorneys, as well as on his appeal on the murder case he has a new retained attorney is my understanding. And because we have three transcripts made, I would ask that the costs for the transcripts be attributed to Mr. Thomas.*

Jeff would make a complete fool of her in not even attempting to cross-examine her irrelevant witnesses:

> NAYLOR: *Okay. I believe those are all my questions at this time. Thank you.*
>
> NORMAN: *All right. Mr. Powell or Ms. Parrish?*
>
> JEFF: *We have no questions, Your Honor... Your Honor, the State's argument was all fine and good, eloquent. Ms. Fuller's testimony was eloquent. There is one reason why I didn't cross examine her. Because her testimony is* irrelevant. *She said only one thing during her direct testimony that is relevant to this case. She said, and I quote, that she sent, I sent a detainer letter May 31st, 2002. They sent a detainer, the State – first of all, let me back up, Judge.*
>
> *Under the IAD there are two ways for the provisions of that IAD to be invoked. And the State is only talking about one way, and that is under Article 3. And that's where the Defendant says, hey, I'm in another jurisdiction but I want to resolve the charges I have in your jurisdiction. Come and get me or dismiss the indictment if you don't want to come and get me. That's the one way, and that's the way the State is talking about and has only talked about. And*

> not only today, but when we had this motion I think January the 7th. Okay.
> But there is a second way that the IAD, the provisions of the IAD can be invoked. And that is if the State says look, we're not going to wait for you, Defendant, to request that we come and get you, we are going to come and get you. We know where you are and we are going to come and get you. That's Article 4. Article 3 is irrelevant in this case because Article 4 is what happened first. They sent a detainer letter May 31st, 2002. That's why the IAD was invoked in this case, under Article 4, not Article 3. And then, Judge, they went to Kentucky and they got him and brought him here August the 28th of 2002 for arraignment. And they arraigned him on August the 29th, 2002. We'll give them the extra day Judge.
> But the 120 day period started to run when they went and got him and brought him here, and he arrived here on August the 28th, 2002. Article 4, Judge, subsection C, says in respect of any proceedings, any proceedings. Certainly an arraignment is a proceeding in this case. In respect of any proceedings made possible by this Article.
> The only reason why they got him from Kentucky to bring him down here for arraignment was under the Article. So there is no question Judge, no question that he deserves the protection under Article C, any respect of any proceedings made possible by this Article.

Jeff was getting riled up now, and you could tell that norman's rotten ass didn't like how he was being talked to. But Jeff was right – we had "the law" entirely on our side in this matter and there was simply nothing that norman nor lisa naylor could do about it. Or so we thought. Jeff continued bashing their heads in with the facts and the law:

> *Trial* shall, *not* should, could, shall *be commenced within 120*

days of the arrival of the prisoner in the receiving state. That's Tennessee. But for good cause shown in open court, *the prisoner or the prisoner's counsel being present in court having jurisdiction of the matter may grant any necessary or reasonable continuances.* No *question that they sent a detainer letter, Judge.* No *question that they got him here because of that detainer.* No *question that the arraignment took place.* No *question that he arrived on August 28th, 2002.* No *question that the arraignment took place August 29, 2002* .No *question that the provisions of Article 4, not 3, were invoked. They had 120 days from August the 28th, and I'll* give *them the extra day, August 29th if you want to. They* had *to try him by December 26th or if I give them the extra day, 27th. They* had *to.*

Two exceptions, Judge. They got two chances, that's it. Two chances to keep this from being dismissed. If they can show one, that a continuance was granted, that it was reasonable and necessary and that it was on the record. And the tennessee supreme court says, at a very minimum, there has to be a verbatim record. Can't be in chambers, verbatim record. The tennessee supreme court also says that the State has the burden of proving that. So they have to show that between August 28th, 2002 and December 26th, 2002 that Mr. Thomas and/or his counsel requested a continuance or the court granted a continuance for a reasonable and necessary cause. And it has to be on the record. And so the transcripts that the State has entered, I didn't object. The reason why, because they are irrelevant. Those transcripts have nothing to do with from December, from August 28th to December 26th, nothing. Okay. Now that's the first one, they can't show that. They can't show it, so they got one chance, Judge, one chance. They had two, they blew one, they have one chance left.

And that is to show that the Defendant was unavailable for trial. They can't show that either. Why, because they had him. He was here the whole time. He wasn't sick, no mental health issues, there was nothing that made him unavailable for trial. So he didn't ask for a continuance, none was granted on the record, that's one exception. And he was not unavailable for trial. He was sitting in jail.

Now the Tennessee — the State is talking about all these things that happened after December 26th, 2002. First of all, they talk about under Article 3, which has no relevance here. Article 4 was already invoked, and they are talking about things that happened outside the 120 days. The Supreme Court says that's irrelevant.

This case is clear, Your Honor. It's clear if you go step by step, it's clear. Letter on May 31st invoked Article 4. They went and got him. See, when they sent the letter they were telling Mr. Thomas and the State of Kentucky we want him. We don't want to wait on him to send us, we are going to come and get him. They brought him here. He was actually here for 14 months, Your Honor. He was here for 14 months. So you go step by step. They brought him here, they arraigned him, he was here, any proceeding. Certainly an arraignment is a proceeding. If you look at the plain language of the statute, Your Honor, it is clear. If they can't show that they continued this case or Your Honor continued this case for reasonable and necessary cause during 120 days or they can't prove that he was unavailable. And they can't prove any one of those, Your Honor. They can't do it.

This Court, pursuant to this statute and also the holdings of the Supreme Court of Tennessee, which says that the trial court **must, shall** dismiss those indictments. We are just asking Your Honor to follow the law in this case and dismiss, no matter how harsh the result is for the State. The LAD was drafted, Your Honor, to protect the defendants. And the State of Tennessee says that the provisions of this article are to be construed liberally. We don't even need that. You can construe it strictly, Your Honor. We don't even need a liberal construction. Strictly, and he still wins on this issue. It's clear. Absolutely clear, Your Honor. And we ask the Court to dismiss the indictment.

Lisa naylor again came with some rigmarole about the State "only sending a letter" and "not a detainer or any other formal request as far as documentation" and Jeff again ate into her:

> Your Honor, the State is missing the boat on that. It's not the letter that we are talking about. The letter did invoke Article 3, there is no question about it. But forget the letter. Even if we give them that, they brought him here, they went and got him. They went and got him and brought him here, and under section C, says that once the prisoner arrives in the receiving state they have 120 days, they must try him within 120 days once he arrives. So forget about the letter, they went and got him and they brought him here for arraignment. It's clear, it says once he arrives in the receiving state. So they can say what they want about it, Article 4 was invoked because they brought him here and they arraigned him and they had 120 days, period, unless they could show one of those two exceptions, and they can't. It's clear.

Checkmate. Norman knew, and naylor knew, that there was no avoiding the fact that I was entitled *by law* to have those two attempted murder charges thrown completely out. *By law.* There was just no avoiding it. Jeff was clear about the facts, the circumstances, and left no doubt that norman had no choice but to dismiss the charges. And everyone in the kkkourtroom could tell that it was eating norman's rotten ass up inside. Jeff also addressed the cost of the transcripts – couldn't let them get away with sticking me with that, either:

> And the other thing I want to address, Your Honor, the matter about the transcripts. The burden is on the State to prove that they requested, a continuance was requested. So we would ask the Court

to deny their request that Mr. Thomas pay for the transcripts. He's entitled to invoke his speedy trial rights under the IAD, and the State has the burden of proving that he continued the case. And the transcripts that they got don't even apply to the time period that it should. So we are asking that you make the State pay for that.

Man, I *love* Jeff and Eileen! You can't even imagine how proud it made me to be represented by the both of them! Never had I witnessed someone stand up to the kkkrooked "judges" found in the majority of kkkourtrooms in bumfukkk nashville, tennessee until I met Eileen, and I never witnessed it again until she introduced me to Jeff. To this day, they are the *only* two attorneys I would ever put my life (or the lives of my loved ones) in having full faith and confidence that a great job would be done, a great fight would be fought, and that I could actually trust them to care! The *only* two. And I've had a lot of attorneys over the years. But it's that serious.

Disdainfully, however, what does the law mean for a Black man in amerikkka when the white folkkks have it in for him? Although norman's bigoted ass was well aware that the case would eventually have to be dismissed, he decided to proceed with trial anyway, just to force me to fight it on appeal. No problem; we were prepared for that more than he thought.

Expectedly – at least by me, that is – Eileen came to me as I was changing into my trial clothes with what she said was lisa naylor and the State's final plea offer: a 2-year sentence on each count to run concurrent to each other and the life sentence I was already serving, in return for my pleading guilty to two counts of felony reckless endangerment; to her surprise and against her better judgment, I rejected it; I had a counteroffer:

"Tell lisa naylor that I'll plead no contest to two misdemeanor counts – time served – if I get the guarantee in writing that the feds won't come in and pick this case up."

No way in hell was I about to be blindsided again like I was in 2000 – thinking the case was completely over only to be charged with a federal crime a few months later. No way in hell.

"*Delo, they're not going to do that.*"

Eileen was certain. I don't know whether she was more concerned that I was requesting two misdemeanors, that I wanted time served, or that I wanted the guarantee of no more fallback off of the case, but she was certain. But so was I. I knew that the State saw the writing on the wall of all that had transpired being a colossal waste of time and money – mine and theirs – and that if they could make it go away somehow while still saving face, they would do so. As far as me, the IAD claims we had previously made and argued had already served notice to the tennessee kkkourts that I wouldn't take that bullshit they were serving lying down. I had it on good word, also, that at least one so-called judge at the kkkourt of criminal appeals was keeping tabs on my case – even though it was technically improper, unethical, and maybe even illegal for him or her to do so. But when has *that* ever stopped an arrogant amerikkkan when dishing out "justice" to a "nigger," right?

"*Try,*" was my only response.

I had the confidence in her that she would sell it, even as she didn't particularly believe that the State would bite. Within ten minutes, however, she was back with an even more surprised expression than before:

"*I cannot believe this – they went for it!*"

"*I told you, Eileen – they don't want to take this case to trial; they know I got 'em! They know I know exactly what I'm talking about and that I got 'em! Guess what, though? I'm not taking it!*"

I was just kidding, of course – and that was totally worth the laugh I got seeing her expression of wanting to kill me…

Have I described to you how deplorable of a person the

so-called "judge" norman is? 200 years ago he would have been the owner of a plantation full of Black slaves; I'm pretty sure one of his direct ancestors was. And that's the attitude he ran his kkkangaroo kkkourt with – warehousing as many defendants as he possibly could at "his" drug court program. Wonder how much money that pulls in for him and his kkkronies every year?

"*All rise.*"

I didn't. Not for norman, this despicable so-called judge.

"*Mr. Delo Thomas,*" (I *hated* when that bastard used my nickname!) he said, "*you're pleading guilty to...*"

I stopped the bastard right there:

"*No! I'm not pleading guilty to* anything *up in here today!*"

With a sour look, he corrected himself:

"*Excuse me – you're pleading no contest to...*"

Yeah, get it right, bastard – no way in hell they would trick me in any shape, form, or fashion ever again. It was obvious to everyone in the kkkourtroom that he couldn't stand the sight of me, and that I could stand the sight of him even less...

My experiences of dealing with those devils served to bolster a truth. I realized in my early childhood after being backed into a corner a couple of times: I *hate* bullies and learned that it's better to fight them and lose, than to not fight at all. And the untied snakes is the biggest bully of them all – historically using its money and military empirically around the world (and domestically in the case of its "Indian problem," "Manifest Destiny," and the use of its so-called "criminal justice system") to subjugate people that are not white anglo-saxon europeans. So I *fight* – and will continue to – until I'm dead or we're all free at last...

"My long-crushed spirit rose, cowardice departed, bold defiance took its place; and I now resolved that, however long I might remain a slave in form, the day had passed forever when I could be a slave in fact..."
Narrative of the Life of Frederick Douglass

PRISON

Monday: trial set culminating in a plea bargain on the two attempted murders of Terrence Freeman; that same Friday: transfer to state prison. The swiftness at which the authorities moved in getting rid of me amazed, even, most of the officers that worked there. But that's how it's always been with me for some reason – procedures and laws not followed, or disregarded, or even just plain violated. And, of course, anything that could possibly be thought of to make my life and time harder. Nothing was ever routine when it came to dealing with me. Hell, I wasn't even finished serving out my federal sentence yet. So I thought if anything, I would have been returned to the federal pen in West Virginia. Instead, however, I was transferred to Charles Bass Correctional Complex in west nashville – what we in the streets referred to as "Cockrill Bend" because of the street it was on.

State prison is a wholly different animal than that of federal prison. The differences are so drastic as to feel as if one has been shipped off to another *planet*. The attitudes are that dissimilar – among the ones "doing time" and the ones turning the keys. Federal prison is Criminal University, with your time spent learning how to become a more productive member of society once free again – whether through licit or illicit means. Whereas state prison is all about *survival,* hoping you can even make it back out into society again *alive.*

In many cases, a person who landed in federal prison got

there because of the inability of the state to get him and it then "siccing" the feds on him. Those in federal prison are used to having things – houses, cars, money. Major money. They're coming in able to call home and get their own money sent to them instead of having to call home to beg. Federal prison is unlike state prison where petty money and petty issues are often the reason for a person being there. Robbing and killing someone for a couple of grand, now doing 30 years? – state prison. Killing an innocent civilian for wearing a color somewhere you don't feel like they should be allowed to? – state prison. You know, brainless shit like that. On the other hand, the federal prisoner mentality is on some *get money* shit.

I spent months fighting my federal (Kentucky/Ohio) case and not once did I hear anything pertaining to a "crack pipe" or "straight-shooter"; transferred to davidson county's criminal justice center county jail and that's one of the first subjects talked about: "Yeah, dey caught me wit da Shootah," or "Yeah, I stabbed da mu'fucka for trying to steal my straight." Just dumb shit. Where county conversations usually revolved around petty and senseless crime related to junkie shit, state prison itself was only just a little bit out of the junkie stage. However, the petty junkie mentality never leaves; although not able to get high as well as they would like to by the time they've made it to state prison, those same grimy cats will still hurt someone for something as small as a dollar.

Shit was crazy. So adjusting to being around that grimy mentality again, I came through the door of classification watching all with a wary eye. Most of the cats at Cockrill Bend already knew or knew of me in one way or another before I walked through the gates; my name had become notorious in the streets long before this point, as a dealer, robber, and killer. Hell, they knew I was coming even before I did, and what's sad to say is that a reputation such as my own is one that's respected within state prison walls. "Respected" or not, however, I still refused to get caught slipping.

A couple of months after the usual tests of "classification" I was transferred an hour or so west of nashville to the turney center industrial prison and farm in only, tennessee. The running joke was it was in "only" because the prison was the only thing in the town and the only thing keeping those bakkkwoods kkklansmen and women that worked there from starving to death.

Which, you know, is really ironic to me: Supposedly the "land of the free" and with only roughly 5 percent of this world's population, the united snakes of amerikkka incarcerates one-quarter of all the world's prisoners and holds a higher proportion of its own population in jails and prisons than does any other country. More so than Russia; more so than China; more so than *any* of the oft-criticized "African" Motherland and/or Islamic countries.

And it's big business, too. I would even go on to say that incarceration of "undesirables" is one of the major underpinnings of this kkkountry's economy – much like slavery was in the not-so-distant past. In fact, all it is, *is* a continuation of slavery. Think about it: Not even counting the myriad number of counselors, probation officers and the such, the united snakes' prison industrial complex employs well over half a million people, making it the kkkountry's biggest employer. Most of these employees are lowly – if at all – educated bakkkwoods "christian" whites who would have no other way to clothe or feed themselves if not for the enslavement and control of Blacks and increasingly Hispanics. Usually the prisons are located in traditional agricultural slave-based counties and towns, who would love to re-fight the Civil War even 150 years after its supposed end. (I say, maybe they shouldn't have laid down like the cowards they were in the first place.) And that's exactly the type of place they sent me...

Dependent upon what one's affiliation (or lack thereof) was, dictated how I perceived them. Matter of fact, I also took it a little deeper: I looked at affiliations, what city you were from, and even what side of town of that city you grew up in. Memphis, Knoxville, or Chattanooga, I took it only as deep as what you claimed usually. But nashville? – what you claimed? Where you hung out? Who you were related to? – all of that and more came into play. Because every side of town – east, west, north, south – felt as if someone on their side of town had died or suffered at my hands in some way. Plus, nashville is so small that it seems like everyone is related in some way or the other. And I had become the Boogie Man, the usual suspect in and out of the streets.

Typical case in point: "Horse" was a cat from south nashville that had been reported as mentioning me as "the dude who killed my homeboy." He further went on to say to whom he was speaking to that I "seem like a cool dude" but that he thought he would "have to get" me. Of course the person who alerted me as to what he said swore me to secrecy that I wouldn't say anything or involve him in any way, and as a man of my word I was bound to keep quiet, but I was just *waiting* on the first opportunity to run into this Horse character and find a reason to take it to him. Finally the day came when the person who alerted me and Horse and I were in the same space as I was working out in front of my cell; somehow or another, the name Alfred Cole came up. I think it was done so to purposely provoke a reaction out of me; I bit on it, however, because I *wanted* to:

"Yeah, man, I really miss old Al. He used to really look out,"

Horse said.

"Yeah, and you know they say I'm the one who killed him, right?"

I wasn't really asking, I was baiting, but fuck it – let me throw it out there and see what he wanted to do.

"Yeah, man, uh, yeah. I heard that. That along with a lot of other stuff," he responded.

There was an awkward pause as we each awaited the other's next move; he was stockier than me, but 3-4 inches shorter – I liked my chances.

"Yeah, man, but I ain't on that. Shid, I'm trying to go home," he finally said.

I thought so. Although I wanted the confrontation to come sooner rather than later if it was going to come at all, I didn't necessarily want to catch another "body" in the penitentiary if I could avoid it so I was cool with that. I wasn't looking for trouble, you see, but I'd be damned if I ever let it sneak up on me again.

After that, we shared a bit more dialogue on whom the other was, what our associations were, the rumors that proceeded me, etc. He let me know that he had been aware of me for the last three months since I had gotten transferred there from classification, and I let him know that I had been aware of him, too, along with any and all other potential threats. I was ready for any and everything at all times. I had gotten caught slipping once on the streets, and fuck letting myself slip again.

After that incident transpired Horse and I actually became sort of cool. Once again, not only is it difficult for people to put the rumors to the face and demeanor, but especially when people actually got to know me, it usually became even more so. And I wasn't even really tripping on how my reputation had people wary of me initially – considering the way the news and ghetto media portrayed me as a despicable motherfucker – a monster to distrust and fear – I can't even blame them.

Another cat that I ended up becoming really tight with stopped me one day after we were both leaving visit:

"Hey cuz, lemme holla at you."

It was Yamamoto, a homie I had seen around the compound and maybe even done a couple of sets on the bench press with, but we had never really conversed besides the standard greeting of "what's cracking?"

"What's good?" I responded.

"They call you Lil' Thomas," he asked.

"Naw, but why? What's up?"

Now – for some strange reason – I was getting apprehensive – and with *him* I *knew* I would have had a problem! Homie was "cock strong!"

"My auntie saw you at visit today... she said you killed her boyfriend."

Aww shit – here this bullshit go! Well let's do it – I got in a defensive stance.

As he continued mentioning a name I wasn't familiar with (not that that really mattered in the streets!), he insisted that it was I whom had transgressed against his aunt:

"She lives on (such-and-such) road, in some apartments."

Then it clicked – Old School!

"Oh shit! Yeah, man, I know what you talking about now – I went to trial, beat the case," I calmly said. He was a street cat like I was, so he knew how shit went.

"Yeah, man, she said you beat it, but that was my auntie's house, though."

"Well what's up?" a bit annoyed now, wanting to get down to whatever we were going to get down to.

Then I guess he thought about it, because like I said he was a street cat just as I was – all he could do was respect it.

Hell, he was locked up himself for murdering the family member of one of my homeboys – as I've said before, nashville is small as hell and everyone has some type of ties in some way it seems.

"*Naw, it's cool, it's straight. I didn't fuck with dude like that, anyway. He wasn't no kin to me. But if my auntie had've been there, shit might-not-a-been-cool."*

"*I guess it's cool for both of us then that your auntie wasn't there, then, huh?"*

He and I became good friends after that incident of understanding...

I quickly realized that one of the major differences between myself and far too many other cats at the prison was that while I was at my worst, a lot of them were actually doing better than they ever had in life. And I'm not just speaking financially – I more so mean in mentality and attitude. A lot of those fools seemed to actually *like it* in prison. No bullshit. Crazy, huh? Contraband – and the petty funds and petty prison cachet that comes with it – made a lot of these cats feel like "big shit." Absolutely, being the "big homie" had a lot of misguided fools feeling "all-powerful." And it was/is heartbreaking to see this "power" misused far too often toward petty and detrimental ends. Especially when it came to other prisoners they thought they could bully or get one over on.[279]

Something else that blindsided me about state prison was the rampant and in-your-face homosexuality – which is actually encouraged by the oppressors.[280]

At any time, and you can (and will!) be thrown in "the

---

[279] Furthermore, instead of equipping their lil homies with the knowledge and tools they needed to get out of prison and stay out, far too many cats sent them out on "dummy missions" and/or encouraged the same destructive behaviors that led the vast majority of us to prison in the first place. I can't begin to tell you how disappointing this all was as a "big homie" myself.

[280] I suspect their mindset is that the more homosexuality, the further all prisoners are emasculated! At least; that's how they act!

hole" for having a nude picture of your wife or girlfriend, but within a few days of getting to turney center I witnessed two swastika-tattooed white supremacists tongue-kissing in full view of kkkorrectional kkkops as we all waited to leave the ball field, yet saw one of those same officers threaten to cancel a cat's "future visits" over a 2-3 second kiss with his wife at the end of visitation. And although the vast majority of prisoners didn't/don't participate in homosexuality,[281] it became not unusual for me to witness kufi-wearing cats walking hand-in-hand (or sometimes, hand around the hip) with effeminate men wearing makeup or hear of gang brawls/wars being started over jealousy surrounding a "boy." The world seemed to have turned upside down, as I had never been around anything like that before then.[282] All in all, I felt the abnormal had become normal. And my only thoughts were to get the hell out of there...

Let me be clear about something, however: I think "homophobia" one of the most ignorant mindsets that this world has ever birthed! What the hell do *I* care whom another person chooses to have sex with?! Woman, man, hermaphrodite, Martian, Casper-the-Friendly-fucking-Ghost, I couldn't give a damn less – *you* just do *you* and *I'll* continue to do *me*! As long as no one steps over that boundary, then I have no problem with *no* one. True enough, I personally feel like there's no more beautifully made creature on this earth than "Woman" (and making love to one is the closest to "Heaven on Earth" that I've ever been), but not everyone *feels* like that, not every man is built/wired like me. And I have to recognize the reality that some men (for whatever reason) choose to live their life sexually differently than I choose to live my own. I further

---

[281] That I know of! But, of course, it's not like I was trying to investigate any other person's sexual habits!
[282] Plus, even things like television were different then – as you never witnessed LGBTQ characters/relationships on the screen like you do now.

recognize that there's absolutely nothing wrong with that. To each his own way of life in my eyes. Although I'll never understand how a man could be attracted to another man, I will never "hate" another simply because of their sexual orientation, proclivities and/or tastes. I mean what does another man's sexual peccadilloes have to do with me? And as such, I just don't get "homophobia" or the "hate of gays." Do they make you feel something that you'd rather keep suppressed, or something? Hmmm, I wonder…

Anyway, because of all this and more, I therefore made a conscious and determined effort not to fall into any of the prison bullshit, or in any kind of way, "slave for the white man," become institutionalized, or especially take my focus off getting my brother and myself home as soon as possible. Nevertheless, it's certainly not that way with everyone. As a matter of fact, after a few months most prisoners fall unconsciously into the routine of the daily prison life and become institutionalized; in fact, most encourage the onset. They don't want to think of anything of the loved ones, the life, the freedom that they left behind and miss. However, I was determined not to be one of these prisoners – I didn't want to look up and realize decades of my life were gone.

Yet as the days and months piled up turning into years and then even (now) almost two decades; as I witnessed my children, nephews, nieces getting older (with even more nephews and nieces and lil cousins born), still, prison eventually got to my mind, too. No matter how hard I resisted it, "time" started "doing me." I battled with keeping my sanity every day; the horrors of prison are bad enough as it is, but for an innocent man it's literally sickening. My mental health quickly deteriorated. I quit protesting my innocence to people, my lawyers included. It didn't take me long to realize that no one gave a fuck about innocence or guilt anyway. Plus, hearing it makes people feel uncomfortable, in fact feel guilty themselves. For how could you say you love and care for someone and stand idly by as they are wrongly accused and incarcerated? The lack of support given to their loved one – emotional, mental, and physical – only serves to make their guilt worse.

Every single day I felt anger, despair, disbelief, lack of hope, depression – usually all within the matter of the few seconds it took me to awaken and contemplate my situation in the mornings. I thought it every time I heard the demoralizing words "chow time" to signal the disgusting meal we're fed like the animals we're believed to be. When I traveled from my cell to the law library to work on and research my case yet inevitably stopped and harassed for my "pass" just as in the days of slavery, I thought about it. When hit with the inevitable "shakedowns" and cell searches, forced to get buck naked like my kidnapped ancestors. And when the doors slammed at 8:30 every night as I lay down living out another day waiting to die.

At different times, I found myself wanting to lash out at the "judge," the jury, the prosekkkutors – hell even my own witnesses – for allowing this sham, this fraud to go on. Here I was, an *innocent man found guilty of a murder that the state of tennessee always knew I didn't commit* languishing in prison!

And it seemed as if it didn't matter to *anyone*! So many times I heard from people – people in my own family and people who at least claimed that they loved me – that maybe I was being punished for something I *did* do and got away with so maybe I should just *accept it*. What??? What exactly kind of bullshit is *that???* It's astounding the bullshit people will come up with (in an attempt!) to justify an injustice! That's like a parent coming home and beating the hell out of his unsuspecting child not for some wrong committed that day, but for some wrong he *may* have committed in the past and "gotten away with." Just how in the fuck is *that* supposed to make a child feel???

Leaves a terrible taste in your mouth, huh? So how in the fuck was what they were telling me supposed to make me feel any fucking better??? Here I was an innocent man sentenced to prison for the rest of my life and I was supposed to enjoy and accept it because of things I "may" have done and gotten away with it??? I think the fuck not! And every single day, every single hour, minute, and second my anger at the world only grew. Furthermore, I learned to despise any and all who have no qualms at all with an innocent man's life being taken away by amerikkka's system of "justice" – family, friends, who-the-fuck-ever!

So many people – including people I thought loved me – wanted me out of the way that I often contemplate whether it would've been better off for everyone if I had the death penalty instead of a life sentence. That way, people could then go on with their lives and guilt.

Each day when I awakened the first question I asked myself was "why?" Why yet another day of misery? Why yet another day of hopelessness? Why yet another day of prison? I had no hope after a while of ever going free again – I was forever a slave. I had no hope of ever being a father to my sons again or an uncle to my nephews and nieces. I had no hope of ever being able to contribute to society. My life was over, yet my body continued to live. Over and over again I had to ask "why?" I tried everything I knew in my mind and heart to convince the Creator to end my misery – I, also, often found myself asking the Creator "why?" I mean, why was I born if it was all to end this way? Why was I allowed to have not one, but two sons just to leave them fatherless? Why was I allowed to affect so many lives, in all the good and bad ways I did so??? Because to be honest, I'd have much rather have been left in that state of nonexistence we proceed from when born. I finally understood the old cliché "ignorance is bliss" because once you know – love, freedom, or just life in general – and that which you know is taken away from you, you mourn it forever. I mourn my life forever...

Looking at magazines, watching television, or even listening to the radio was (and continues to be!) hard. You're constantly being bombarded with the images and sounds of all you're missing in the "free world" and being reminded of how society has left you behind – the "Lifer." Every holiday that passes, every event that takes place, every new start to a sport season is like a blade in your side being twisted and turned; it hurts. It's a reminder that you and your life are essentially nothing – you're a slave.

Sometimes – regretfully – I would sit around and *wish* I had done some of the things I was accused of. You think I killed Duck and Al? I *wish* I did. You think I killed Youngsta? Well fuck it I'm doing the time for it anyway, so I *wish* I had done it. Pasheni thinks I did that bullshit she and her mother out-of-nowhere accused me of? Well, hell, I *wish* I had the thought to do so way back then! My thoughts were that maybe I'd feel better about the situation I'm in *if* I had done all of the awful things subscribed to me. Thankfully, however, I would quickly come to my senses.

Yet for many a day and night I would find myself praying for death. Whether it came in my sleep, a knife in my chest or back, I didn't care. I just needed to stop the pain and misery of serving this life sentence. A lot of people got it twisted, and a lot of people would call me crazy, but still I'd much rather have the death penalty than the sentence of "life." Why? Because both result in the same end – death in prison – yet one is a slower, more torturous death than the other. At any time you can drop your appeals in a death penalty case and force the end.[283] But with "life," you could spend 20, 30, 40 years or more waiting for the day in which it would all be over. You tell me who's better off? The man who dies after 10-15 years of imprisonment, or the man who dies after 20-30 years of being worked as a slave serving "life?" Personally, I've witnessed a man who had served over 25 years of enslavement, the last 5 or so taking whatever pittance of pain medicine the pigs may have given him for cancer (like, for instance, Tylenol 600 mgs), only to drop dead one day of a heart attack. A life sentence. I've celled with a man who's given over 40 years – 40 YEARS OF HIS LIFE!!! – to various prisons in tennessee and Mississippi. He loses himself to bouts of insanity, having conversations with and dreams of people that have long since been dead decades ago. A life sentence. A life sentence. A life sentence. It should more appropriately be called that what it is – a slower, more torturous death penalty. Because at the end of the journey that's all you have to look forward to – death…

I'm not the kind of man, however, whom will, by virtue of the fact that everything in my life has been taken away from me, turn to religion to somehow make things better. From what I've seen, attendance of church in prison really exposes you to the theatrics of it all – style over substance. Through the tens of "thank you Jesus's," "thank you, Lords!," "Amens," and "Hallelujahs!," it's really damn near impossible to figure out just what the point of the sermon is a lot of times. If there even *is* a point, ya know? And the same fervent worshippers one would find in the chapel at every service are usually the same cats you have to watch the most from sticking a knife in your back or

---

[283] Although, you may have some sadistic liberal that "cares about you" attempting to pick them up on your behalf – ironically, they may be allowed to do so by proving that you're "insane" by wanting to die.

snitching you out to the "kkkorrectional kkkops."

Yet let me be fair and clear here and say that although I recognize the right of *anyone* to practice their religion and/or philosophy of life (as long as you do *no* harm to *others*), there is no "organized religion" that I would ever personally subscribe to. *No one* is going to tell me how, when, and where to pray, how, when, and/or where to worship, what's right and/or wrong for *my* life – when I'm doing no wrong to others. No One. Not any preacher, any priest, any pope, any imam, any sheikh, any monk, or any llama. No one. None of these people or anyone else could ever *force* me to their ways of life. Besides, to each his own and what may be perfectly fine for *you* could, in fact, be the very throes of hell for *me*. And vice-versa. So again, to you your way of life and to me my own. And as long as we do no harm (especially and primarily physical) to one another, then I can't see how anyone would/could have a problem with this "live and let live" attitude.[284] My own "religion" is very simple: I respect and "do right by" as I demand others respect and "do right by" me. Moreover, we all *live* by what we truly "believe." Yet the wicked amongst us can't tolerate leaving people be – their "religion, their philosophy of life seems to cause them to want to *force* all manners of bullshit on others: women should dress, walk, talk, and play only *this* way – and are only allowed to do [fill in the blank scenario] with *their* bodies; men *and/or* women are only allowed to have intimate contact with people that look like [fill in the blank] or under the guise of [fill in the blank scenario]! However, what the fuck do you *or* I care about what another chooses to do with their bodies as long as it's consensual and not forced upon a child or animal (because,

---

[284] Nevertheless, let me be clear by explaining that just because I have an inherent tolerance of others living their life as they so choose, this *doesn't* mean that I automatically have to like, enable, support, nor participate in those choices! Can you dig it?

don't forget, this *is* tennessee) that doesn't know any better and/or can't resist?! What the hell do you *or* I care what the next man or woman does if it affects no one other than themselves?! Whatever floats whatever kind of boat you're riding in, is my way of thinking.

Nevertheless, my tolerance (or maybe I should say "my respect") does *not* extend to hypocrites – the preachers and church deacons that constantly espouse the "sanctity of marriage" while putting penis to every woman, child, and even man he can get his hand on in the congregation; the priests, bishops, and cardinals that have molested countless thousands of children in just this kkkountry alone; the Muslim sectarians whom view all others as "infidels" deserving of annihilation if not "converted" to their own sect despite being "no compulsion in Islam"; those monks and rabbis (dependent upon the area of the world) whom espouse "enlightenment" and/or "peace" yet participate in and/or support the genocide of hundreds of thousands (if not millions!) of innocent people! Hypocrites all! Just fucking hypocrites!

Just the same are those amerikkkan hypocrites that scream off the rails about "animal rights" yet look for any flimsy excuse to sanction the beating and/or killing of any random unarmed Black or Brown person (you know, human fucking beings!), or espouse the "sanctity of life" in regards to abortion but just love the hell out of the death penalty (and not unsurprisingly, especially when it comes to, again, the Black and/or the Browns!); or scream to be the biggest "patriots" yet worship at the altars/statues/monuments of coward confederate *traitors*!! Hypocrites all!!

But a special distaste for hypocrisy I have is homegrown, indeed – and that's the dislike I have for Black "christians" in the mold of my Aunt Nancy. I mean, this woman in particular is one of the loudest "shouters" at every church service, wearer of some of the biggest and elaborate (and ugly as hell, too!) "church hats," constant caller of the kkkops on me – yet she forever turns a blind eye to the child molester in her own household that she knows for a *fact* has even stuck dick to some of her own grandchildren under her care![285]

So yeah, I look at *all* "christians" – especially the Black ones! – with a wary, skeptical and suspicious eye, as I've only witnessed a precious few that actually *walk* what they talk/teach. And I (honestly!) thank my "family" for that nugget of wisdom. I honestly do…

Politics has not always been my favorite subject, but any man with even an ounce of sanity and intelligence would turn "political" in prison. Prison has a way of highlighting the injustices in one's life, in the world, and in turn, this forces one to change and attempt to change the world around him. Or at least rage undamned.

I chose the former, but never kept the latter far from the back of my mind. In choosing the former I taught awareness (but *never* "hate" – I feel like any person with two eyes, two ears, and a mind to think with like we were *all* "blessed with" can come to their own conclusions!) to any that seemed receptive, or sought me out for legal advice or inquired why I moved the way they noticed me "move." In prison it doesn't escape notice

---

[285] If I've said even *one* thing untrue, then *please* sue me! I *welcome* it! Y'all know what it is! Hell, he's probably got a little boy sitting in his lap right now as I write this – while you sit there *watching* talking about "I *know* Delo killed Duck; I know he did!" Pitiful! And so very "christian-like" of you, huh?! I don't know *why* y'all keep wanting to fuck with *me* over something *your snake ass son did to me,* but from *here on out* I *promise* to hit back *every single time* you motherfuckers (or anyone else) throw a blow at me! Over 21 fucking years you've been spitting this bullshit, and that tells me that I've been Mr. Nice Guy for far too fucking long! But no more! The truth is the *truth*! Let's *see* who has it on *their* side!!? Cool with you, "Auntie?" Because it's perfectly fine with me!

when someone has the humble confidence to be different, and I always respected myself and all others (yet never ran from an unwarranted aggression from prisoner or pig), never indulged in drugs or homosexual activities (but conversed with the "junkies" and/or "boys" just as I did anyone else if they came at me on some righteous shit), and never had to move and/or run with a crowd. I was just being myself. I never unethically attempted to impose my will on others; never took advantage of even one person; and was always open to conversing with anyone – no matter their race, color, ethnicity, religion,[286] sexual orientation, "affiliation," whatever – as long as they came at me on some respectful and righteous shit as opposed to "penitentiary dumb shit" and/or gossip. And word quickly got around (as it's want to do in any captive environment) that I was the man to see to borrow or get recommended a good book to read, or if you wanted help learning the law and/or how to research your case without being charged anything (besides a promise to teach at least one other person what you learn!) like you faced with most other cats. So I became *that* guy – always to be found spending my "free time" in the library helping someone help themselves get home when I wasn't on the ballfield lifting weights and/or shooting ball to "stay in shape. Even with the constant shipping in and out of different prisoners, I'm positive that at least a few times (over the years) I probably had helped 200 (or more) of the 2,000 prisoners housed there with their appeals, pending cases, record exonerations, divorces, parole hearings, and other legal issues. No bullshit. And there are more than quite a few cats that are at home right now to this day (that otherwise *wouldn't* be) that can attest to how effective I was/am.

---

[286] Although I continued to be wary of christians – yet my wariness could be erased if I sensed in them a personal righteousness as opposed to hypocrisy.

Nevertheless, what I was doing (helping teach others to *think for* and *help themselves*) was not to be met without suspicion and/or resistance from the oppressors, of course! And more than a little "resistance" I did receive in myriad ways. (Although I technically wasn't breaking any "rules" in empowering people to do for self!) But I'll save the details for another day...

I want to say this, however: A harsh reformation of thinking should occur not only in our own Black and Brown communities but in the united snakes as a whole when dealing with issues pertaining to prisons and their population. Prisons have long been used as warehouses to stock us, the "undesirables," however some of us same individuals currently have within ourselves the potential to produce great works that could benefit "needy" countries and communities worldwide.

And this kkkountry should strongly consider that; send us "back" to the Motherland and/or Mexico or Central America[287] as you stupid white supremacists are quick to scream! Hell, set up liaisons with the countries you rotten bastards kkkidnapped our ancestors from and allow them to pick and choose those of us they would/will accept in their lands as the free and clear actual citizens that we've *never* been, nor will *ever* be in this land you've stolen "fair and square!" Hell, throw in a year's worth of the money you pay (bakkkwoods whites!) to enslave us so we can even more quickly get situated in our new land, and I can almost guarantee that you'll never see even one of our Black or Brown faces again! Hell, some of our *families* might leave with us, so that's even less people you'll have to call the kkkops on for barbequing in the park! Think about it! Doesn't that sound great!?!

However, don't think that I'm ignorant of the fact of how

---

[287] Although the vast majority of us have never been to any of these places because we were born in *this* land, I'm sure a lot of individuals in *my* position would *love* to go!

Prison

some white folkkks are adverse to ever letting "their" nigras and/or wetbacks go if they can help it; I realize that most of these bumfukkk bakkkwoods kkkommunities where most prisons are located wouldn't be able to support themselves without the pay from the enslavement of us "undesirables," so I offer yet another proposal: How about every single person automatically retains/regains the right to vote a mere 3-6 months after their convictions?! Whatdayya say??? And I mean for every local, state, and national election where the prison is "housed." That way a person retains the right to always have a say in his/her own life and the communities in which they live! That's only "right," right?! That's what a *true* democracy is, isn't it?! And I know how "trikkky" "you people" can be,[288] so I propose that even if shipped somewhere the day before any election, every prisoner should be supplied with an absentee ballot for the locale they "lived" in in the previous 3 months! Let's see how many of these places want prisoners then, when good ole' nigger Ray-Ray and spic Jose has a say so in who Lil' Suzie's director of schools is?!

And I'm a fairly reasonable man so I'll throw you doggish motherfukkkers *one* bone: Maybe persons shouldn't be allowed to vote (only!) for the time in which they're incarcerated for *treason*?! You know the crime those coward ass confederates committed yet are still praised 150 (plus) years later for in the south?! I mean, we *can* take away the vote for *that* – but now that I think about how you wikkked motherfukkkers will quickly change the meaning of the word if given half the chance, *only* for a prescribed period of time and never for more than a year! You, know, just like the majority of the confederate traitors you love so much! Even *they* didn't lose their "right" to vote for too long!

---

[288] I know all about your poll taxes, grandfather clauses, reading tests, voter ID laws, registration purges, closing of polling places, etc. you trikkky devils, you! I see you!

So, what say you?! Want to have a *real* democracy where even Blacks and Browns universally have the right to vote and a say in their own lives?! How righteous would *that* be, right?! Come on now, you can do it; you can do it! There's absolutely nothing to be afraid of! Hypokkkrite motherfukkkers!

And one more thing: Considering all these amerikkkan "holidays" named after tyrants and/or their tyranny, how glaring is it that *Election Day* is *not* a federal holiday?! I mean, this is (supposed to be!) a democracy, isn't it?! And the height of a democracy is people expressing their views through votes, right? So tell me why this kkkountry has forever been making it harder (indeed impossible and/or detrimental to the health of!) for the "undesirables" to vote instead of *easier*?! Let's cut the bullshit and just call it what it is!...

"Without willing it, I had gone from being ignorant to being aware of being aware. And the worst part of my awareness was that I didn't know what I was aware of. I knew I knew very little…
I Know Why the Caged Bird Sings by Maya Angelou

AWAKENING

It's amazing how intense pressure in the proper conditions can result in a flawless diamond. And not that I claim to be "flawless" by any means, but the more pressure and pressure-packed situations my enemies submitted/submit me to, the more I became/become the man they always feared I would. The more I've been allowed to reflect back while simultaneously looking forward, the clearer my path is set out. Indeed, sometimes the only way forward is by looking back properly – realizing how we got to the place we are in our lives, place we are in the world. Then, and only then, will our eyes, hearts, and minds be shown the road forward, and that's what my traumas and travels have done for me over these years since fighting my way into the world at birth. Now I'm ready – and I thank my enemies for awakening me…

Although (admittedly) horrible for me to have lived through and/or witnessed, I had to understand empathetically the even more horrific torments and nightmares experienced by a young man mourning the loss of a father (Old School); a father torn apart over the unrighteous death of his teenage son (Youngsta); a mother having lost a child but being unable to receive any closure (my aunts Paulette and Nancy); worries of losing a beloved brother (myself and my other siblings); the heartaches of a mother and father with children in prison (my own and far too many others); the suffering of children with an imprisoned parent (my own, my nieces, nephews and little cousins and far, far too many others).

I had to personally experience the harmful hardships of federal and state prison, solitary confinement, being wrongfully accused and other injustices of the "justice" system – just as much as I had to understand every facet/allure of "the streets."

Just as I felt hopeless sometimes amidst the throes of a struggling marriage, tumultuous love, a contemptuous family, and Black lives mattering little to even my own Black people – I was given hope and humbled by the joys of fatherhood and the Heavenly Black Love I was blessed to experience a time or two.

So all in all, I have no "regrets"; although not instantaneous, my transition from "thug" to the man my people have always needed me to be is/was, however, complete. Reflecting this transformation, I long ago changed my name,[289] as I understood instantly from reading brother Malcolm's book that names do and should mean and symbolize something; and although the names were picked out by mother herself, I am not an english man,[290] nor am I italian,[291] and from that point forward I was searching for names that fit my essence, soul, and character. But it took a little longer than I thought it would.

In the meantime, the Universe shared with me the names

---

[289] I knew from the very moment I finished reading the autobiography of Malcolm X (for the first time!) at the age of 15 I couldn't/wouldn't for too much longer wear the "slave name" given to me at birth that represents the barbarian bastard who considered himself as "owner" of my ancestors. To HELL with him and his name! In fact, I had a mind then and still have it in anger and disgust to this day, to trace all of the progenitors of the various "slave names" that my loved ones wear or have worn: Thomas, Walden, Davis, Clay, Kennedy, Clark, Chubb, Radley, McLemore, Johnson, Webster, and Robinson among them so that I can personally go and piss on their graves! But I digress...

[290] In the case of "Kenneth," no matter that it supposedly means "Handsome." Moreover, how could I dare wear the name of, and thereby honor, the uncle whom I later discovered had abused at least one of my female cousins?! The hell with that!

[291] In the case of "Deangelo."

"Kyree Diya" for my oldest son, and a few years later the names "Kalii Dayani" for my youngest. "Kyree" is an Islamic name that means "radiant" or "shining,"[292] as is also "Diya" which means "beneficent." "Kalii" is a Kiswahili name/word that means "strong," "sharp," and "fierce," and "Dayani" is the name of a clinic at the hospital where my son was safely born in my presence despite my actively being hunted by the feds at the time. And true enough to the importance of names, both of my sons (I can say proudly!) have grown up to be beneficent, kind, and caring souls, with a charm and charisma that radiates from deep within and naturally attracts others, with sharp and strong and intelligent minds. Along with fierce angers if ever wrongly pushed or provoked. Their names profoundly and proudly fit their personalities.

As far as my true name, it was finally revealed to me as I sat/lay in CJC on "maximum security" awaiting transport to federal prison after being wrongly convicted of murder and sentenced to life imprisonment.

"Kamaj" was adopted from the Kikuyu of Kenya tribal name "Kamau" which means "quiet warrior" – although with the "j" instead of the "u" on the end of my name, I feel as if, ultimately, I will come to define my name. And I want/wish for "Kamaj" to mean among other things "enlightened warrior," "humble soul," and "fighter for his people." Because only after having my life taken for a crime my enemies/accusers always knew I was innocent of, did I finally realize what amerikkkan society knew even before my conception: I (and all of my kind) am a threat. Existential, terrifying, nightmare inducing threat. Because my very existence and that of every other Black, Brown, and Native man, woman, and child serves to shine light on the amerikkkan lies of "truth, justice, and equality" and its greatest

---

[292] Although I chose to spell it differently from how it's usually done.

moral crimes. And only by being humble yet enlightened warriors who (righteously) fight back, will we survive and finally defeat our unjust enemies in this immoral amerikkkan system...

"Dakari" references Dakar, Senegal and Goree Island, which was the point of "no return" for at least some of my kkkidnapped ancestors. This way, they (the Ancestors) know that I'll always remember...

My last name, I feel, is my most important as I hope to pass it on to many descendants: "Tawhid" is the concept of monotheism in Islam, and as it relates to me, it is also the doctrine of the "Oneness" of God. This doctrine holds that God (or "Allah" in Arabic) is one and unique, the single and absolute truth that transcends the world, an independent and indivisible Being (for lack of a better word) who is independent of the entire creation. The indivisibility of God implies the indivisibility of the Creator's sovereignty which, in turn, directs one to the concept of a just, moral, and coherent universe, as opposed to an existential and immoral chaos. And that is something I really need to believe, in order to keep on pushing on. Because if there's no true justice and righteousness to be found in the Universe, then Life has all been one cruel, sick, and sadistic joke.

Yet with all of that being said, what truly chose my name for me was the specific notion of "Tawhid al-ibada" which means "declaring God one through our service" by worshiping God and only God both in those actions that are visible to others and in those actions and thoughts that are hidden from other men. This requires one to worship God alone, with pure and sincere intent and dedication,[293] and this is what I wished to pass on to all my loved ones. So, "Kamaj Dakari Tawhid" is a

---

[293] Worship includes any action done in servitude to the Creator including prayer, sacrifice, vowing, love, supplication, and respect of *all* living creatures.

Awakening

name I strive to live up to every single moment of every single day...

Likewise, not long after I got to state prison in early 2005, I covered up the "Delo" tattoo on my left arm with an iconic picture of Harriet Tubman soon to be found on the amerikkkan $20 bill; her portrait along with a quote kept all in perspective for me – if and when I retook my own freedom back, I was returning as she did for any others who wanted to go. Keeping her as close to my heart as possible symbolized how I would never turn my back on all the brothers and sisters that find themselves enslaved like I was (am); no way could I not return for my people. No way would they not be in my heart until I helped destroy the system that enslaved us all. I would fight for them as I fought for myself, and as Sister Harriet said (in the quote I have permanently sketched on me in ink), "I should fight for my liberty as long as my strength lasted, and when the time came for me to go, the Lord would let them take me."

Along with the Black Panther on my chest and the Black Power fist on my right arm that I've rocked since the mid-90s, I also decided to go ahead with the ink that I had been contemplating long before my incarceration: my backpiece. Along the top of my shoulders stands "The Struggle" as I carry the struggle of all the ancestors on my back. That is my responsibility. That is the burden I bear in this life. I owe this not only to the ancestors, but my family and friends and our people of even today. And most importantly, I owe to myself to fight this struggle until *all* of my people are free once and for all in this kkkountry. The bottom of my back says "Continues..." as in "The Struggle Continues." As it does. As it does.

In the middle of this frame you have Marcus Mosiah Garvey and El-Hajj Malik El-Shabazz (a.k.a. "Malcolm X") on either side left to right, respectively of Huey Percy Newton,

Amerikkka

cofounder of the Black Panther Party. Marcus, Malcolm, Huey. My brothers. My elders. My ancestors. My mentors. The ideals I strive to hold myself up to. Brothers who fought for us as a people, even as sometimes we didn't even fight for ourselves. I carry the burden of their struggles, our struggle, on my back.

Nor could I forget about Brother Raymond Lee Washington and my comrades who have supported me throughout the years from afar in California. So they, too, I carry on my back in symbolism...

Even more so than my name change and tattoos, a surer sign than (a lot of) others that my mindset had changed was how I began to view "conflict resolution" – and especially amongst us "brothers." In opening my eyes, it didn't escape my notice how (generally speaking, of course!) Blacks deal with conflict with another Black as opposed to all others; our "default" seems to be "violence" whenever there's a Black-on-Black "disagreement," and I, too, sadly, used to be a practitioner of this madness. Blacks have been known to kill one another simply for accidently stepping on another's shoes or bumping them in clubs, yet will give a White person (or pig of *any* race!) a "pass" for far more egregious (and purposeful!) insults. Learning how this mindset directly stems from the Willie Lynchism of slavery, I consciously resolved to eradicate this foul way of thinking from my mind.

To highlight the transformation, an example: Unabashedly, my brother Carvin and I each had a bad habit, in our youthful past, of reacting (but not over-reacting, I would say) without completely thinking through all of the consequences whenever we felt the other was in harm's way. This stemmed from our mutual protectiveness of each other from childhood on. In fact, Carvin and I were also extremely protective of not just our other siblings, but also our extended family members and friends, even those much, much older than we were. I guess it's just a gene we carry. I loved (and love) him so much as my "little brother" and he loved (loves) me so much as his "big" brother that consequences be damned, and many times we'd find ourselves in big trouble trying to "save the other" somehow. That's how strong our bond was and continues to be to this day. You harm him means you harm me — and I'm coming. You harm me means you harm him — and then he's coming. That's just the way it is.

Carvin is the "Strength" of us four siblings that were raised in the same household[294] and has always been the strongest and most needed among us even if he doesn't realize it a lot of times. Our sister Devonne is our "Heart," and even more importantly in my opinion, our "Backbone," the one who holds us all together like so many other Black girls, women and matriarchs before her.[295] Our youngest brother John is our family's "Eyes and Ears," forever observant, watching and listening and learning and not making so many of the mistakes we others have made. For that very reason, he's probably the "smartest" among us. And me? – I'm our family's "Soul" or maybe, I should say, "Conscience" but only because I came first. Even though these are our dominant positions in the family, each of us have elements and qualities of the others and none of us would be truly who we are and should be if one of the others was missing.

Yet, due to the injustice of the amerikkkan "justice"

---

[294] Our other sister, Shawanda, was raised by her mother; also our cousin Justin (my mother's nephew by her sister Mookie) was raised with us from his birth.
[295] Unfortunately, our "Backbone" she is no more. Sadly, Devonne along with my brother John have over the years allowed small disagreements and misunderstandings to morph into larger ongoing conflict (helped along greatly by outside agitators, of course) that is adversely affecting a younger generation. This does no more than perpetuate an awful cycle that has already proven itself detrimental to our own extended family and the Black community at large. However, beyond all reason I hold out hope that they'll finally take the steps necessary to heal themselves, and, in turn, our immediate family.

system, I went over 15 years without being able to hug or even see one of my favorite people in this life — my younger brother Carvin. Only hours after my acquittal and release from CJC in August of 2000, I returned to the jail to visit with my brother still trapped there, and I would continue weekly until forced to stop going on "the run" after the feds "hit" (May 2001) searching for me. From there it was my eventual capture in Kentucky, Carvin's bogus convictions at trial and subsequent transfer to a tennessee state prison, then my numerous kkkourtroom battles in both federal and state kkkourts resulting in my being imprisoned in at least eight different county jails, and four different federal and state prisons [two each not counting the one I'm currently enslaved at] in four different states in 11 different cities until I was finally "settled" for a few years at turney center. From there, for years Carvin and I tried to get transferred to the same prison to be together while simultaneously being as close as we possibly could be to (the majority of) our loved ones in nashville. We finally got our wish – or so we thought – in late 2010/early 2011 when Carvin was re-classified from the CCA-run for-profit prison where he was in whiteville, tennessee to the turney center where I was. However, CCA is extremely "reluctant" to release people, since they generate profits from a "body in a filled bed," and stalled Carvin's transfer for months. Finally, in an ultimate slap in the face, a kkkorrectional kkkop whom was also a widely known (by the "administration") "gang member" opened Carvin's cell door (while he was unknowingly asleep) so that the kkkop's "brothers" (i.e., fellow gang members) could assault my brother in an attempt to rob him, which resulted in Carvin being badly stabbed, hospitalized, and finally placed on maximum security in nashville for defending his life! I was murderously pissed![296]

What would have been the reaction of cats had I pushed the button on the plan I quickly put in place after those fools did harm to my brother? If all the "hitters" I had in place in every prison in the state (including the women's) and on the streets had been directed to simultaneously strike their targets? Would cats have been prepared for all the bloodshed? Would the fools have ever understood what had befell them? Would they have ever been able to mentally function once the chaplain started to visit? All over a little funky ass $20 phone that one could buy at any Walmart, Dollar General store, Family Dollar, etc. But really over envy, and jealousy, and some wanna be bully bullshit because they felt my brother was by himself and had no one that loved him as deeply as our family does, I guess. Because that move they pulled was stupid, absolutely stupid any way you looked at it. For one, it was petty and completely unwarranted, unjustified, and uncalled for. Two, they didn't know their enemy, which was obvious by the way they reacted, not expecting my brother to immediately strike back and stab their asses up. Anyone with any sense would be able to tell within minutes of meeting my brother that he's never been one to back down from a fight no matter the odds, nor has he ever had a fear of death. So them not preparing for his reaction was totally moronic. But lastly and damn near most detrimentally for them, the idiots gave no consideration whatsoever to the mind, the way of thinking, of not only my brother but also myself and

---

[296] From there Carvin fought to get off maximum security while I awaited at turney center so that we could finally somehow get transferred to the same prison. Finally, it happened in early 2016, when my brother surprised me waiting for me in the library (where I worked as an editor of the prison's newspaper) after I returned from lunch. I couldn't believe it was him — my brother! And no words in the English language can describe how I felt. And from there we made it a point to somehow see each other and hug every single day if we could until we were separated again a year later by this bullshit that I'm currently going through.

others that love us and would kill and die for us. Because if they did, they would have protected their flanks inside and outside of the prisons walls. And because they didn't, because of the ease with which I was able to find out all the information I needed and put in place a plan for retaliation the likes of which a lot of people can't even fathom within 24 hours of them pulling that bullshit, I knew those cats "knew not the evil that which they do." Because had they known, had they ever suspected, then no way would they risk all that/whom they were about to lose over a $20 phone. No way in hell, right? One would think so anyway.

So, after finalizing the details of my move, I laid my head to rest for a couple of hours, then took another hour or so in the shower to make sure I had thought it all through. And slowly, distressingly, I had to admit that I was ignoring an irritating lil gnat that kept popping up in the back of my mind; that I was somehow being a hypocrite and falling right into my *real* enemy's — *our* real enemy's — traps. That if I took it straight to more bloodshed – somewhat indiscriminate but by design *buckets* of bloodshed – then I was serving to my people and my community all the harm I had been preaching and teaching against when maybe it could be avoided. Because my family members in the offending organization did offer that it could be taken care of "in house" as the offenders were "in violation" of one or more of their bylaws by pulling the move, and Carvin did in fact stab three or four of the principal perpetrators back, so I decided (*extremely* reluctantly!) to give diplomacy a chance. Therefore, they "handled" it within, and I took my finger off the button.

But of course, I never threw that "button" away and for the longest time kept it "hot" and "at the ready" along with a couple of contingency plans just in case they were needed. Because had I thought the diplomacy was some bullshit or a stall for time to fortify defenses, or if my brother wasn't healing up as quickly as he did or heaven forbid got worse, then I would have felt righteously justified in serving up at least ten times worse what had come his way. He was minding his own business living his life, not bothering anybody, when those fools brought harm to him. So for that, they deserved any and all the punishment that came their way even if it led to the losing of their lives.

And unlike them (it seems), I was prepared for whatever fate befell me behind my retaliation. I've always been a big proponent and student of "mutually assured destruction" [M.A.D.] or as I refer to it, "mutually assured death." Let's all die, is my way of thinking; if I'm not bothering someone and they attempt to do me harm, let's do it. Let's see if you're ready to take it to the level I'm prepared to for you fucking with me. Come on, let's go there. I'm perfectly prepared to dance when/if you decide to cut on the music.

M.A.D. is the concept that kept the united snakes and the Soviet Union fighting proxy wars instead of going head to head. M.A.D. is what keeps the bully-prone u.s. from "taking it" to Russia or China directly even to this day. M.A.D. if practiced by our Ancestors is what would have kept the arabs and europeans from enslaving and murdering our people and carving up and stealing our continent. And M.A.D. is what will finally once and for all allow us Blacks and Browns to throw off the yoke of white supremacy and all its manifestations: police brutality/assassination, enslavement/incarceration, medical experimentation, etc. I mean think about it, when did President Obama finally speak out and the police assassinations (lynchings) of Blacks finally stop, or at least slow down? Not after the choking of Eric Garner. Not after the shootings of Mike Brown or Walter Scott in the back, not after the murders of Alton Sterling, or even Philando Castile in front of his wife and child. But only, only (to my knowledge) did the then president of this kkkountry, the first *Black* president, in fact choose to make mention of our uncounted deaths when heroes martyred themselves by gunning down some pigs in Baton Rouge and Dallas. Only then was the major outcry.

And that should tell you something. In fact, that should tell you a lot. How many more dylan roofs would there be if someone had gone to *his* church and gunned down as many parishioners as they could, including *his* parents and siblings? How many more Tamir Rice's would we have to mourn if those two pigs' children were shot in the head the next time we caught them with a super soaker water gun or a BB gun shooting at birds? How many? How many more Aiyana Jones would we have to bury if a mob of the "retaliatory righteous" would bust down the doors of every single one of those pigs involved in the raid and gun their kids down? How many? How many? Just think about that ... Seriously, seriously think about that.

I think if we as a people are once and for all sick of all the bullshit we've had to and continue to endure since we were kkkaptured and kkkidnapped to these shores then we should organize Seven Day cells[297] in every single city and town in this kkkountry with a sizable Black and/or Brown population. And the next time there's the unjust death of a Trayvon Martin, a Jordan Davis, a Sandra Bland, a Freddie Gray, a Leon Fisher, an Oscar Grant, a Sean Bell, Breonna Taylor, Ahmaud Arbery, George Floyd, etc., then the Seven Days in every city and town should strike back at once. And then see how quickly the enemy of the people will be begging for mercy. Call me "radical" or "militant" all you want. I just call it realism...[298]

---

[297] In the mold of the "Seven Days" from the novel *Song of Solomon* by Toni Morrison.
[298] For the record, I agree when the (thinly-veiled) white supremacists proclaim that "white" and/or "blue" lives matter, also. But what *they* and everyone else kkkountry

"May we meet again in the light of understanding..."
El-Hajj Malik El-Shabazz
(b.k.a. "Malcolm X")

With nothing but time, my thoughts have many times now turned to things that years ago had not even occurred to me. For one thing, I never thought about the impact my recurring and constant incarcerations had on my father. No man wants to feel a failure raising his sons; no man wants his son made into slaves. A man wants the best for his children, sons especially; he wants his children to have all that may have been denied to him for whatever reason in life. I knew. Once I was finally able to look into my sons' faces, I knew the love that my father felt for me when first looking into my own. And I finally understood him. I love him like no other.

Nor did I ever consider the pain I've for so many years put my mother through. All of the time she's gone through the indignities a person faces when enduring the rigmarole of coming to visit me throughout my various incarcerations, my court dates, my probation visits, etc. My own and my brothers Carvin's and John's. Think about what that does to a mother. I even remember one time of her crying out through the tears of how it seems she "only had sons to give to the white man." Sad, isn't it? As my mother has gotten up in age, she expresses time

---

has to realize is *no* white life, *no* cop life, is any more important than a *Black* one! This is a kkkountry in which a solitary black male surrounded by a squad of pig police with no more than a cell phone in his hand is deemed "dangerous" (and thus marked for death!) as opposed to an entire troop of white "ranchers" with *loaded guns* trained on *federal agents*! Think about that! For far too long this kkkountry has perpetuated a false sense of white life sanctity and superiority, but to hell with all of that! The uncomfortable yet unconditional truth is that *our* lives (along with everyone else's) matter just as much — or just as little — as yours do, so either deal with it get *dealt* with!

and time again how her only wish is to have all of her children at home with her before she dies. How many of our Black mothers throughout the history of this kkkountry have felt the same? Is today any different from those mothers that had their beloved children sold away to another plantation? Is it any different when one child is in this prison (plantation) hundreds of miles away and another is in the opposite direction in another?

Not to mention how my mother has time and time again sacrificed the life she wanted for the wishes and needs of my brothers, sister and I. My mother was only sixteen-years-young when she was pregnant with me; I entered this world three weeks to the day after she turned seventeen. From there on, she's been a parent, a mother entrusted by the Creator with raising and nurturing the beings she chose to bring into this world. But what of *her* dreams, wishes, and wants *before* she had us? And what of them after? Even to this day after we are all grown? Did they just dissipate into nothing? Is all she is and all she'll ever be is the mother and grandmother of someone else? Not to discount what a mother and grandmother means to us, but when does she get the chance to live *her* life *for her* without putting us or other people first? When does my mother get to just *be* as she *wants* to be???

And how many other women – Black and Brown women the world over, especially – feel much the same way? To be disappointed to think that her life is unimportant, it seems, or only important in relation to those she birthed?

Words could never adequately explain how much I empathize with my mother; she is of a generation of Black Women that birthed and raised children with the deaths of Emmett Till, Malcolm X, Martin Luther King, and the children in Atlanta never far from their minds. Only after I became an

Awakening

adult myself – indeed, a parent also – could I appreciate what witnessing the "riots" after King's death, enduring the traumas of forced school "de-segregation," and living every second as a two-way target in this kkkountry (Black *and* a woman), had on her psyche and (thus) the way she raised us. I don't blame her nor my father for *anything* – and I pray that they'll finally realize that...

My awakening has not been without its missteps, of course. Nor has it always been with the complete support and/or understanding of those around me.

For example, my aversion to – and refusal to "celebrate" – the typical holidays generally observed by most Blacks in this kkkountry. Although my father understood where I was coming from even before I could articulate my views, it took longer for my mother and even younger siblings not to ridicule me for what I felt. (Hell, sometimes they still do – but only in good fun now!) However, I'm wondering now how they – or my mother in the very least – couldn't have foreseen where I would get to even long before I, myself, did.

Much to my mother's chagrin, even as a child, I've never been much of a holiday kind of guy. I was always too observant, a quiet yet reasoning and inquisitive kind of child, so I always inquired as to "Why?" "*Why* do we celebrate Christmas Mama? But *why* does Santa bring *us* gifts for the birth of Baby Jesus???" "Mama, why *I* gotta wear this ugly suit to church (on Easter)? And *how* does a bunny lay eggs anyway???"

So, as you can imagine, I really worked my mother's nerves, right? And my questioning nature only worsened as I entered my adolescence.[299]

---

[299] Probably my most frequent and irritating question to my mother back then: "But, Mama, how can a man 'save' *me* two thousand years after he *died*, when he couldn't even save *himself* when he was *alive*?"

Moreover, growing up, I looked up to two men as my role models: my Father, and my older cousin Raymond. Men of Principle. Men of Honor. Men of Respect. And they taught me to *always* be true to myself, to *never* be afraid to go against the grain when following my heart, and that *principles* and the *relevancy* of things *always* mattered. So although I enjoyed the gifts of Christmas, the chocolates and painted eggs of Easter, and the fireworks of the 4th of July, I had to let it all go once I became "aware."

Aware that the day history has chosen for Christmas actually has no historical basis as being the day of Jesus of Nazareth's birth; *aware* that both Christmas and Easter have both become debased into days of commercialism without meaning; and *aware* that upon the founding of this kkkountry, millions of people who looked just like me continued to be enslaved for over another hundred years while its "founders" were all the while espousing ideals such as liberty, justice and freedom for all.

So how could I not? How could I look myself in the mirror and consider myself a *man* of *principle* if I didn't do so?

So around the age of fifteen or so I let the holidays of my childhood go, let them pass year after year without my active celebration or participation. And I never missed them at all because I knew in my heart and soul that I was doing the right thing for me and my principles.

But what *was* missed was the family togetherness, the meals and cookouts, and our personal family traditions. Thankfully, anticipating the birth of my oldest son, I discovered, along with Juneteenth, Kwanzaa, which allowed me to stay true to myself and my principles, and to establish new family traditions relevant to my people's culture and history.[300] Umoja, Kujichagulia, Ujima, Ujamaa, Nia, Kuumba, and Imani – unity, self-determination, collective work and responsibility, cooperative economics, purpose, creativity, and faith – the Nguzo Saba, principles I vowed to share with my children, my extended family, my friends, and my community. Principles that I believe if embraced by only even one other person, will make the world that much of a better place. So instead of the hollowness and commerciality of Christmas that was forced down my throat in my childhood, I lit the mishumaa saba – the seven candles, each one symbolizing one of the Nguzo Saba – each day in celebration of Kwanzaa. And I felt all the better for it.

I feel all the better too, also, for all of my romantic relationships throughout the years. I'm thankful for every single relationship that I've been in – for every woman that I've loved. I simply wouldn't know myself without them – my wants, my needs, my wishes and my boundaries. Nor would I know Black women well enough – to be the man I need to be for them in my own family and community. So again, I'm thankful.

I'm thankful, too, to come to the realization (now as I've gotten older) that I never got over the pain of losing my cousin Putt, then my cousin Duck a few years later, both to violent deaths. Black lives don't really matter it seems — seemingly also to our own kind — so my loss, my family's losses were never really addressed either by my family, my community, or society at large. Think about what that teaches a young adolescent. Consider, too, that my cousin TC's "craziness" only manifested itself after losing his own father to a violent death, gunned down

---

[300] Along with "Hood Day" in April, Mother's Day in May, and Father's Day and Blue June in June, Juneteenth every June 19th and Kwanzaa every December 26 - January 1 are the *only* "holidays" (Holy Days) I choose to celebrate. The rest you can have in my opinion…

(as an unarmed Black man) by some racist pig, metro police officers — who of course, were never charged or even reprimanded. Could there be a coincidence here?

And you won't get any objection from me saying that my (early) life was in large part that of a violent existence, but what came first, the chicken or the egg? Was I born and bred violent — was/is violence inherent in the nature of my kind? Or was I (were we) *made* violent in response to the violence of the world around me (us) so that I (we) might have even a miniscule chance just to exist at all? And if the violence that surrounded my life was/is a learned behavior, then where did it all come from? Because there *was* no violence in my own individual home. It was a safe and loving place; I was loved and safe within my family's embrace and the *only* violence I witnessed as a child/adolescent were the violent police raids of the neighborhood in which *all* of us young children would regularly see the pigs coming in beating down our neighborhood men and/or boys and disappearing a few of them away. Remember at the beginning of this where I said even as a child we had all heard about the big, bad police? Or would a young crazy TC have become what he became regardless of the fact that his unarmed father (still a big, black nigger in the eyes of those with the guns) was murdered in cold blood by a couple of nashville's finest pigs. Think on that...

> "Silence in the face of injustice is complicity with the oppressor..."
>
> Ginetta Sagan, prisoner rights activist

APPEAL

After witnessing the way Jeff performed and was prepared in norman's kkkourtroom, I retained him in the appeal of my murder conviction and fired my previous "representation." No return of even one hot penny of my money, of course, from either the NLPA[301] out of Cincinnati or attorney robert brooks[302] from Memphis, yet no doubt a complete waste of my time and funds that could have purchased someone a new car. However, that's what I get for falling for the NLPA's propaganda/marketing materials that were floating around the feds soliciting themselves out as the ones to hire, as neither they (the NLPA) nor robert brooks seemed to know their ass from their ankles in my needed area of law.[303] Compounding my mistake, I had convinced Carvin to hire the same "representation" in his appeal, also – costing him, too, a new car – yet he ultimately netted the same results I received from them: nothing at all worth the money.[304] All in all, this and other experiences made me realize that I should have taken my ass to law school as the "game" they were/are running is one of the best hustles going – right up there with preaching, pimping, and politics.

However, just as there are a *few* sincere and righteous

---

[301] National Legal Professional Associates – supposedly a "legal research" firm.
[302] The only attorney from tennessee listed in the NLPA's materials that it would like to work with.
[303] The IAD and wrongful convictions in spite of violations of it.
[304] In fact, nothing worth the price of a pair of decent socks! So buyer beware! Of the NLPA and "attorney" robert brooks of Memphis!

preachers and politicians in the world, there are also a few honest, just, and even effective attorneys. And Jeff was/is one of those — right alongside Eileen. Jeff was, by then, extremely knowledgeable about the IAD, its procedures, and caselaw in general – along with how it pertains to my case in particular – so he quickly hit the ball rolling filing briefs (documents) to the tennessee kkkourt of criminal appeals spelling out how it was "clear" that my case should have been dismissed. His oral arguments in front of the kkkourt, made it just as clear. And it *was* clear — I/we had not only the facts, law, but even my *innocence* on my/our side – so Jeff and I were both confident that my case would soon be overturned and dismissed.

But not so fast. In the first instance of Jeff experiencing what he described as (and I'm paraphrasing here) "a duck quacking like a duck, swimming and flying like a duck, clearly looking like a duck and having two duck parents," nevertheless the tennessee kkkourt of criminal appeals *still* found a way to say it was a "cow" and "thus the IAD didn't apply" to my case. Unfucking believable.

No – I take that back. Entirely believable because I am, of course, a Black Man in amerikkka so I never should have been surprised that this was/is happening to me. My case is no more surprising than Dred Scott's in that I have "no rights that a white man (amerikkka) is bound to respect."[305] Jeff suppositioned that "the kkkourt just couldn't bring itself to let Delo Thomas go free no matter what"[306] and I could tell that it really shook his

---

[305] But don't take my word for it – you can look it up for yourself: State of tennessee v. Kenneth D. Thomas, 2006 jWL 521426 (Tenn Crim App). You can also look at my subsequent appeals to so-called "higher kkkourts" that ostensibly were there to "enforce the law" when lower kkkourts like the bumfukkk tennessee kkkourt of criminal appeals so blatantly violated/ignored the law like in my situation" Thomas v. Fortner, 2009 WL 649733 (M.D. Tenn.); and most recently, Thomas v. State, 2015 WL 1568235 (Tenn.Crim.App.).

[306] Like, who the fuck am I?! And especially to those rotten hypokkkritical bastards?!?

"faith in the law." Me? – it just made me take the rest of the blinders off my eyes and face what I knew (inherently) about amerikkka and its "law" all along. And as long as I continued to have breath in my body, I vowed to do all I can/could to help expose and destroy it...

"As the struggle intensifies, and reaches toward higher levels, the power structure responds with increased levels of repression..."

To All Brothers of Misfortune
(The Black Panther)

I started to question myself more and the conditions in which I and my people have consistently and constantly found ourselves in this kkkountry; and my questions came unceasingly. No longer could I stand idly by doing nothing – or even worse, make our situations more grim in helping to destroy my own kind – while looking at myself in the mirror as a man. Something had to be done. And I vowed to make myself one of the ones that would help do it.

So I started speaking to the brothers and conveying with them my philosophy of life. As opposed to acquiring knowledge and keeping it amongst myself and my own close personal circle, I made a conscious effort to share it with all that seemed receptive. Not that I became preachy or anything – because I don't believe in beating someone over the head with something – but I just shared, ya know? Some of the Nation brothers even convinced me to speak at service a time or two:

"Last Saturday night on the CBS television show 48 Hours, as I watched the special on violence in Chicago, I found myself getting angrier and angrier. I mean, I got pissed to the point where there

were almost tears in my eyes! And you know what – or should I say whom I found myself angry at??? Us!!! You and I!!!... But why, right??? 'Why get upset at us?,' you might be now saying to yourself. Because we are the ones causing all of those tears to be shed by our Black mothers and fathers – our Black mothers and fathers – over the loss of their children to early graves or incarceration!!! We are the ones at fault in the deaths of Porsche Foster and Hadiya Pendleton and countless other children and young men and women in not just Chicago, but Atlanta, L.A., Knoxville, Nashville, Memphis, Chattanooga, Jackson, and every other major city in this nation! We are!!! We are the causes of their deaths!!! Because we aren't standing up as Men... Men protecting our communities! Men protecting our children! Men protecting our women, our elderly, ourselves!!! Not savages making it unsafe for our people to walk the streets!!!... Taking a look at the histories of the different organizations coming out of Los Angeles, Compton, or Chicago that some of us in here claim as a part of ourselves we see that every single one without fail came into being out of the want and need to protect and better our communities; now we – these same organizations – are the ones that are absolutely terrorizing them!!! How crazy is that??? And just how in the hell did this come to be??? Somehow or another something has went terribly wrong!!!... We are the ones that should be spreading smiles and tears of joy and not the tears of anguish that we saw on the faces of Porsche's and Hadiya's parents! We are the ones that should be caring enough about ourselves and what's going on in our streets to start making some type of positive difference! All of us in here – us – should make it our missions to teach the young locsters, the young dawgs, the young playas, and the young macs about how it's their jobs to make our communities safe for our people to live in, not turn them into war zones!!! Or are we that callous that we don't care about our own extinctions???... The more I hear or read of the state of our

Appeal

communities and listen to the seemingly braggadocios comments of cats talking about how it's 'going down' in Chicago or Memphis or Nashville or Chattanooga or wherever, I think to myself: How pathetic does it make us to be proud of that??? And I ask, throughout all of this madness, where are we, the shot-callers, the OGs, the Top Hats, the Chiefs??? Are we *the ones encouraging this insanity by instructing those that look up to us to 'put it down' or by being all on Facebook lying about how this 'shit ain't half bad' because once a week we can order a few overpriced generic-ass cakes and chips, or finally done came up on some chump change that you really can't buy a decent pair of shoes with??? Are* we *the ones supporting this madness by saying 'this is the place to be' like those fakes-ass rappers/C.O.s??? Raymond and Mac and Tookie and Tam and Puddin and David and Jeff and Larry and the Original 21s have to be looking down on us from their graves or their prison cages with* disgust*!!! What a waste we've been to their legacies, huh? It's got to hurt that their lives and works were all in vain..."*

As well, I would also never fail to express my sentiment letting the brothers know how I felt it was *us* each holding a personal responsibility to change our communities and own lives for the better:

"Sometimes I think 'man you just care too damn much,' but then I realize, these are my *daughters that are dying, these are* my *sons, these are* my *nieces, nephews, uncles, aunts, brothers, sisters, friends – these are* my *people!!! These are* my own people *that I –* we *– are killing in cold blood!!!... Madness!!! Doing the devils' bidding for them ourselves!!! How stupid is that??? Do we hear of the Natives of this stolen land at constant war amongst themselves on the concentration camps know as 'reservations?' No!!! Because they* love *and* care *for themselves, for their people, to never allow that to happen!! But* we *do it.* We *do it... So yes, I should care; yes, you should care! More so than we have ever shown!!!*

I would even speak on the fact that we should "police" our own selves and our own communities instead of allowing our enemies to have an excuse to come in and dominate us:

> "We as men should police ourselves and our own homes and communities so as not to give the enemy an excuse to come in and do it for us! We should be doing it! Even here at Turney Center, at this prison, there should never be a reason for the enemy to regulate the disputes we have amongst ourselves!... Don't call on our enemies to police and regulate the problems we have amongst ourselves – whether through that coward-ass 'kite dropping' shit or whether by allowing whatever the problem is to get out of hand. Because we're MEN, aren't we? Well, show and prove then!... Because I never want my enemy – my one true enemy – to feel like I need for him to come in and regulate and/or mediate the problems that I may have with my brother!!! Do I look that stupid??? Do I look like I would dare give him the chance to come in and help me neutralize and/or defeat my brother, just to turn around and then have him do the same with me on that divide-and-conquer shit??? I know the true history of the so-called 'settlers' and the theft of this land!!! We're all witnesses to the genocide of the Natives!... And now our time, our turn is upon us. And look at how we so senselessly help them. Pathetic..."

But always, always I was looking for solutions to what ails us and our communities – and I would implore for the brothers to do the same:

> "So what is the solution, you say??? I wish I knew; I wish I knew. I'd be a lie if I stood up here and said I had them all. What I do know is that the solutions, the solutions must come from us, must come from within our people. We have to be more of the solution and less of the problem, ya dig? Maybe a part of it that will go a long way in finding some salve as to what ills us is wanting for your brother what you want for yourself – Peace!"

Appeal

Yet, when I would get the opportunity to speak, I would always keep it Gangsta and completely honest with the brothers – no time or use in sugarcoating what sometimes needed to be done:

"And don't get it twisted because I recognize that there are some foolish souls that we may come across that need a killing, ya know? I'm not naïve to think that we must save everyone. Those that mean ill-will to everyone and everything, including themselves, I say give them what they want. But not by shooting into a crowd of innocents; not in ways that serve to terrify our own people. There has been more than enough of that. But you can dig what I'm saying. And well, you know, I've said more than enough on that so let me shut up – I've still got cases and appeals pending..."

That usually brought more than a few knowing smiles and laughter.

I once even had the opportunity to speak on the Nation's "Holy Day of Atonement" shortly after a stabbing incident that resulted in an extended lockdown and a whole lot of cats getting hospitalized, shipped, and/or "maxed out":

"As-Salaam Alaikum! I won't take up a lot of you brothers' time, but first I'd like to thank the Brothers for allowing me to speak on this Holy Day of Atonement. Because I feel like there's a lot that we need to atone for this particular year in this particular penitentiary. I know that some of you brothers haven't been here long, but those of us that have, have witnessed – or even participated in – brother against brother, cousin against cousin, comrade against comrade violence. We've seen cats that have known each other their entire lives – grew up together, ate at one another's tables, slept in one another's homes during childhood – stab each other in the back, even attempt to take one another's lives. And all for what? Mostly petty gripes; or petty money; or petty issues such as jealousy or envy. None of it for righteousness... You know, the older you get, the more

you're supposed to mature – in mind, body, and spirit. I say that to say this: If you've got even an ounce of decency in your soul, you'll eventually recognize when you've transgressed against your fellow human being; you'll eventually realize when you've done wrong. True enough, it may not necessarily be at that very instant that the wrongful deed is done, or even a week, a month, or a year later, but eventually, you'll see. And when that time comes is when you should honor your responsibility as a MAN and take that first step towards atonement's... Now, I'm a realistic man and I recognize that we as MEN will always have our disagreements with one another. But understand, not every dispute need be handled with violence. As a matter of fact, violence should be our last resort and not our first. And I say "handled" instead of solved because the majority of the time violence doesn't solve the dispute, only increases it. Besides, that's the way of the barbarian, the way of the devil, not the way of righteous MAN, ya dig? We have to start upholding our responsibilities to one another as MEN and start solving our disputes as MEN – even when it's not the 'popular' thing to do. All that should matter to us is that it's the RIGHT thing to do... The wise Prophet Muhammad once said that 'an Arab is not better than a non-Arab nor is a white better than a black or a black better than a white except in piety.' He said that 'the noblest among you all is the one who is most pious.' So I say to you all here now that a Rider is not more righteous than a Damu, and a Player not better than a Mac. And vice-versa. We're all community revolutionaries; we're all brothers of the struggle; we're all brothers leading our own destinies. True enough, to you your way of life and to me mine, but us taking different routes to get to the same Paradise doesn't make us enemies. Think about it. I leave you as I came – As-Salaam Alaikum!"

    I would speak on damn-near whatever question/issue that the brothers requested my thoughts on; when I didn't know enough about a subject to express an opinion, I would say so clearly, but usually chose to educate myself on it later. Never did I stray from my philosophy that each person to his or her own way of life, however – and to do no harm unless clear harm is being done (or attempted to be done) to you and/or your loved ones or others. Never will I deny to *all* the right to self-defense and the right to live your life in peace; nor will I ever advocate turning the other cheek.

I never failed to point out hypocrisy, not just in the oppressors, but also, within ourselves; I made sure I expressed how weak it was/is that we run and/or hardly ever put up a fight when the "authorities" run roughshod over us, yet we – Blacks especially – are so territorial towards each other, especially regarding "our" neighborhoods, "our" streets, "our" cities, and other shit that *we* don't "own" I expressed how pathetic I feel it is the we fight, hate, and even kill one another over this bullshit time and time again.

I made clear my lack of tolerance, love, or respect for anyone who chooses to prey upon the people, and how these individuals need to be "dealt with" harshly until they "learn the error of their ways." So, too, I expressed my animus towards the man (father) who feels his duty/responsibility ends at conception, just as equally I feel towards the woman who feels as if a man (father) has no import to a child's life...

The brothers at the prison all dug what I was saying – Black, White, Hispanic, Asian, and Natives, too; regardless of race, affiliation, or religion, the prison never failed to show up whenever I was rumored to speak. People (especially us "cynical prisoners") can tell when you're speaking and moving genuinely, sincerely from your spirit with the purest of love, and I was.

As I will continue to. Despite the increasing oppression I started experiencing because of it...

Black love – my love for our people and our community – is what sustains me in this journey for liberation…
                                   Dante Berry, social justice activist

HOPE

"Dad, I'm telling you – he's going to win!"

I hated bursting my 10-year-old's bubble, but I had to temper his expectations – because I *knew* the kkkountry in which we live. There was absolutely no way this kkkountry would ever elect a Black man President – or at least in my lifetime. Maybe at the end of my son's, but nowhere any time soon. I hated knowing the disappointment he would soon feel. But, hell, he had to grow up one day, right? Right?

Shows what I know, huh? Little Bush had so fukkked up the kkkountry – hell, the world even! – by leading it into an unrighteous war in Iraq (and the resultant "Great Recession") after the "chickens came home to roost" on 9/11, that it actually elected someone with the name *Barack Hussein Obama*?! What, am I in the *Matrix*, or something??? Or is my mind just fucking with me? Maybe there was hope for this kkkountry yet. As Brother Eldridge (Cleaver) once said "If a man like Malcolm X could change and repudiate racism, if I myself and other former Muslims can change, if young whites can change, then there is hope for America."

But not so fast; President Obama's election re-awakened[307] a virulent and violent strain of racism/white supremacist thought that some fools unwisely felt had long since been dead. How they (the fools) had come to this dangerous misconception, I'll never understand – what with the increasing

---

[307] Not least of which at/in prisons such as the one I was then "housed" at: turney center.

dire straits of the average Black, Brown or Native man, woman and child as compared to "main-stream America." Critics (including many of my fellow prisoners) would/will point to a few elites that they felt/feel had/have "made it" (athletes, rappers, singers, actors and/or other entertainers usually), but I would counter that this is a well-worn tactic (allowing a few "special ones" success in order to mollify the masses) and question if they knew of anyone *personally* to have "made it" in their eyes? Especially someone who was/is not an "entertainer" of others,[308] but instead, a *thinker, producer* (of actual products), *manufacturer*, or *entrepreneur*? How many of the Black, Brown or Native men did/do *they* know that had/has never been arrested and/or harassed or beaten by the police?? How many? Leaving cats to their thoughts after throwing those and/or similar questions would/will more times than many open their eyes: Racism/white supremacy hadn't/hasn't died, it had just gotten comfortable (and somewhat lazy) in its entrenchment.

However, don't get it twisted – I recognize the value in the election of President Obama, I love what it represents about the younger generations. They see more the content of a person's character rather than a skin color compared to my generation and (especially!) those older. Gives me hope that after we older generations die off completely, then amerikkka will finally be *America* and a much more righteous place for everyone living in it. Yet only if we/they face the bullshit – once and finally for all – that we all see, smell, and can tell that's stinking up the place.

As it stands, however, nothing is ever an issue in this kkkountry until it in one way or another affects *white* people. Whether it's fucking with their money – which in actuality means interference with their exploitation of others – fucking

---

[308] Not to discount entertainers, but people *do* know that we/you *can* do other things, right?

with their children, or most dangerously, fucking with their pride, that's the *only* time in which a "problem" is actually a problem.

Yet that shit can no longer fly. What would be the uproar if a rash of unarmed White men, women and/or children are killed by trigger-happy pigs, "community watchmen," or self-appointed (armed!) parking place patrollers?!

You think it escaped my notice that more whites started pushing for LGBTQ rights as more of *their* loved ones started "coming out of the closet"? Or that #Me Too became a "movement" instead of "just a hashtag" to the lamestream media and/or "general public" once it became embarrassingly apparent how many *white* women had been/are being sexually harassed, demeaned, and/or assaulted?

Yet, Tarana Burke had been pushing #Me Too for a decade (plus!) before then, nevertheless some *still* want to give all the credit to Alyssa Milano and/or Rose McGowan?! Hilarious. Yet indicative of the mindset of amerikkka. Tell me, what makes the "opioid epidemic" any different than the crack epidemic besides the skin color of those most affected?? Why all of a sudden the (almost) nationwide acceptance of the decriminalization of marijuana? Could it be because "they" can longer (or are not willing to!) hide the fact that more and more *white* children/people smoke and sell the "drug" than Blacks ever did, and besides, there's a way to make *billions* off of it?? How many of the budding weedpreneurs (both puns intended) such as Woody Harrelson and others are making as strong a push to free (and make right/whole!) all those "unfortunates" imprisoned behind marijuana as they did/do for its legalization??

Speaking of imprisonment, isn't it amazing how the cries for "criminal justice" reform have died down (especially from the "fiscally kkkonservative right") since the ekkkonomy has improved and there are no longer any worries about how to pay for the kkkontrol and enslavement of undesirables??[309] In fact, just bring up the subject of shutting down a prison and watch the outcry of bakkkwoods whites over the possible loss of their jobs and livelihoods! What does it say that it's more important that a (white!) slaver has a "job" than (the Black and/or Brown!) enslaved goes free and/or is never enslaved in the first place?? What a kkkountry, huh? And you demand that *we* "salute *your* flag?!" It's not even worth wiping my/our asses with!...

Furthermore, this kkkountry has no moral standing whatsoever to impose upon other countries and peoples its values – and for the record, it never has. Look at what's going on with Black males such as myself nowadays – hell, look at the history of our time in this land *in totality*. Amerikkka's attention is currently directed at "illegal aliens" and "religious radicals" (i.e. "Islamic terrorists" in the words of President Obama) when every day it continues to "radicalize" the poor, underprivileged, marginalized minorities of *this* kkkountry. *Every* time you send an innocent man to prison like me, you make an enemy. *Every* time you overcharge and over punish someone like my brother, you make a potential enemy. *Every* time you imprison and steal years from a person's life for nonviolent drug offenses, an *enemy* is growing within your midst. Every death of a Trayvon Martin, Eric Garner, Michael Brown, Tamir Rice, Walter Scott, Freddie Gray, Sandra Bland and others, you make hundreds, if not thousands or even *millions* more enemies who sooner rather than later will say "no more! We will not tolerate any more the shedding of our Innocents' blood!" and will seek the long-

---

[309] Although as I now edit this in July of 2020, the push for fundamental change has been even more so strongly renewed in the uproar over the murders of George Floyd, Ahmaud Arbery, Breonna Taylor, and Rayshard Brooks. May they all rest peacefully with the Ancestors and their lives not be in vain...

awaited retribution. Consider yourself forewarned. My message is really simple to amerikkka: Respect and "do right by" all others as you *demand* all others respect and "do right by" you.

While you still have the time to, anyway. Because as of now, in my opinion, we're not pissed off enough as a people; too much of the collective anger we had in the 60s and 70s has dissipated as a precious few of us have had the luck to taste a little bit of what this kkkountry considers "success." But for the most part, our people are doing just as bad – if not worse – in most of the categories that actually matter: wealth, health, employment, "employability," education, home ownership, being victims of police brutality, suicide, being victims of gun violence, etc. Yet all we do is bitch, moan and complain as others constantly transgress us as a people – if, in fact, we even do *that*. However, we never *do* anything about it. No retaliation, no "push-back." And that's the express thing we need.

Serving time in prison, I've witnessed numerous times the fact that even the most racist of kkkorrectional kkkops would respect considerably those whom they know will match their aggressions. Why? Everyone respects a fighter – no one a coward. And that's what we seem to be as a people: a race of cowards. Pigs and others have for years and continue to constantly murder us and our children, kidnap our men (and increasingly our women) on trumped up "charges," yet still in this 21st century we sit idly by. Where is our naacp, our urban league, or rainbow coalition, etc. while all of this is going on? Probably begging our enemies for a buck as always. I say we need to reconstitute the BLA, the BGF, the Black Panthers and others of their ilk from only a few decades ago to at least match and turn back the aggressions of our enemies. Furthermore, how about we turn the aggressions of our Crips, Bloods, Vice Lords, Gangster Disciples, Latin Kings, Mexican Mafia, etc.

around from one another to our true and declared enemy once and for all? Think of how revolutionary this would be, and how much respect we would garner from both our enemies and our unspoken allies. Just imagine how we could rock the world…

"While a person is locked away in distant netherworlds, time seems to stand still; but it doesn't, of course. Children left outside grow into adulthood, often having children of their own. Once loving relationships wither into yesterday's dust. Relatives die, their loss mourned in silent loneliness. Times, temperaments, mores change, and the caged move to outdated rhythms…"

Live From Death Row

by Mumia Abu-Jamal

With all of the missteps I've taken over the years, a lot of people no longer believe in me; and honestly, I can't really even blame some. How many times can you allow someone to disappoint you, to break your heart, to disappear from your life for years at a time due to imprisonment? Good thing I still believe in myself, though.

However, I finally accepted that there were just some things that life would never allow me to have and some people that were just not good for *me* and my life and my purpose. And just because something – or someone – were not good for me did not mean that they were not good for something or someone else. A woman may be a good, even great woman for someone else, but just the wrong fit for me and my life. That's just the way it is. It doesn't make something "wrong" overall because it's wrong for me. Can you dig what I'm saying?

For example, in each of my serious relationships, I feel as if each of us came out a better person than we were before we met — although at the end, at the time, that may have been hard to think, feel, and/or see; with Soyayya this was all doubly true. She was the woman to whom I opened up to emotionally and spiritually like no other; she knew all of my hopes, fears, loves, likes, wishes, and dreams nevertheless eventually, she ended up breaking my heart through desertion and unfaithfulness. We were young, however, only teenagers, so there are no hard feelings, and I soon forgave her and we're now good friends even though we haven't spoken in years. With Soyayya, most importantly, I saw the possibilities of what love could be, and for that, I'll always love and care for her.

Nevertheless, I recognize that I legally married Soyayya as a way of hurting her or of being close enough to hurt her back, I should say, and I'm glad that she realized this (even if only, instinctually) before I was given that chance. Even though I loved her, I truly did, I was still too hurt and damaged from my misunderstanding of her actions and reactions in and towards our relationship that my intentions were not good in accepting her proposal. And that was wrong; all I could have done was cause more (unnecessary!) damage to her, her newly born child, and even to myself. And how terribly evil and foolish was that? So, I'm glad she disappeared on me again shortly before my (unbeknownst to her) release, making me finally realize "enough [was] enough" so that I finally had the wherewithal to put our relationship behind us even as she begged me back. Because at that time, at that age,310 in those circumstances, with everything we had already put ourselves through we would not have been good for or to one another. We had to let it go...[311]

---

[310] I had turned 19 three weeks prior to my release, she would still be a few weeks shy of 17.
[311] Besides, is a woman your "comfort when only convenient?" Or is that woman actually your complement and conscious commitment." Someone you've actually dedicated a part of your life to in some meaningful way? That's what Soyayya was to me, my complement, my comfort even when it was inconvenient for us both, and the woman (albeit young, true enough) to whom I consciously committed myself to for

And just as I've changed over the years, so too has the world and others in general – whether in ways that I personally consider positive or negative – as nothing nor no one is ever static nor stagnant. Distressingly, my relationship with the mothers of my (now-young adult) children I would describe (at best!) as "less than ideal" so that is something I would clearly square in the "negative," while other relationships and friendships have strengthened in ways that I never would've imagined…

Pasheni will seemingly never admit to people the truth of why we broke up (and never rekindled our relationship) nor the lies she and her mother propagated about me, and until we get past that, well hell, how "cool" could we ever be? Nonetheless, I too, will love the person Pasheni is/can be once I (force myself to) look past the lies…

As far as Tsawa, I don't really "like" the person that she puts herself out to be nowadays (mean spirited, conniving, devious, non-loving, malicious, materialistic, extremely selfish, vindictive), yet I'll always love the person beneath (deeply beneath) all of the bullshit…

And Zara? – (As I've said before) I sincerely wish I had the capacity to *unlove* someone, as her moves have continued to become more repulsive towards me even as we've had no reason/need to communicate in over a decade besides to get some paperwork taken care of. Yet I still wish her all the best. And hopefully (one day) she'll recapture that woman I first

---

the rest of our lives if she truly wanted. This we did at the ages of 16-17 (me) and 14-15 (her) and I/we considered ourselves as having been "married" even before we were able to legally do so. Because "commitment" and "marriage" doesn't particularly mean having a piece of paper to me, necessarily, but instead concrete and clear actions, thoughts, and feelings expressed – a piece of paper can be easily torn up and discarded not so much the others. So, Soyayya and I were "married" long before we were "legally" and our marriage was in fact over by the time we were. The irony of it all.

kissed so many years ago...

Sadly, neither Pasheni, Tsawa, nor Zara's paths in life complement my own now (or rather, my discovered purpose, I should say) for a variety of reasons, but that doesn't necessarily mean that their paths are not what's best for *them*. Although I'm of the opinion that all three women have a lot of healing to do to discover their "best selves," neither woman particularly has shown a receptivity to the man I've become (since the little boy's tears), so I've accepted the reality for that which it is. And although it pains me to realize that I've contributed in any way to their degradations (even if it was just by "being with" them at unrighteous times in either of our lives – or allowing ourselves to become involved in unrighteous situations), I can't be involved in their upliftment unless they *want* me to be, therefore, please forgive me if I don't harp on the pain I may have caused (them). Besides, as with anyone (or anything) else, nothing nor no one before its/their time...

Jannah, however, was so strong in her womanhood (even way back then) that my troublesome life never derailed her growth as a woman, and even still today I'm astounded at the strength of her spirit. Besides my friend Freckles, Jannah is the only other woman I've ever been in complete awe of. She never ceases to amaze me, and I consider her one of the greatest friends of my life...

Speaking of great friends, remember the young lady that joked on my shoes in high school? Well that was Nasiha – and over the years she's become my most consistent, dependable, and loyal female friend. We've been "rocking hard" as friends since I had to chase her down in '94 for snatching my flag out of my back (left) pocket. Throughout our various relationships and children with others and all the struggles that life brings, we've been there for one another and there's no denying that we'll always love and care for each other. I consider her a blessing. Just as I do all my other great and supportive friends...

I recognize, also, that blessings abound in unexpected ways and in unexpected areas. For instance, my cousin Renee: She's converted to Islam, left the streets alone, married a good man, and generally gotten her life together – and she and I even put all the bullshit concerning Terrence Freeman (her daughter's father) behind us. Although I still say she never should have taken his side after the fool pulled those moves on my teenage sister and brother, I can dig her dilemma (that he, of course, placed her in!) as she didn't want the father of her child to die...[312]

Other blessings are the various loved ones of mine that have "struggled mightily" over the years, yet have pulled themselves together since I've been gone. Not that they're looking for my approval or anything, but I never fail to express how proud of them I am and for them to "keep on pushing on." I recognize how far each of them have come, and how a kind word and encouragement can go a long way towards keeping them motivated despite the wikkkedness inevitably coming their way. They'll *always* have my support traveling a righteous path – and to hell with anyone that tries to diss them because of their troubled pasts...

Notwithstanding the (precious few) blessings, however, don't get the impression that I haven't had to weather more than a few vicious storms over the years. I've already discussed with you my brother's stabbing (that almost pushed me to become again that person I don't like to be!), but I've also had to face

---

[312] Speaking of that child, can you believe that she and my own son are pretty close? Hell, I guess I shouldn't be surprised as they *are* cousins and even my sister and Terrence are cordial to one another now. Moreover, he (Terrence) understands that I no longer hold any malice towards him so (as we say in "hood") "it's all good." Everyone can live in peace now that he knows the boundaries not to be transgressed.

(both) my parents failing health and silently mourn the deaths of an untold number of family members and close friends. That hell is unimaginable for the average person to have to deal with alone, yet is the bleak reality that I and every other prisoner has to contend with. It's emotional/mental torture at its hardest. Nevertheless, we're just "rotten prisoners" anyway, so we deserve that and then some, right? Right?

"Man is the individual who is able to shape his own character, master his own will, direct his own life and shape his own ends..."

Marcus Mosiah Garvey

In an unexpected twist, Paul Talley finally came around and told the truth that I wasn't involved in any way whatsoever with the death of Youngsta. As he got older and had children and grew into a man, he (rightly) wanted to rectify the wrongs of his past. First, he went to his pastor in church, I think, then he approached a cousin of mine with what really happened. I didn't wish to hear anything he said, nor did I believe that he would tell the truth after what happened at my trial and all the years I had by then been locked up, so I told my cousin to "miss me with that bullshit." I mean my cousin might have believed that dude had changed but all I harbored was hate and suspicion in my heart. I mean, how could I trust it? After once again being implored to hear what the guy had to say, I told my cousin to have him tell it to my lawyer if he was serious. Or put it in writing. Or do both, as a matter of fact. I knew then that that was the end of it.

But it wasn't. While in the hole for yet another thirty days, I received the notarized affidavit from Paul Talley (via my cousin) admitting to the fact that I was entirely innocent of the crime for which I was serving life imprisonment and that he had lied on me with the express permission and prompting of the district attorney and detectives. Everything I had been expressing and shouting to people all along. All I could do was cry on the inside. It seemed like I had begun to awaken from a sick nightmare that had been going on forever. But was I having a dream within a dream? Was my mind only manufacturing Paul telling the truth because it was something I had wished and prayed and hoped for, for so so long? Probably just the hole getting to me again. That's all it was.

But it was true. I wasn't dreaming; I wasn't wishing it had happened; it was all real. It was all real. Still I wouldn't call and talk to the man. What could I say? What would I say? I still harbored hate in my heart. Every day I awakened in prison unjustly, how could my bad feelings just dissipate? So instead of talking to him, I talked to my lawyer; what could we do? Is there any way for this to get in front of a judge or jury? Was it true that the "truth shall set you free?

As soon as I got out of the hole, I hit the library hard researching wrongful kkkonvictions; (prosekkkutor sanctioned/coerced) lying witnesses; prosekkkutorial misconduct; recanted testimony; and the exonerations of innocent prisoners. The horror stories were even more dire than I had imagined (and I was living it!) and I quickly familiarized myself with the cases of Glenn Ford, Ronald Cotton, John Edward Smith, Dale Beckett, the Exonerated Five and so many others[313] growing ever angrier and more determined to expose

---

[313] It amazes me what this kkkountry has gotten away with doing to us undesirables and how for so long so many have been turning a blind eye to it! I was already well versed on the wrong perpetrated upon the late, great Geronimo Ji-jaga Pratt – former Black Panther who was convikkkted of killing someone hundreds of miles away from where the FBI had him under active surveillance! (I guess he was one of these "Super Negroes" like I'm supposed to be – able to physically be in two places at one time! What the hell is in the water for amerikkka to be breeding so many of us, anyway??

(and hopefully destroy!) the kkkorrupt system that has wronged so many of us. Within a matter of weeks I gathered all of my evidence and facts, case law and other research, then typed and filed a motion to judge norman's kkkourt (where the law instructed I had to go) to re-open my case and/or grant me a new trial. And although I was in bumfukkk, tennessee,[314] and forced to present my case to a rednekkk who despised me almost as much as I loathed him, I had the truth, law, evidence (new and old!), and justice on my side so there were no worries going into that bastard's kkkourtroom. I also had Jeff [315] and I knew he would present my case, facts, evidence, and the law better than almost anyone. Hell, he even interviewed Paul before the hearing (to determine for himself the veracity of Paul's newly expected testimony) and shared with me his (Paul's) determination to finally free his conscience and tell the truth so things were looking good, indeed.

Nevertheless, after the surprise of Paul's "come to Jesus" moment, came another development that should have been a surprise, but after what I've been through, it didn't surprise me at all: The so-called judge's outright rejection of what he always knew to be the truth. That was it. I pushed things to a head: I wanted my liberty or my death. Point-blank as that.

Therefore, I made a monumental decision – a decision that only a man who was experiencing the torment of hell would make. After I was denied by the so-called appeals kkkourt, I petitioned to be euthanized – put to death as serenely as possible

---

Figure that shit out and I'm pretty sure you can sell it!!!) Only through his sheer will and determination to expose the truth (along with the help of late, famed attorney Johnny L. Cochran) would he finally be freed after 27 years of his life were taken! This is amerikkka for you…

[314] Which had only found cause to exonerate only *8 people* – *eight fucking people!* – out of the over 2,000 that had been exonerated nationwide in the preceding 25 years!

[315] Whom I had hired after filing my paperwork myself – followed by the kkkourt (unsolicitedly) appointing me an "attorney" – like I would fall for *that* trikkk again?? You devil bastards need to come better prepared!

as you would a beloved pet – by the state of tennessee.[316] And so that they couldn't sweep my appeal under the rug like so many others, I also wrote and sent a copy of my petition to most local and national "major news agencies." CNN, the Associated Press, the New York Times, USA Today – none of these felt as if my story was of enough interest to the public[317]– but locally, the affiliates of ABC, NBC, and CBS all showed interest, with ABC News 2 showing the most and running with my story. Joseph Pleasant, the correspondent who investigated my story, really did a good job of showing the truth of my situation and of how I wanted to give of myself even in death, with the story months later on NBC News Channel 4 really being a "hack job" and only warranting broadcast after a *white* friend of mine decided he would rather die, also, than continue being unjustly incarcerated. That's amerikkka for you – nothing is ever of interest until it affects *white people* in some shape, fashion, or form. But I digress.

You know what, no I don't. Because this has to be said. How is it that with all of the (*hundreds* now!) exonerated Black and Brown individuals in this kkkountry, Steven Avery and Amanda Knox have been made to be the faces of wrongful conviction??? Are you fucking kidding me??? Seriously, though! *These* two individuals??? And even locally here in tennessee,

---

[316] Unsurprisingly, I told almost no one what was coming until I was days away from filing my petition as I didn't want anyone to worry nor foolishly attempt to talk me out of it. Because how many people would have or could have understood my feeling that the only value and purpose in my life is wrapped up wholly in my *death*?? At least that was my way of thinking then and most of the time even now. And not just that my organs can allow others to truly live – because what I experience now and for the last couple of decades is *far* from it! – but also in the condemnation of this kkkountry for having taken another innocent man's life, I can inspire those *left* to live, to finally fight for the *right to be able to do so*! Maybe that's my contribution to the world, is what I was/am thinking. Much like in the life of martyr George Floyd…

[317] However, it was picked up online by People Magazine, the Chicago Sun-Times, the National Review, and many others nationally and internationally that I never even thought to contact. I have no idea how they found the story.

Hope

Noura Jackson, another *white* girl!!! With all of the Black and Brown people that I know *personally* having been wrongly convicted of some bullshit, this is yet another slap in the face to us!!! So all of our lives matter not at all??? *We* don't warrant public interest stories, or blogs, or podcasts, or 60 Minutes profiles, etc., etc.??? Not *us*! Not *we* the ones who continue to be set up and wrongly convicted of the harshest crimes and sentenced to the longest and toughest sentences whether warranted or *not*. Not *us*. Not us. *Them*. *They* merit all of the scrutiny and investigation into how they were wronged in their case but *not us*. Not us. If only we could be so 'lucky" as to have paler skin, ya know? Maybe Michael Jackson had the right idea all along, huh? Bullshit.

And I'm not even trying to put all of the disinterest off on the "mainstream" media, either. Because *we* should be the ones telling our stories, highlighting our injustices, investigating when *our* people have been wronged, exposing the hypocrisies of the (in)justice system in relation to *us*. *We* should. So I kind of don't even blame the lamestream media for its ignoring of our cases. Because if *we* don't care, then why the hell should they? If *we* don't show interest then what sense does it make for them to? I mean, the latest "rap/internet beef" or european's new clothing, shoe, or makeup line is way more important in our lives than the continual yet insignificant kkkidnapping of our people. Pitiful.[318]

Just so you know, in our priorities we scream to the world what's important to us, and in our negligence our screams are only heard that much louder. Neglect of "our own" seems to be

---

[318] However, I do have to give props of late to those such as Jay-Z and the since disgraced Harvey Weinstein for their work on the documentary for Kalief Browder, and Marc Lamont Hill and BET for their coverage of the so-called Black Lives Matter movement and "mass incarceration." Also John Legend and Jesse Williams for their activism. I have to admit that things *are* improving. Yet, until we as a common people care about the individual injustices in our own communities and neighborhoods that we live in, then no other people will either.

one of the strongest legacies of (the horror known as) slavery, and, in my opinion. The biggest failure of the Black community in my lifetime. I, too, have been (both) victim and progenitor of this awful mentality of disregard of our people, but long ago I learned to recognize the responsibilities we all hold. Personally, we are responsible for our own actions, the way we treat others, and the way we allow others to treat us individually, but collectively we hold familial, community, and even societal responsibilities to ensure the protection, safety, freedom, and dignity of us all. Furthermore, our most degrading negligence is to be found in our actions and inactions towards our own family members, friends, and those at risk of harm in our community and society in general and is manifest in the miserable state in which we find ourselves. You would think that our self-styled "leaders" and "venerable" civil rights and/or religious organizations would be at the forefront of our needed battles, but most seem more interested in status quo and/or not displeasing their oppressive benefactors…

Speaking of certain "venerable" organizations and/or leaders, I strongly recommend that the masses of the Black, Brown, and Native people in this kkkountry should give neither their money nor their time nor even their acknowledgment to those "civil rights" organizations and/or "leaders" that really care nothing for nor especially *do* anything about the problems facing our and our families' everyday lives! To hell with them including their pat on the back "awards" shows. In my observances and experiences, the "black church" and "venerable" organizations such as the naacp specifically, are so *un*supportive of the people they purport to serve, that most people are embarrassed to ever bring their problems/issues to them! So I ask you, what are they even there for except to look pretty and solicit a check so as to sustain their own existences?!

Preaching the same tired ass sermons saying nothing while doing nothing. Nothing at all. These "reverends" are accomplishing nothing but getting next year's Cadillac[319] and his (because it's usually a "he") mansion paid for! Pitiful! The urban league and most of those puppets in the pulpits of the "black church" only show up when there's a chance to get in front of a camera and/or when they can solicit (beg) for the money that we really don't have to give. I mean, of course we see them drive by in their Bentley's — sometimes never stopping to give any of the elderly parishioners lugging groceries down the street a ride home; or sometimes creeping out of the vulnerable lady congregants' (and sometimes the men, young boys, and young girls, too!) homes at 3:00 a.m. after giving them some "special" late night, hands on "ministering" and/or "mentoring"; or even on television at their uppity awards shows. But other than that? Naw, they're never there, they're never around, we can expect nothing but general bullshit from them regarding what we face and/or experience every day in the real world.

So, for those "interested parties" that may be reading/listening, these organizations and/or "leaders" can no longer be used to kkkontrol the masses of the people – to prevent change in the conditions of the people and/or community they "serve." For my generation (and those that follow us) are not of (early) Martin Luther King, Jr. and his ilk; there will be no peaceful suffering, hat in hand begging to do us "justice." So, again, to hell with them. Soon, if possible…

A few weeks after my story first hit the news, I released an open letter to those that supported me:

> *I want to thank everyone and anyone that may have taken an interest in my case since it's been in the news this last month. And*

---

[319] Well, Bentley's and/or Maserati's in today's time.

although I've had some people to question my sanity and/or the sincerity in my request for a "Death With Dignity" in the form of "euthanasia," I want you all to know that I am entirely sincere in my plea and I'm at peace with the decisions that I've made in regards to my appeal. My soul is now at ease, and that reinforces to me that I'm doing the right thing. Soon no more will I have to suffer the indignities of being an innocent prisoner, and (in fact) I've slept more serenely since I've filed my petition than at any other time ever in my life. There is no longer anything that "the system" can do to harm me (that hasn't already been done in taking my life for a crime that I'm innocent of), nor could I possibly help my parents in any better way than allowing them to live on through the gift of my organs. I am at peace…

As well – no matter what – I don't want anyone that supports me to discount the fact that a young man lost his life in the incident I was wrongly sent to prison for. The crime was senseless – and the young man had a family, friends, and a community that loved and cared for him. He could have possibly grown up to be President of this country, or perhaps found a cure for cancer or Alzheimer's, or perchance even raised a family of his own. Yet he was senselessly murdered. His death should cause uproar in our communities in much the same way that Tamir Rice's, Freddie Gray's, Trayvon Martin's, Eric Garner's, Michael Brown's, Oscar Grant's, and Jordan Davis' did. His death was as senseless as the Charleston church murders, as Aiyana Jones', as Hadiya Pendleton's, as 15-year-young Kenneth Jones' of Nashville was just last month. My point is to say, his life should matter to us – his life matters to me *– and never should we overlook the loss of him, Andrew Lewis Titus, and all that we lost* with *him…*

Last but not least, I want you all to know that I forgive those whom wrongly prosecuted, persecuted, and/or accused me of this crime and sent me to prison. I would like to especially inform Paul E. Talley that I forgive him, and – although I could never understand or agree with what he did in the past – I admire his bravery in admitting to the fact that I was in no way involved in the taking of young Mr. Titus' life. While I never in fact expected it to happen, I'm grateful for him that he turned his life over to God, found love and started a family, and furthermore had the courage to attempt to right one of his wrongs. Not a lot of people can admit when they've transgressed against someone, but he was courageous enough to do so, and for that, I'm appreciative...

Can you believe it? I actually *admired* this cat Paul now. Seriously. He helped teach me that redemption is available to us all...

"Tyranny is very strange. The tyrant, despite the access that he or she may have to instruments of power and control, always fears the individual who will speak out against their prerogatives or their tyranny – whether this individual is armed or just has the clothes on his or her back... But when an individual does not care about the coercive instruments of the state, and calls into question the moral and ethical credibility of the tyrant, then the tyrant has a very serious problem. And the way that they deal with this problem is by isolating this individual as if he or she has a virus, as if he or she has something that's contagious..."

Dhoruba Bin Wahad

TO LIBERATION OR *DEATH*

So here I and my brother lay as prisoners, not of politics or circumstance, but of society. Our lives are ones that are actually the norm for Black males growing up in amerikkka. We reject the title of "victim," but victimized is what we have been and continue to be. We have been failed by this world, by our communities, our leaders, and especially ourselves. And things are only getting worse it seems…

On April 9, 2017, some shit went down and I (again) made national (and probably international) news along with 15 other cats at the prison where we were enslaved. The day started off like any other, besides the fact that my brother and I were expecting a visit from his two sons along with my oldest son Kyree. However, things didn't begin *nor* end as my brother and I expected, which can most clearly be illustrated by this letter I was able to somehow get to him a few weeks later despite prison pigs (illegally) intercepting and throwing away the mail I attempted to send out:[320]

My May, 20, 2017 letter to my brother Carvin

I *love* you, bro, man! I *love* you, I *miss* you and I know that you know that I would *never* do anything to purposefully sabotage our fight to regain our freedom or to be separated again. It's been forty-two fucking days since I've seen you — forty-two fucking days! I thought that we would never again in life have to go through more than a couple of days without seeing one another but I guess the Universe or God or the Devil, or whatever the fuck you want to call it had other plans again! This is some real sick, sadistic assed shit no matter which way want to look at it. You and I have been done (or are being done) like so many of our ancestors of the not so distant past who have been sold to different plantations.

And I have replayed over and over again how God could have ensured that things would have turned out differently that day, at least in regards to (you and myself) or I could have already been moved back to the top of the hill like I was supposed to. Darieon and Deangelo could have come to visit as planned and I know that we would have more than likely could've stayed until the end. Or I could have just stayed to the end with Kyree but I could tell he was getting tired and he already had to drive back

---

[320] And although this letter doesn't "name any names" besides those of the pigs involved (which is public information), don't get it twisted and let it be clearly understood that *I* would *never* blaze the other cats entangled in all of this bullshit as *they* will tell their own stories when and if *they* want to. As a matter fact, I strongly recommend for someone with a genuine interest in truth, righteousness and justice to go interview these cats as to what *really* happened and, more importantly, *why* it happened. I can guarantee that they are *eager* for the public to know the truth. Furthermore, there were at least 100 witnesses to what I write about; there are a minimum of 4 hours of uninterrupted surveillance video backing up what I say; and most of the other cats have already been pressured to plead guilty to various charges related to their conduct in the situation. (And again, that's public information so look it up if it's that serious for you.)

by himself. Or when all that shit went down while I was asleep in my cell it could quickly have been placed under control by the officers. My cell door could have stayed locked like it was and no fucking prisoners would have been able to get the key. The officers/captain, warden shouldn't have used *me* (for whatever reason) to ensure the safety of those officers. Or, which is the most important thing — the shit shouldn't have happened in the first fucking place!

Shit's crazy, bro, shit's crazy. I mean I'm really pissed off the more and more I think about it. I'm very frustrated, I'm depressed... I miss you, I miss our sons, and Mama and Daddy and Devonne and although I appreciated what you said in your letter — I have almost no faith whatsoever left in God. All of this, bro, all of this shit, got me (and in essence, you too!) got us caught up in some madness not of our/my choosing and didn't have shit to do with me/us!

Do you even know what happened? Have you been getting my messages from Daddy, Mama, Devonne, John, Christa and the universe?

From the beginning to the end, here's what happened:

After leaving visit about 1-1:15, I went back to the pod and called John so we could reach out to Darieon to see why they didn't come. After talking to him and Kyree then promising to get up on time to come visit that Good Friday, John then told me nonchalantly that Daddy was at the Emergency Room about his heart.

That just ruined my whole entire mood of having a good visit with Kyree because now I'm wondering if we're about to lose Daddy and I was depressed/frustrated because I knew if I was out and/or somehow able to give him a kidney, then his heart wouldn't be straining so bad. So I went back to the cell and lay down on the bunk and put my jacket over my head and went to sleep. (It was almost 1:30 lockdown for shift change, anyway.)

Bro, I got awakened to a whole lot of thumping and shouting and shoes squeaking that seemed like it was right outside my cell door. I thought I was dreaming, though, so I was slow to come out of my sleep but I kept hearing the shit. Then I heard, "3A, officer needs assistance." That, right there is what really kind of brought me almost all the way out of my sleep. I was still somewhat groggy.

So as I got up off the bunk and am walking towards the door, my door opens and my cellie runs in and the door slams HARD. I'm like, "What the fuck?" and then I really hear thumping and fighting right against my door (and now I think that's what slammed the door so hard.).

Then the fighting against my door stops but now there's even more shouting going on in the pod and the officer says again — even more frantic this time — "3A officer requests assistance! Where is my help in 3A?"

My cellie then says, "They out there fighting with the officer and everything."

You know what I do? I say, "Well, we'll be locked down for a while" and grab my remote, sit down and turn on the TV. I don't even go to the window to look out the cell to see *who* is fighting and shouting and shit. Why? Because it has nothing to do with *me* and there's nothing *I* could do about it even if I *did*. I even tell my cellie, to "Fuck that bullshit," and come off the cell door, and that we might as well "get comfortable." Because again, I know the pod is going to be locked down for a while.

After about five minutes (if not ten or more) of complete

pandemonium in the pod, my cellie says, "I think I just heard someone say your name."

I say, "My name? Why the fuck someone say my name for?"

Then I hear somebody come to the side of the door (I still don't know the fuck who) and say that they want me at the door.

I say, "What? Who the fuck want me at the door and for what!?"

But, I guess, whoever it was had got off the door or didn't hear me because I didn't get an answer. Now I'm really fucking confused. Like what in the hell is going on out there!? Then, Bro, I hear some more shouting and thumping and arguing and what sounds like fighting in the pod and then a few minutes later my *door* gets opened! But check this out, bro. It wasn't a motherfucking *officer* who opened my door but a fellow *prisoner* who did and with the *keys*! Now that instantly let me know at least a couple of things: that there's got to be some absolute crazy shit going on if a *prisoner* has the keys to the doors and that since a prisoner *does* have the keys and wants you to come out then you better bring your ass out because people can sure as hell get the fuck *in* on you. Ya know? For real! And I didn't know *what* I was walking out to, an ambush, or anything! I honestly didn't know what the fuck was going on or who was at odds with who. (I remember thinking at the time that maybe two prisoners had got to fighting and the officer was possibly hurt trying to break it up. Boy, was I *wrong*!)

So when I tentatively came out looking around to see what I was walking into I instantly saw a whole mess of blood (and I think a couple of officer's hats) like right in front of my door; I make sure that I don't step in any of it, and then I look around to see what looks like the whole pod out wearing shocked and stunned and scared expressions on their faces — and I also noticed a whole lot of movement, like people running around frantically shouting with what seems to be no rhyme or reason. And I instantly go into survival mode to where I see shit but *couldn't* see shit to where I hear shit but *don't* hear shit and all I can really see or hear actually is people's energies. So, I could feel if I was around nervous energy, or dangerous energy or fearful energy or angry energy etc. I notice that people keep on saying that "they want [me] at the door." I still have no fucking idea who "They" are or why in the fuck they would want me. So, I make my way down the stairs and towards the door. By the time I get near the tables I'm hit with some shit where I can't breathe so I ask someone for a towel. (I guess one of the officers had sprayed something in the pod, I guess and you know I had just had the worst asthmas attack of my life, what not even two weeks before that?) While I'm waiting I can tell that an officer is trying to wave me to the door. But to be honest, I'm not too quick to go over there because cats on this side of the door were arguing with officers on the other side and I just feel real bad fucked up energy all around. Ya know? But I go over there after I get the towel to wrap my face and get my breathing together. Once I get closer, I notice the officer who's waving me to the door is Sergeant Gilbert and he's cool. I mean he does his job and will bust ya if you in the wrong, but he wasn't going out of his way to fuck with you or make your life a living hell like a lot of the rest of them will. So when I get there he keeps saying something about "the officers" or "his officers," and "are they all right?" I'm dumbfounded because I don't know *what* he's talking about and I say I don't know what he's talking about I didn't see any officers in the pod and he wanted to know if they were hurt or not. I thought he really didn't know what he was talking about because I didn't see any other officers in the pod and I told him there were no officers in the pod but I can't really hear him from all of the shouting and arguing going on at the door. (At least not completely.)

I think that he and one of the prisoners basically told me at the same time that yeah they were in there, the prisoner said that they (the officers) had locked themselves in somebody's cell. I told Sergeant Gilbert what they told me, and he asked me to see if they were alright. See if they needed medical attention, see if I could get them out. I think he could sense the apprehension on my face, but he convinced me to do it. I don't know if it was him or the Universe or God or just because it was the right thing to do and I asked the pod "Where are the officers?"

Come to find out, they were only a few doors down from my cell on the top walk. When I walked back up there, I could clearly see the blood trail leading to the cell they were in. I don't know *how* I missed it when I first came out of my cell, it was so much. I guess I was just so super-focused on figuring out just what in the hell I was walking into and when I looked through window, Bro, it was bad! That's when I really knew it was two officers (come to find out later it was actually *three* officers that got hurt but I never, *not once*, saw the *third*).

Now I could really tell that they got beat bad but I still didn't actually know that they had been stabbed, ya know? I think I might have said out loud, that "We got to get them to medical" because a prisoner (who had come up to the cell also) produced the keys and opened the door. The younger officer (I think his name might be Shockley but I'm not sure – he had worked the pod a time or two) was cradling the other officer (Now *his* name I remember — that was Ball and you would remember him no matter *who* you are even if he only worked the pod once while you were in it!) and raised a pencil when the door opened and said, "If y'all come any fucking closer I'll kill you." Or something like that... Ball didn't move or say anything and for a minute I feared the worse. I told him, "Look into my eyes, I'm not here to hurt you. I'm here to help. Your officer told me to check to see if y'all were alright and if I can get y'all out of here. And y'all need medical attention." I guess he could sense my sincerity. Because he and the other prisoner (I don't remember who but I do remember his energy. Soon as I get around someone I think who knows, I'm going to ask them,) helped Ball up (who instantly snapped to life cursing up a storm!) and they were soon following me down the stairs. Ball was screaming things like, "Where's that punk who beat me up? Where's that coward who stabbed me?"

This was when I first got the idea that the officers got stabbed. Out of nowhere comes this energy and it seems like it's going right at Ball and tell the energy (I suspect I know who that was, but I'm not absolutely sure. I'm going to ask who he was too) to be cool and I tell Ball to be cool. "I'm trying to get you out of here and to medical. We got to get you to the nurses." (I realize now how crazy and stupid that was and that I could have been stabbed but I wasn't thinking about that at the time – my instinct was to protect – what a fool I am. Right?)

So, somehow or another I continue to lead them to the door to get them out of the pod where there is a crowd of both prisoners on our side of the door and officers (including Captain Clendenion with the gun who I think might have been there for some reason). I'm just now noticing on the other side all yelling, pointing, arguing and shouting at one another. I yell through the crowd and the noise something to the effect of, "Hey we've got to get these officers to medical."

That gets everybody's attention because I don't think anybody wanted either one of these officers to die and I know sure as hell, *I* didn't because I *knew* it would have been hell to pay for whoever caused them harm and whoever got caught up in the penitentiary lynching that was sure to come. We all know how turney center gets down when they got it out for you. Even though all this is crazy enough do you want to know an even crazier part? *All the fucking keys to the door were on our side of the door in the pod! So, none of the officers on the other side of the door could get the door opened to let the officers out!* I think I kept stressing that *somebody, anybody*, needed to get that door opened so those officers could get to medical. But I was *begging* Clendenion to please not shoot that gun when it did. Gilbert and Clendenion both assured me that he wouldn't shoot that gun and to his credit he kept his word. Finally, one of the prisoners produced a set of keys and opened the door.

I had stepped off to the side away from the door when it was about to be opened so I wouldn't get hit from gunfire or mace and die with an asthma attack. And wouldn't you know it? They only let Ball out into the hall into C pod. I think the other officer is either sitting in a chair or at the table. I honestly can't tell you whether he sat down on his own or was forced to sit down or what the fuck happened. That's how fucking chaotic all this shit was.

So, now all of the arguing and shouting and pointing starts up again, this time even worse if that can be believed.

Gilbert calls me back up to the door (I think I was over by the phones near the showers) and asks me to ask them prisoners arguing with Clendenion and the rest of the officers through the door what they want. So, I turn around and ask and everybody starts hollering shit out to me at the same damned time. I can't understand shit, Bro! One of those motherfuckers could have been asking for a dinner date with Rihanna and I wouldn't have been able to tell the difference! So I turn back to Gilbert and tell him that I can't understand what they are saying and he says, "Write it down. Write it down. Write down their demands,"

I couldn't believe I was hearing what I was hearing so I asked him again to be sure and he told me again to write down their demands. I didn't understand why, but I understand now because there was nothing but hate and harsh invectives being unleased from both sides of the door to the point where anybody could understand what anyone else was saying. It seems like Sergeant Gilbert and I and eventually Captain Clendenion were the only ones attempting to keep cool calm heads amidst the chaos. So I asked around the pod and eventually somebody gave me a pen and paper and I ask them — the pod really — "what they wanted?"

Again, everybody starts speaking all at once and I can't hear what anybody is saying. I tell everybody to "be cool and talk one at a time" and eventually they told me what they wanted. Which was basically not to be put in handcuffs and then be beat up and assaulted, for a bus to take them to Riverbend (because they knew they couldn't stay at turney center anymore without being hurt or killed) and for Ms. (Warden) Johnson to come down there with the bus to insure their safety. I gave them the list. Gilbert discussed it with Clendenion and said that they would make it happen.

I was thinking that now maybe I would be able to go back to my cell and prepare for the shakedown from the Strike Force that I knew was coming for the pod and then be locked down for however long we were going to be locked down. Remember, I don't have anything to do with this shit that was going on and was still completely in the dark about what, exactly, transpired and why. I didn't beat up or stab anybody. I wasn't holding anybody against their will. I never had any weapon or participated in any bullshit. Ya know? Not for one fucking second. So I wasn't worried about any harm coming my way unless some of the bad energy in the pod decided to take it upon themselves to do me harm.

I don't know why but there was all kinds of shit breaking out in that pod for reasons I couldn't understand and I stayed on edge like everybody else and kept my distance from whatever energy didn't seem right for whatever reason.

But all that started to change when Lieutenant Woods came through the unit's door, seemingly drunk and cussing and pointing at me (or so it seemed) and had *murder* in his eyes! I couldn't understand or really hear what he was saying, but I could *feel* it, Bro! I think that whatever had happened that he may have been a part of it beforehand or a catalyst for it or something because when the prisoners at the door saw him, they went *ballistic*! I mean if he could've got to them or they got to him, then *somebody* was going to die brutally! These motherfuckers wanted to *kill* each other something awful and we all should be thankful that closed doors were between them. Shit was already crazy enough, but once Woods showed up it started to get even crazier by the second! I thought that shit maybe was starting to calm down and be resolved but Woods ratcheted up the tension level by a *thousand*! I asked Sergeant Gilbert, "What did Woods say to me?"

He told me, "Don't worry about it," and eventually pushed Woods out the unit door.

But now I'm starting to get worried even more than I already was because Woods kind of showed me that for one, they had murder on their minds (which I kind of understood because some of their officers had been hurt) but two, when they came in there to kill they would kill indiscriminately first and sort out the innocent later. Because there was no way in hell that anyone — least of all the officers — should have wanted to do *me* harm because *I* had done everything asked of me to get the situation peacefully resolved.

I know this is kind of off subject but this reminds me how in the not so distant past when one Black person has done something or pissed off a white person by being "uppity" or reckless-eyeballing or even just minding their own fucking business, then the lynch mentality inherent in of a lot of whites comes out and a lynch mob forms to kill *any* Black person found guilty of something or not! But I digress.

I think I asked Gilbert at that time, "How long before Warden Johnson gets here so this can be over, and can we

get Nicky Jordan down here faster or something?"
I wanted to get that shit over before things got even more crazier that it already was! Can you believe, Bro, that I still somewhat thought I was just having a nightmare or something and none of that shit was really happening? Hell, sometimes, I *still* do! If so then God needs to quit fucking sadistically playing with me and allow me to wake the fuck up! I even tried to ask Clendenion what Woods had said and if we could somehow resolve this shit as quick as possible. But Gilbert told me to talk only to him and to deal with him. He kept telling me that everything was already worked out, the bus was on the way and Ms. Johnson will be here.

By this time, I'm literally *begging* them, Bro, for them to work this shit out and to please get this situation resolved. While I'm begging Clendenion and Gilbert to hurry up and resolve the situation, I'm also literally *begging* the prisoners in the pod for them to be cool and don't make everything worse.

Eventually most of them seemed to start listening and taking heed. And then, bro, I think right after Woods left Sergeant Gilbert, again asked me to see if the officer was alright and if he needed water or anything.

So I leave off the door with Gilbert to go to the table were the officer is sitting. I can't remember if he was sitting or at the table when I was writing down their demands; he might have been there and I didn't notice because of tunnel vision or he might have been in the chair or somewhere else or I don't know. But I know he was at the table when Gilbert asked me to check on him again.

Looking at him, I felt compelled to tell him, "I promise you I am going to get you out of here safely and to your family. I promise you I am going to get you home to your wife and kids."

The man looked at me and told me that I was his best friend right now and that his life was in my hands.

Somebody had brought us some water (my mouth was parched) and I repeated the same thing I had told him, shaking his hand and then going back to the door with Gilbert. And I swear to you, Bro, if I could have somehow got him safely out of the pod, without myself getting stabbed or beaten, or the whole pod being beaten or killed as a result I would have. You could have easily seen how badly hurt he was, although he was being real, strong about it but trying not to show it.

So I'm again asking Gilbert how long before Ms. Johnson got here and got shit resolved when here comes flying in Sergeant Mackin and he instantly comes pointing at me, threatening me to the point that *spit* is flying out of his mouth.

Gilbert has to hold him back like he did Woods and eventually got him to leave.

But now I'm thinking that I *know* for sure that my life is in danger (and yours too, because they *know* we are brothers) because I *know* what kind of a rotten person *he* is! He had written me up once before on a bogus charge of receiving two food trays when I in fact *gave away* the food on the tray that I rightfully received because I was in the cooking class but he *still* made that shit stick just to show his authority over me. He also participated in the handcuffed beating of Lorenzo Shelton that not only didn't get him fired or demoted but it got his ass *promoted* and to a higher position! That's turney center for you. Show that you will kick a little Black prisoner ass even or especially when they are cuffed up and you'll quickly rise up the ranks.

So I think I knew it then, after Mackin did that, even if I still didn't want to admit to myself that for whatever reason my life was now in danger at turney center and that I might not make it through the night alive. I had already noticed that the whole pod was on the phones telling their families what was happening and telling them to call the news media and that the media was showing the shit on TV.

I asked Sergeant Gilbert if I could get off the door. I knew he wanted me to stay there and talk to him because, as I said, everybody else, it seemed wasn't thinking all that rationally for the most part.

I wanted to call my family and he said that was cool but to use the phone over near the showers.

I got there and tried lil bro, but of course he's never there when we need to rap with him. Right? Eventually I got Nasiha on the line. She told me that since I got to Morgan County that the first thing I said to her was that "If I die tonight it's because they killed me." And to tell y'all, you, Mama, Daddy, Devonne, John, our children that I love them all and that I miss y'all. But so much was going on that I don't know if I even remember that, but that sounds about right. I think I was trying to explain to her all that was going on and asking her if she saw it on the news like the people in the pod were saying and to contact the news herself because if they wanted to know the truth then I would tell them because they were the only thing that could keep innocent people like me, alive with the way Mackin, and Woods had murder on their minds.

She called them and I talked to a reporter named Cherish

Lombard for a few minutes and that is the clip that somebody (just got here from Trousdale) told me they played on the news for a couple of weeks.

The interview was interrupted first by an incident at the door. Come to find out that the stupid fake drunk white supremist said he wanted to use the officer to "take over the whole prison!"

What is wrong with these people? And by then Sergeant Gilbert was telling me that Warden Johnson was about to call the pod phone and wanted to talk to me.

So, I told Nasiha and the reporter to hang on (eventually the phone either disconnected or they turned it off) and somebody brought me the phone so I could wait for the Warden. I didn't even know how to use the motherfucker. It's been so long since I held a regular cordless phone that somebody had to show me how to answer when she called.

Lol. But she called, and I identified myself and told her how she remembered me and she also asked me what was going on and I told her as best I knew but I really didn't know too much. A couple of times I had to ask people to quiet down a little, so I could hear what she was saying since a million and one people were in my ear trying to tell me to tell her certain things. But I just let her know that they said that they would let the officer go if they got a bus to transport them (and now me and maybe even you because I was scared for us to stay at turney center too!) to Riverbend and they saw her face because they were scared of being hurt. A lot of people were scared of staying there and being hurt after it was all over, Bro, they kept saying that they wanted to leave too! Black, white, Hispanic, 20 year olds 30 year olds, 40 and 50 year olds, all affiliations and non-affiliates too.

She said she was on her way so everybody, prisoners and officers just waited. But the tension level in the meantime kept rising and falling. The prisoners thought that the officers and security forces were coming in through the back door, through the roof, through the windows etc. I just kept praying to the Universe to *please* let Ms. Johnson hurry up get here and resolve the situation and to *please* keep the wounded officer alive. Also to keep the innocent people (even the guilty ones in spite of themselves) unharmed. And to *please* just work things out as quickly and as best as possible.

I was just praying, praying, praying in my head, and begging, begging, begging, out loud for everyone to be cool. And re-assuring, re-assuring, re-assuring the officer that it was almost over with and he would be safe and re-united with his family soon.

But I expected a sniper round to hit me in the head almost every single moment.

Eventually Gilbert asked how many people were getting on the bus. Warden Johnson also asked later when she called back but he asked first.

I think that was the first time I mentioned your name to him. For that I mean to apologize. But I was just afraid for you to continue to stay there with knowing how vindictive and evil officers like Mackin and Woods and a few others could be. So I asked Gilbert to see if you were alright and to see if you wanted to get on the bus with me to where I thought was Riverbend until this bullshit could be sorted out.

I felt the turney center would forever be unsafe to us through no fault of our own, but in trying to keep you safe, I actually gave them the pretext needed to fuck with you.

So, again, I apologize, Bro and I hope you forgive me for any bullshit they are putting you through.

Eventually Warden Johnson called the pod back saying she was on the compound and wanting them to release the officer. I told the pod what she said but they wouldn't do it till they saw her face. Ya know? They thought it was a trick or something.

So she told me to say something to them. Whatever it was I don't even remember.

I told her that I couldn't say that to them.

Whatever it was she wanted me to say I got the feeling that it could have and would have got me hurt. Then she asked me who was in charge here.

Well, it wasn't *me* and *I told her so*.

The whole time that bullshit was going on if you could tell me who was in charge then you were a better man than me. *Nobody* and *everybody* was in charge! It was *pure fucking chaos* in there! I told her that *she* was in charge because *she* was the one they wanted to see and who could resolve the situation. I put her on speaker phone. Somebody had to show me how. She said what she had to say and somebody took the phone and talked to her personally. They gave the phone back to me and she said that she was on her way down there. I felt so relieved. But not as much as I did as when she walked in the door. Now as I think about it, the officer kept saying to her, "Get me out of here." That's when she said she was coming to the unit.

I thought for sure she was Moses delivering us from the clutches of Pharaoh and certain death, Harriet Tubman guiding us to sure passage to the North. For real. For real.

That shit was about to end peacefully, and I would again get to hold, kiss and hug y'all.

But still it had to be some shit. Right?

She wanted them first to send the officer out by himself but certain cats felt that this was a trick and he wasn't going. They argued and negotiated back and forth until I said, "Look, we have to trust her. She isn't going to let anything happen or she wouldn't have come all the way down here."

Still, those fools weren't trusting nothing.

So, finally I said, "Fuck it. I'll be the sacrifice and go out first but the officer has to come out right behind me."

And that's what I did, Bro. Sacrifice. To get the shit over with and ensure the safety of all.

I was the first one cuffed, searched and placed in the van. Everyone who wanted out got out, I assumed without being assaulted. The wounded officer made it to the hospital. But now I am going to be made to suffer for it all.

Shit's so crazy. Of course when I made it to Morgan County I was threatened with getting my ass beat three times within the first twenty four hours. But for some reason they didn't beat my ass. As far as I know they did something awful to three or four of the other cats that got on the bus with me.

I guess they were surprised that I didn't have one scratch or a drop of blood on me or my clothes. I was still wearing my visit gear, shirt tucked in and everything. I didn't have any contraband on me like some of the other cats, nor did I fail a drug test. You know how I feel about the stupidity of drug use! Or even have a STG history or jacket. Although they have since bogusly labeled me even though

Amerikkka

I never had an STG related write up my entire time in the system!

I plan on fighting that later after I fight all this other shit first.

But still, these evil devils didn't feed me, or anyone else who came on the bus with me. They are also now doing the same shit to a couple of cats who just came from Trousdale. Matter of fact, the only people that I know who got fed every meal he was supposed to get from day one was this white guy! Now what does that tell you?

For the first four days I was here the only way I survived was by other people saving their bread and sides and sending them to me when and however they could. I ate some very disgusting looking disgusting tasting shit and was locked up (constipated) for over a week!

The only way I had something to wear besides just a pair of boxers was because Ant was in the pod (he sends his love as does Shooter from Knoxville/Oklahoma.) I didn't get my property for 11 days and when I did it was destroyed. Also, a lot of stuff was missing or sliced down the middle. My clothes were all fucked up with what I figured out was cinnamon poured all over them. I only received one Danish out of all the Commissary I had. My TV was just returned last week, but it was mysteriously broken and will not turn on.

Dirty rotten, stinking ass evil malice hearted bastards!

I wasn't even allowed to go out for rec the first 31 days. The only reason I am now wearing shoes is that a brother, feeling sorry for me, got a pair of Chuck Taylor knockoffs to me after seeing me walking barefoot to the barber after I had been there two weeks.

Shit's crazy, Bro. Shit's crazy. But it's cool. These evil ass people got that right now. But you better believe that I have been documenting everything and the first chance I get I'm filing a lawsuit! Even if I lose it at least I'll expose the practices of these devils and maybe make it harder for them to do the next person like this!

I still haven't received any write up or any paperwork besides two extensions of p.i. memos, nor can I find out any information besides I'm pending investigation. Although officers calling themselves being hard on me like not wanting me to use the phone and tearing my commissary sheets up for the first four weeks kept saying I was punitive but they can never tell me why or produce a copy of the paperwork.

So, now I'm just preparing for what comes next and to fight any and all administrative punishments, writeups or street charges all the way to the fullest! I wouldn't give a fuck if it was a class C writeup verbal warning or a misdemeanor street charge, I'm going to trial and appealing it if I have to and fighting it as long as far as I can fight it and telling any and everybody who will listen, what happened. Also what happened and *is* happening to me because of it.

Like I said, *I* didn't assault or stab anyone. The fact is all of that happened while I was sleeping or locked in a cell as far as I can tell. *I* didn't hold anyone against their will and in fact put my *own* life in danger to keep those officers safe and get them out of there to get medical help. *I* never had a weapon or participated in any bullshit and I did *every single fucking thing* that not only Sergeant Gilbert but also captain Clendenion and even Warden Johnson asked of me. Matter of fact I never even left the door *one time* unless Sergeant Gilbert *said* I could whether that was to get some

Amerikkka

water, use the phone or even pack my shit after Mackin came in making his threats! *Never*! Not *once*, Bro! Not once! So, what should or *could* I be written up or charged with? What did *I* do wrong? *Somebody* needs to tell me *that*. And it's not like I'm looking for a fucking award or pat on the back or something. "There you go boy, Good boy." But I sure as *hell* and *you* sure as hell *shouldn't* be getting *punished*! Whether it's this max bullshit they've currently got us both on in essence or us being sent to two separate prisons (sold off to different plantations) or us being shipped off further away from Nashville and making it even harder for Mama, Daddy (well making it impossible for them because of their medical conditions) and our sons to be able to come see us!

There is just no moral or ethical justification or righteousness in that in any shape, form or fashion. And if there was truly anything just or merciful, righteous or good about God then it wouldn't happen either! But let me not get started on that because I'd be writing a thousand more pages and I'd have to burn up ten or twenty more pens. And shit would be so much easier to fight if I had a lawyer on it but of course I don't.

It's cool though, it's cool. I'm prepared to represent myself even at trial if I have to. And everything I've told you in this letter is on pod video/audio surveillance footage and should be backed up by the TBI interviews of everyone that was in the pod when shit was happening. I already have a list of 40 something people that I plan to subpoena to trial — over a third of the pod!

Plus the interviews of the cats that got on the bus with me (and I think at least a few of these cats are completely innocent, like me — like I said, some people just wanted to leave because they were afraid of staying there with the way the officers were acting). Plus the interviews of Gilbert, Clendenion, Warden Johnson, Officer Ball and Officer Shockley. I'll hope I can count on them to tell the truth. I hope so anyway. Plus, I want the — well never mind right now. You get the idea. I'm preparing to fight this, however and for however long it takes. Shit, what do *I* have to lose? I already don't even become eligible for parole for another 45 years and I'm already determined to make them euthanize me legally within the next couple anyway. So what do I have to lose? So fuck it, Bro. Let's see how all of this now turns out.

So there it is. There's everything. There was even more I wanted to express to you and tell you but I'd be writing for a month straight if I did and you'd never get this letter. Plus I want to make sure that you do get this one. So call Devonne or Mama or Daddy or even John or maybe even Nasiha. Her number is… … … they changed the last four to my pin number so I couldn't even call out until I got that. Then they very rarely want me to use the phone and let one of them or all of them know when you finally receive this letter. It took 12 days from the time you wrote yours for me to receive it; there is no reason for them not to give you this or for them to delay it; everything I said to you is all on camera and already known to the TBI and DOC internal affairs. And shit, we (you and I) don't have anything to hide.

So I love you, Bro. *Love* you and *miss* you. Be *safe*, be *careful*, move around *cautiously*, not trusting too many and hit me back when you can. Love always…

So, there it is; the overseers were either unable, unwilling, or (in my estimation!) not brave enough to resolve the shit that went down without seeking out and enlisting *me* to bring calm to the situation. That was the only way those in charge could see getting it resolved as peacefully as possible. Now, unsurprisingly, these amerikkkans are now extremely embarrassed by their cowardice. They used me to their advantage, knowing that I respected everyone so everyone in turn respected me (including the vast majority of their coworkers), and that once I assessed the situation I would do my best to make sure "cool heads" would prevail so as to prevent the unnecessary loss of life (prisoner nor overseer) if it could be avoided. And the pod – I'm sure every prisoner in there if they were being completely honest – would tell you that they were just as happy to see that I had become involved in the resolution of things as the overseers were. That's not bragging, that's just a simple fact.[321]

And although I had a jumble of emotions, thoughts, and feelings swirling around in my head (as clearly shown in my letter to my brother) as any normal person would have in a highly charged situation like this, no one on the outside could see any more than the "cool, calm, and collected" self that I have always presented. Yet, in the mind of investigator nicky jordan,[322] this evidently makes me the "leader" of what went down on April 9th. A "leader" with enough power to "order" enraged and armed grown men (other prisoners) around as I've come to find out the young overseer I saved told investigators – although I was unarmed myself and never knew I could "order" others around by *begging* them to "be cool." I also discovered more

---

[321] I've had more than quite a few prisoners and officers at this new prison (whom, I assume, heard about it through their own grapevine somehow) to unsolicitedly share with me that they were "glad [I] was there so things didn't get worse." So what does that tell you?
[322] You know, the same person whom I mentioned in my letter to my brother as having requested to get down there to help resolve the situation when it seemed as if it was taking too long to find Warden Johnson. Nicky jordan had just the year before "resolved" a potential Crip-Aryan gang war that had jumped off in the prison's cafeteria.

"Super Negro" superpowers (that I never knew I had) as I'm able to command men *in my sleep* to stab and attempt to kill others and I honestly appreciate these devils enlightening me of this power by charging me with 3 counts of the attempted murders of the overseers (along with 6 counts of their kidnapping and especially aggravated kidnapping in addition to 1 count of aggravated riot), all of which occurred while I was *asleep locked in a cell having nightmares of losing my father* – which not only the surveillance cameras show, but the actual perpetrator has *admitted and pled guilty to*! And even though my fellow prisoner is a *well-trained military veteran with a mind of his own*, maybe neither he nor I were aware of how I (evidently) took over his mind and body with simply the power of my *dreams*. Good thing the devils have pointed out to us how I'm the "leader" and "cause" of what happened, as he and my Black asses would've never had any idea...

Yet, the truth of the matter is all I can ever be to others is the "voice of reason" and all my fellow captives have already admitted as much. When being interviewed in a matter of 24-36 hours of being bussed away from turney center, cats admitted that I was simply enlisted to "de-escalate the situation" because I "know how to talk to people" and even my fellow prisoner who did the stabbing accepted all responsibility and explained why it all went down. Yet, that doesn't fit the devils' narrative does it?[323] So I just have to be made to be the bad guy...

Disdainfully, the general public realizes that, as prisoners, we've already been stripped of our freedom and supposed "civil rights," but does the general public also know that we have been essentially severed of all familial and community connections

---

[323] I mean, in this era of Fuhrer Combover, what are you going to believe? What "they" tell you? Or your lying eyes and ears when watching the video of the (at least!) 6 surveillance cameras that recorded it all? Maybe I should have just "grabbed someone by the pussy"?!

and rendered as legally invisible and incommunicado as the "slaves" were in antebellum times? And we prisoners and our "issues" are generally ignored by both the media and those venerable "civil rights" organizations that purport to advance the interests of all "colored people." As a wise man once observed, "riots are the language of the unheard." Is it too much for t.d.o.c. (tennessee department of correction) prisoners to ask not to be indiscriminately beaten (sometimes to the point of death), dehumanized, abused, and just generally mistreated? And if it is, then this kkkountry really needs to take a serious look at itself and quit rushing to judge other countries in the world for supposed "human rights abuses." Because I, myself and other prisoners in the jails and prisons countrywide but especially here in tennessee experience and/or see human rights abuses every single day. Every single day! And one day soon one way or another there *will* be reckoning. There has to be. People have been pushed too far, and we just can't endure it anymore…

By no means could I ever minimize the harshness and horrors of prison – any "prison" in amerikkka will share with every other the basic dehumanizing and warehousing of souls – and this, usually us "minorities," the Blacks and Browns. No matter the prison where I have been "housed" at different points in my life – the juvenile prison known as "Woodland Hills Youth Development Center," the county prison "Metro-Davidson County Detention Facility" run by Corrections Corporation of america (or "C.C.A.," now known as CoreCivic), the "Federal Correction Institution – Beckley" in Beaver, West Virginia, or the three plantations overseen by the tennessee department of kkkorrections called "Charles Bass Correctional Complex," "Turney Center Industrial Prison and Farm" (now "Complex") and, now (racistly worst of all), "Morgan County Correctional Complex" – each was/is a misery pit of captive brothers (and sisters, in the case of "Woodland Hills" and "C.C.A.") snatched away from our families, being told when and where to eat, sleep, shit, and "play"; derided as a number, something much less than an actual human being. I could never understand the senselessness of fools who not only minimize the loathsomeness of jail or prison, but in fact glorify it. They are some of the ones I think should first be sent to the pits of hell.

Matter of factly, let me be clear by expressing to you that I advocate the complete abolishment of jails and prisons throughout this entire kkkountry; whether by force *or* choice, this kkkountry *will* soon be forced to find another "solution" to "crime." Our people can no longer endure the enslavement and indignities forced upon us on trumped up bullshit ass charges that have affected millions of us through multiple generations.

Furthermore, I advocate the burning of the racist united snakes' kkkonstitution and every kkkonstitution of every single state in this land. Replace them all with inclusive, libertarian constitutions in which Natives, Blacks, Browns, women and other "minorities" actually have a *say-so* in the governing of their *own* lives, ya know? And to hell with the blatantly arrogant and hypocritical amerikkkan white male supremacist attitude (and those that support this implicitly *or* complicitly!) and the rest of those that have a fear of losing the power that was *never* rightfully theirs in the first place.

I feel as if we're living in an incomparable historical moment in time, which presents to us all an opportunity to foment change the world over for the greater good of *all* people and not just the precious few. Our focus this time just needs to be sustained, and not again put off by divide-and-conquer tactics, drug abuse, or a few crumbs dropped from the table to a chosen few like what happened in the 60s and 70s.

And I understand that none of us from the Turney Center 20 (which includes my brother Carvin) are necessarily sympathetic figures, and have thus been pilloried in the media as "convicted murderers, robbers, and/or drug dealers." However, the lack of concern for our well-being and the root cause of what went down on April 9, 2017 speaks volumes about not just us, but also society at large. Furthermore, the near future forecasts many more (and more deadlier, I'm afraid!) incidents like this to come nationwide unless something drastically changes starting with the lack of concern for those like myself and my brother who have been grievously wronged by this kkkountry's system of injustice and incarceration.

So, that's why you had the prisoner uprising in Delaware in early 2017 that resulted in 18 prisoners currently facing indictment, that's why I currently find myself on "maximum security" here in tennessee along with at least 18 others from turney center facing over a combined 300 felony charges ourselves! That's why four officers ultimately lost their lives in the prisoner uprising on October 12, 2017 in Elizabeth, North Carolina. And why at least two correctional officers were held hostage for a time a little over a month later (on November 25, 2017) in an Arkansas prison! *That's* why!...

"For I had reasoned this out in my mind: there was one of two things I had a right to, *liberty* or *death*! If I could not have one, I would have the other..."

Harriet Ross Tubman

Shortly after being placed on "max" again because of April 9, my appeal to reopen my case or be euthanized was suddenly rejected again. Yet another slap in the face but I have no doubt that my new predicament played a part in my denial coming when it did. Funny thing, too, was the "judge" who initially sent me to federal prison was "specially appointed" for some reason to hear my appeal. What a strange "coincidence," huh?

Last time my appeal was denied, Carvin was there in the cell with me and helped me through my brokenness and depression with his very presence, however this time I have no one nor anything to do so. But, this, too, I will get through…

In my retort to the state of tennessee's response in opposition to have my case reheard in federal court, I wrote this:

2015 was yet another year in which the record was reset in this country in regards to innocent men and women having been exonerated from wrongful convictions — in spite of that, the State of Tennessee's response serves as yet another callous disregard for an innocent *man having had his life wrongfully taken away from him for a crime he* didn't *commit. Petitioner has been incarcerated —* suffering *— for well over a decade… for a crime he* didn't *commit. Petitioner has been denied the opportunity to be an asset to his community and world, and rectify the wrongs he served upon it as a misguided youth… for a crime he* didn't *commit. Petitioner has been unable to live, eat, and go as he* chooses *to — which should be his unassailable right as a human being —* for a crime he didn't commit.

As is implicit with the tone and tune of the State's response, Tennessee realizes that no just and moral jury would have convicted Petitioner had it known of the evidence that we now have in front of us: the fact that the State's main and most crucial witness *has "turned [his] life over to God" and now acknowledges Petitioner's* complete and actual innocence, *and the fact that that same* witness *all along had an illicit deal with the State for his now-admittedly perjured testimony. No jury would have. None. Not in Russia. Not in China. Not in Iran. Not in North Korea. Nowhere. The evidence speaking to Petitioner's innocence is that*

Amerikkka

strong – *in spite of the State's clandestine moves to subvert it. Furthermore, it is simply untrue that Petitioner is only* now *newly making claims of innocence – a cursory glance of Petitioner's trial testimony transcripts will show Petitioner's adamant assertions of his complete and actual innocence from the* very beginning of this nightmare, *along with his bewilderment as to why* he *was accused of and charged with the murder of the unfortunate victim in the first place. Petitioner has from the* very *onset been* shouting *and* screaming *of his innocence from the rooftops for all to hear, yet been ignored for over 14 heartbreaking years.* To anyone and everyone *whom would listen – his children, his parents, his siblings, and other family members;* every single attorney *he's had helping to fight this unjust misfortune;* multiple *"innocence" projects and prisoner-assistance organizations; and* numerous media personalities, representatives, and organizations *– literally* hundreds *of people have heard Petitioner* constantly *and* consistently *protest his innocence since this nightmare started – sometimes to the point of* tears. *So for the State of Tennessee to assert that Petitioner is only newly-now asserting his innocence is an insult of the most* galling *and* disparaging *kind. The only major differences between now and the beginning is that the State's main and most crucial witness has made an unsolicited acknowledgment of what Petitioner has been crying out all along, and more people are starting to finally listen...*

And lastly, again, Petitioner places the ball back squarely in the State of Tennessee's court in that this matter can end to everyone's possible satisfaction by simply putting Petitioner to death and out of his misery. No more, then, will the State hear any more appeals / motions / pleadings, etc. from Petitioner, and it will have satiated its bloodlust for innocent Black *men if only for a moment. Petitioner again makes the unrescindable vow herein that if afforded the opportunity to be euthanized or allowed a Constitutionally-*

warranted new trial with the death penalty as the only available sentence, Petitioner will not appeal anything else and will quietly go off into the annals of history after his death. Petitioner is unaware if the State of Tennessee (or any other state, for that matter) has ever been presented with this opportunity in the past, but Petitioner suspects that his offer is a unique one, indeed, that the State should jump at. However, what cannot and will not happen is for Petitioner to quietly go about continuing as an innocent imprisoned slave for Tennessee for any more longer. Enough is enough. Petitioner refuses to continue being finagled into another drawn out and useless process of back-and-forth with "the law" with the people that perpetrate these injustices for a living. Petitioner has no more to give and the State of Tennessee should recognize this as such...

In an effort to come to some type of compromise, I even wrote the assistant attorney general responsible for fighting against my appeal:

I'm not sure if this letter to you is "appropriate" or not, but to be honest, what exactly do I have to lose? In no way can I possibly imagine my condition getting "worse" for me, as "living" here in prison as an innocent man is the worst hell I could ever contemplate experiencing.

But I know you don't believe that. My understanding is that it's your view that I'm just a "criminal" trying to "get away with murder" off of a technicality. I'm not sure if you honestly believe that or not, or if you're just "toeing the company line," but in any case that's simply not true. I think if you or anyone else in this world placed yourself in my shoes – if what has happened to me with arrest, indictment, conviction and imprisonment on such bogus unfounded charges happened to one of you – then your sense of outrage and despair and loss of hope would be much the same as my own. Place yourself in my shoes, look at it from my point of view, feel what I feel every single second of every single day. Much as I have forced myself to do with you and your office and Mr. Titus's family. And that's why I came to the conclusion I did. And I hope that we can work something out.

Simply put, if you and the state of Tennessee and Mr. Titus's family still feels as if I'm guilty of this tragic and terrible crime despite all of the evidence – new and old – that says otherwise then there's nothing whatsoever in the world I can do to convince you to the contrary. There's simply nothing I can do and I begrudgingly accept that.

But you, too – yourself, the State, Mr. Titus's family – must *accept that I* refuse *to continue suffering for something I did not do so I ask that you all drop any opposition that you may have to me being humanely put to death. At this moment I cannot commit suicide for a multitude of reasons that I wished I cared nothing about, but my condition as an innocent prisoner is so tragic that my continuing life will only bring me unnecessary pain, so I pray that you all will be merciful and support my death. That is the* only *way I can foresee all interested parties getting what we want out of this life, this situation (you, the State and Mr. Titus's family someone to blame; me the end of my suffering), and to be honest, I can't foresee any reason whatsoever why any of you would be opposed. If I'm the "big bad badguy" that I've seemingly been made out to be, then I'm not deserving of life – even if it is imprisoned, right? Less heinous crimes have warranted the death penalty so what makes this any different?"*

And so it went. But of course I got no response.[324] Most people in those types of jobs have no compunction about allowing an innocent Black or Brown person to languish in

---

[324] Over the years I've reached out to various "Innocence Projects" explaining my plight and even filed a complaint with the United Nations Human Rights Commission, neither of which had any positive effect (if even netting a response!) on my struggle's outcome.

prison.³²⁵ So much evil we allow to run this world. And that's why I wouldn't mind checking out...

You know, despite what my parents and others have sometimes said in reference to my supposed intelligence in relation to the struggles of my life, it's not that I didn't/don't have "common sense," it's that for far too long I didn't have purpose nor a sense of direction. Can you dig it? For far too long I lived only for the day or maybe even just the moment most of the time. I was just *existing* like far too many cats that come up like me. Because much like most other Brothers, had I *had* a purpose that I felt deep down in my soul, then I, too would have went full-fledged at it. *Full-fledged.* Therefore I now surmise that a major reason for a lot of the "troubles" I had when younger was this lack of direction, this lack of purpose – coupled with an inherent rambunctiousness and need to rebel against what I saw and felt was unjust yet I just couldn't articulate at the time. But now I'm good; I've got it now. Now I realize what I should have been working towards all along: the final, once-and-for-all liberation of my people. Starting with myself and those closest to me...

In the meantime, I'll continue to do my part in leaving this world, leaving people in a better condition than I find them. No matter where "they" try to hide me. Mindfully, I hold no delusions nor do I harbor any intimations as if I'm anything "special"; I'm simply a man striving to become a better person than the one I was yesterday — no more (nor any less) than that. Not only for myself, but also for my family, my community and "my people." You can either dig it or not dig it. Either way, it won't stop my stride...

Until we, finally, overcome, the struggle *will* continue...

---

³²⁵ Look at what happened to the young brother Kalief Browder of New York – 16 years young when first imprisoned – who suffered for over three years after being wrongly accused of stealing a backpack. A backpack!

Amerikkka

I am a Black man
An Afrikan man
Fighting for the future / heading for home
Manhood
Be my momentum
Nationhood
Be my challenge
Familyhood
Be my reward…

I Am a Black Man
by George Edward Tait

AFTERWORD & PROPER RESPECTS

The great Paul Robeson expressed that "artists are the gatekeepers of truth – (they) are civilization's radical voice," and I couldn't agree with him more. That thought stands out in my mind as to why I somehow kept pushing on to complete this book in spite of the oppression and (attempted!) censorship and silencing I continue to experience on solitary confinement in an overtly white supremacist maximum security prison. But I have to admit, it was hard – *damned hard!* – and more than once I felt like giving up. So although I initially had misgivings about being misunderstood in "giving proper respects" in this forum, I believe that people will understand that this is the *only* platform at my disposal at the moment as I say "thank you" to all those artists, activists, author's, truth-tellers, awareness-raisers, and thought-provokers whom inspired me to "keep pushing" without them even knowing:

- filmmaker Ava DuVernay
- filmmaker Jordan Peele
- filmmaker Lena Waithe
- all-around artist Donald Glover
- Angela Rye of *IMPACT Strategies*
- Van Jones of *The Redemption Project*
- Samantha Bee of *Full Frontal w/*
- Trevor Noah of *The Daily Show w/*
- W. Kamau Bell of *United Shades of America*
- activist Bree Newsome
- Alicia Garza of *Black Futures Lab*

Afterword & Proper Respects

- activist Patrisse Khan-Cullors
- activist Amani Sawari & all the other contributors of the *SF Bay View*
- Amanda Nguyen of *Rise*
- activist Linda Sarsour
- activist Ana Maria Archila
- comedian Jim Jefferies
- Akiba Solomon of the *Abolitionist*
- Judges Greg Mathis, Lauren Lake & Lynn Toler
- journalist Jemele Hill
- comedian Jordan Klepper
- journalist Jamilah Lemieux
- journalist Kierna Mayo
- actress & activist Danai Gurira of *Love Our Girls*
- Prof. Marc Lamont Hill
- all-around badass Janelle Monae
- Rasheedat Fetunga of *Gideon's Army*
- journalist April Ryan
- writer Ta-Nehisi Coates
- writer Ntozake Shange
- actress/activist America Ferrera
- activist Shaun King
- activist Tarana Burke of *Girls for Gender Equality*
- activist Nina Turner of *Our Revolution*
- Prof. Brittney Cooper
- writer Nikole Hannah-Jones
- writer Michelle Alexander
- DeRay McKesson of *Pod Save the People*
- Stephen A. Smith, Max Kellerman & Molly Qerim-Rose

- of *First Take*
- Shannon Sharpe & Skip Bayless of *Undisputed*
- Dr. Raymond Winbush
- Prof. Anita Hill
- Prof. Nikki Giovanni
- The Ladies & Gentleman of *Essence* magazine
- The Ladies of *Red Table Talk*
- The Ladies of *The View*
- comedian Robin Thede
- Alphonso David of the *Human Rights Campaign*
- Arusha Hatch of *Color of Change*
- MiAngel Cody of *The Decarceration Collective*
- Brittany K. Barnett of the *Buried Alive Project*
- author Ruth Wilson Gilmore
- founder Taliah Waajid of *Taliah Waajid Natural Hair & Body*
- founder Pinky Cole of *Slutty Vegan*
- filmmaker Melina Matsoukas
- rapper/activist/entrepreneur Killer Mike Render
- rapper/activist/entrepreneur Clifford Tip Harris
- rapper J. Cole
- hoopers/activists Maya Moore of the *Minnesota Lynx*, Renee Montgomery of the *Atlanta Dream* & Trae Young of the *Atlanta Hawks*
- activist Tamika D. Mallory
- writer Luvvie Ajayi
- Prof. Roxane Gay
- activist Symone D. Sanders
- rapper Kendrick Lamar
- Kesha Cash of *Impact America Fund*

Afterword & Proper Respects

- Kimberly Bryant of *Black Girls Code*
- actress/activist Anna Deavere Smith
- Vivian Anderson of *Every Black Girl*
- writer Eve L. Ewing
- activist Mariame Kaba of *Project NIA*
- Lisa Lucas of the *National Book Foundation*
- proprietor Noelle Santos of *The.Lit.Bar*
- actress/activist Amanda Seales
- Emil Wilbekin of the *Native Son Initiative*
- proprietors Derrick & Ramunda Young of *Mahogany Books*
- Aisha Oyebode of *#BringBackOurGirls*
- Dr. Joy Harden Bradford of *Therapy for Black Girls*
- Spirits Wright, Kali Wilder & Safon Floyd of *EstroHaze*
- Wanda James of *Simply Pure*
- Kebra Smith-Bolden of *Women Grow*
- writer Feminista Jones
- author Chimamanda Ngozi Adichie
- actress/activists Abbi Jacobson & Ilana Glazer
- activist Opel Tometi of *Black Lives Matter*
- author Jabari Asim
- author Tomi Adeyemi
- Charlene A. Carruthers of *Black Youth Project 100*
- Glory Edim of *Well-Read Black Girl*
- Kalimah Johnson of *Sasha Center*
- author/journalist Aliya S. King
- YOLO Akili Robinson of *BEAM*
- Brittany Braithwaite & Kimberly Huggins of *Kimbritive*
- director Barry Jenkins

Afterword & Proper Respects

- actress/director Regina King
- author Camille Acker
- Morgan DeBaun of *Blavity*
- Kathryn Finney of *DigitalUndivided*
- author Amber Scorah
- actor/activist Billy Porter
- actress/activists Ellen Pompeo & Alyssa Milano
- the next generation of actress/activists such as Yara Shahidi, Chloe & Halle Bailey, Amanda Stenberg, Zendaya & Marsai Martin
- comedian Roy Wood, Jr.
- author/activist Janet Mock
- The Honorable Rachel Bell, (St. Louis, MO) prosecutor Kim Gardner & (Baltimore, MD) prosecutor Marilyn Mosby
- Jalen Rose, Fab Five legend & founder of *The Jalen Rose Leadership Academy*
- journalist Soledad O'Brien, *BET News*, and the *Black Economic Alliance Presidential Forum*
- activists Kenyette Barnes & Oronike Odeleye
- columnist Solomon Jones of the *Philadelphia Daily News*
- Rick Tulsky, journalist & co-founder of *Injustice Watch*
- actor/activist Jesse L. Williams
- recording artist H.E.R.
- Stephen Colbert of *The Late Show w/*
- Jimmy Kimmel of *Jimmy Kimmel Live*
- founder Charlene Izere of *Melanin & Money*
- Angelou Ezeilo of the *Greening Youth Foundation*
- commentator Bomani Jones
- actor/host Arturo Castro of *Alternatino*

Afterword & Proper Respects

- the activists of the *Sunrise Movement*
- Prof. Kathleen Belew
- founder Destiny Thomas, Ph.D. & the rest of *Thrivance Group*
- Sokhnadiarra Ndiaye & all the other student-activists of *Teens Take Charge*
- educator Julia Torres
- Joe Thomas Baker Jr., writer, author & publisher/founder of *XCON Magazine*
- Marley Dias of *#1000BlackGirlBooks*
- Tyah-Amoy Roberts of *March for Our Lives*
- *The Movement Family* in Atlanta & all the other *Cop Watchers*
- *The Freedom from Religion Foundation*
- founder Grand Master Jay & the rest of the *(NFAC) Not Fucking Around Coalition*
- founder Fred Swaniker of the *African Leadership University*
- Prof. Yaba Blay
- and finally – despite my wariness, skepticism, and suspicion of the vast majority of most politicians in this kkkountry (which rivals only that which I have for preachers and other pimps of the people!) – I have to give props to the newly-elected Progressive and Courageous Representatives of the *116th Congress* (Squad Up!); 2018 Georgia gubernatorial candidate Stacey Abrams; and 2020 presidential candidates Tom Steyer, Andrew Yang, Corey Booker, Kamala Harris, and Marianne Williamson.

Just knowing that there are people in the world like you working towards making this planet a better place (for *all*!) gives those like me a semblance of hope. And although I'm clear in

Afterword & Proper Respects

my understanding that I know not even one of you personally – nor do neither of you "need" props given from "the likes of me" – I want you all to know how you inspire, encourage, and give optimism to an unknown number of cats that you may not even realize are watching you fight that good fight. So stand strong and keep on pushing on – you're very much appreciated...

Last but not least, some of you may be wondering as to why I refer to myself as a "conscientious thug" in this book's subtitle? Well, I've always known "conscientious" to mean "honest" and "upright" – to, in essence, describe someone whom strives to do what's "right" – and long before I knew what any of those words meant, a sense of conscientiousness, honesty, and uprightness were somehow imbued in me by my family and community. And those character traits have never left me – even throughout my "craziest" times, experiences, and/or misdeeds in the streets. Not bragging, but conscientiousness is simply a part of who I am, who I've always been, and who I'll always be – no matter the bullshit, treachery, malevolence, devilishment, etc., that comes my way...

And as far as "thug," well – no matter what *Webster's* or *Merriam's* dictionaries may express – the *actual* "mainstream" definition of "thug" is as follows:

Thug. Any random Black, Brown, or otherwise non-white male[326] between the ages of 5 and (at least!) 50 whom sometimes has the audacity to attempt to move about society as if they're actually *free*. These animals must *always* be viewed with extreme suspicion, approached with extreme fear and caution, and be met with the utmost aggression – especially by law officers, "community watchmen," gun-toting self-appointed "parking space patrollers," and/or all *real* amerikkans. At *all* times, one

---

[326] However, increasingly this can even refer to *white* males, also, whom are considered "urban" or "Black-identified" due to their style of dress, speech, mannerisms, etc.

should be prepared to call upon the power of law enforcement against these "sons of bitches" as they have been known to attempt disguising their nefarious natures by doing normal shit such as walking down a street; jogging or otherwise exercising; driving a vehicle following all the traffic laws; entering a store, coffee shop, or restaurant to spend money and/or use the restroom; birdwatching in NYC's Central Park; minding their own business, etc, etc, etc (see, i.e., Jordan Davis, Sean Bell, Trayvon Martin, Walter Scott, George Floyd, Ahmaud Arbery, Rayshard Brooks, Freddie Gray, Philando Castille, Eric Garner, Timothy Thomas, etc, etc, etc, etc, etc, etc……..) Along with the terms "gang member," "drug dealer," and (the catch-all!) "criminal," "thug" is the most widely used euphemism for "nigger" in "politically correct" circles.

Can you dig it? In the eyes of this kkkountry I was considered a "thug" to be targeted for neutralization and/or extermination *long before* I could wrap my head around rules and laws – let alone before I could contemplate "breaking" any of them. I would surmise that I and all of those like me were considered "thugs" before we were ever even *conceived*. Our mistake – *my* mistake – was in subconsciously believing all of the awful things pretextually subscribed to us without questioning *whom* was doing that subscribing and to what agenda. But I'm wiser now. And I pray that with this book I did an adequate enough job of helping those that think/thought "thuggishly" as I did, wisen up as well.

Until we all overcome, the struggle continues…

Favorite Books

- *The Autobiography of Malcolm X* as told to *Alex Haley*... Simply put, the most profound book to have had an impact on my life. Sent to me by my Aunt Tricia when I was fifteen and living in a group home fresh out of a juvenile prison, Brother Malcolm's musings were the catalyst for my opening my eyes to the world in which we live, wanting to do something to better it, and also, for my therefore stopping the eating of not only pork, but all animals and becoming a vegetarian. Over the years I've read Malcolm's book at least 10 more times since then and never do I fail to discover something new about myself and my people in doing so. It simply is the greatest book to shape my life...
- *Assata: An Autobiography* by *Assata Shakur*... There's no other way to say it besides I *love* this woman. I absolutely love her. Sister Assata's autobiography has been the most important book I've ever read that has helped me to understand what our sisters go through in our struggle for freedom...
- *The Color Purple* by *Alice Walker*... Although the film is in itself powerful and compelling, it doesn't do nearly enough justice to the book which more so explores Celie's and Shug's relationship. Simply a classic...
- *Midnight: A Gangster's Love Story* by *Sister Souljah*... It's a damned shame that the 7-years-young protagonist of this book can teach a lot of cats 20-30 years his senior how to be a man. (Not to mention the fact how both his mother *and* his (eventual) wife are the epitomes of womanhood.) Sister Souljah is by far my favorite author

of all time – and this is my favorite book of the six that she's written (five novels, one memoir). Check it out and enjoy...

- *Blue Rage, Black Redemption: A Memoir by Stanley Tookie Williams*... Don't believe all the disparaging propaganda put out there about us – this is Crippin and Bloodin from one of the Originals. Check out how something that sparked to life with the purest of intentions became twisted, misguided, and ultimately metastasized into our destroying ourselves and one another. (But we'll get it together. I promise.)...

- *Monster: The Autobiography of a L.A. Gang Member* by *Sanyika Shakur (a.k.a. "Monster Kody" Scott)*... An in depth discourse on "gang culture." Read it and understand why some of youth and neighborhoods are in the state that they're in...

- *Roots: An American Saga* by *Alex Haley*... Both versions of the miniseries are cool and all, but we all know that the books are always way better. *Roots* is the universal story of almost every Black American family. Read it and understand yourself, your family, and your ancestors more...

- *Makes Me Wanna Holler: A Young Black Man in America* by *Nathan McCall*... I almost decided not to release *Amerikkka* to the public after re-reading Brother McCall's memoir in late 2018 – so much of stories are so similar and I can only *hope* that my own is at least half as well-written as his. But then I thought of how much his book affected me upon first reading in 1995, and it pissed me off how so many things in our communities, this nation, and my people are so detrimentally the same or worse even 25 years after he first published *Holler*, that I decided that my story, too, needs to be heard. All the same, I would be remiss if I didn't implore you to please check out Brother McCall's deeply insightful book (a national bestseller!), and I thank him for his words of encouragement to me even though I was just another stranger on the internet...

- *The New Jim Crow: Mass Incarceration in the Age of Colorblindness* by *Michelle Alexander*... Probably the most important book that will be written during my lifetime – there should be *no* politician voted for (Black, White, Hispanic, Asian, Native, whatever!) for *any* elected position (from President down to neighborhood dog catcher!) if they can't expound on their familiarity with this book and the issues and facts discussed within. Furthermore, it should be required reading in every law school, and police, sheriff's and/or correctional officer's academy long before graduation is ever contemplated! (Hell, let's require it in all of this "great country's" military academies and teacher's colleges, too, for great measure!) That's how deep it is...

- *Brotherman: An Anthology* ed. By *Herb Boyd*... Such a well-organized and conscientious anthology of book excerpts and other writings by and for Black men. It exposed me to such illustrious compositions as *The Father's Pledge* by *Haki Madhubuti* and other prose that helped me to more understand our long-standing struggle for justice and equality in this kkkountry. Kind words and encouragement from Brother Boyd was, too, instrumental in helping me make the decision to publish this book...

- *Raw Law: A Hip-Hop Guide to Criminal Justice* by *Muhammad Bashir, Esq.*... It is simply what it says it is:

the law at its "rawest." Mr. Bashir holds no punches about what we as "minorities" are up against in the streets and kkkourtrooms of this kkkountry. He gives anecdotes of cases he's handled that highlight the injustices and biases that are inherent in the kkkriminal "justice" system, and uses a passionate (but common sense) approach to explaining how to fight back when faced with a lot of the common "traps" we find ourselves susceptible to. If you have a Black or Brown loved one in your life, *please* read this book yourself in addition to sharing it with them...

- *Soledad Brother: The Prison Letters of George Jackson*... I didn't realize it at the time, but in reading Comrade George's book of letters, I was inadvertently strengthening myself spiritually, mentally, emotionally, and physically for all of the hells I to this day experience in solitary confinement. Along with his younger brother Johnathan, Brother George was wise beyond his years, both revolutionary *and* gangster *to the core*, and his light couldn't be dimmed even in death at the hands of the pigs. Check this out and understand why he not only inspired Tupac lyrics, but also continues to live on in me and an untold number of other cats...

- *A History of God: The 4,000-Year Quest of Judaism, Christianity and Islam* by *Karen Armstrong*... Very well-researched and put-together tome. This book helped me to understand the histories of most of the main "religions" of the world and how they've changed over the years; it also reinforced a lot of the things I always suspected, and opened my eyes to the perspectives and reasoning behind why a lot of things are the way they are in this day and age. I recommend it for any seeker of

Favorite Books

knowledge about our world. Use it as a companion piece to your Torah, Christian Bible, or Qur'an…

- *Worse Than Slavery: Parchman Farm and the Ordeal of Jim Crow Justice* by David M. Oshinsky… Want to know why there are so many prisons dotting the rural united snakes? Well, read this book. You'll then understand why after ratifying the 13th Amendment that solidified slavery for those "duly convicted of a crime," those "undesirables" like myself have been "duly convicted" for dubious bullshit time and time again. It was because slave labor was still needed to support bumfukkk kkkommunities such as Parchman,[327] Angola, Turney Center, Wartburg, etc. Read the book and open your eyes…

- *The Willie Lynch Letter: The Makings of a Slave*… Why "Black America" exists in the comparatively miserable state in which it does. Don't be surprised if, in reading it, it helps to grow your awareness of your own unconscious biases and where/what they stem from…

- *Cocaine Nation: How the White Trade Took Over the World* by Tom Feiling… Ever wondered why cocaine, heroin, and even marijuana have been demonized the world over when other drugs of equal or even more harm-potential such as tobacco, alcohol and (overly!) prescribed opioid are "legal"? This book will help you to understand the geopolitical policies and reasoning behind the "Drug War" and how it is no more than a control mechanism to keep "undesirable" peoples and "developing" countries "in their place": submissive to the united snakes…

---

[327] Which was recently in the news in early 2020 because of at least 9 prisoner murders in less than two weeks!

- *Inside a Thug's Heart* by *Angela Ardis (with Original Poems and Letters by Tupac Shakur)...* I don't know who had more "game" – Pac or Angela – but I could dig it from them both. If you've ever loved (or been!) a "thug," you'll love this also...
- *The Collected Poetry of Nikki Giovanni, 1968-1998...* Any doubts that Black women have *always* been the most righteous and bravest Souljas in our struggle to survive in this kkkountry? Then please check out (Fiskite!) Sister Nikki G. and recognize what's real...
- *Black Love is a Revolutionary Act* by *Umoja...* If there's only one book on this list that you decide to check out, then please let it be this one. Although (most of) you may not necessarily agree with *all* that this "politically incorrect" book posits, I can almost guarantee that one way or another you'll be profoundly changed in word and deed once you're finished with it. Count on it...
- *The Art of War* by *Sun Tzu...* A study of human nature in the realm of war...
- *The 48 Laws of Power / The Art of Seduction / The 33 Strategies of War* by *Robert Greene...* In depth studies of "human nature." No more, no less. Despite what the fearful will tell you...
- *The Black Panther Party, Reconsidered* ed. By *Charles E. Jones...* Pay no mind to what those Beyonce-SuperBowl halftime-haters will spit out to disparage her salute to the Black Panther Party. Check out this tome as a *proper* introduction to the Panthers and enjoy how it will inspire you to seek out more knowledge concerning Brothers and Sisters such as Huey, Bobby, Eldridge, Elaine, Angela, Kathleen, Assata, Afeni, George, Geronimo, David, Big Man and numerous others. This

book is a foundational tome that belongs in every freethinking household (in my humble opinion). Check for it – you *won't* be disappointed...

- *Nigger: The Strange Career of a Troublesome Word* by Randall Kennedy... Referring to someone as a "nigger" (*or* "nigga") is just as offensive (if not more so) as calling someone a "bitch" (how ironic coming from me, right?) or referring to me as a "crab" (in a bucket), therefore I eliminated the term from my vocabulary by the time my teenage years were in the rearview.[328] However, I admit to it being an arduous process of forever staying conscious of how, why, and when others and I used the nefarious word – and I can't say that my Black community and culture made things particularly easy on me. Nevertheless – no matter how hard the road – I understood after reading Brother Malcolm's autobiography at 15 that this vocabulary elimination was necessary in order to escape (and not propagate!) the negative connotations of the word's clutches. Pick up Brother Randall's well-researched but to-the-point discourse on the word and its history, and maybe you'll understand why I myself and increasingly a lot of others feel as if its elimination in *our* conversations and hearts is so important. Take that courageous leap... [329]

- *The Dekkklaration of Independence / The Kkkonstitution of the United Snakes*... Not books exactly, but ever wanted to see the truest definitions of "hypocrite" possible? Then

---

[328] Take notice of when and how it was used in this book at my welcome.
[329] NOTE: It's just as easy to spit "brother," "homie," and even "sucka" (if you're trying to diss!) in a rap song as it is "nigga." Or in the alternative, how about becoming an equal-opportunity offender and saying "cracker," "wetback," "kike," or "honkie," etc. a thousand times in the same song and see how *that* goes over! I'm just saying! Thought so!...

take an actual look at the documents that serve as the foundation for this so-called "great" nation. Instead of listening to demagogue politicians and/or racist "judges" wax poetic about these bullshit documents when it serves their kkkrooked agendas, *read them for yourselves* and ask if the ideals the "Founding Fathers"[330] espoused were actually truly believed and fought for, or just some self-serving bullshit the united snakes still trots out for subterfuge while it runs roughshod over the rest of the world...

AUTHOR BIO

Known as prisoner Kenneth D. Thomas #262443, Kamaj Dakari Tawhid is currently enslaved "for life" in the tennessee department of correction for a crime he has always maintained his complete innocence of. No stranger to local, national, and even international news, Kamaj continues to fight for his exoneration (or in the alternative, to be "euthanized") in *that* case, while also fighting 16 *current* felony charges related to the April 9, 2017 prisoner uprising at turney center industrial prison & farm in only, tennessee. To learn more about Kamaj, his cases, or to in any way support and/or contribute to his cause, please visit www.JusticeForCarvin&Kamaj.org or the Justice for Kenneth D. Thomas Facebook page. Thank you...

---

[330] Take note that there were no Founding "Mothers" nor any Blacks or misnamed "Indians" in the formation of these documents!